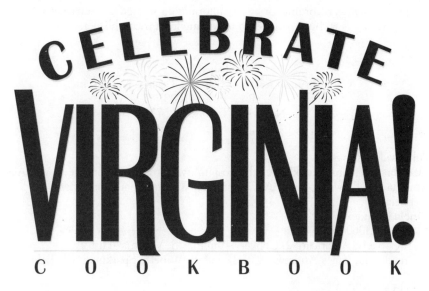

CELEBRATE VIRGINIA!

COOKBOOK

The Hospitality, History, and Heritage of Virginia

Copyright 2002
James A. Crutchfield
Rowena Fullinwider
Winette Sparkman Jeffery

All Rights Reserved. No part of this book may be reproduced or transmitted
in any form, or by any means, electronic or mechanical, including
photocopying, recording, or by any information storage and retrieval system,
without permission in writing from the publisher.

Published by
Cool Springs Press, a Division of Thomas Nelson, Inc.
P. O. Box 141000
Nashville, Tennessee, 37214.

Fullinwider, Rowena J.
  Celebrate Virginia! cookbook : the hospitality, history, and heritage of Virginia /
Rowena J. Fullinwider, James A. Crutchfield, Winette Sparkman Jeffery.
    p. cm.
  Includes index.
  ISBN 1-930604-96-3
    1. Cookery, American. 2. Cookery--Virginia. 3. Virginia--History.
I. Crutchfield, James Andrew, 1938- II. Jeffery, Winette Sparkman. III. Title.

TX715.F946 2003
641.59755--dc21

                                                              2003040914

First printing 2003
Printed in Colombia
10 9 8 7 6 5 4 3 2 1

Managing Editor: Billie Brownell
Designer: James Duncan Creative
Production Artist: S.E. Anderson
Illustrator: Dean Shelton

Visit the Thomas Nelson website at www.ThomasNelson.com

VIRGINIA'S FINEST

Virginia's Finest

This registered trademark identifies Virginia agricultural products of the highest quality.
It may be used only on those products which meet standards set by the industry and are approved
by the Virginia Department of Agriculture and Consumer Services. The blue "check" and
the red "A" of the trademark assure you that you are buying the finest agriculture product
Virginia has to offer. Look for this trademark on specialty foods, beverages, fresh produce,
meats, fish, poultry, and other top-quality Virginia products.

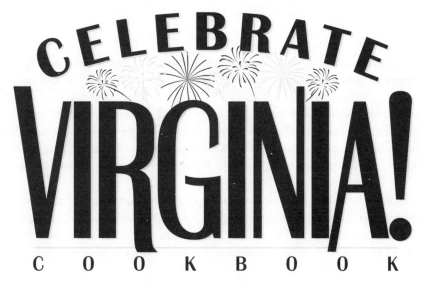

CELEBRATE VIRGINIA!

COOKBOOK

The Hospitality, History, and Heritage of Virginia

Rowena J. Fullinwider
James A. Crutchfield
Winette Sparkman Jeffery

COOL SPRINGS PRESS

Nashville, Tennessee
A Division of Thomas Nelson, Inc.
www.ThomasNelson.com

Acknowledgments

For Regena, the love of my life, and for my Commonwealth Crutchfield family: Sam and Sylvia; Firmadge and Mollie; Elizabeth and Steve; and all of the kids, Emma, Ian, Sydney, and William.
—Jim

I dedicate the love and encouragement of this project to my mother, Edwina Clendenon Sparkman, an angel among us until recent time . . . now an angel above watching over me in Virginia.

I am grateful to my husband, Tom Jeffery, for bringing me to Virginia to share life with Matt, Brent, Allison, Daniel, and Trey beside the Bay. His dining journeys with me across the Commonwealth and his late night keying of historic recipes (which always made him hungry) are much appreciated. Also, affectionate thanks to my little dog, Katie the Corgi, for company on the long writing nights.

Countless thanks to all historic site curators, public relations staff, restaurant owners and managers, chefs, librarians, and historians throughout Virginia. Special thanks to Mary V. Thompson, Research Specialist, Mount Vernon; Susan R. Stein, Curator, Monticello; and Carol C. Godwin, Public Relations, Colonial Williamsburg for allowing the use of their extensive materials.
—Winette

This book would not have been possible without Becky Alejandrino, Joan Place, and my husband, Peter Fullinwider. They cheerfully deciphered my handwriting, putting it all on computer files, and stayed up to the wee hours of the morning to meet deadlines. A big thank-you also goes to the "family" of Rowena's Jam and Jelly Factory, who helped in so many big and little ways.

I have lived in many places in our world, and chose Virginia as my home. Throughout my many years here, I have crossed paths with countless, wonderful people. It is to those people that I would like to express my gratitude—to friends, both business and personal, to family members, and to leaders of our Commonwealth. They have been such a huge support to me over the years, especially with this endeavor by contributing recipes and anecdotes.

And a special thank-you to the ladies of the DAR, whose sense of history and enthusiasm was infectious.
— Rowena

To be a Virginian either by birth, marriage, adoption, or even on one's mother's side, is an introduction to any state in the Union, a passport to any foreign country, and a benediction from the Almighty God.
—Anonymous

Contents

Introduction

Most of us have fond memories from our childhood that center around foods served in our family kitchens. With my Lithuanian maternal grandparents, we had our share of potato pancakes and galumkees that differed greatly from the snaps and fried chicken my Southern paternal grandmother "fixed up." Whatever the dish, eating a meal prepared with a pinch of work and a big dash of love made for happy times.

I learned a great deal from my mother, who prided herself on presentation and perfected her talents by attending Asian cooking courses. She had her own specialties that none of us have yet mastered, including flank steak, wontons, and fondue. Experiencing such a variety of foods would later serve me well in my roles as First Lady of Virginia and now as the wife of a U.S. Senator, as duty has called us to travel to other countries and sample many cuisines.

Traveling across our great Commonwealth of Virginia has provided similar opportunities to expand my appreciation for the infinite range of choices one has in selecting menus for any event, from a simple lunch to a multicourse dinner. Virginia's varied geographical regions— from the seashore of the Atlantic Ocean and Chesapeake Bay, through the Piedmont and the Great Valley, all the way to the lofty mountains of the west — have provided a wonderful fabric for people of all nationalities and ethnic backgrounds to pursue their culinary skills much as they did in their native lands.

As its title suggests, *Celebrate Virginia!* does just that. It is a cookbook that includes recipes suitable for every occasion from noted Virginians, as well as history that represents every corner of the Commonwealth. Norfolk's very own culinary expert, Rowena Fullinwider, gathered recipes from family, friends, and businesses, as well as their unique histories, from across our beautiful, multicultural state. Historical sites and recipes were delightfully covered by Winette Jeffery, a Poquoson educator. Historian James A. Crutchfield, who calls Alexandria his "second home," handled the greater history and little known tidbits from Virginia's past.

We should thank these three for pulling together and creating this entertaining, educational, and delicious sampling of Virginia now and then. Thank you, and *Celebrate Virginia!*

Susan Allen
Former First Lady of Virginia (1994-1998)

Susan Allen and Family

CHAPTER ONE

Hors d'Oeuvres
and
Refreshing Beverages

In olden days, glasses were hand blown, thus flat bottomed glasses were difficult to produce. Those with curved bottoms would tend to tumble over when placed on the table, and too many tumblers of whiskey would make you a little bit tipsy.

Hors d'Oeuvres

Avocado and Cheese Dip

2 ripe avocados, peeled,
   cut into halves, seeded
2 tablespoons lemon juice
1 clove garlic, crushed
1 small onion, grated

1 (3^1/$_2$-ounce) package
   cream cheese, softened
Salt and freshly ground
   black pepper to taste
Paprika for garnish

- Mash the prepared avocados in a bowl. Add the lemon juice, and mix well. Blend in the garlic, onion, and cream cheese. Season with salt and pepper. Sprinkle with paprika. Serve with savory biscuits, crisps, and crudités.
- Makes 6 servings

NANCY THOMAS, a nationally known artist and thirty-year resident of Yorktown, Virginia, contributed this recipe.

Chile Tomato Dip

1 small onion, chopped
1 can diced mild green
   chiles

8 ounces cream cheese,
   softened
1 tomato, chopped

- Sauté the onion in a small saucepan until tender. Add the chiles and cream cheese, stirring until smooth. Remove from the heat. Stir in the tomato. Serve warm with tortilla chips.
- Makes variable servings

This recipe has been a long-time favorite of the Salem community. It originated with the staff of Roanoke College, located in Salem, and was sent to us by SANDY and BOB ARCHER, who live in Salem. Bob is president of the Blue Ridge Beverage Company, which dates back to the post-prohibition era, when it was founded in 1938 as a small wholesaler of beer and soft drinks. Since 1958, the company has been under direct ownership and management of the Archer family. It now is one of the largest wholesale beverage distributors in Virginia. Bob also has worked diligently for businesses in Virginia and was chairman of the Governor's Small Business Advisory Board for years—a chairmanship to which I succeeded him. —Rowena

DID YOU KNOW THAT:

The first permanent school exclusively for American Indians was established at Williamsburg (1720)?

ROWENA'S KITCHEN TIPS

If your brown sugar dries out and hardens, put an apple slice or piece of bread in the box or bag.

Virginia's Eight (Plus One) Presidents

The Commonwealth of Virginia has furnished an unprecedented eight men to the presidency of the United States, more than any other state in the Union. Beginning with our first chief executive, George Washington, the list includes Thomas Jefferson, James Madison, James Monroe, William Henry Harrison, John Tyler, Zachary Taylor, and Woodrow Wilson. Additionally, native son Sam Houston served as president of the Republic of Texas.

For thirty-two years out of the country's first five decades of nationhood—64 percent of the time—Virginians held the power of the presidency. During that first half-century, the very foundations of the United States—the political structure and institutions that are taken so much for granted today—were formed and placed into action. And during the administrations of all eight of these men, events occurred that so influenced American and world history that even a mere listing of them boggles the mind.

GEORGE WASHINGTON (1732-1799) was, no doubt, the most famous man in America when he was elected to the presidency of the new nation in 1789. Born in Westmoreland County, the hero of the Revolution had, for more than six years, successfully guided the rag-tag American army to victory over Great Britain's elite fighting machine, culminating with his defeat of Lord Cornwallis at Yorktown in October 1781. While in the presidential office from 1789 till 1797, Washington witnessed the invention of the cotton gin, a feat that had monumental effects on the predominately agricultural South. Other events during his administration were the moving of the nation's capital from New York to Philadelphia, the founding of the New York Stock Exchange, and America's first successful flight of a hot-air balloon.

THOMAS JEFFERSON (1743-1826) was already well known before he served as the country's third president from 1801 till 1809. He was born in Albemarle County, and when he was in his early thirties, he became the primary author of the Declaration of Independence. Jefferson also was secretary of state in George Washington's first administration, as well as vice president to President John Adams. During his two terms as president, Jefferson vastly expanded the size of the United States by his purchase of the Louisiana Territory from France in 1803. He was the brains behind the successful Lewis and Clark Expedition from St. Louis to the Pacific Ocean and back again during 1804 to 1806. Jefferson remained active after his presidency, helping to establish the University of Virginia, providing his book collection for the cornerstone of the Library of Congress collection, and maintaining his plantation at Monticello.

Thomas Jefferson's successor was JAMES MADISON (1751-1836), who served as president from 1809 till 1817. The "father" of the United States Constitution and founder of the Democratic-Republican Party was born in King George County. America's second war with Great Britain was fought during Madison's two terms in office, and he and his wife, Dolley, witnessed the burning of Washington. Two significant milestones in science occurred during Madison's presidency. In Kentucky, Dr. Ephraim McDowell removed an ovarian tumor weighing twenty-two-and-one-half pounds from Jane Crawford, who tolerated the thirty-minute operation, the world's first ovariotomy, without anesthesia. And the rapid development of the steam engine allowed the first successful navigation of the Mississippi River by a steamboat.

JAMES MONROE (1758-1831) was the nation's fifth president and the fourth to herald from Virginia. Born in Albemarle County, Monroe served two terms, 1817-1825, during a period sometimes referred to as "the Era of Good Feeling" due to the strong and successful dealings of his administration. Monroe expanded the size of the United States by the purchase of Spanish Florida, he established an unarmed U.S.-Canadian border that persists to this day, and he oversaw the passage of the Missouri Compromise. The achievement for which he will always be remembered, however, was his enactment of the Monroe Doctrine, which defiantly proclaimed to the world that the countries of the Western Hemisphere "are henceforth not to be considered as subjects for future colonization by any European powers."

When **WILLIAM HENRY HARRISON** (1773-1841) became the nation's ninth president in 1841, he was best remembered as the "hero of Tippecanoe," an Indian battle that occurred in Indiana Territory in 1811, and as the victor over the famous Shawnee Indian chief Tecumseh during the Battle of the Thames in 1813. Harrison was born in Charles City County, but moved from Virginia at an early age, eventually ending up in Indiana Territory, where he became governor. Harrison served only briefly as president; he took ill with pneumonia shortly after his inauguration and died one month later. Harrison was the first president to die in office and the last president to be born in British-ruled America.

JOHN TYLER (1790-1862), William Henry Harrison's vice presidential running mate and successor, was also a Virginian, also born in Charles City County. Legend has it that Tyler received word of President Harrison's death at his Williamsburg home while he was shooting marbles with his children. Tyler's less-than-one-term administration (1841-1845) was highlighted by his successful pursuit of the Texas annexation issue. During his years in the White House, the world's first telegraphic message was transmitted between Washington and Baltimore by Samuel Morse, and the great showman P.T. Barnum began his long career as a circus impresario.

ZACHARY TAYLOR (1784-1850), known to his friends and enemies alike as "Old Rough and Ready," was catapulted into the presidency in 1849 following his military successes during the recently ended Mexican-American War. Born in Orange County, Taylor was raised in Kentucky. A career soldier, Taylor was poorly prepared for the responsibilities of president, yet during his sixteen-month tenure that ended with his death in July 1850, the old warrior demonstrated his resolve when he advocated statehood for California and promised military intervention against any state that pursued secession.

WOODROW WILSON (1856-1924), the nation's twenty-eighth president, served two terms, from 1913 till 1921. Wilson was born in Augusta County, and he was an educator, his career culminating with an eight-year stint as president of Princeton University. At the 1912 Democratic Convention, Wilson finally won the party's nomination on the forty-sixth ballot and went on to defeat his Republican opponent in the fall elections. Wilson's two terms were highlighted by the establishment of the Federal Reserve Act, World War One, the Clayton Antitrust Act, the passage of the Nineteenth Amendment allowing women the right to vote, and his pursuit of a League of Nations. For his work in trying to reestablish and preserve world accord, he was awarded the Nobel Peace Prize in 1919.

SAM HOUSTON (1793-1863) was born near Lexington and later migrated to Tennessee where he served as governor and a member of the U.S. Congress. Moving to Texas in 1833, he was appointed commander-in-chief of the Texas army and became the Republic's president in 1836. When Texas was annexed to the United States ten years later, he was elected to the U.S. Senate and, later, to the Texas governor's chair. He was ousted from office in 1861 for refusing to take the oath to the Confederacy.

Chutney Cheese Dip

1 (8-ounce) package cream
  cheese, softened
1 cup grated sharp cheddar
  cheese
1 teaspoon curry powder

1 teaspoon (or more) sherry
1 jar Major Grey's Chutney
3 tablespoons chopped
  green onions

- Combine the cream cheese, cheddar cheese, curry powder, and sherry in a serving bowl, and mix well. Spread the chutney over the top. Sprinkle with the green onions. Serve with thin wheat crackers.
- Makes approximately 12 servings

PEGGY BEALE of the Great Bridge Chapter of the Virginia DAR shared this recipe. Peggy cares a great deal about her community and is very involved.

Hot Crab Dip

1 (8-ounce) package regular
  or light cream cheese,
  softened
1 tablespoon mayonnaise
1¹/₂ teaspoons lemon juice
¹/₄ cup finely chopped onion

2 dashes of Tabasco sauce
2 (6-ounce) cans lump
  crabmeat
4 ounces Swiss cheese,
  shredded

- Preheat the oven to 325°F. Combine the cream cheese, mayonnaise, lemon juice, onion, Tabasco sauce, crabmeat, and cheese in a bowl, and mix well. Pour into a baking dish or serving dish. Bake for 45 minutes or until bubbly. Serve warm.
- Makes approximately 3 cups

The recipe is easily doubled and is always well received at a potluck or buffet.

The recipe is from ANN MALINIAK, Chesapeake Chapter of the Virginia DAR.

FOOD PRESERVATION

Historically, the preservation of food was truly a life-or-death issue. The early colonists used salting and smoking as forms of preserving their meats and fish. Sugar was essential in keeping fruits for long periods. Vinegar and lemon also helped in maintaining the freshness of most vegetables. Of course, preserving foods in jars has been used for centuries.

THE DAWN OF A VIRGINIAN DAY

Offshore from the Virginia coast, lobsters in the cool, dark Atlantic waters are claimed as Virginia Lobsters. As the first minute ray of sunlight glistens across the waves toward the land, the sandpipers on the Eastern Shore coastline and barrier islands— where some small towns that used to be are no more—anticipate running to and fro on the beach that beckons in the dim light. The sunray gleams across the back of an Assateague pony that stands in the wind scanning the horizon before beginning a scavenge of the beach for a sea oats breakfast. Soon the watermen of Chesapeake Bay see the ray, as well, for their day of fishing and oystering in the largest estuary in the world is already underway. Farther inland, the spires of colonial buildings glisten as ships nearby are shined and cleaned with readiness in the U.S. Navy. Remnants of contrails linger in the now rosy and yellow Virginian sky as the U.S.A.F. First Fighter Wing has taken off on yet another mission. The roadways near the capital city of Richmond and the busy area of Fredericksburg are now more ably seen in the full dawn as motorists travel to work. Sunlight now dapples the peanut farmer's cap in the field as hog producers feed their future Virginia hams. The rays of light reach to the apple orchards in the Shenandoah Valley and touch the leaf of the tallest tree in Bath County. It is the start of a new Virginian day!

CRACKING OF THE LIBERTY BELL

One of President John Adams' last official acts in office occurred on January 20, 1801, when he appointed John Marshall to the post of Chief Justice of the United States Supreme Court. Marshall, who at the time was serving in the Adams administration as Secretary of State, was a Virginia-born attorney who had seen active duty in the American Revolution and had served as a U. S. congressman. During his thirty-four year tenure on the high court, Marshall addressed many legal challenges, among them the interpretation of the court's role in the judicial review process. The story goes, that when Marshall died on July 6, 1835, the Liberty Bell in Philadelphia's Independence Hall tolled so many times that it cracked.

Curry Dip

2 cups (16 ounces) mayonnaise
2 tablespoons ketchup
3 tablespoons honey, such as Sweet and Sassy

$^1/_2$ red onion, finely grated
7 to 9 dashes of hot sauce
$1^1/_2$ teaspoons lemon juice
$1^1/_2$ tablespoons curry powder

- Combine the mayonnaise, ketchup, honey, onion, hot sauce, lemon juice, and curry powder in a medium bowl. Stir by hand, or beat lightly with an electric mixer. Store, covered, in the refrigerator.
- Note: This dip can be refrigerated for up to 10 days.
- Makes 1 pint

This is a wonderful dipping sauce to use with veggies, or apple and pear slices. Be creative, and serve it with fresh asparagus or cauliflower to enliven vegetable dishes. We must admit, modestly, that this is the one dish that is repeatedly requested when we are invited to potluck suppers, picnics, and church socials. Best of all, it is so quick and easy.

This was sent by KAREN REED LOWE of Lowelands Farm. Lowelands Farm is the family farm in the hunt country of Middleburg, Virginia. Their first products were introduced in 1984, when their youngest child was two years old. There are now three generations living and working on the farm along with horses, dogs, cats, cows, pygmy goats, chickens, and a miniature donkey.

VIRGINIA AGRICULTURE
Virginia's Finest

Hot Virginia Dip

4 teaspoons butter or margarine
1 cup pecans, chopped
4 teaspoons minced onion
$^1/_4$ cup minced green pepper
$^1/_4$ cup milk

2 (8-ounce) packages cream cheese, softened
2 (2.25 ounce) jars chopped dried beef
1 teaspoon garlic powder
1 cup sour cream

- Preheat the oven to 350°F. Melt 2 teaspoons of the butter or margarine in a medium skillet, and sauté the pecans. Melt the remaining butter or margarine in a separate skillet, and sauté the onion and green pepper.
- Combine the milk, cream cheese, dried beef, garlic powder, and sour cream in a large bowl, and mix well. Stir in the onion and green pepper. Spoon into a $1^1/_2$-quart casserole, and top with the pecans. Bake for 20 minutes. Serve warm with crackers or toast points.
- Makes approximately 3 cups

A real hit at parties, this recipe was shared by DEBBIE WALDROP, a member of the Botetourt County Chapter of the Virginia DAR.

LuLu Paste

1 pound sharp cheese, shredded	1 teaspoon mayonnaise
2 onions, grated	1½ tablespoons lemon juice
1 (12-ounce) bottle seafood cocktail sauce, such as Crosse and Blackwell	1 teaspoon Worcestershire sauce
	Dash of Tabasco sauce

- Process the cheese, onions, cocktail sauce, mayonnaise, lemon juice, Worcestershire sauce, and Tabasco sauce in a blender until smooth, and serve with crackers.
- Makes approximately 12 servings

This is the famous LuLu Paste recipe. I understand it originated decades ago at a social club in Richmond. We obtained it from my wife's sister and were sworn to secrecy. I am now released from this oath, and I can pass on the true ingredients. There is never any left over, and guests frequently ask for the recipe. Absolutely wonderful.

MATT WERTH from Norfolk, Virginia, a really fun guy with a twinkle in his eye, shared this recipe.

MORAN'S
Delectable Dip

1 soft avocado, peeled, seeded	1 (1.4-ounce) package chili or taco seasoning
1 medium tomato	1 (13.5-ounce) bag nacho chips
1 pound cheese, grated	
2 cups sour cream	

- This recipe is concerned with appearance as much as taste. It is very important to make it in the following order.
- Dice the avocado into small pieces, and spread over the bottom of a clear 8×8-inch dish. Dice the tomato, and spread over the top of the avocado. Add a layer of the grated cheese, reserving some to sprinkle over the top as the finishing touch.
- Combine the sour cream and ¾ of the chili or taco seasoning in a medium bowl, and mix until well blended. The sour cream should take on a pinkish tint. Spread the sour cream mixture over the top of the cheese layer. This is actually tricky. The object is not to disturb the cheese. As the finale, sprinkle the reserved cheese over the top. Serve with the nacho chips.
- Makes about 3 pints

This recipe is generously provided by CONGRESSMAN JIM MORAN, who has served in the U.S. House of Representatives from the Eighth Congressional District since 1990 and before that as City Councilman, Mayor, and Vice-Mayor of Alexandria.

VIRGINIA TIMELINE

1584—Captains Philip Amadas and Arthur Barlowe are commissioned by Walter Raleigh to make a reconnaissance of the land soon to be named Virginia, after England's monarch, Elizabeth I, the Virgin Queen.

1585—Elizabeth bestows knighthood upon Raleigh and appoints him to oversee the colonization of Virginia. Sir Richard Grenville plants the first colony on Roanoke Island, part of present-day North Carolina.

1587—Although Raleigh's goal is to colonize the Chesapeake Bay area, a permanent settlement, soon to become known as the famous "Lost Colony," is established instead on Roanoke Island when the fleet's pilot refuses to go farther.

1590—Delayed because of England's war with Spain, an attempt to rescue Roanoke Island's stranded colonists fails when no sign of the settlement is found.

1607—After a seventeen-year hiatus, England finally establishes its first permanent settlement in the New World at Jamestown under the auspices of the newly formed Virginia Company of London.

1610—By the end of winter, more than four hundred residents of Jamestown die from malnutrition and disease in what is called the "starveing time."

BY JOHN LEDERER IN HIS THREE MARCHES.

BYERS STREET BISTRO
Spinach Artichoke Dip

2 tablespoons butter	1 pound ricotta cheese
1 cup finely chopped onion	2 tablespoons salt
2 pounds spinach, chopped	1 tablespoon black pepper
1¹/2 pounds canned artichoke hearts, drained, chopped	1 cup mayonnaise
	2 tablespoons lemon juice
3 pounds cream cheese, softened	2 teaspoons garlic powder
	Mozzarella cheese

- Melt the butter in a large skillet, and sauté the onion until soft. Add the spinach, and sauté until wilted. Place the spinach mixture in a fine mesh sieve, and press out the excess moisture.
- Combine the spinach mixture with the artichokes in a large mixing bowl, and mix well. Add the cream cheese and ricotta cheese, and mix well. Stir in the salt, pepper, mayonnaise, lemon juice, and garlic powder. Season with additional salt and pepper if desired. Spoon into 6-ounce serving dishes, and wrap with plastic wrap. Microwave for 1 1/2 minutes before serving. Sprinkle with mozzarella cheese, and bake until golden brown. Serve with a split, toasted hoagie roll.
- Makes approximately 20 (6-ounce) servings

Byers Street Bistro is a popular gathering place with many regulars. They even have a Mug Club. You can leave your personal mug to use whenever you are there. It is located in the historic warehouse row in the wharf area of historic Staunton, Virginia.

This recipe was obtained through the efforts of E. JANE SHERMAN, Regent of the Colonel Thomas Hughart Chapter of the Virginia DAR.

Boursin Cheese Ball

1 (8-ounce) package cream cheese	1 teaspoon oregano
	1/2 teaspoon basil
2 tablespoons butter or margarine	1/8 teaspoon salt
	1/4 teaspoon cayenne
2 large cloves garlic, crushed	2 tablespoons fresh parsley
1/2 teaspoon fresh lemon juice	Coarse black pepper

- Process the cream cheese, butter, garlic, lemon juice, oregano, basil, salt, cayenne, and parsley in a food processor until blended. Place on waxed paper sprinkled with black pepper. Shape the mixture into a ball. Serve with crackers or thinly sliced French bread.
- Makes about 6 servings

This is a favorite with HARRIET M. GALBRAITH of the Cricket Hill Chapter of the Virginia DAR.

Cheese Torte

8 ounces cream cheese, softened

12 ounces goat cheese, crumbled

¹/₂ pound butter or margarine, softened

1 (10-ounce) bottle of basil pesto, drained

1 cup sun-dried tomatoes, drained, minced

- Beat the cream cheese, goat cheese, and butter or margarine in a bowl until well blended and fluffy. Line a springform pan with cheesecloth, leaving enough so that you can lift the completed torte for serving.
- Layer ¹/₃ of the cheese mixture over the bottom of the pan. Top with half the pesto. Repeat layers. Spread the remaining cheese mixture over the top, and cover with the tomatoes. Place a piece of plastic wrap over the top, and cover with the cheesecloth. Place the pan on a dinner plate lined with paper towels to absorb any excess moisture. Refrigerate overnight so that the torte may become firm.
- To serve, remove the torte from the pan, using the cheesecloth It is possible to do this using two plates (place one plate wrong side up on top, turn the springform pan upside down, remove the pan bottom/cheesecloth, and replace it with the desired serving platter). Serve with crackers or a toasted, sliced French baguette.
- Serves 15 to 20 as an appetizer or cocktail food.

This recipe comes from the family of MARGARET C. TUTTLE, a member of the Albemarle Chapter of the Virginia DAR in Charlottesville, Virginia. Sallie Claudia Pittman, Margaret Tuttle's grandmother, was born in 1863. She was the great-granddaughter of James Pittman, born in 1756 in Amelia County, Virginia, a Revolutionary Patriot who later served as a private and a lieutenant in Georgia. James married Martha Taylor in 1781 in Henry County, Virginia.

ACCOMACK COUNTY

Accomack County—"accomack" is American Indian for "across the water place"—was established in 1634 as one of the Colony's original eight shires. In 1643, its name was changed to Northampton County, and twenty years later, present-day Accomack County was formed out of Northampton. Accomack County contains five hundred two square miles, and the latest census reports a population of 38,305. The county seat is Accomac.

Accomack County is the birthplace of Henry Alexander Wise (1806-1876), governor of Virginia from 1856 until 1860, and at various times a Confederate general, U.S. congressman, and U.S. minister to Brazil. The first theatrical presentation within the boundaries of today's United States was performed at Fowkes' Tavern in this county on August 27, 1665.

CAPTAIN JOHN SMITH ON INDIAN FOOD

In his book, *The Generall Historie of Virginia, New-England, and the Summer Isles*, published in London in 1624, Captain John Smith, the fourth president of the Jamestown Council, described the dining habits of the surrounding Indian tribes.

In March and Aprill they live much upon their fishing wires [weirs, or fish traps]; and feed on fish, Turkies, and Squirrels. In May and June they plant their fields, and live most on Acornes, Walnuts, and fish. But to mend their dyet, some disperse themselves in

Four-Cheese Pâté

3 (8-ounce) packages cream cheese, softened	1 cup shredded Swiss cheese
2 tablespoons milk	1 (4½-ounce) package Camembert or Brie cheese, softened
1 cup toasted chopped pecans	Grapes, apple wedges, and gingersnaps, optional
1 (4-ounce) package blue cheese	

- Line a lightly greased, 8-inch round cake pan with plastic wrap. Combine 1 package of the cream cheese and the milk in a medium mixing bowl. Beat at medium speed with an electric mixer until smooth. Spread the mixture into the prepared pan, and sprinkle evenly with the pecans to the edge of the pan. Chill, covered.
- Combine the remaining cream cheese, blue cheese, Swiss cheese, and Camembert or Brie (including rind) in a medium bowl, and beat until blended. Spoon the mixture over the pecan layer, and spread to the edge of the pan. Chill, covered with plastic wrap, for at least 4 hours or up to 1 week.
- To serve, invert the pâté onto a serving plate, and remove the plastic wrap carefully. Garnish with grapes, if desired, and serve with apple wedges and gingersnaps.
- Makes 4½ cups

This recipe was sent by SUE C. MURRAY, a member of the Front Royal Chapter of the Virginia DAR. Sue Murray and her husband, Joe, live in *Erin* circa 1840, a Virginia Historic Landmark located seven miles north of Front Royal. It is a wonderful example of a three-part, Greek Revival, plantation house. It has a sweeping spiral staircase, semi-circular hall, and handsome woodwork.

Shrimp Butter

2 (5-ounce) cans shrimp, finely chopped	¾ cup (1½ sticks) butter or margarine, softened
1 tablespoon minced onion	8 ounces cream cheese, softened
Juice of 1 lemon	
¼ cup mayonnaise	

- Combine the shrimp, onion, lemon juice, mayonnaise, butter or margarine, and cream cheese in a large bowl, and beat at low speed. Spoon into a greased, medium-size mold. Refrigerate, covered, for several hours. Serve with crackers. May be frozen.
- Makes about 4 cups

This was sent by JEAN KEMP of Roanoke, a member of the Colonel William Preston Chapter of the Virginia DAR.

small companies, and live upon fish, beasts, crabs, oysters, land Tortoises, strawberries, mulberries, and such like. In June, July, and August, they feed upon the rootes of Tockwough [green arrow arum] berries, fish, and greene wheat [corn]. It is strange to see how their bodies alter with their dyet, even as deere and wilde beasts they seeme fat and leane, strong and weake. Powhatan, their great King, and some others that are provident, rost their fish and flesh upon hurdles . . . and keepe it till scarce times.

Artichoke Nibbles

2 (12-ounce) jars marinated
  artichoke hearts
1 small onion, chopped
1 clove garlic, minced
4 eggs
1/4 cup fine dried bread
  crumbs

1/2 teaspoon salt
1/8 teaspoon pepper
1/8 teaspoon oregano
1/8 teaspoon Tabasco sauce
1/2 pound cheese, shredded
2 tablespoons minced
  parsley

- Preheat the oven to 325°F. Drain the marinade from 1 jar of artichokes into a frying pan. Drain the remaining jar, and discard the liquid. Chop the artichokes. Add the onion and garlic to the frying pan. Sauté until the onion is soft. Beat the eggs in a medium bowl, and add the bread crumbs, salt, pepper, oregano, and Tabasco sauce. Add the cheese, parsley, artichokes, and onion mixture.
- Spoon into a greased 7×11-inch baking dish, and bake for 30 minutes. Let stand until cool. Cut into 1-inch squares. Serve cold, or reheat in a 350°F oven for 10 to 12 minutes.
- Makes about 70 (1-inch) squares

This was sent by MARY PRESCOTT, Regent of the Colonel William Preston Chapter of the Virginia DAR.

POOR MARINER'S SHANTY
Crab Appetizers

1 pound crabmeat, back-fin
  or claw meat, or a mixture
1 medium onion, chopped
1/4 to 1/2 cup mayonnaise, or
  enough to moisten
  crabmeat

1 tablespoon horseradish
Salt and pepper
1 (1-pound) package party
  rye bread, toasted
8 to 12 processed cheese
  slices, such as Velveeta

- Place the crabmeat in a large bowl, and remove any bits of shells. Combine the crabmeat and onion in a bowl. Blend in enough of the mayonnaise to moisten. Add the horseradish, salt and pepper to taste., and mix well. Place the rye bread on a baking sheet. Spoon the crabmeat mixture onto the rye slices. Top with 1/4 slice of Velveeta cheese. Broil until the cheese melts. Serve warm.
- Makes 35 to 45 single servings

This is from SALLY LLOYD, who, with her husband, Jerry, is the owner of Poor Mariner's Shanty in Coles Point, Virginia. Poor Mariner's Shanty was founded in 1996 to showcase bay buoy products. Lobster and crab pot buoys are hand painted by artisans of the Chesapeake Bay. Bay buoys are the same buoys used by watermen. They make great gifts, express your nautical persona, and bring the friendly greetings of the waterways to home and hearth.

CHESAPEAKE BAY BRIDGE TUNNEL

A manmade phenomenon surrounded by the natural beauty of the Chesapeake Bay makes the Bridge Tunnel a favorite travel route and a popular tourist attraction. Following its opening on April 15, 1964, the Chesapeake Bay Bridge Tunnel was selected as "One of the Seven Engineering Wonders of the Modern World," and in 1965 it was distinguished as "The Outstanding Civil Engineering Achievement" by the American Society of Civil Engineers. In 2000, the Bridge Tunnel was recognized by *Structural Engineer* magazine as one of "The Seven Structural Engineering Wonders of America for the 20th Century." Measuring seventeen and six-tenths miles from shore to shore, the crossing is considered one of the largest bridge tunnel complexes in the world. Sea Gull Island, one of the four manmade islands, offers a 625-foot, handicap-accessible fishing pier, where travelers cast lines for bluefish, trout, and croaker (the Bridge Tunnel may be the only major highway in the world offering free fishing). Visitors may also enjoy the scenic view of the Hampton Roads harbor, one of the world's busiest seaports, where U.S. Navy and commercial ships ply the waters. Sea Gull Island also offers a seaside restaurant and an adjoining gift shop.

Fun Day on the Bay, an annual free event that allows bicyclists and walkers to cross portions of the eighteen-mile structure, started in 1998 to celebrate the completion of a $250 million expansion project. The inaugural Trigon Bay Bridge Marathon, a unique opportunity for marathoners to run across the Chesapeake Bay Bridge Tunnel, took place in October 2002. Participants ran fourteen and one-half miles of the twenty-six-mile marathon distance over and under the magnificent waters of the Chesapeake Bay, including running through two tunnels. This event marked the first time that a sanctioned marathon had ever been run over a bridge and subsequently through a tunnel along a major highway route.

Pan-Seared Tuna with Curry Dipping Sauce

TUNA

1 pound fresh tuna, dark portions removed, cut into bite-size cubes	1 teaspoon white pepper
	3 tablespoons vegetable oil for searing
1 cup all-purpose flour	30 (6-inch) wooden skewers
2 teaspoons salt	Curry Dipping Sauce

- Combine the tuna with the flour, salt, and pepper in a mesh strainer, shaking off any excess flour. Pour 2 tablespoons of the oil into a hot sauté pan. Sear the tuna quickly, about 6 pieces at a time, browning on all sides.
- Add the remaining oil as needed. Place each piece of tuna on a wooden skewer, and serve warm with the curry dipping sauce.
- Note: As always when browning, be sure not to overcook or overcrowd the sauté pan. The tuna is best left a little pink inside.
- Makes 30 servings

CURRY DIPPING SAUCE

1/4 cup Major Grey's Mango Chutney	1/2 cup plain yogurt
	1 teaspoon curry powder
1/2 cup mayonnaise	1/2 teaspoon Dijon mustard

- Process the chutney in a food processor for 10 seconds or until puréed. Combine with the mayonnaise, yogurt, curry powder, and Dijon mustard in a bowl.
- Refrigerate the dipping sauce, covered, until ready to serve.
- Note: The chutney's color will intensify after several hours.
- Makes 1 1/2 cups

Unmistakable, exotic, and extraordinarily versatile. No wonder Major Grey and his compatriots brought curry home in triumph from the far reaches of the Empire. Married to its longtime companion chutney, curry provides the basis for a sauce that is exceptionally good with chicken or seafood.

The recipe is shared by PETER COE of Taste Unlimited, a specialty food and wine retail business in Norfolk, Virginia Beach, and Chesapeake, Virginia. Founded by Coe in 1973, Taste Unlimited is known for carefully chosen specialty food products, prepared foods, and wines, as well as being one of the leading caterers in southeast Virginia. Coe recently authored and published a cookbook called *Entertaining With Taste* and he also started a Taste Unlimited cooking school. This particular recipe is an all-time favorite in the Taste Unlimited catering repertoire. Taste sensations may come and go, but this is one hors d'oeuvre that clients never stop requesting. It inevitably precipitates a huddle of guests who gather as each tray full is brought from the kitchen.

FORMER GOVERNOR AND MRS. LINWOOD HOLTON'S

Cheese Dreams

1 cup (2 sticks) melted
butter or margarine
$^1/_2$ pound sharp cheddar
cheese, grated
Dash of cayenne

$^1/_2$ teaspoon salt
2 cups all-purpose flour
2 cups crisp rice cereal,
such as Rice Krispies

- Preheat the oven to 315°F. Combine the butter or margarine, cheese, cayenne, salt, and flour in a bowl and mix well. Gently mix in the cereal.
- Shape the mixture into small balls, and place on a lightly greased baking sheet. Press to the desired size with your finger or a fork. Bake for 20 to 30 minutes.
- Makes about 50 dreams

This recipe was generously shared by VIRGINIA R. HOLTON, former First Lady of Virginia (1970 to 1974). She and her husband, former Governor Linwood Holton, live on the Northern Neck of Virginia. When not making Cheese Dreams, she has devoted herself to a continuous variety of worthwhile civic activities. She is currently focusing on organizations for children, her church, the Chesapeake Bay Foundation, and Habitat for Humanity. She is also the mother of four successful children and the grandmother of six. Her honors are numerous. Governor Holton remains very active throughout the state, and, of course, as an attorney. He served as president for the Center for Innovative Technology until 1994 and at the same time chaired the Metropolitan Washington Airports Authority. He is currently a member of the Amtrak Board of Directors. Education and opportunities for children, as well as all people, remain a constant focus for the Holtons.

ALBEMARLE COUNTY

Albemarle County was organized in 1744 from land in Goochland County. Named for the governor of Virginia at the time, the Earl of Albemarle (1702-1754), the county's present size is seven hundred fifty-one square miles. Its latest population figures show 79,236 residents. Charlottesville is the county seat.

Thomas Jefferson, Meriwether Lewis, and General George Rogers Clark were all born and raised in Albemarle County, and James Monroe maintained his residence, Ash Lawn, there for nearly twenty years. Dr. Thomas Walker, an early explorer of Cumberland Gap, built his house, Castle Hill, in the county in 1765.

VIRGINIA'S HISTORIC COVERED BRIDGES

Starting almost two hundred years ago, covered bridges in Virginia could be found crossing rivers and streams throughout the countryside. Though covered bridges were vital to travelers for years, today only eight remain. Five have been preserved as landmarks, while three are on private property.

Virginia's Bridge Lady, Leola Pierce, an energetic engineer seventy-nine years young from Portsmouth, has, along with her son, Stephen Pierce, researched, measured, sketched plans, and fallen in love with these remaining covered bridges. In her book *Covered Bridges in Virginia*, she describes and tells the history of each one in vivid and picturesque terms. Pierce brings these "Old Ladies," as covered bridges are often referred to, alive for each of us.

Humpback Covered Bridge, built in 1857 over Dunlap Creek, is located in Alleghany County. The oldest covered bridge in Virginia, it is the only one in the United States with the Kingpost trussed arch or "humped" design.

Meems Bottom Covered Bridge, built in 1894, is the longest covered bridge in Virginia and the only one carrying modern-day traffic over the North Fork of the Shenandoah River in Shenandoah County.

Jack's Creek Covered Bridge was built in 1914 over the Smith River in Patrick County. It was built to serve a church and has a very unusual design.

Sinking Creek Covered Bridge, built in 1916 over Sinking Creek in Giles County, has a tiny underpass for animals to travel through rather than go up over the elevated roadway approach to the bridge.

Bob White Bridge, built in 1921 over the Smith River in Patrick County, has two spans and leads to a church. It was named after the Bob White Post Office, but no one knows why.

These bridges are located on private property:

- Biedler Farm Covered Bridge was built in 1896 over Smith Creek in Rockingham County.
- Link's Farm Covered Bridge, built in 1912 over Sinking Creek in Giles County, is decorated for Christmas with a wreath over her entrance.
- C.K. Reynold's Covered Bridge, built in 1919 over Sinking Creek in Giles County, is the shortest historic bridge in Virginia.

Covered Bridges in Virginia
Leola B. Pierce

Horseradish Meatballs in Orange Sauce

MEATBALLS

2 egg yolks, or 1 whole egg
1/2 cup water
1/2 cup dried bread crumbs
2 tablespoons horseradish
1 cup finely chopped water chestnuts
1 1/2 pounds ground chuck

ORANGE SAUCE

1 teaspoon cornstarch
1/3 cup water
2/3 cup orange marmalade
2 cloves garlic, minced
1/4 cup soy sauce
2 tablespoons lemon juice

- To prepare the meatballs, preheat the oven to 375°F. Beat the egg yolks and water in a large bowl. Add the bread crumbs, horseradish, water chestnuts, and ground chuck, and mix well. Shape into small balls. Place the meatballs in a shallow pan. Bake for 12 minutes.
- To prepare the orange sauce, combine the cornstarch and water in a small saucepan, and simmer until blended, stirring constantly. Combine the marmalade, garlic, soy sauce, and lemon juice in a medium saucepan, and mix well. Add the cornstarch mixture. Bring to a boil over high heat. Cook until thickened, stirring constantly.
- To serve, place the meatballs in a chafing dish. Pour the orange sauce over the meatballs. Use wooden party picks to spear the meatballs.
- Double the recipe for a large group of more than eight people, and enjoy.
- Makes 6 to 8 servings

This recipe sent by JOAN GOODENOUGH, member of the Fauquier Court House Chapter of the Virginia DAR.

ALLEGHANY COUNTY

Alleghany County, named for the Alleghany Mountains, was established in 1822 from sections of neighboring Bath, Botetourt, and Monroe Counties. It covers four hundred fifty-eight square miles and is home to 12,926 residents. Covington is the county seat.

The noted Shawnee Indian chief Cornstalk attacked Fort Breckenridge in this county in 1763 during Pontiac's War. Alleghany County was an important producer of iron in the nineteenth century, and several furnaces are scattered across its face.

ROWENA'S KITCHEN TIPS

If you have trouble keeping your flour dry, put a bay leaf in your canister. It absorbs the extra moisture.

Pineapple Sunset

2 tablespoons butter or
  margarine
1/4 cup firmly packed brown
  sugar
2 tablespoons mild curry
  powder

1 tablespoon sherry
1 fresh pineapple, cut into
  bite-size pieces
Mint leaves for garnish

- Combine the butter or margarine, sugar, and curry powder in a small saucepan, and mix well. Simmer over low heat until the mixture becomes a smooth glaze. Stir in the sherry. Add the pineapple, coating the pieces with the syrup. Serve warm or chilled. Garnish with mint.
- Makes 6 to 8 servings

This recipe came from DOROTHY FAGAN, who is creator of original pastel paintings and limited edition prints inspired by Virginia landscapes, including one of Laurel Bluff, which in turn inspired the recipe called Pineapple Sunset. Laurel Bluff, a tranquil sanctuary with glorious sunsets, overlooks the Warwick River in southeastern Virginia. Dorothy's paintings have been represented in some of the nation's most prestigious art exhibitions and collections, and she is a very special lady.

Spinach Cheese Delights

1/4 cup (1/2 stick) butter or
  margarine
3 eggs
1 cup flour
1 cup milk
1 teaspoon salt
1 teaspoon baking powder

1 pound Monterey Jack
  cheese or other mild
  white cheese, grated
2 (10-ounce) packages
  chopped, frozen spinach,
  thawed, drained well

- Preheat the oven to 350°F. Melt the butter or margarine in a 9×13-inch baking pan. Remove the pan from the oven. Beat the eggs in a large mixing bowl. Add the flour, milk, salt, and baking powder, and mix well. Stir in the cheese and spinach. Pour into the prepared baking pan, and bake for 35 minutes. Let stand for 45 minutes to cool. Cut into bite-sized squares for appetizers or large squares to serve with a meal.
- To freeze, place the squares on a baking sheet, and allow to freeze. Store in plastic bags in the freezer. To serve, place the squares on a baking sheet and heat at 325°F for 12 minutes.
- Makes 25 appetizers or 12 dinner servings

DORIS LUGAR WHITSON, a member of the Great Bridge Chapter, Virginia DAR, sent this recipe.

Beverages

Mulled Apple Cider

8 cups fresh apple cider
1 cup firmly packed light
  brown sugar
$1/2$ cup lemon juice

$1/2$ teaspoon grated nutmeg
1 cinnamon stick
8 whole cloves

- Combine the cider, sugar, lemon juice, and nutmeg in a large saucepan, and mix well. Tie the cinnamon stick and the cloves in a cheesecloth bag, and place in the saucepan. Simmer over medium-high heat for 10 minutes. Remove the bag of spices and serve hot.
- Makes 10 to 12 servings

A special thank-you to CHOWNING'S TAVERN for sharing their recipe.

COFFEES AND TEAS
FIRST COLONY
EST. 1902

Special Irish Coffee

2 teaspoons (or more)
  sugar
2 ounces Bushmill's Irish
  whiskey

5 ounces First Colony
  Coffee, brewed at full
  strength
Whipped cream, chilled

- Place the sugar in a mug made especially for Irish coffee. Pour in the whiskey and the hot coffee. Stir until the sugar is dissolved. Top with a dollop of the whipped cream.
- Makes 1 serving

Whipped cream should stand on top and the drink enjoyed while sipping through the cream. The secret is in the coffee: Always use First Colony Coffee—a Columbian Supremo, Special House Blend or our new Centennial Blend will work beautifully.

VIRGINIA AGRICULTURE
Virginia's Finest

The Brockenbrough and Gill families have supplied the Tidewater area households and restaurants the finest coffees since 1902. TOM BROCKENBROUGH is a member of the fourth generation to head First Colony Coffee and Tea Company, Inc., from the same warehouse in Norfolk's Ghent area that his great-grandfather operated. This coffee drink is Tom's favorite, as it was his father's before him.

YORKTOWN'S NANCY THOMAS

Nancy Thomas is a contemporary artist whose works are found in magazines, decorator books, museums, Hollywood films, Broadway productions, television, and homes across the country. She is versatile enough to design for the White House, Colonial Williamsburg, and the Museum of American Folk Art, as well as refrigerator magnets! Her work is prized through the country for its wonderful color, its warmth, and its style.

Thomas has lived and painted in historic Yorktown for over thirty years. Her splendid fences and herb gardens greet visitors to her shop and studio. Thomas also has a shop in Market Square of Williamsburg adjacent to Colonial Williamsburg and her good friends at the Trellis restaurant. Her joint creation with Trellis chef Marcel Desaulniers—the book *Alphabet of Sweets*, includes reproductions of twenty-seven original dessert-inspired paintings.

Long a passionate collector of beautiful antiques, Thomas has a studio and shops filled with the treasures she has gathered through the years. She likes to see her works coupled with antiques for a style that is exciting, yet warm and inviting. Her way with celebrating food in art led her to be commissioned to honor chef Julia Child on her ninetieth birthday. Thomas proudly unveiled the piece in San Francisco for Child as well known restauranteurs around the world joined in the celebration.

POCAHONTAS AND JOHN ROLFE

During the year 1613, affairs in Jamestown, Virginia were not going well for the newly arrived English colonists, primarily because of Indian hostility toward the newcomers. Matoaka, whose nickname was Pocahontas—loosely translated as "the naughty one" for her playful nature—was the daughter of the powerful chief Powhatan, and a familiar figure to the colonists. As a defensive move, Pocahontas was captured and held hostage until the Indians ceased their warring activities. In the meantime, the lovely Pocahontas and the Englishman widower, John Rolfe, who had advanced the economy of the colony by the introduction of tobacco, fell in love. The couple was married on April 5, 1614. Two years later, Pocahontas and Rolfe, along with their infant son, Thomas, sailed to England. The Indian princess died a few years later upon the eve of her return to Virginia.

Christiana Campbell's
TAVERN

Wassail

1 cup sugar	2 cups orange juice
4 cinnamon sticks	$1/2$ cup lemon juice
3 lemon slices	6 cups dry red wine
$1/2$ cup water	1 cup dry sherry
2 cups pineapple juice	Lemon slices for garnish

- Combine the sugar, cinnamon sticks, lemon slices, and water in a large saucepan, and bring to a boil over high heat. Boil for 5 minutes and strain. Discard the cinnamon sticks and lemon slices. Pour the pineapple juice, orange juice, lemon juice, wine, and sherry into a large saucepan, and simmer over medium heat. Do not boil. Combine the wine mixture and sugar syrup in a serving bowl. Ladle into mugs, and garnish with lemon slices. Serve hot.
- Makes 20 servings

Ves heill *is Norse for "be in good health." The early English toast to someone's health has become a popular part of the special Christmas celebrations at Colonial Williamsburg. Whole cloves, allspice berries, or shavings of mace can be added or substituted.*

CHRISTIANA CAMPBELL'S TAVERN sent us this recipe.

Frozen Daiquiri

1 (6-ounce) can frozen limeade	1 (12-ounce) can frozen pink lemonade
12 ounces light rum	36 ounces water

- Combine the limeade, rum, lemonade, and water in a large container, and mix well. Freeze, covered, for at least 12 hours. Stir well. Freeze for an additional 12 hours. Stir and serve immediately. Frozen daiquiris will keep in the freezer for several months.
- Makes 10 to 12 servings

My husband and I moved to Virginia Beach in 1986, following his retirement from the U.S. Navy and my eight-year tour as a Foreign Service Officer. While serving as the Cultural Attaché at the U.S. Embassy in Ottawa, Canada, a newspaper reporter once described me as "the Daiquiri Diplomat" because my daiquiris were so popular. To this very day, some Canadian friends will, upon arrival in our home, peer into the freezer to look for daiquiris.

CATHERINE COLGAN, one of the most organized and dedicated women I know, shared this recipe.

Dandelion Wine

4 quarts boiling water	4 oranges, sliced
4 quarts dandelion blooms, yellow centers only	4 lemons, sliced
	4 pounds sugar

- Pour the boiling water over the dandelion blooms, orange slices, and lemon slices in a large crock, and let the mixture stand, covered, for 24 hours. Strain (do not squeeze) the mixture, and add the sugar. Let stand, covered, in a warm place until fermentation ceases, approximately 1 week.
- Strain the wine into containers. (I store mine in large, glass pop bottles.) Cork the containers with cotton, and store in a cellar or cool basement for 3 weeks. Decant and cork tightly. Can use when winter comes.
- Makes approximately 4 quarts

This is Uncle Paul Bruce's recipe as given to Zared Earnest, his niece, by his wife Beulah. PAUL BRUCE and ALMA SHUFFLEBARGER shared this recipe with us. Their forebears, William and Anna Ballard Bruce, came to the region known as Bland County from Albermarle County after the American Revolution. Alma E. Shufflebarger is a member of the Fort Maiden Spring Chapter of the Virginia DAR in Tazwell, Virginia.

Peach Toddy

1 cup smashed fresh peaches	4 ounces bourbon
1 cup crushed ice	

- Refrigerate two silver cups (a must). Fill the cups with the fresh peaches. Add the crushed ice, and pour in the bourbon. Stir with a silver teaspoon (a must).
- Sit on the porch and rock, and then go take a nap. Get up and start again.
- Makes 2 servings

The recipe was given to me by an elderly DAR member.

DEBORAH WILLIAMS CHAPPELL of the Constantia Chapter of the Virginia DAR located in Suffolk, Virginia, shared this recipe.

DID YOU KNOW THAT:

Cider was enormously popular with the "middling sort" in early Virginia. Apples grown on plantations near Williamsburg provided the juice, which was fresh when first pressed, but quickly fermented.

YES, VIRGINIA, THERE WAS A REAL DR. PEPPER

In our sister state of Texas, there's a place in Waco that says it is the "home of Dr. Pepper." True, the beverage was concocted there at a drug store in 1885. True, Dr. Pepper is the oldest major manufacturer of soft drink formulas and syrups in the United States. True, it was invented by a young English pharmacist, Charles Alderton, while he was working behind the fountain at Wade B. Morrison's Old Corner Drug Store. But the owner of the drug store and the namesake of the popular drink were Virginians!

As a teenager in the 1870s, Wade Morrison lived with his family in the Christiansburg and Wytheville areas (Montgomery County). He worked as a druggist clerk for Dr. Charles T. Pepper, graduate of the University of Virginia Medical School in the class of 1855. Dr. Pepper practiced medicine within his pharmacy in the Rural Retreat community.

Seventeen-year-old Morrison was very much in love with Dr. Pepper's sixteen-year-old daughter, Minerva A. Pepper.

The Morrison family moved away to Round Rock (Williamson County), Texas, by 1880. Poor Wade had to leave his love behind. But he did well enough by 1885 to own his own drug store. When his clerk Charles Alderton mixed carbonated water with some flavorings one day in Waco, the customers really liked it. Morrison is thought to have named the drink for Dr. Pepper—back in Virginia. Some say he was trying to impress the doctor enough to get Minerva's hand in marriage across the miles. But others say the drink was named for his horse, Dr. Pepper. Even so, the horse had been named for the same man!

By 1891, Morrison decided to bottle the drink, and by 1904, it was introduced at the St. Louis World's Fair. He did not get to marry Minerva, but Rural Retreat, Virginia, can also claim to be the "home of Dr. Pepper!"

Mint Julep Iced Tea

BROWN SUGAR SYRUP

1 cup firmly packed light brown sugar	1 cup cold water

- Heat the sugar and water in a small sucepan over medium heat. Bring to a boil, stirring occasionally. Simmer for 6 to 8 minutes. Remove from the heat and cool. Store, covered, in the refrigerator.
- Note: The syrup will have a medium brown color.
- Makes about 1 cup

ICED TEA

2 tablespoons (6 tea bags) mint tea	2 ice cubes
1 quart cold water	Mint leaves
Brown Sugar Syrup	Confectioners' sugar,
1 to 1¼ cups bourbon	optional

- Place the loose tea or bags into a large glass container. Add the cold water. Stir well, and chill, covered, in the refrigerator overnight. Strain the tea through a fine sieve or remove the bags. Note: Strain the leaves through a sieve lined with a coffee filter.
- Press the leaves or bags to extract all the liquid. Sweeten to taste with the Brown Sugar Syrup, and chill, covered, in the refrigerator until serving time. To serve, pour the sweetened mint tea into a 2-quart pitcher, add the bourbon, and stir. Add the ice cubes and a few bruised mint leaves. Pour into ice-filled glasses, and garnish with mint dusted with confectioners' sugar, if desired.
- Makes 6 (8-ounce) servings

I have always loved Mint Juleps—in fact, we served them at our wedding reception in Leesburg. This variation features the best of the South, iced tea and juleps. The brown sugar syrup complements the bourbon quite nicely. This drink must have been very refreshing on that hot July day.

This comes to us from MARTHA CRIMMINS, who established Perfect To A Tea in 1999 in Fredericksburg, Virginia. As tea mistress, she conducts presentations and lectures for organizations, fundraisers, and business or social occasions on the legend, lore, and etiquette of "taking tea." Perfect To A Tea also features many fine tea accoutrements so you may savor this timeless ritual at home.

DID YOU KNOW THAT:

Former U. S. presidents, Thomas Jefferson and John Adams, both died within hours of each other on the same day, July 4, 1826—the fiftieth anniversary of the signing of the Declaration of Independence?

Rummer

1¹/₄ ounces dark rum
³/₄ ounce peach brandy
³/₄ ounce apricot brandy
Ice cubes

Orange slice for garnish
Maraschino cherry for
garnish

- Pour the rum, peach brandy, and apricot brandy into an 8-ounce glass. Add ice cubes as desired. Garnish with the orange slice and maraschino cherry.
- Makes 1 serving

SHIELD'S TAVERN generously provided this recipe.

Coffee Punch

1 pint milk
2 quarts brewed strong
  coffee
2 tablespoons vanilla
  extract

¹/₂ cup sugar
1 quart vanilla ice cream
Whipped cream

- Combine the milk, coffee, vanilla extract, and sugar in a large pitcher. Chill until serving time, stirring occasionally.
- To serve, break the ice cream into chunks, and place in a punch bowl. Pour the coffee mixture over the ice cream. Cover the surface with whipped cream.
- Variations: Sprinkle the punch with nutmeg or shaved chocolate. You may substitute chocolate ice cream. Or the whipped cream may be flavored with ¹/₂ tablespoon brandy or sherry.
- Makes 10 servings

This recipe submitted by MARY BROWNE, Regent of the Cameron Parish Chapter of the Virginia DAR. This great punch was served at a dedication ceremony in April 2002, honoring Francis Lightfoot Lee, the only resident of Loudon County to sign the Declaration of Independence. The plaque is installed in the main terminal of Washington Dulles Airport, which is now on land once owned by Francis Lightfoot Lee. The commemorating plaque was provided by the Cameron Parish Chapter of the Virginia DAR.

DID YOU KNOW THAT:

Virginia became the first state in the nation whose population passed the one million mark (1820)?

JOHN FONTAINE ON CONVIVIALITY

Conviviality has always been a Virginia tradition. Good reasons to celebrate ranged from witnessing a bountiful growing season to triumphing in a political race to the successful conclusion of a military campaign. In some cases, however, one apparently needed very little stimulus to party. John Fontaine, a British army officer who accompanied Lieutenant-Governor Alexander Spotswood with an expedition to explore the Blue Ridge Mountains, wrote about one such occasion in his journal. Spotswood and his followers had just breached the wilderness fastness of the Blue Ridge Mountains, crossed over to the western side, and spied the Shenandoah Valley. On September 5, 1716, when the group chanced upon the spring that was the headwaters of the James River, "where it runs no bigger than a man's arm . . . we drank [to] King George's health, and

all the Royal Family's, at the very top of the Appalachian mountains." The following day, after making more discoveries, the men of Spotswood's expedition:

> *. . . had a good dinner, and after it we got the men together, and loaded all their arms, and we drank the King's health in Champagne, and fired a volley—the Princess's health in Burgundy, and fired a volley, and all the rest of the Royal Family in claret, and a volley. We drank the Governor's health and fired another volley. We had several sorts of liquors, viz., Virginia red wine and white wine, Irish usquebaugh, brandy, shrub, two sorts of rum, champagne, canary, cherry, punch, water, cider, etc.*

My Favorite Punch

3 (12-ounce) cans frozen orange juice concentrate, undiluted
3 (12-ounce) cans frozen lemonade concentrate, undiluted
2½ pounds sugar

Water
6 (46-ounce) cans pineapple juice
1 (8-ounce) bottle lime juice concentrate
Ginger ale, chilled

- Thaw the frozen orange juice concentrate and lemonade concentrate. For simple syrup, place the sugar in a medium saucepan, and add enough water to cover. Bring to a boil, remove from the heat, and let stand until cool.
- Combine the orange juice concentrate, lemonade concentrate, pineapple juice, lime juice concentrate, and simple syrup in a large container. Pour into gallon jugs, and store in the refrigerator for at least 3 days.
- To serve, add 3 quarts ginger ale to each gallon of juice mixture, and mix gently.
- Variation: For spiked punch, add 1 quart or more of whiskey to each gallon of juice and ginger ale mixture at serving time.
- Note: The flavors of this punch are enhanced if prepared several days in advance.
- Makes approximately 40 to 50 servings

The recipe is shared by MARTHA D. JAMES of the Northampton County Chapter of the Virginia DAR.

THE
KING's ARMS

Berry Shrub

3 cups cranberry juice
¾ cup apple juice
1 pint raspberry sherbet

8 sprigs of fresh mint for garnish

- Combine the cranberry juice and apple juice in a large bowl, and chill thoroughly. Pour into tall glasses, and top each serving with a scoop of sherbet. Garnish each serving with a sprig of mint.
- Makes 8 servings

THE KING'S ARMS TAVERN kindly sent us this recipe.

AD FOR A BAR-KEEP

A young man qualified to act as bar-keeper, that writes a tolerable good hand, and understands something of accounts. Such a one, coming well recommended, will meet with proper encouragement from John Pullett.

—Virginia Gazette, *August 7, 1766*

DOUMAR'S
Lime (or Orange) Freeze

2 large scoops lime (or orange) sherbet
1 large scoop vanilla ice cream

2 teaspoons sugar
2 teaspoons water
2 ounces carbonated water

- Combine the sherbet, ice cream, sugar, water, and carbonated water in a blender. Add more carbonated water if the freeze is too thick.
- Makes 1 serving

DOUMAR'S is the home of the original waffle ice-cream-cone machine. Doumar's still has, and uses, the original machine daily. As direct descendants of the inventor of the ice cream cone, the Doumar family continues this great American tradition at the Norfolk location. Doumar's may be one of the last real drive-ins from the 1930s. Girls with big smiles deliver cones, thick, creamy milkshakes, delicious homemade burgers, and sandwiches. And they still use trays that latch on the car window. You feel well treated at Doumar's of Norfolk.

(Almost) Orange Julius

$^1/_2$ can (3 ounces) frozen orange juice concentrate
$^1/_2$ cup milk
$^1/_2$ cup water

$^1/_4$ cup sugar
$^1/_2$ teaspoon vanilla extract
5 to 6 ice cubes

- Combine the concentrate, milk, water, sugar, vanilla extract, and ice cubes in a blender and blend well.
- Note: For adults, try adding a little vodka.
- Makes approximately 2 servings

This is a real favorite of my son. He likes it almost anytime, but the recipe generally comes out when he has friends over so he can impress them.

JANE MIHALYKA GIBSON of the Chesapeake Chapter of the Virginia DAR contributed this recipe.

DID YOU KNOW THAT:

The water just off Cape Henry was the site of the world's first jet airplane landing on a ship (July 21, 1946)?

ROWENA'S KITCHEN TIPS

Add a little grated carrot or raw potato to meatloaf or burgers. It really improves the moisture.

YES, VIRGINIA, YOU CAN CLAIM MOUNTAIN DEW!

It took three years for Marion, Virginia area resident William H. (Bill) Jones to come up with the right formula for his lemon-lime drink base. When his children came home from school in the afternoons, he would have the "tastings" ready on the kitchen table. Their opinions did not always agree with Bill's, yet he kept experimenting with the flavors and coaxed friends to try them as well. The employees at Flossie Richardson's Florist shop (where his wife worked) were candidates for "tastings" as were the folks at the Tip Corporation of America where Bill's friend, Clay Church, was the owner. Bill knew his friend, Wythe Hull, who worked at the local Pepsi plant, would want to try it as well.

At first, bottlers turned Bill down when he tried to peddle his final formula. He helped refinance the Tip Corporation and used the name of an old lithiated lemon-lime soda that his friend Ollie Hartman had used years before. The words "Mountain Dew" on the bottles of that product referred to the slang used for the moonshine coming out of the hills of Virginia. The original formula had been called "zero proof hillbilly moonshine." Bill hurriedly sought attention for his drink as Pepsi scrambled to invent a competitor called "Teem." Pepsi would not allow any affiliated bottler to manufacture a similar tasting drink, so Bill added enough orange juice to his formula for it to be considered as a different category. He also reduced the amount of carbonation in his version, added more sugar, and was extra generous with the caffeine!

He was finally able to convince Charles and Herman Minges in North Carolina to bottle the drink. The catch was it still had to be called "Mountain Dew" because they had been stuck with old bottles of Ollie's product from the 1940's. In April of 1961, Mountain Dew was introduced and became an instant hit. Soon America's bottlers were demanding the formula! Within three years, the Tip Corporation was supplying forty bottlers, and they sold over 10 million cases of Mountain Dew a year! By 1964, Pepsi offered Bill an offer he couldn't refuse, and then the drink became Pepsi's second-best selling drink.

Alpenglow
Sparkling Cider

Freezeland Float

1 (25.4-ounce) bottle of
  Alpenglow Virginia
  Sparkling Cider

Cinnamon to taste
1 pint vanilla ice cream,
  softened

- Combine the cider and cinnamon in a bowl, and mix well. Pour the cider mixture into tall glasses and top each with a scoop of ice cream. Sprinkle with additional cinnamon.
- Makes 4 to 6 servings

Virginia's Finest

Shared by DEBBIE HUNTER of Linden Beverage Company, home of Alpenglow Sparkling Cider, located in the beautiful Shenandoah Valley. Freezeland Float is the namesake of the original Freezeland Orchard (named for the fact that it was protected from freezing), which has been in the Lacy and White families for ninety years. Mr. Ben R. Lacy III, inventor of Alpenglow Sparkling ciders and owner of Linden Beverage Company, uses Virginia winesap apples. These apples are known to make the finest-tasting apple juice. They are one variety of apples used in blending Alpenglow Sparkling ciders in four delicious, non-alcoholic varieties. His father, Dr. Ben R. Lacy, a Presbyterian minister who was president of Union Theological Seminary in Richmond, Virginia, always brought home sparkling cider while attending Oxford as a Rhodes Scholar. This gave Ben a dream to invent.

Debbie Hunter adds this wonderful story about the company.

As you know, young companies experience many growing pains, and one of our experiences was unique. We were excited about our unique product and so very proud to have our Alpenglow occupy the shelves of the Wythe Candy Company in Williamsburg, Virginia. The shelves looked beautiful, and they placed us in the front window of the store. Then one day, we got a phone call from the manager telling us that our bottles were exploding. What a blow. We rushed to the rescue a Belgian microbiologist, who discovered that our beautiful Alpenglow was growing yeast. Fortunately, we have not had this problem since our early beginnings, almost twenty-five years ago, but it was a startling event in our days of a start-up company.

DID YOU KNOW THAT:

The first cyclone ever recorded in the New World occurred at Jamestown (August 27, 1667)?

Berkeley Plantation

Virginia claims many American "firsts" including the "First Thanksgiving" at Berkeley in 1619. Two American Presidents claim Berkeley, as it was the home of the Harrisons. It was also here that "Taps" was composed and first played as troops were encamped along the banks of the James River.

Berkeley Plantation was first settled on December 4, 1619, as the 40-ton ship *Margaret* arrived from Berkeley Parrish, England, with a crew of thirty-eight brave men. Captain John Woodleaf led the voyage, which had taken two and one half months. He and his men gave thanks as he read a prepared ordinance given in the Charter of the Berkeley Company to be revealed as they landed. The document proclaimed the following:

Wee ordaine that the day of our ships arrivall at the place assigned for the plantacon in the land of Virginia shall be yearly and perpetually keept holy as a day of thanksgiving to Almighty God.

About a year after the settlers arrived, the first bourbon whiskey in America was made from a brew of "maize." But by 1622, the settlement was "wiped out" due to a massacre by Indians.

Benjamin Harrison III purchased Berkeley in 1691. He established the first commercial shipyard on the James River. Tobacco was shipped from the plantation to England from Berkeley Plantation, and 18-gun battleships were built here for the Revolutionary Navy. Benjamin Harrison IV built the Georgian brick manor house on the property, which still stands today. It is said by some that this is the oldest three-story brick house in Virginia. The house also boasts the first pediment roof in Virginia, according to many historians. Benjamin's wife was the former Anne Carter, daughter of the famed Robert "King" Carter. The couple's initials are etched with a heart above the date 1726 on a round datestone carved above a side door.

Benjamin Harrison V inherited the home when his father died suddenly by being struck by lightning; he was just out of the College of William and Mary. He served on the Committee of the Whole House, which secured the support of Lafayette to join the Revolutionary Corps. He also signed the Declaration of Independence,

and served as Virginia's Governor three times. His sons Benjamin VI and William Henry were born at Berkeley Plantation.

William Henry Harrison spent most of his life as a soldier, senator, representative, and then as Governor of the area that was then known as the Northwest Territory. He became the ninth President of the United States in 1841, but only lived a month after his inaugural. His grandson, also named Benjamin Harrison, became the nation's twenty-third President.

After the Harrison family lost control of Berkeley Plantation in the 1840's, it changed hands several times. During the Civil War, General George McClellan's Union troops occupied the acreage. President Abraham Lincoln visited here on two occasions when the entire U.S. Navy brought food and supplies to 140,000 troops. General Daniel Butterfield composed the familiar melody "Taps," the Army's call for "lights out," for his bugler, O.W. Norton, to play here one evening.

John Jamieson bought the house and 1400 acres in 1907. His son, Malcolm, inherited Berkeley in 1927, with the plantation in ruins. In 1933, he married Grace Eggleston. Her expertise in antiques and decorating was important as the couple restored the home and grounds. Today, Berkeley Plantation shines as a stop along Highway 5 beside the James River with other lovely plantation homes such as Evelynton, Shirley, and President John Tyler's home, Sherwood Forrest.

CHAPTER TWO

Bountiful Breads
and
Breakfast

Bread was a staple, but the division of that bread was determined by your status. Field workers would often get the burnt or harder bottom of the bread, the family got the middle, and guests got the top or "Upper crust."

Breads

GRACE SHEPHERD'S
Angel Biscuits

4¹/₂ cups all-purpose flour
1 tablespoon sugar
1 teaspoon baking soda
1 tablespoon baking powder
1¹/₂ teaspoons salt
1 cup shortening

2 (¹/₄-ounce) packages
  active dry yeast
¹/₄ cup warm water (105°F
  to 115°F)
2 cups buttermilk

- Preheat the oven to 400°F. Mix the flour, sugar, baking soda, baking powder, and salt in a large bowl. Cut in the shortening with a pastry blender. Dissolve the yeast in the warm water in a bowl. Add the yeast mixture and buttermilk to the flour mixture, mixing well.
- Turn the dough onto a floured surface, and knead for 8 to 10 minutes or until smooth and elastic. Roll the dough 1 inch thick, and cut into rounds with a 2- to 3-inch biscuit cutter. Place the biscuits on a greased baking sheet, and bake for 12 to 15 minutes.
- Makes approximately 2 dozen biscuits

These biscuits will melt in your mouth. They are a Christmas tradition at the 300-acre Shepherd Farm, which has been owned by the Shepherd family for over 50 years. Grace Shepherd and her daughter, Joanie Shepherd, are very well known and loved in Nokesville, Virginia.

The recipe was sent by LOLA YODER, a good friend and admirer of the Shepherd family. Lola is a native Virginian and owns, with her husband, Yoder Steel Corporation in Manassas, Virginia.

Grandmom's Rich Biscuits

2 cups all-purpose flour
2 tablespoons sugar
1 tablespoon baking powder
¹/₂ teaspoon salt

¹/₃ cup butter or margarine,
  softened
Cream
Fruit and whipped cream

- Preheat the oven to 400°F. Combine the flour, sugar, baking powder, and salt in a large bowl, and mix well. Cut in the butter or margarine with a pastry blender. Stir in enough of the cream to blend, forming a soft dough that can be easily handled.
- Roll the dough about ¹/₂ inch thick on a floured surface, and cut into 2- to 3-inch rounds. Place 1 inch apart on a baking sheet. Bake for 10 to 12 minutes. Split the biscuits, and add fruit and whipped cream for shortcake.
- Makes 8 to 10 servings

The recipe comes from the family of JOAN LITTLEY CLARK of Fairfax Station, Virginia. She is Regent of the Providence Chapter of the Virginia DAR.

The Life of a Baker

The following description of the baker's profession comes from *The Book of Trades, or Library of Useful Arts*, originally issued in London, but also released in Richmond in 1807. The volume was apparently published as a children's book that, according to a critic of the time, provided material that was "very proper for young minds to be occupied with in their hours of amusement, when they are not proposed in too scientific a way."

The chief art of the BAKER consists in making bread, rolls, and biscuits, and in baking various kinds of provisions.

It is not known when this very useful business first became a particular profession. Bakers were a distinct body of people in Rome nearly two hundred years before the Christian era, and it is supposed that they came from Greece. To these were added a number of freemen, who were incorporated into a college, from which neither they nor their children were allowed to withdraw. They held their effects in common, without enjoying any power of parting with them.

Each bake house had a patron, who had the superintendency of it; and one of the patrons had the management of the others, and the care of the college. So respectable were the bakers of Rome, that occasionally one of the body was admitted among the senators.

Even by our own statutes the bakers are declared not to be handicrafts; and in London they are under the particular jurisdiction of the lord mayor and aldermen, who fix the price of bread, and have the power of finding those who do not conform to their rules.

Bread is made of flour mixed and kneaded with yeast, water, and a little salt. It is known in London under two names, the white or wheaten, and the household: these differ only in degrees of purity; and the loaves must be marked with a W or H, or the Baker is liable to suffer a penalty.

The process of bread-making is thus described: To a peck of meal are added a handful of salt, a pint of yeast, and three quarts of water, cold in summer, hot in winter, and temperature between the two. The whole being kneaded, as is represented in the plate [the accompanying engraving], will rise in about an hour; it is then moulded into loaves, and put into the oven to bake.

The oven takes more than an hour to heat properly, and bread about three hours to bake. Most bakers make and sell roll in the morning: these are either common, or French rolls: the former differ but little from loaf bread: the ingredients of the latter are mixed with milk instead of water, and the finest flour is made use of for them. Rolls require only about twenty minutes for baking.

The life of a baker is very laborious; the greater part of his work is done by night: the journeyman is required always to commence his operations about eleven o'clock in the evening, in order to get the new bread ready for admitting the rolls in the morning. His wages are, however, very moderate, seldom amounting to more than ten shillings a week, exclusive of his board.

The price of bread is regulated according to the price of wheat; and bakers are directed in this by the magistrates, whose rules they are bound to follow. By these the peck-loaf of each sort of bread must weigh seventeen pounds six ounces avoirdupois weight, and smaller loaves in the same proportion. Every sack of flour is to weigh two hundred and a half; and from this there ought to be made, at an average, twenty such peck-loaves, or eighty common quartern-loaves.

If bread were short in its weight only one ounce in thirty-six, the baker formerly was liable to be put in the pillory; and for the same offence he may now be fined, at the will of the magistrate, in any sum not less than one shilling, nor more than five shillings, for every ounce wanting; such bread being complained of and weighed in the presence of the magistrate within twenty-four hours after it is baked, because bread loses in weight by keeping.

The process of biscuit-baking, as practised at the Victualling-office at Deptford, is curious and interesting. The dough, which consists of flour and water only, is worked by a large machine It is then handed over to a second workman, who slices it with a large knife for the bakers, of whom there are five. The first, or the moulder, forms the biscuits two at a time; the second, or marker, stamps and throws them to the splitter, who separates the two pieces, and puts them under the hand of the chucker, the man that supplies the oven, whose work of throwing the bread on the peel must be so exact, that he cannot look off for a moment. The fifth, or the depositer, receives the biscuits on the peel, and arranges them in the oven. All the men work with the greatest exactness, and are, in truth, like parts of the same machine. The business is to deposit in the oven seventy biscuits in a minute; and this is accomplished with the regularity of a clock, the clacking of the peel operating like the motion of the pendulum. There are 12 ovens at Deptford, and each will furnish daily bread for 2040 men.

By referring to the plate [the engraving], we see the baker represented in the act of kneading his dough: the bin upon which he is at work

contains the flour: on his right hand [actually his left] is the peel, with which he puts in and takes out the bread: at his back we see the representation of the fire in the oven, and in the front [in the left of the engraving] is the pail in which the yeast is fetched daily from the brewhouse; and by the side of the flour-bin on the ground is the wood used to heat the oven.

A Soldier's Favorite Fare: Hardtack

During the Civil War, food varied from well-supplied garrison troops to the fast moving armies that rapidly out-marched their supply system. Generally, the food was just plain bad or an insufficient amount for a soldier's needs. Salt pork, dried beans, rice, hardtack and coffee were the soldier's staples. Often, soldiers would prepare their meals in grease and one doctor campaigned vigorously to save his men from "death from the frying pan." Hardtack was the staple bread ration for the Civil War soldier. It was a plain flour and water biscuit about 3 inches by $2^{1}/_{2}$ inches and $1/_{2}$ inch thick. More often than not, these crackers became moldy and filled with worms, weevils and maggots. One Union soldier remembered: "All the fresh meat we had came in the hard bread . . . and I, preferring my game cooked, used to toast my biscuits." Soldiers called hardtack "teeth-dullers" or "sheet-iron crackers." To eat these crackers, soldiers might crumble it up in soup or coffee where the weevils would rise to the top to be skimmed off. Hardtack could also be soaked in water to make it elastic and then fried brown in pork fat, making a dish called "skillygelee." Confederates enjoyed "lob scouse," a dish made of flour and cornmeal mixed with bacon grease with broken crackers stewed into it.

If you want to try making your own hardtack, use this recipe: Mix together $1^{3}/_{4}$ cup flour, $1/_{4}$ tablespoon salt, and $1/_{2}$ cup water to form a dough. Roll out on a floured surface to about $1/_{2}$ inch thick. Place a pattern on dough and cut around it with a knife (or use a biscuit cutter). Place each cracker on a baking sheet, poke holes in the top with a fork and bake at 400°F. for 20 to 25 minutes until lightly browned.

—John V. Quarstein, Director
The Virginia War Museum

Sweet Potato Biscuits

³/4 cup canned or mashed cooked sweet potatoes	²/3 cup milk
¹/4 cup shortening, melted	4 teaspoons baking powder
3 tablespoons sugar	¹/2 teaspoon salt
	1¹/2 cups all-purpose flour

- Preheat the oven to 400°F. Heat the sweet potatoes in a medium saucepan. Stir in the shortening and sugar. Add the milk, baking powder, salt, and flour, stirring to make a soft dough. Pat the dough into a ¹/2 to 1-inch thickness with hands, and cut into 2 to 3-inch rounds. Place on a lightly greased baking sheet, and bake until brown.
- Makes approximately 24 biscuits

This recipe was sent in by KAY WILSON from Virginia Beach, Virginia, a member of the Lynnhaven Parish Chapter of the Virginia DAR.

Batter Bread

2 cups boiling water	1 cup milk
1¹/2 cups sifted yellow cornmeal	2 teaspoons baking powder
2 teaspoons salt	Cold water
2 eggs	3 tablespoons shortening, melted

- Preheat the oven to 450°F. Pour the boiling water over the cornmeal in a large bowl, and blend well. Add the salt and eggs, beating well. Stir in the milk. Dissolve the baking powder in the water in a bowl, and stir into the batter.
- Heat a 9×9-inch pan in the oven until hot. Pour the shortening into the hot pan, and add the batter. The shortening will rise to the top. Stir to evenly distribute. Bake for 30 minutes or until golden brown.
- Makes 8 servings

This is from my paternal grandmother, Grace Walthall Turner. My mother, Fannie Turner, served it every Sunday for thirty years. Although they used the same recipe, her batter bread and my grandmother's turned out quite differently. They could never figure out why.

Fannie Turner is in her 90s and is becoming a member of the DAR. Shared by her daughter, GRACE KARISH, who is a member of the Fairfax County Chapter of the Virginia DAR.

DID YOU KNOW THAT:

The first theater to open in America began operations at Williamsburg (1718)?

WHY IS VIRGINIA A COMMONWEALTH?

There is no such entity as the "State" of Virginia. While generically categorized as a state, Virginia has been the "Commonwealth" since independence from Great Britain. Virginia is the first of four states that are commonwealths, including our daughter Commonwealth of Kentucky, which was formed from Virginia in 1792.

Our first Constitution, adopted on June 29, 1776, directed that "Commissions and Grants shall run In the Name of the Commonwealth of Virginia, and bear teste by the Governor with the Seal of the Commonwealth annexed." The Secretary of the Commonwealth to this day issues commissions in this manner. Among other references, the Constitution furthermore dictated that criminal indictments were to conclude "against the peace and dignity of the Commonwealth."

It is Virginia's Declaration of Rights, adopted on June 12, 1776, that sets forth our rights and philosophy of government. Virginia's founders viewed government as a contract between people who are "created equally free and independent." The underlying theory held that personal sovereignty was given over in order to create society, which then in turn facilitated individual pursuits. As "all Power is . . . vested in, and consequently derived from the People," government was created to be the servant of the people.

Of greatest importance, Virginia's founders envisioned that the people would possess certain traits, namely, "a firm Adherence to Justice, Moderation, Temperance, Frugality and Virtue." No concept was more central than that of public or civic virtue. The civically virtuous citizen was self-reliant and self-determinative while recognizing a duty to the general welfare, or common good of the community. It is the figure of Virtue, standing over the dead body of Tyranny, that dominates the Great Seal of the Commonwealth.

Virginians, as members of the Common-wealth, enjoy a high degree of sovereignty. The continuing existence of the Commonwealth requires that each citizen be an active participant in government. All citizens must likewise be practitioners of civic virtue, dedicated to conducting themselves in a socially responsible manner.

A state may or may not reflect the will of the people, but a commonwealth simply cannot exist without the people's express consent. The common-wealth is an extraordinary form of government based upon the collective genius of its citizens. The Common-wealth is distinguished from, and superior to, a mere state by the greatness of the people of Virginia.

—The Honorable Thomas M. Moncure Jr.

THE LYNNHAVEN HOUSE
Herbed Cornbread

3 cups stone-ground white
  cornmeal
1 teaspoon salt
1 teaspoon dried sage

2 eggs
1 cup (or more) boiling
  water

- Combine the cornmeal, salt, sage, eggs, and boiling water in a saucepan, and mix well. Add additional boiling water, $1/4$ cup at a time, until the dough is stiff enough to shape with your hands.
- Shape the dough into a loaf. Cover the bottom and sides of a preheated (about 15 minutes) greased Dutch oven with large cabbage leaves to prevent sticking, and place the loaf in the middle. Cover with more cabbage leaves, and place a lid on the Dutch oven. Cover the top with hot coals, and place on hot coals. Bake at what feels like 400°F for 30 to 40 minutes or until the cornbread is crusty. Let stand for 15 minutes before serving.
- Makes 8 to 10 servings

The bread does not pick up the flavor of the cabbage leaves. Yellow cornmeal may be used, but white was more available in the South. If you don't have a hearth and a Dutch oven, a modern oven will do.

This recipe is from the LYNNHAVEN HOUSE, built circa 1725 by Francis Thelaball. This historic house is a $1^1/2$-story, brick, late-medieval manor house consisting of four rooms-two downstairs and two upstairs. Originally, tobacco was grown on the property along with cattle, sheep, and hogs. Today 80 percent of the brick is original, and costumed docents inform visitors about life in the eighteenth century in Tidewater Virginia. The infor-mation includes food that was available and how it was prepared and eaten. Here is one of the most interesting medicinal recipes.

1) Collect crab claws from the beach—provide calcium
2) Slice ginger very thin—settles stomach
3) Cinnamon sticks—provide flavor
4) Crush all this up finely and put it in any liquid of your preference, and you have an eighteenth century remedy for nausea or upset stomach.

Spoon Bread

2 cups milk
1 cup self-rising white
  cornmeal

¹/4 cup (¹/2 stick) butter or
  margarine
4 eggs, separated

- Preheat the oven to 375°F. Scald the milk in a double boiler. Stir in the cornmeal gradually. Cook until thickened, stirring constantly. Stir in the butter or margarine. Beat the egg whites in a medium bowl until stiff. Beat the egg yolks without cleaning the beaters in a separate bowl until thick and lemon colored. Fold the cornmeal mixture into the egg yolks gradually. Fold in the egg whites. Pour into a greased 2-quart casserole dish, and bake for 35 minutes.
- Makes 6 to 8 servings

This recipe was sent by ANNA JAMES SMITH BOWEN. Anna Bowen was raised in Smithfield and moved to Maiden Spring when she married a Bowen. Her sister-in-law, Anne Bowen Smith, after being raised in Maiden Spring, married Anna's brother and moved to Smithfield in Russell County, Virginia. Both homes, Smithfield and Maiden Spring, are historic landmarks and are about twenty miles apart.

A PINCH OF THE PAST
Buttermilk Bran Muffins

4 cups raisin and bran cereal
2¹/2 cups all-purpose flour
1 cup sugar
2¹/2 teaspoons baking soda

1¹/2 teaspoons salt
2 eggs, beaten
2 cups buttermilk
¹/2 cup vegetable oil

- Preheat the oven to 400°F. Combine the cereal, flour, sugar, baking soda, and salt in a large bowl, and mix well. Stir in the eggs, buttermilk, and oil, and mix well. Spoon the batter into generously greased muffin cups, filling the cups ²/3 full. Bake for 20 minutes or until golden brown.
- Makes 1 dozen muffins

CATHY STINEBAUGH of A Pinch of the Past Antiques, Poquoson, Virginia, shared this recipe.

CABBAGE PUDDING
from Mary Randolph's *The Virginia House-wife*

Get a fine head of cabbage, not too large, pour boiling water on, and cover it till you can turn the leaves back, which you must do carefully; take some of those in the middle of the head off, chop them fine, and mix them with rich force-meat [veal and suet made into balls]; put this in and replace the leaves to confine the stuffing; tie it in a cloth and boil it; serve it up whole with a little melted butter in the dish.

AN EARLY VIRGINIA COOKBOOK

THE

VIRGINIA HOUSE-WIFE.

METHOD IS THE SOUL OF MANAGEMENT.

WASHINGTON :

PRINTED BY DAVIS AND FORCE, (FRANKLIN'S HEAD,)
PENNSYLVANIA AVENUE.

1824.

In 1742, a volume of recipes released in Williamsburg entitled *The Complete Housewife*, written by E. Smith, became the first cookbook ever published in North America. But Smith's volume was a reprint of an older one published in London fifteen years earlier. It thus remained for a true daughter of Virginia, Mary Randolph, to write the book that not only became a blockbuster bestseller in its time, but that generations of women religiously relied upon for guidance in the kitchen.

The Virginia House-wife was issued in 1824 by the publishing house of Davis and Force, located on Pennsylvania Avenue, in nearby Washington, D.C. The book's author, Mary Randolph, was a member of a socially and politically prominent Virginia family. She was born in 1762 near Richmond, the daughter of Anne Cary and Thomas Mann Randolph. In 1782, Mary married David Meade

Randolph, and the couple soon became known for their lavish style of entertaining at their charming Richmond home Moldavia.

Randolph's popular cookbook quickly became a mainstay in kitchens across Virginia. In fact, it has been ranked by modern authorities as the most influential such volume of its day. Its *raison d'etre*, according to the author herself, was to assist "the young inexperienced housekeeper." Recalling her own early days as a newlywed, she wrote, "The difficulties I encountered when I first entered on the duties of a House-keeping life, from the want of books sufficiently clear and concise, to impart knowledge . . . compelled me to study the subject, and by actual experiment, to reduce every thing, in the culinary line, to proper weights and measures." Most of the book's recipes were written from Randolph's memory, where "they were impressed by long continued practice."

The facet of Randolph's book that leaps out at the modern-day cook is the vast variety of recipes it contains. From instructions on how "to grill a calf's head" and how "to pickle sturgeon," the volume's informative pages go on to detail procedures for preparing cuisine that one might read about in the living section of today's newspaper — fried oysters, corn bread, strawberry ice cream, and apple pie, for example.

SAPLING GROVE
Sourdough Muffins

2 cups all-purpose flour	1 teaspoon cinnamon
1 cup sugar	3 eggs
1 (5-ounce) package vanilla instant pudding mix	1 cup oil
	1 teaspoon vanilla extract
1 1/4 teaspoons baking powder	1 cup Sourdough Starter
	1 1/2 cups diced dried fruits
1/2 teaspoon baking soda	and apples
1/2 teaspoon salt	1/2 cup chopped nuts

- Preheat the oven to 350°F. Combine the flour, sugar, vanilla pudding mix, baking powder, baking soda, salt, cinnamon, eggs, oil, vanilla extract, Sourdough Starter, and diced fruits in a large bowl, and mix well. Pour the batter into greased muffin cups. Bake for 15 to 20 minutes.
- Makes 18 muffins

SOURDOUGH STARTER

3 1/2 cups unsifted flour	1 package active dry yeast
1 tablespoon sugar	2 cups warm water

- Combine the flour, sugar, and yeast in a large bowl, and mix well. Beat in the water gradually until smooth. Let stand, loosely covered with plastic wrap, at room temperature for 2 days. Refrigerate if not used immediately after standing time.
- Sourdough starter should be "fed" 1 teaspoon sugar every 10 days. It will last and last if properly "fed."

The recipe was submitted by MUSSER W. WARREN, past Regent of the Fort Chiswell Chapter of the Virginia DAR in Bristol, Virginia. Sapling Grove Sourdough Muffins are a sweet treat for holiday giving. One of Bristol's finest cooks very generously shared this recipe with the Fort Chiswell DAR Chapter. Sapling Grove was the name of the early settlement that later became Bristol, Virginia. The Sapling Grove post office was first established in the 1817 mansion that has been for more than 100 years the residence of the chapter's oldest living member.

HARE SOUP
from Mary Randolph's *The Virginia House-wife*

Cut up two hares, put them into a pot with a piece of bacon, two onions chopped, a bundle of thyme and parsley which must be taken out before the soup is thickened, add pepper, salt, pounded cloves, and mace, put in a sufficient quantity of water, stew it gently three hours, thicken with a large spoonful of butter, and one of brown flour with a glass of red wine; boil it a few minutes longer, and serve it up with the nicest parts of the hares. Squirrels make soup equally good, done the same way.

ROWENA'S
Refrigerator Bran Muffins

1¹/₂ cups sugar
¹/₂ cup (1 stick) butter or
  margarine
2 eggs
2¹/₂ cups all-purpose flour
2¹/₂ teaspoons baking soda

¹/₂ teaspoon salt
2 cups buttermilk
1 cup water
1 cup 100% bran cereal
1¹/₂ cups seedless raisins
2 cups all-bran cereal

- Preheat the oven to 375°F. Beat the sugar and butter or
  margarine in a large mixing bowl until creamy. Add the
  eggs one at a time, mixing well after each addition. Beat
  in the flour, baking soda, salt, and buttermilk until smooth.
- Bring the water to a boil in a medium saucepan. Add the
  100% bran cereal, and let stand until the cereal has
  absorbed the water and cooled slightly. Blend the 100%
  bran mixture into the batter. Add the raisins and all-bran
  cereal, and mix well. Spoon the batter into prepared
  small muffin cups, and bake for 20 minutes.
- Makes 100 small muffins

*My children loved these. They thought they were a special treat.
They didn't know they were also good for them. And now, my
grandchildren are eating them. Mary Frances Bellman, our
daughter who lives in Hong Kong, remembers these muffins with
great fondness, and now they are a great treat for her twin girls.
—Rowena*

Herb Bread

¹/₂ cup (1 stick) butter or
  margarine
1 teaspoon grated fresh onion
  or instant minced onion
2 cloves garlic, crushed

¹/₂ teaspoon each basil,
  rosemary, and oregano
1¹/₂ teaspoons dried parsley
1 (20-ounce) package frozen
  roll dough, such as Rich's

- Melt the butter or margarine in a 2-cup glass measuring
  cup in the microwave. Add the onion, garlic, basil, rosemary,
  oregano, and parsley, and mix well. Dip the frozen rolls in
  the herb mixture. Place in a greased bundt or angel food
  cake pan. Pour any remaining herb mixture over the rolls,
  and let rise, covered with a clean cloth, for at least 2 hours
  or longer. Preheat the oven to the temperature indicated
  on the frozen dough package, and bake for approximately
  30 minutes.
- Makes 6 to 8 servings

The recipe was submitted by KATHLEEN L. DEEGAN, past
Regent and a member of Cameron Parish Chapter of the
Virginia DAR. Parishes were created in Colonial America by
the Church of England.

VIRGINIA WINEMAKING

Although early settlers at Jamestown
tried their hands at making wine using
wild grapes growing in abundance in
the tidewater areas of Virginia, results
were unsatisfactory. Later experiments
with imported, cultivated grapes yielded
a similar, dismal outcome.

It was not until the years immediately
before the Revolution that Phillip Mazzei,
a vintner from Tuscany, succeeded
in attaining a fine grape crop—but
his dreams were dashed by a fungi
epidemic, compounded by the
destruction of his vines by the British.
As the locally cultivated "Norton" grape
gained popularity among Virginians
during the nineteenth century, winemaking finally got its real start in the
Commonwealth.

Prohibition put the skids on the
industry, and after the legislation's
repeal in 1934, interest in American
winemaking shifted to California. A
renaissance occurred in the 1970s,
however, and today, Virginia ranks sixth
in the nation in wine production, with
several domestic varieties having
gained both national and international
attention.

NAT TURNER'S REBELLION

Nat Turner, a Virginia-born slave whose religion led him to organize and lead one of the most infamous revolts in American history, was born in 1800 in Southampton County. Turner's religious zeal persuaded him that he was God's instrument to free the slaves, and on August 21, 1831, he put his plan for freedom into action. With five other slaves, Turner killed his master's entire family. About sixty other slaves quickly gave Turner their support. But when the state militia was called out, Turner's riot lost organization and fell apart. More than fifty white neighbors were killed in the affray. Turner eluded the law for six weeks before he was captured, tried, convicted, and hanged at Jerusalem, New York.

Turner's slave revolt also had another Virginia connection. The incident became the setting for William Styron's best-selling novel of 1967, *The Confessions of Nat Turner*, which was awarded the 1968 Pulitzer Prize. Styron, born in Newport News in 1925, published his first novel, *Lie Down in Darkness*, in 1951. This first effort was set in tidewater Virginia and chronicled the life of a mentally-disturbed woman who eventually took her own life.

MARY DODD LANGHORNE'S
Nut Bread

1 egg	1 teaspoon salt
1 cup sugar	1 tablespoon baking powder
1 1/2 cups milk	1 cup chopped or ground
3 cups all-purpose flour	English walnuts

- Preheat the oven to 350°F. Beat the egg in a large bowl until light and fluffy. Add the sugar and milk, and mix well. Combine the flour, salt, and baking powder in a separate bowl, and mix well. Add to the egg mixture, and blend well. Fold in the English walnuts.
- Pour into a well-greased 5×9-inch loaf pan, and let rise, covered, for 1 hour. Bake for 1 hour or until bread tests done.
- Makes approximately 8 servings

The recipe is shared by EDYTHE H. LANGHORNE. This is a very old recipe from her mother-in-law, Mary Dodd Langhorne, who didn't join the DAR until she was 90 years old. Edythe is a member of the Great Bridge Chapter of the Virginia DAR.

Apricot and Brazil Nut Bread

1/2 cup dried apricots, rinsed, drained	1 tablespoon baking powder
	1/4 teaspoon baking soda
1 egg	3/4 teaspoon salt
1 cup sugar	1/2 cup orange juice
2 tablespoons butter or margarine	1/4 cup water
	1 cup chopped Brazil nuts
2 cups all-purpose flour	

- Preheat the oven to 350°F. Mince the apricots finely with a knife or food chopper. Beat the egg in a large bowl until light colored. Add the sugar, and beat well. Beat in the butter or margarine.
- Combine the flour, baking powder, baking soda, and salt in a medium bowl. Add the flour mixture to the apricot mixture alternately with the orange juice and water. Fold in the Brazil nuts. Spoon the batter into a well-greased 5×9-inch loaf pan. Bake for 1 1/2 hours.
- Makes 1 loaf

This is from my mom and grandmother. The bread was always in our home, as well as a pound cake, on top of the refrigerator.

This is from the family of DOT and JIM WOOD. She is the founder of the well-known JD & W, Inc., a construction company in Virginia Beach. They are Virginians by birth, through four generations in Upperville for his family and elsewhere for hers. They have lived their entire lives in Virginia. Theirs is a Virginia "family affair."

Banana Nut Bread

1/4 cup shortening	2 teaspoons baking powder
1/2 cup firmly packed	1/2 teaspoon salt
brown sugar	1/2 teaspoon baking soda
1 egg, beaten	1/2 cup chopped nuts
1 teaspoon vanilla extract	1 1/2 cups mashed banana
1 cup cooking bran	2 tablespoons water
1/2 cup all-purpose flour	

- Preheat the oven to 350°F. Beat the shortening and sugar in a large bowl until creamy. Add the egg, vanilla extract, and bran, and beat well. Beat in the flour, baking powder, salt, and soda. Fold in the nuts. Combine the bananas and water in a small bowl, and mix well. Stir into the batter. Pour into a greased 9×13-inch baking pan. Let stand for 30 minutes, and bake for 30 to 35 minutes.
- Makes 8 to 10 servings

This recipe from the late 1800s, stuck into a daughter's cookbook, was on a slip of paper in the handwriting of Anna Taylor Younger (1861-1941), whose four daughters, Mary Y. Stone, Sallie Y. Baker, Linville Y. King, and Cora Y. Smith, were all DAR members.

The recipe is shared by the family of MARY CARTER STONE of Danville, Virginia. Mary Carter is a member of the Thomas Carter Chapter of the Virginia DAR.

'39 Nut Bread

2 cups whole-wheat flour	1 cup chopped nuts, such as
1/2 cup unbleached flour	pecans or walnuts
1 tablespoon baking powder	2 cups milk
1/2 teaspoon salt	1 egg, beaten
1/2 cup sugar	

- Combine the whole wheat flour, unbleached flour, baking powder, salt, sugar, and nuts in a bowl, and mix well. Blend the milk and egg in a separate bowl. Add the milk mixture to the dry mixture, stirring to combine.
- Spoon the mixture into a greased 5×9-inch loaf pan. Let stand for 20 minutes. Preheat the oven to 350°F, and bake for 40 minutes.
- Makes approximately 8 servings

The original version of this particular recipe was printed in 1939, but nut breads have been popular much longer than that. I modified the old recipe, making it more healthful.

The recipe comes from PATRICIA B. MITCHELL of Chatham, Virginia, author of *Waking Up Down South: Southern Breakfast Traditions*, Mitchells Publications, and owner of the Sims-Mitchell House.

SIMS-MITCHELL HOUSE

How did Patricia B. Mitchell land in Chatham, Virginia, to write over a hundred titles about food history? The recipe is simple: she came home! Mitchell began food writing as a contributor to the *Community Standard* magazine in New Orleans in the early 1970s after leaving her hometown of Chatham. She and husband Henry returned in 1975 to restore an old house and begin a bed and breakfast operation. At the coaxing of her guests through the years, Mitchell began to compile her recipes into book form and research food history.

Mitchell pored through letters, diaries, old books, and microfilmed records in her search for clues to American eating habits and cooking techniques. She has sold over half a million copies of her books at historic sites, bookstores, museums, and shops in forty-nine states, as well as in other countries. Her website, www.foodhistory.com, is a guide familiar to many cooks and food enthusiasts. Her own stocked kitchen is located in her restored retreat in Chatham.

The Sims-Mitchell house had a long history involving several families before Patricia and Henry Mitchell found it. The main house was originally the home of Colonel William E. Sims (one of Virginia's most controversial postwar politicians), his wife Matoaka, and their family in 1875. Matoaka was the daughter of local State Senator James Whittle. The house has eleven fireplaces, a raised English basement, shiplap siding with brick kilned on the premises, and fifteen rooms!

William and Matoaka Sims had three children. Matoaka's responsibilities for the management of the home were many, while her husband had a very active political life that eventually ended with his withdrawal to Washington, D.C., and finally Colon, Colombia. Matoaka continued to live in her large home; at her death in 1901, she was survived by her two adult sons and her half-sister "Miss Mary" Whittle of Eldon.

By 1906, the home housed the first Chatham Episcopal Institute after the Institute's building burned. The addition of a telephone and battery-house electricity made the facilities modern for the times. When the Institute moved back to its campus, the Warren Training School (later Hargrave Military Academy) enlisted use of the home. In time, a Southern Railroad engineer bought the house. Mrs. Victor Adkins of Chatham relates that "the tin roof was torn off by a tornado" while her family lived there in 1937. A Ford dealer, apartment dwellers, and a Danville bank eventually had holdings on the structure.

In August 1975, Henry and Patricia happened to "find" the house in nearby Cherrystone Creek valley. The house reminded them of one they had regretfully left behind in New Orleans—so much so that within a few days, transfer of the Sims property was completed and the Sims-Mitchell house came to be!

One-Bowl Gingerbread

1 egg
1/2 cup sugar
1/2 cup molasses
1 1/2 cups all-purpose flour
1 teaspoon baking soda
1 teaspoon ginger

1/2 teaspoon salt
1/2 teaspoon cinnamon
1/4 teaspoon cloves
1/2 cup canola oil
1/2 cup boiling water

- Preheat the oven to 350°F. Beat the egg, sugar, and molasses in a large bowl until well mixed. Add the flour, baking soda, ginger, salt, cinnamon, and cloves, and mix well. Stir in the oil and water. Pour into an 8×8-inch baking pan, and bake for 35 to 40 minutes.
- Makes 6 to 9 servings

This tastes great with freshly whipped cream after the gingerbread has slightly cooled. This recipe was given to me by my grandfather, Mark G. Richmond, and has been a longtime favorite, especially at holidays.

The recipe comes from the family of ISONA C. HECKEL, a member of the Bill of Rights Chapter of the Virginia DAR.

Superior Soft Gingerbread

1 cup sugar
1 cup (2 sticks) butter or
  margarine
2 teaspoons baking soda
1 cup sour milk or
  buttermilk
1 cup dark molasses

3 eggs, separated
3 1/2 cups (or more)
  all-purpose flour
1/2 teaspoon salt
1 tablespoon ginger
1 teaspoon allspice and/or
  nutmeg

- Preheat the oven to 350°F. Beat the sugar and butter in a large bowl until creamy. Stir 1 teaspoon of the baking soda into the sour milk in a cup, and place in a bowl. Stir the remaining baking soda into the molasses in a separate cup, and place in a bowl.
- Beat the egg yolks in a bowl until well mixed. Beat the egg whites in a separate bowl until stiff. Add the egg yolks to the creamed mixture, and mix well. Stir in the molasses and milk mixture.
- Combine the flour, salt, ginger, and allspice and/or nutmeg, and mix well. Add to the creamed mixture, and blend well. Fold in the stiffly beaten egg whites. Spoon into a well-greased and floured 9×9-inch baking pan. Bake for 1 hour or until the gingerbread tests done, being careful that the gingerbread does not scorch.
- Makes approximately 9 servings

This recipe came from ANNIE BELL WHITLOW COLES from her friend Mrs. A. H. Plecker. Mr. Plecker took the famed photograph of Robert E. Lee on his horse, Traveller, from which the statue was done.

Northern Neck Brown Bread

1 cup whole wheat flour
1 cup all-purpose flour
1 cup white cornmeal
2 cups buttermilk

1/2 cup molasses
1/2 cup sugar
2 teaspoons baking soda
2 teaspoons salt

- Combine the whole wheat flour, all-purpose flour, cornmeal, buttermilk, molasses, sugar, baking soda, and salt in a bowl, and mix well.
- Pour the batter into 2 greased and floured 1-pound coffee cans, and cover tightly with foil. Secure the foil with rubber bands. Add 2 inches of water to a large Dutch oven or tall multi-purpose pot with a tight-fitting lid. Insert a steaming rack or clothespins in the bottom of the pan to prevent the cans from touching the bottom. Bring the water to a boil. Place the bread cans foil side up in the water, and reduce the heat to low. Steam, tightly covered with a lid, for 3 hours, adding additional water as necessary.
- Makes approximately 16 servings

This recipe was given by MAJOR RUSSELL E. MILLER, JR. USMC, Ret., in honor of his grandmother. Major Miller resides in Lancaster, Virginia.

Pumpkin Bread

3 cups sugar
1 cup vegetable oil
4 eggs
3 1/2 cups all-purpose flour
1/2 teaspoon mace, optional

1 teaspoon nutmeg
1 teaspoon cinnamon
2 1/2 teaspoons salt
2/3 cup water
1 (15-ounce) can pumpkin

- Preheat the oven to 350°F. Beat the sugar, oil, and eggs in a large mixing bowl until smooth. Add the flour, mace, nutmeg, cinnamon, salt, water, and pumpkin, beating at low speed. Increase the mixer speed to high, and mix well. Pour into a greased tube pan, and bake for 1 hour or until the bread tests done.
- Makes 14 to 16 servings

This recipe was shared by EUGENIA McGROARTY to honor her grandmother. It is from the kitchen of Lucille Patterson Rizor, a founding member of a DAR Chapter in Middle Tennessee (General Daniel Smith's Rock Castle Chapter) and the fraternal grandmother of Eugenia Rizor McGroarty, a member and former Regent of the Anna Maria Fitzhugh Chapter of the Virginia DAR. She is a descendant of Thomas Pettus, who was born on December 12, 1712, in Hanover County, Virginia. He was a member of the House of Burgesses and was a signer of the protest against the importation or purchase of British-manufactured products.

NELLY CUSTIS' RECIPE FOR HOECAKES

George Washington's typical breakfast has been described both by members of his immediate family and by several of their guests as well. One of the best descriptions was left by Martha Washington's youngest granddaughter, Nelly, who was raised at Mount Vernon after the death of her father:

He [George Washington] rose before sunrise, always wrote or read until seven in summer or half past seven in winter. His breakfast was then ready—he ate three small mush cakes (Indian meal) swimming in butter and honey, drank three cups of tea without cream... These "mush cakes" were also called 'Indian Hoe Cake,' 'Cake of Indian Corn,' 'Indian Cakes,' and 'Indian Corn Cake.'

At right is Nelly's *Original Recipe for Hoecakes,* which may be similar to what was served at Mount Vernon during her childhood. A modern adaptation of her hoecake recipe is on page 66.

[Excerpted from a letter written at Woodlawn Plantation by Nelly Custis Lewis to her longtime friend, Elizabeth Bordley Gibson of Philadelphia, January 7, 1821]:

...the bread business is as follows—if you wish to make 2¹/₂ quarts of flour up—take at night one quart of flour, five table spoonfuls of yeast & as much lukewarm water as will make it the consistency of pancake batter, mix it in a large stone pot & set it near a warm hearth (or a moderate fire) make it at candlelight & let it remain until the next morning then add the remaining quart & a half by degrees with a spoon [sic]—when well mixed let it stand 15 or 20 minutes & then bake it—of this dough in the morning, beat up a white & half of the yolk of an egg—add as much lukewarm water as will make it like pancake batter, drop a spoonful at a time on a hoe or griddle (as we say in the south)—when done on one side turn the other—the griddle must be rubbed in the first instance with a piece of beef suet or the fat of cold corned beef...

THE HUNTER HOUSE VICTORIAN MUSEUM
Season's Best Strawberry Bread

STRAWBERRY BREAD

2 cups fresh strawberries and juice	1 teaspoon baking soda
Sugar	1 tablespoon cinnamon
3 cups all-purpose flour	4 eggs, beaten
2 cups sugar	1¹/₄ cups vegetable oil
¹/₂ teaspoon salt	¹/₂ cup chopped pecans

GLAZE

1 cup confectioners' sugar	1 tablespoon strawberry juice
2 tablespoons lemon juice	

- To prepare the bread, sprinkle the strawberries with sugar in a freezer container, and freeze overnight. Defrost the strawberries, but do not drain. Reserve 1 tablespoon strawberry juice for the glaze.
- Note: The secret to moist strawberry bread is the sprinkling of sugar on the fresh strawberries before freezing.
- Preheat the oven to 350°F. Combine the flour, sugar, salt, baking soda, and cinnamon in a medium bowl, and mix well. Combine the eggs and oil in a separate bowl, and mix well. Stir in the flour mixture, and mix well. Add the strawberries and pecans, and mix just until blended. Pour into two greased and floured 5×9-inch loaf pans. Bake for 1 hour or until bread tests done.
- To prepare the glaze, combine the confectioners' sugar, lemon juice, and strawberry juice in a small bowl, and mix until smooth.
- To assemble, drizzle the glaze over the warm loaves. Remove the loaves from the pans when cool.
- Makes 2 loaves

The fabulous Season's Best Strawberry Bread recipe was used at a tea that recreated a "Strawberry Tea" offered in an 1890s issue of the Ladies' Home Journal.

The recipe was sent to us by THE HUNTER HOUSE VICTORIAN MUSEUM, the 1894 home of James and Lizzie Hunter in Norfolk, Virginia. The museum perpetuates the Victorian fascination with tea by hosting teas throughout the season. And the museum uses these recipes when entertaining today. The themes and menus are inspired by ladies' magazines of the 19th century and carried out with aplomb by the wonderful volunteer staff. Surely Mrs. Hunter would have considered these recipes as appropriate for afternoon tea in her parlor.

Gadsby's Tavern

Sally Lunn Bread

³/4 cup (or more) milk
¹/2 cup melted shortening
3¹/4 cups all-purpose flour
³/4 cup sugar
¹/2 teaspoon salt

¹/4 cup warm water
1 (¹/4-ounce) package active
  dry yeast
1 large egg, beaten
Butter for brushing

- Heat the milk and shortening in a small saucepan to the temperature of a warm baby bottle. Combine the flour, sugar, and salt in a large bowl, and mix well. Add the water to the yeast in a separate bowl, stirring to dissolve. Stir the warm milk mixture into the flour mixture, mixing well. Add the beaten egg and dissolved yeast, and mix well. Beat until mixture comes away from the side of the bowl (sides should be clean). Let rise, covered, in a warm (non air-conditioned) place for 1¹/2 hours or until doubled in bulk.
- Turn the dough onto a floured surface. Punch the dough down, and shape into a round loaf. Place on a baking sheet sprayed with nonstick vegetable cooking spray, and let rise for 45 minutes or until doubled by half. Preheat the oven to 350°F, and bake for approximately 45 minutes, brushing the top of the bread after 30 minutes with the butter, and again after baking has finished.
- Makes 1 loaf

There are several old accounts of the origin of the name "Sally Lunn." One of the more appealing is about an English girl who sold bread on the street crying "Solet Lune!" to advertise the buns. The sun and the moon, soleil et lune, as it is in French, were the images evoked to describe the golden tops and white bottoms of the buns. By the time soleil-lune reached America, it had become Sally Lunn and, rather than a bun, was a baked bread in a Turk's-head mold.

GENE MOSS of the famous Gadsby Tavern, an eighteenth century tavern in Alexandria, Virginia, shared this recipe. The building, originally built in 1792 as a city hotel, is noted for its exquisite Georgian architecture, and has been preserved and restored to a late-eighteenth century appearance and now houses Gadsby Tavern. The original Tavern, built circa 1770 and adjoining the current tavern, is today home to the Gadsby Tavern Museum. For nearly a century, Gadsby Tavern was a center of political, social, and cultural life in this important colonial seaport community. It hosted patriots, high society, and Presidents, including George Washington. Even today, the restaurant steps back in time and faithfully replicates the food, serving pieces, furnishings, costumes, and entertainment of the period.

DOROTHEA HENRY'S SALLY LUNN BREAD

(As copied from the Red Hill archives)

Beat 4 eggs well; melt a large tablespoon of butter in a teacup of warm water; pour it to the eggs with a teaspoon of salt and a teacup of yeast; beat in a quart of flour stiff enough for a spoon to stand in. Put it before the fire to rise the night before. Beat it over in the morning, grease your cake mold and put it in time enough to rise before baking. Should you want it for supper, make it up at 10:00 in the morning in the winter and 12:00 in the summer.

Twenty-first century substitutions: Substitute 1 cup milk for the teacup of water; substitute 2 packages of dry yeast softened in 1 cup of water for the teacup of yeast. Allow the mixture to double, punch it down, place in a greased Bundt pan, allow to double again, and bake at 350°F for 30 minutes. It takes 4 to 5 hours to prepare this modified version.

Sally Lunn is one of the most famous Virginia hot breads. It was named for a young woman who sold her breads on the streets in eighteenth-century Bath, England, and it was very popular in the Colonial South. The story goes that a "respectable baker and musician" bought Sally's business and wrote a song about her. The crumbly bread has become a Virginia favorite. It's delicious served warm with softened butter.

Dorothea Dandridge Henry, wife of Patrick Henry, used this recipe when they retired to Red Hill, from 1794 until his death in 1799. His family and friends "sought him out," and it was not unusual to have twenty to thirty people (twenty-four family members) for any meal, which consisted of fruits and vegetables from the garden, beef, pork, and poultry raised on the plantation, homemade bread made from home-grown grain, and often wild game. Beverages included milk, perhaps tea and coffee, and water from "Cool Spring," his favorite of the eight springs on the plantation. Visitors described the food as tasty and abundant.

This information was obtained through the efforts of curator Edith Poindexter of the Patrick Henry Memorial Foundation and Serena Green, Regent of the Red Hill Chapter of the Virginia DAR.

OUR DAILY BREAD
Portuguese Sweet Bread

2 cups warm water
5 eggs
$3/4$ cup ($1^1/2$ sticks) butter or margarine, softened
3 tablespoons active dry yeast
1 cup sugar
$2^3/4$ pounds high-gluten bread flour
$1/4$ cup non-fat dry milk powder
1 tablespoon salt

- Combine the water, eggs, butter or margarine, yeast, and sugar in a large bowl, and mix well. Combine the flour, dry milk powder, and salt in a separate large bowl, and mix well. Add the flour mixture to the egg mixture, and mix well. Knead lightly on a floured surface. Note: The dough will be sticky, but do not add much additional flour or the bread will not be "cake-like."
- Place the dough in a lightly oiled large bowl, turning to coat the surface. Let rise, covered, until doubled in bulk. Shape the dough into 3 round loaves. Let rise until almost doubled in bulk. Cut slits in the tops of the loaves with a sharp knife before baking. Bake at 325°F for 1 hour or until the bread is golden brown.
- Makes 3 ($1^1/2$-pound) loaves

Virginia's Finest

Portuguese Sweet Bread has been a favorite in Blacksburg, Virginia, for 22 years. It makes great French toast, sandwiches, or toasted bread with your favorite jam on top. Our Daily Bread Bakery and Café makes this wonderful Portuguese Sweet Bread. The café opened in 1980 and is the family owned business of KAREN GENO and FRANCESCA IANNACCONE. Karen was a chemist, like Rowena, who followed her love for baking.

AMELIA COUNTY

Amelia County was formed in 1734 from parts of Prince George and Brunswick Counties. It was named in honor of Princess Amelia, the daughter of King George II. Its present-day size is three hundred seventy-one square miles, and its population is 11,400. The county seat is Amelia.

Here, in April 1865, following the Battle of Sayler's Creek during the War Between the States, Confederate General Richard S. Ewell was forced to surrender his corps consisting of about seven thousand men and hundreds of supply wagons to Union troops. General Robert E. Lee also retreated with his army across much of the county in April 1865, just before the Confederate surrender.

Sweet Yeast Bread

$^1/_2$ cup (1 stick) butter or margarine	1 ($^1/_4$-ounce) package active dry yeast
$^3/_4$ cup sugar	$^1/_4$ cup lukewarm water
1 egg	1 teaspoon salt
2 cups milk	7 cups all-purpose flour

- Preheat the oven to 350°F. Beat the butter or margarine and sugar in a large mixing bowl until creamy. Add the egg, and beat well.
- Heat the milk to lukewarm (120°F) in a small saucepan. Dissolve the yeast in the lukewarm water, and add to the milk. Combine the salt and flour in a bowl, and mix well. Gradually add the milk mixture to the creamed mixture alternately with 4 or more cups of the flour mixture, beating well at low speed after each addition. Stir in the remaining flour by hand. Place dough in a greased bowl, turning to coat the surface. Let rise, covered, until doubled in bulk.
- Knead the dough flat, and divide into three portions. Shape into loaves. Place in greased 5×9-inch loaf pans, and let rise.Bake for 30 minutes. Remove from the pans, and cool on wire racks.
- For variety, roll the inside of the loaves with cinnamon and sugar or extra-sharp cheddar cheese, dried fruits, or chocolate.
- Makes 3 medium loaves

Get-togethers and holidays in our family always feature classic loaves of Sweet Yeast Bread. There is something about the aroma and taste of freshly baked bread that gives everyone a sense of home, well-being, and celebration.

MAGGIE CASTELLOE, who lives among the rolling meadows of northern Virginia's hunt country, shares this family recipe. From this setting she has created a specialty food company that makes Best of Luck Horseshoes and Nail Shortbread Cookies and Horseshoe Chocolates. The most recent addition to Hunt Country Foods stable of products is a chocolate Jazz! Bar. These products can be found nationally in gourmet stores, gift stores, equestrian shops, museum shops, and catalogs.

DID YOU KNOW THAT:

Richmond had been the seat of Virginia's government since 1780?

ROWENA'S KITCHEN TIPS

Sprinkle salt in your frying pan to keep fat from splattering. This is especially useful when frying hamburgers.

LEE HALL MANSION

Lee Hall, an Italianate-style manor house, was completed by an affluent planter, Richard Decauter Lee, in 1859. Lee, a scientific farmer, learned how to revitalize the worn-out soil of the tobacco-growing Virginia Peninsula with the 'four-field farming system.' He amassed over 2,000 acres and operated a tide mill, Lee's Mill, on the Warwick River.

When Virginia left the Union in 1861, R.D. Lee became a strong supporter of the Confederacy. His elegant mansion was used as headquarters by Confederate generals John Bankhead Magruder and Joseph Eggleston Johnston during the early stages of the Peninsula Campaign. It was from Lee Hall that Magruder orchestrated his brilliant defense of the Yorktown-Warwick River Line blocking the huge Union army's path to Richmond for over a month. A Confederate hot air balloon was sent aloft to spy on the Union army from the earthen redoubt that still remains on the manor's front lawn.

R.D. Lee lost his property in the war's aftermath. However, his stately antebellum home has been restored and decorated to its pre-Civil War splendor.

—John V. Quarstein, Director
The Virginia War Museum

MAE'S ORIGINAL WHOLE WHEAT BREAD

Add 2¹/₂ cups boiling water over 3 tablespoon Crisco (or shortening), 1 cup sugar, 2 teaspoons salt in a bowl. Soften 1 package yeast in ¹/₂ cup water. Add spoon of sugar. Let stand until above cools to lukewarm. Add yeast first, next 4 cups whole wheat flour, next 4 cups white flour. Put out of bowl on board and knead 10 minutes hard. Use flour if needed.Cover, set to rise in warm place free of draft. When above doubles in bulk punch down. Let it rise again until double. Knead well. Divide in 3 loaves or 2 big ones. The last Kneading is to free dough of air bubbles. Set to rise in pans covered. Bake in preheated 325 degree oven 45 minutes. If too thick, could bake 10 minutes longer. Turn out and grease well with butter. I grease my bowl with oil so bread doesn't stick before I let it raise.

—Mae Girling

Mae's Whole Wheat Bread

REVISED VERSION
2¹/₂ cups boiling water
3 tablespoons shortening
1 cup plus 1 spoon sugar
2 teaspoons salt
1 (¹/₂-ounce) package active dry yeast

¹/₂ cup warm water
4 cups whole-wheat flour
4 cups all-purpose flour
2 to 3 tablespoons butter or margarine

- Pour the boiling water over the shortening in a large bowl. Add 1 cup of the sugar and the salt. Dissolve the yeast in the warm water in a separate bowl, adding the remaining sugar. Let stand until the shortening mixture cools to lukewarm. Add the yeast mixture to the shortening mixture, and mix well. Stir in the whole-wheat flour and all-purpose flour. Place the dough on a floured surface, and knead hard for 10 minutes.
- Place the dough in a greased bowl, turning to coat the surface. Let rise, covered, in a warm place free of drafts until doubled in bulk. Punch the dough down. Let rise again, covered, until doubled in bulk. Knead well, and divide the dough into 2 or 3 portions. Knead to remove air bubbles. Shape the dough into loaves, and place in greased loaf pans. Cover and let rise. Bake, uncovered, in a preheated 325°F oven for 45 to 55 minutes. Invert the loaves onto wire racks, and brush well with butter.
- Makes 2 or 3 loaves

This recipe was submitted by LORRAINE SHIELS GIRLING (Mrs. Rowland Lea Girling) of the Blue Ridge Chapter of the Virginia DAR. This is Mae Girling's recipe from Speed the Plough Farm in Elon, Virginia. Speed the Plough Farm was a tobacco farm with several tobacco barns scattered over its 295 acres. As recalled by the present owner, Rowland Lea Girling (whose great Uncle Rowland Lea purchased Speed the Plough in 1925), milk and cream were stored in the Spring House, which dates back to the 1700s. The main brick mansion was built circa 1845 in the Georgian style. For decades, the apple and peach orchards attracted people from surrounding cities and counties to "Pick Your Own" fruit. Dr. Girling's parents managed the farm from 1938 to1998. Mae's bread was a favorite of many. Presently, the rolling hills at the base of Tobacco Row Mountain provide pasture for beef cattle. The Girlings are restoring the house and grounds.

DID YOU KNOW THAT:

From 1607, when it was settled, until 1820, Virginia was the most populous colony or state in America?

GREENWAY HAVEN
Party House Rolls

1½ cups warm water
½ cup shortening
¼ cup sugar
2 teaspoons salt
2 eggs
⅓ cup milk powder
2 (¼-ounce) packages
  active dry yeast

5 cups sifted unbleached
  all-purpose flour
½ cup (1 stick) butter or
  margarine
½ cup shortening

- Pour the water over the shortening, sugar, salt, eggs, and milk powder in a large bowl. Add the yeast, and mix together with your hands or a mixer. Add the flour gradually, mixing well after each addition. Place in a greased bowl, turning to coat the surface. Let rise, covered with a towel, for 1 hour or until doubled in bulk.
- Roll the dough on a well-floured surface, and cut with a biscuit cutter. Melt the butter or margarine and shortening in a small saucepan, and dip the rolls in the mixture. Fold the cut dough over the thumb to form a Parker House roll. Place the rolls touching in a pan. Do not crowd or leave an open space in the pan. Let rise, covered with a lightweight towel, for 1 hour or until doubled in bulk. Bake in a preheated 400°F oven for 15 to 20 minutes or until golden brown.
- Makes about 35 to 40 rolls

The recipe was shared by MARY ANN JOHNSON, owner of Greenway Haven Party House of Abingdon. The Greenway Haven, located on White's Mill Road, was built in 1874 by John G. White. In 1954, Mr. and Mrs. Robert Smith acquired the property and started the Greenway Haven Party House, which is owned and operated today by their daughter, Mary Ann Janson, and grandson, Robert Janson. It caters parties of eight or more in one of Abingdon's loveliest old homes.

AMHERST COUNTY

Amherst County was named for General Sir Jeffery Amherst (1717-1797), the British commander in North America during the French and Indian War and, later, the governor of Virginia (1759-1768). The county was formed in 1761 from part of nearby Albemarle County. It covers four hundred seventy square miles and has a population of 31,894. Amherst is the county seat.

Patrick Henry's mother, Sarah Henry (née Winston), is buried in Amherst County. Sweet Briar College for women was established in the county in 1901 and presented its first bachelor of arts degree in 1910.

VIRGINIA TIMELINE

1612—John Rolfe, a young Jamestown resident, contributes to the salvation of the colony by demonstrating that the variety of tobacco he has been growing since his arrival is a valuable and marketable product. The export of tobacco literally saves Jamestown from extinction.

1614—John Rolfe and Pocahontas, daughter of the powerful chief, Powhatan, are married.

1619—The House of Burgesses, the first body of legislative representatives organized in the New World, holds its premier assembly at Jamestown. At Jamestown, also, a boat carrying the first slaves to arrive in North America docks.

1622—Indians massacre scores of colonists in villages and plantations situated along the James River, including the one at Wolstenholme Towne.

1633—Middle Plantation, later renamed Williamsburg, is first settled.

1650—Four Virginians—Edward Bland, Captain Abraham Wood, Sackford Brewster, and Elias Pennant—depart Fort Henry, present-day Petersburg, on an exploration trip that takes them almost to what is today's North Carolina border.

Madisons (Potato Rolls)

4 medium potatoes, peeled	8 to 9 cups flour
3 cups water	4 eggs, lightly beaten
1 1/2 (1/4-ounce) packages	1 cup milk
active dry yeast	1 cup (2 sticks) butter or
1/4 cup sugar	margarine, softened
1 1/2 teaspoons salt	

- Cook the potatoes in water in a medium saucepan until tender, and drain, reserving 1 cup of the cooking liquid. Mash the potatoes.
- Dissolve the yeast in the reserved cooking liquid in a large bowl. Add the sugar, salt, and 3 cups of the flour, and mix well. Stir in the eggs, milk, butter, and remaining flour. Beat until the dough is soft and light. Let the dough rise, covered with a greased cloth, for 2 hours or longer. Place the dough in the refrigerator to cool.
- Shape dough into balls, and place 3 balls in each greased muffin cup, or roll out, and cut with a biscuit cutter. Let rise, covered, for 2 hours. Bake in a preheated 400°F oven for about 15 minutes.
- Makes about 4 dozen rolls

Marshal Duretté, (Junior to us), worked for my family practically since his birth. He and my father were playmates in the early 1920s. We're not sure where Junior got this wonderful recipe, but he made the rolls for us as frequently as we could persuade him. Be sure to serve them warm with lots of real butter.

CAMERON SMITH FOSTER, one of the most creative cooks I know, sent this recipe. She even serves her family pink mashed potatoes on Valentine's Day. She is the creative director at Rowena's, Inc., Creators and Producers of Gourmet Foods in Norfolk.

APPOMATTOX COUNTY

Appomattox County was organized in 1845 from parts of Buckingham, Campbell, Charlotte, and Prince Edward Counties. It is named after an American Indian tribe that originally lived in the area. Appomattox County has a population of 13,705 and covers three hundred forty-two square miles. The county seat is Appomattox.

Joel Walker Sweeney (ca. 1810-1860), credited with the invention of the five-string banjo, is buried in Appomattox County. The Confederacy had its last "hurrah" in April 1865 in this county as General Robert E. Lee prepared his Army of Northern Virginia for surrender to General Ulysses S. Grant at the McLean House on the ninth of the month.

1670—From a vantage point several miles northeast of present-day Charlottesville, John Lederer, a young German physician, becomes the first European to sight the Blue Ridge Mountains.

1676—Supporters of Nathaniel Bacon, a backwoodsman who had repeatedly failed to gain Governor William Berkeley's support for defending the frontier, burn Jamestown to the ground during a short-lived revolt called "Bacon's Rebellion."

1693—The College of William and Mary at Middle Plantation becomes the second institution of higher learning to be organized in the American colonies.

1699—Virginia Colony's capital is moved from Jamestown to Middle Plantation, and the village is renamed Williamsburg.

MISS GIBSON'S
Refrigerator Rolls

1 cup water
3 tablespoons shortening
1/2 cup sugar
1 tablespoon salt
4 cups all-purpose flour

1 egg
2 (1/4-ounce) packages
  active dry yeast
1/4 cup warm water
Sugar

- Heat the water in a medium saucepan until hot. Remove from the heat. Stir the shortening, sugar, and salt into the hot water. Add 2 cups of the flour and the egg, stirring well. Dissolve the yeast in warm water in a saucepan, sprinkling the mixture with sugar. Add 1 cup of the flour and the yeast mixture to the dough, and mix well. Add the remaining flour as needed to make a soft dough. Place in a greased bowl, turning to coat the surface. Let rise, covered, for 90 minutes.
- Punch the dough down. Refrigerate, covered, for 8 to 10 hours. Knead the dough until the bubbles are worked out when ready to bake. Shape into 30 rolls. Place on greased baking sheets, and let rise, covered, for 3 to 4 hours. Bake in a preheated 400°F oven for 10 minutes or until brown.
- Makes 30 rolls

This recipe came from a grand cook in Front Royal. Miss Gibson boarded single schoolteachers. Her dinner table was a delight.

The recipe is shared by SHELLEY LINGAMFELTER of Woodbridge, Virginia. She is the wife of Scott Lingamfelter, delegate to the General Assembly for the 31st District, which is comprised of parts of Fauquier and Prince William Counties. He is a graduate of Virginia Military Institute and the University of Virginia, and a Colonel, United States Army (retired).

ARLINGTON COUNTY

Arlington County was originally called Alexandria County. Organized in 1847 from land retroceded to Virginia by the Washington, D.C. government, it received its present name in honor of the Arlington Estate in 1920. The county covers thirty-one square miles and has a population of 189,453. The county seat is Arlington.

The noted statesmen Henry Clay of Kentucky and Virginia's John Randolph participated in a duel in this county in 1826 in which neither combatant was wounded. The world's first public passenger airplane flight took place here in 1908, when Orville Wright carried a friend on a six-minute, twenty-four-second excursion.

Breakfast

MABRY MILL
Grits

1 cup Mabry Mill grits	2 tablespoons butter or
1/2 teaspoon salt	margarine
3 1/2 cups water	

- Combine the grits, salt, and water in a medium saucepan, and mix well. Cook over low heat for 25 minutes, stirring frequently. Add the butter or margarine, and cook for 5 minutes longer, stirring frequently.
- Note: May be served hot, chilled, or sliced and fried in butter or pork drippings.
- Makes 6 servings

The recipe was sent by SHELBY CLIFTON COCHRAN, Regent of Colonel Abraham Penn Chapter of the Virginia DAR. Mabry Mill lies along the Blue Ridge Parkway located in Meadows of Dan, Virginia. The restaurant serves buckwheat cakes and other southern recipes. Mabry Mill is typical of the ingenuity of the pioneer people who settled in the southern highlands. Ed Mabry first started his enterprises with a blacksmith shop, and later expanded his operations to include a sawmill, gristmill, and woodworking shop. From about 1905 until 1935, this community center provided for the needs of the families in Floyd and Patrick Counties. Mabry Mill is still a working mill, where flour or corn meal is ground daily. The mill ships buckwheat flour all over the world.

Crock Pot Beef Hunt Breakfast

2 pounds lean chuck roast, cut into 1-inch cubes	1 package dried onion soup mix
1 (10 3/4-ounce) can cream of mushroom soup	1 (4-ounce) can drained mushrooms
1/2 cup red wine, optional	

- Combine the chuck, soup, wine, soup mix, and mushrooms in a crock pot, and mix well. Cook on Low for 8 to 12 hours. Serve over buttered cooked egg noodles.
- Makes 6 to 8 servings

The recipe can be doubled to feed a crowd.

The recipe was submitted by ANNE STEELE SKIDMORE from Madison, Virginia, a member of the Montpelier Chapter of the Virginia DAR.

"THE LARGEST HAM BISCUIT IN THE WORLD"

On September 28, 2002, history was made in Smithfield, Virginia—along with a 2,200-pound ham biscuit—proving that Smithfield truly is the Ham Capital of the World!

The day Smithfield Foods made a biscuit that weighed over a ton, the company and its hometown of Smithfield made headline news all over the world! CNN touted it all day, while the BBC in London did live radio interviews. Indeed, radio, television, magazines, and newspapers reported the spectacular event on front pages and in in-depth interviews featuring the art of making a biscuit!

Biscuit making is truly an art, according to Smithfield Foods representative Betty Thomas, who graciously explained that many Southerners have fond memories of Mother or Grandmother in the kitchen rolling out flour, never using the same

Largest Ha...
In Smit...
"The Ham

recipe twice, yet always producing fluffy, moist homemade biscuits that put a "taste of home" in the mouths of the family.

When a gentleman from the BBC asked, "This biscuit, is it a dumpling?" Virginians within earshot grinned and knew some educating about biscuits needed doing. Life has many necessities, and true Virginians know that making a warm biscuit and placing Smithfield ham inside is one of them.

The recipe for the World's Largest Ham Biscuit is both a wonder and a science. The Ham Biscuit Team's efforts were recognized by Guinness World's Records and Ripley's Believe It or Not with the following recipe and cooking instructions that were carried out that beautiful Saturday when Smithfield made a story to be told for generations to come!

1,000 pounds flour	80 gallons buttermilk
32 pounds baking powder	14 pounds salt
7½ pounds baking soda	500 pounds genuine
75 pounds butter	Smithfield ham, sliced
75 pounds Luter's lard	

- The total amount of time required to prepare 5 batches of dough is 2 hours. A special oven is necessary in order to bake the biscuit. The baking time is more than 14 hours using the special oven!
- Cooling time for the biscuit is 4 hours. It takes an additional 1¼ hours to remove the top of the biscuit to place the ham slices.
- Makes an enormous number of servings

An accompanying cartoon appeared in "Ripley's Believe It or Not" and was published in 200 major newspapers in 37 countries.

BETTY THOMAS of Smithfield Foods, Inc., Smithfield, Virginia, shared this recipe for the World's Largest Ham Biscuit.

ROWENA'S

Sausage Breakfast

1 pound bulk sausage	1 teaspoon dry mustard
1 cup grated sharp cheddar	1 teaspoon salt
cheese	8 slices white bread, crusts
8 eggs	removed, torn into pieces
2 cups milk	

- Brown the sausage in a medium skillet until cooked through and crumbly. Drain any excess drippings. Combine the cooked sausage with the cheese in a large bowl, and mix well. Beat the eggs and milk in a medium bowl. Add the mustard and salt.
- Arrange the bread pieces in a greased 9×13-inch pan. Layer the sausage mixture over the bread pieces. Pour the egg mixture over the sausage layer. Refrigerate, covered, overnight.
- Preheat the oven to 350°F, and bake for 45 minutes.
- Makes approximately 12 servings

Easy to make for a big breakfast; everybody loves this recipe. I even made it for my husband's 75th birthday when we had all the children, grandchildren, and our sisters for a reunion breakfast— thirty-six people in all. —Rowena

Blueberry French Toast Strata

STRATA

12 slices day-old bread, crusts removed, cut into 1-inch cubes

2 packages cream cheese, cut into 1-inch cubes

1 cup blueberries

12 eggs

2 cups milk

1/3 cup maple syrup

BLUEBERRY SYRUP

1 cup blueberries, about 6 ounces

1/2 cup pure maple syrup

1 tablespoon fresh lemon juice

- To prepare the strata, place half the bread cubes in a greased 9×13-inch baking dish. Place the cream cheese cubes over the bread cubes. Top with the blueberries and the remaining bread. Beat the eggs in a large bowl. Add the milk and maple syrup, and mix well. Pour the mixture over the bread cubes. Chill, covered, for 8 hours or overnight.
- Remove the strata from the refrigerator 30 minutes before baking. Bake, covered, at 350°F for 30 minutes. Bake, uncovered, for 25 to 30 minutes longer or until golden brown and the center is set.
- To prepare the syrup while the strata is baking, cook the blueberries and maple syrup in a small saucepan over moderate heat for 3 minutes or until the berries burst. Pour the syrup through a sieve into a heatproof pitcher, pressing on the solids, and stir in the lemon juice.
- The syrup may be made a day ahead and chilled, covered, in the refrigerator. Reheat the syrup before serving with the strata.
- Makes 6 servings

The WILSON-LEE HOUSE B&B on Virginia's Eastern Shore shared this recipe.

AUGUSTA COUNTY

Augusta County, one of Virginia's largest, derives its name from Augusta of Saxe-Gotha, the mother of King George III. The county covers one thousand six square miles, and its population is 65,615. The county seat is Staunton.

The eminent American painter George Caleb Bingham (1811-1879), was born in Augusta County, as were John Colter (1775-1813), the discoverer of present-day Yellowstone National Park, and Woodrow Wilson (1856-1924), the twenty-eighth president of the United States (1913-1921).

THE WILSON-LEE HOUSE

On Virginia's Eastern Shore

Cape Charles became the largest and most prosperous town on the Eastern Shore in the late 1800s. Incorporated in 1886 at the southern end of Delmarva, the town was "planned" by and for the railroads and the commerce they brought. The large harbor of Cape Charles was also an attraction. It was the terminus for various ferries in operation bearing freight and passengers between Norfolk and Maryland.

In 1906, James W. Lee, a highly distinguished and sought-after architect from Norfolk, came to Cape Charles to design the house that stands at 403 Tazewell Avenue for James W. Wilson, son of W.B. Wilson, founder of Wilson's Department Store. Today, the house is an Eastern Shore bed and breakfast. Resident Innkeeper Leon Parham has restored the original integrity of the Wilson-Lee House (named for the builder and architect). Each of the six guest rooms has a private bath. The rooms vary in historical allusion from Classical, Victorian, and Art Deco through Post-Modern.

Breakfasts at the Wilson-Lee include a choice of juices, fresh fruit, hot bread, a tantalizing main course, and a choice of specially blended coffees. Superb cook David Phillips has perfected the Oven-Baked Pancake with Apple and Créme Brulee French Toast. Guests continually ask for the Inn's recipes.

FRENCH AND INDIAN WAR ACTION

In March, 1754, Edward Braddock was commissioned a major-general in the British Army and given total command of all British forces in North America. Nine months later, Braddock was dispatched from England and sent to Virginia to accept his new post during the early months of the French and Indian War. Arriving at Hampton Roads on February 20, 1755, Braddock was accompanied by the 44th and 48th Infantry Regiments, neither of which had a particularly good reputation as crack unit.

On April 20, 1755, General Braddock departed Alexandria, Virginia, with orders to capture French-held Fort Duquesne, located in the peninsula formed by the Monongahela and Allegheny Rivers. At Wills Creek, about 130 miles north of Alexandria, Braddock organized a fighting force consisting of about two thousand professional Redcoats and Virginia colonial militia. By July 8, the army had finally arrived at a point fifteen miles from Fort Duquesne. The following day, July 9, 1755, the men started on the final leg of the journey. Then, as the combined British and American force-marched noisily along the previously cleared road through the dense forest, the French and Indian attack came. Within minutes, Braddock was dead, Colonel (later General) Thomas Gage was severely wounded, George Washington had had two horses shot out from under him, and nearly eight hundred officers and men of the British column were killed, captured, or wounded.

Breakfast Quiche

5 large or 6 medium eggs
1 unbaked (9-inch) deep-dish piecrust
2 tablespoons butter or margarine
2 tablespoons diced onion
1/3 cup diced ham

8 ounces coarsely grated mild cheese
1/3 cup crumbled cooked bacon
1 cup light cream
Salt and pepper

• Preheat the oven to 425°F. Beat the eggs in a medium bowl until blended. Pour the eggs into the piecrust, covering the surface, and then quickly back out into the bowl. Place the piecrust in the oven for 1 to 2 minutes to seal the crust.
• Melt the butter or margarine in a small skillet, and sauté the onion and ham. Spread the ham mixture and bacon in the piecrust. Stir the cream into the eggs. Add salt and pepper to taste. Pour the egg mixture over the top.
• Bake for 15 minutes. Reduce the oven temperature to 300°F, and bake for 30 minutes longer or until a knife inserted 1 inch from the edge comes out clean. Let the quiche stand for 10 minutes before cutting.
• Makes 8 to 10 servings

This quiche can be refrigerated if it's covered. Use a slice at a time, and warm it in the microwave. Great for the family that needs to eat at different times.

The recipe comes from the kitchen of JANE W. BACON of Lynchburg, a member of the James River DAR.

Huevos Rancheros

8 ounces bulk chorizo sausage
Vegetable oil
6 (10-inch) flour tortillas
1 1/4 cups warm salsa
12 fried eggs

1 1/2 cups shredded cheddar cheese (see Note below)
1/4 cup black beans
Avocado, peppers, grape tomatoes, and sour cream for garnish

• Cook the sausage in vegetable oil in a skillet until brown and crumbly, and drain. Wrap the tortillas in foil, and place in a warm oven. Spread each tortilla with 1 tablespoon of the salsa. Place 2 eggs on each tortilla. Top with 1 scant tablespoon of the salsa, 1/4 cup of the sausage, another tablespoon of the salsa, and 1/4 cup of the cheese. Sprinkle each with the beans, and garnish with sliced or chopped avocado, chopped peppers, grape tomatoes, and sour cream.
• Note: Six ounces of shredded Mexican four cheeses can be substituted for the cheddar cheese.
• Makes 6 servings

DAVID PHILLIPS, innkeeper and owner, submitted this recipe from his Wilson-Lee House Bed & Breakfast, Cape Charles, Virginia.

Bed & Breakfast
at

The Historic
PAGE HOUSE INN
Circa 1899

Eggs à la Stormi

8 slices toasting bread, such as Pepperidge Farm, crusts removed
$1/4$ cup ($1/2$ stick) butter or margarine, melted
$1/2$ teaspoon minced garlic
1 pound each hot and mild Italian sausage, casings removed
2 cups shredded Monterey Jack cheese with peppers

$3/4$ cup finely chopped sun-dried tomatoes, drained
7 eggs
$2^3/4$ cups milk
1 teaspoon dry mustard
$1/4$ teaspoon oregano
1 teaspoon salt
Papaya slices, mango slices, strawberry slices, and sprigs of rosemary for garnish

- Arrange the bread slices in the bottom of a lightly greased 9×13-inch baking dish. Melt the butter or margarine in a saucepan. Add the garlic, and mix well. Brush the top side of the bread slices with the butter mixture. Brown the sausage in a skillet until cooked through and crumbly, and drain. Layer the sausage, cheese and tomatoes over the bread slices. Beat the eggs, milk, dry mustard, oregano, and salt in a bowl, and pour over the layers. Refrigerate, covered with foil, for 8 to 10 hours. Let the baking dish stand at room temperature for 45 minutes before baking.
- Preheat the oven to 350°F. Bake for approximately 45 minutes or until puffy and browned on top. Remove from the oven, and let stand for about 10 minutes. Cut into servings. Garnish with papaya, mango, and strawberry slices, and sprigs of rosemary.
- Makes approximately 9 to 12 servings

So easy to make. Assemble the night before, and present an elegant "all-in-one" dish to your breakfast guests. Place on your very finest breakfast china, and garnish with papaya and mango slices, rosemary sprigs, and fresh strawberry halves. Accompany this wonderful dish with lightly toasted scones or muffins served with apple-honey butter.

Thanks to CARL ALBERO, of the Page House Inn in Norfolk, Virginia, for sharing Stormi's recipe.

DID YOU KNOW THAT:

Williamsburg's Public Hospital was America's first publicly maintained institution for the mentally ill (1773)?

PAGE HOUSE INN

At the Page House Inn in Norfolk, Virginia, breakfast is a stellar affair. Amid the grandeur of pre-Civil War furnishings and elegant Willoware, hearty breakfasts are served each morning by the inn's capable staff. An atmosphere of genteel calm reigns as Stormi, the chatelaine of Page House Inn, surveys her domain. Stormi, the 8-year-old Yorkshire terrier who charms each and every guest with her delightfully open personality, is particularly fond of the breakfast hour. Not only is she able to greet each guest enthusiastically, but also she is able to police the dining area to ensure that no morsels of food are spilled and left to stay on the highly polished, oak floor. And on those days when guests are especially careful, Stormi rewards them with biscuits from her special apothecary jar, which is displayed prominently on the hearth in the parlor.

The Page House Inn, immersed in history and imbued with elegance, is surrounded by stately homes and imposing mansions. It is centrally located in Ghent's tree-lined streets amongst charming restaurants and small shops conveniently situated near downtown Norfolk, Virginia. Originally built in 1899 by Herman L. Page, a wealthy real estate tycoon, the property was sold by the Page Family in 1989. Following a complete restoration of the mansion in accordance with the "certified historic rehabilitation" guide-lines, the Page House Inn Bed and Breakfast was then opened. The three suites and four guest rooms at Page House are the epitome of comfort and elegance, and the décor of each room is unique and welcoming. In 2001, the Inn was acquired by the Albero Family and is under the management of Carl Albero, the owner of Stormi.

Brunch Eggs Supreme

1 pound fresh mushrooms, cleaned, cut into quarters
³/4 cup plus 1¹/2 tablespoons unsalted butter, at room temperature
¹/2 tablespoon salad oil
¹/2 cup all-purpose flour
3 cups simmering milk
1 cup plus 1 tablespoon heavy cream, no substitutes
1¹/2 teaaspoons salt
Freshly ground white pepper
Few drops of lemon juice
12 large eggs
¹/2 cup grated Parmesan cheese

- Sauté the mushrooms in 2 tablespoons of the butter and the oil in a skillet. Set aside, and keep warm.
- To prepare a béchamel sauce, melt 5¹/2 tablespoons of the butter in a heavy saucepan. Blend in the flour, stirring constantly. Stir in the simmering milk, cream, 1 teaspoon of the salt, a pinch of white pepper, and the lemon juice. Cook until thickened, stirring constantly. Float 1 tablespoon of cream on the top of the sauce to prevent a "skin" from forming. Reheat the béchamel sauce and the mushrooms.
- Beat the eggs with ¹/2 teaspoon of the salt and pepper to taste in a bowl. Pour the egg mixture into a 9-inch skillet. Add 3 tablespoons of the butter. Cook over medium heat, stirring until the eggs are scrambled into large underdone curds. Remove the eggs from the heat, and stir in 2 tablespoons of the butter. Layer the béchamel sauce, Parmesan cheese, mushroooms, and eggs, ¹/2 at a time, in a buttered shallow glass baking dish, about 12 inches long. Dot the top with the remaining butter.
- Makes 4 to 6 servings

The recipe can be prepared ahead and refrigerated for 6 to 8 hours or overnight. Let the dish return to room temperature. Preheat the broiler, and watching carefully, broil about 1 minute before serving.

DORA BELL, who lives in Mount Vernon, Virginia, and is a member of the Nelly Custis Chapter of the Virginia DAR, submitted this recipe.

BATH COUNTY

Bath County was organized in 1790 out of territory from Augusta, Botetourt, and Greenbrier (in present-day West Virginia) Counties. It was most likely named for the township of Bath, England. Bath County covers five hundred forty-five square miles, and its population is 5,048. The county seat is Warm Springs.

The site of Terrill Hill, home of brothers William R. and James B. Terrill, is located in Bath County. William graduated from West Point and was a general in the Union Army, while James was a Virginia Military Institute graduate who became a Confederate general. Both brothers were killed during the War Between the States, prompting their father to erect a monument in his sons' memories proclaiming, "God alone knows which was right."

THE GREY HORSE INN
Herb-Baked Eggs

4 thin slices Virginia ham
4 large eggs
1 teaspoon Dijon mustard
1/4 cup plain yogurt
1 teaspoon snipped fresh dill

1/2 teaspoon McCormick
  Vegetable Supreme
  Seasoning
3/4 cup shredded Swiss
  cheese

- Preheat the oven to 375°F. Spray two 6-ounce ramekins with nonstick cooking spray. Line the ramekins with 2 ham slices each. Beat the eggs, mustard, yogurt, dill, and vegetable seasoning in a medium bowl. Stir in 1/4 cup of the cheese. Divide the mixture between the prepared ramekins. Top with the remaining cheese.
- Bake for 25 to 30 minutes or until golden brown and set. Loosen from the ramekins, and invert onto serving plates. Serve with biscuits or crusty country bread.
- Makes 2 servings

This recipe was provided by JOHN and ELLEN HEARTY, innkeepers, The Grey Horse Inn, The Plains, Virginia.

MAGNOLIA HOUSE TEA ROOM
Maple Pecan Scones

3 cups all-purpose flour,
  such as White Lily
1/2 cup sugar
2 1/2 teaspoons baking powder
1/2 teaspoon baking soda
1/2 teaspoon salt
3/4 cup (1 1/2 sticks) firm
  butter, cut into small
  pieces

3/4 cup finely ground
  pecans
1 cup low-fat buttermilk
1 teaspoon maple extract
1/2 teaspoon vanilla extract
2 tablespoons turbinado
  sugar

- Combine the flour, sugar, baking powder, baking soda, and salt in a large bowl, and mix well. Cut the butter into the flour mixture using a pastry blender until the mixture resembles coarse cornmeal. Stir in the pecans. Make a well in the middle of the flour mixture.
- Combine the buttermilk, maple extract, and vanilla extract in a bowl, and pour into the well of the flour mixture. Mix the ingredients with a fork, forming a ball of dough. Note: The mixture will seem dry, but will soften as you continue to mix with a fork.
- Preheat the oven to 425°F. Roll the dough 1/2 inch thick on a floured surface. Cut out circles or hearts, and place on a greased heavy-duty baking sheet. Sprinkle with the turbinado sugar, and bake for 12 minutes.
- Makes 6 to 8 servings

KAREN GLASS of the Magnolia House Tea Room, Hampton, Virginia, contributed this recipe.

THE GREY HORSE "INN" THE PLAINS

Nestled in a quaint village called The Plains, surrounded by old plantings and original outbuildings, stands the Grey Horse Inn.

A glimpse of the "Old South" awaits you in the beautiful Grey Horse Inn. The restored mansion, circa 1880s, situated on four acres in the heart of Virginia Hunt Country is furnished with family antiques from the antebellum era and has five elegantly appointed guest rooms, the King George, Marshall, Shenandoah, Blue Ridge, and Piedmont, available. A country breakfast is ready for guests each morning.

John and Ellen Hearty are proud to welcome visitors to this retreat, which is close to many Civil War sites, vineyard tours, fine shops, and restaurants. Just beyond the Inn grounds is open pasture and views of unspoiled farmland with the Blue Ridge Mountains and vivid sunsets filling the skies.

The Grey Horse Inn is convenient to the Northern Virginia and D.C. weekend-getaway crowd, as well as the visitor to Virginia who plans to relax and see the countryside.

MAGNOLIA HOUSE

One of the best surviving examples of late-nineteenth-century architecture reflective of the Victorian era in Hampton is the Magnolia House on South Armistead Avenue. Built in 1885 by William Walter Scott, a Virginia Harbor pilot, the mansion boasts twenty rooms. William and his wife, Cora, had five children in their bustling home. Each of the children lived in the home for a while after they were married, and at one point, all five children and their families lived there at the same time. This large group required two dining rooms for meals. William prospered well as he went into the "moving pictures" business—bringing movies to the peninsula area of Virginia in Hampton Roads for the first time.

The home was converted into five apartments and remained so until 1997 when Karen and John Glass purchased the property. Decorative white mantles with gold inlay are distributed through the house. Columns in the interior reflect the Victorian times when their number signified social prominence and wealth. Upstairs rooms feature art and antiques. The downstairs now houses a beautiful location for luncheon or tea. Many weddings and events take place in the elegant setting within walking distance of downtown Hampton. A visit guarantees one a warm look at a home that offered good food for many long, long ago.

Toffee Coffee Cake

$^1/_4$ cup ($^1/_2$ stick) butter or margarine
2 cups firmly packed brown sugar
$^1/_2$ cup sugar
2 cups all-purpose flour
1 teaspoon baking soda

1 egg, beaten
1 cup buttermilk
1 teaspoon vanilla extract
1 (6-ounce) package toffee candy chips, such as Heath Bar

- Preheat the oven to 350°F. Blend the butter or margarine, brown sugar, sugar, and flour with a pastry blender in a large bowl. Set aside half the mixture.
- Stir the baking soda, egg, buttermilk, and vanilla extract into the remaining mixture until moistened. Pour into a greased 9×13-inch baking pan. Combine the toffee candy chips with the reserved mixture, and mix well. Sprinkle over the top. Bake for 30 minutes.
- Makes 10 to 12 servings

This recipe was sent by JOYCE HAYTER FERRATT, owner of Shepherd's Joy.

Cottage Cheese Pancakes

2 eggs
$^1/_2$ cup cottage cheese
2 tablespoons wheat germ
2 tablespoons whole wheat flour or all-purpose flour

$^1/_8$ teaspoon salt
Fruit jelly, optional
Confectioners' sugar, optional

- Process the eggs, cottage cheese, wheat germ, flour, and salt in a food processor until smooth. Pour a small amount of the batter onto a lightly greased pan or griddle, and cook until brown.
- The pancakes are similar to crêpes. They are good by themselves or spread with a fruit jelly and rolled up. Sprinkle with confectioners' sugar, if desired.
- Makes about 6 pancakes

This recipe was shared by EDNA SARA LAZARON, an artist extraordinaire who created a tiny and very special four-generation recipe book for her family called *Family Fare*.

DID YOU KNOW THAT:

The country's first successful Caesarean section was performed by Doctor Jesse Bennett at Edom (January 14, 1794)?

Grandma's Old-Fashioned Buckwheat Pancakes

2 cups buckwheat flour
1 cup cornmeal (do not use
    cornmeal mix)
1 teaspoon salt
1 (^{1}/4-ounce) package active
    dry yeast

1^1/2 cups (or more) water
2 tablespoons molasses
^{1}/4 cup milk
1 teaspoon baking soda
Shortening for frying

- Combine the flour, cornmeal, salt, yeast, and enough water to make a fairly thick batter in a large bowl, and mix well. Let the batter stand, covered with waxed paper, overnight at room temperature to rise.
- Stir in the molasses, milk, and baking soda 1 hour before serving time. Let rise, covered with waxed paper. Heat enough shortening in a cast-iron skillet to fry the pancakes. Fry until the pancakes are bubbly. Turn the pancakes over and brown the other side.
- Makes 12 to 15 large pancakes

Serve with molasses or maple syrup and cooked sausage. Enjoy!

This was the recipe of PAULINE HOLLOWAY's grandmother, who lived in Bland County. Pauline is a member of the Roanoke Valley Chapter of the Virginia DAR.

Old Chickahominy House
Williamsburg, Virginia

Miss Melinda's Pancakes

6 eggs
^{1}/2 cup oil
^{1}/2 cup sugar

4 cups self-rising flour
4 cups buttermilk

- Beat the eggs, oil and sugar vigorously in a bowl with a stiff wire whisk. Add the flour alternately with the buttermilk, beating well after each addition. Pour a large amount of the batter onto a hot griddle. Bake until brown on both sides.
- Note: Beating well is one of the secrets. Add additional buttermilk if the batter is not light enough.
- Makes 8 to 10 large pancakes

We make them plate-size at the Chick.

MAXINE WILLIAMS, owner of The Old Chickahominy House, Williamsburg, Virginia, shared this recipe.

OLD CHICKAHOMINY HOUSE

The home of Old Virginia Ham Biscuits, the Rebel Cocktail, Brunswick Stew, Buttermilk Pie, and a cat named Biscuit.

Regular customers of the Old Chickahominy House in Williamsburg, just down the road from the College of William and Mary, know that parking at "the Chick" is a challenge. From the moment the old screen door (with the glimpse of a cat's tail swiftly dashing by) greets them on the big front porch, guests feel transported back to an earlier, easy-going time when it was all right to "wait." Indeed, they sometimes plan the "wait" for a table so as to have ample time to browse in the antique and gift shop. It is not unusual to find just the perfect item for one's home or next gift. One begins to believe that Biscuit, the resident cat for over ten years, has the right idea—curling up under the table, with its lavender and silver, until it is time to sit and enjoy the Colonial decor in the dining area.

Maxine Williams and her staff greet visitors and provide the wonderful service at the Chick. For breakfast, the Rebel Cocktail sparks the morning with ingredients that include tomato juice and beer. Biscuits are large, flat, rectangular, and crusty. Virginia ham can be placed inside the biscuits or they can be enjoyed with just butter. For lunch, the most popular selection is Miss Melinda's Special, named for the lady who started the business over forty years ago. This feast includes Brunswick stew, Virginia ham biscuits, fruit salad, a choice of homemade pie, and a beverage. The chicken and dumplings are "something to write home about."

Moved from its original location along the Chickahominy River a few miles away, this mid-eighteenth-century house is actually out of the restored area in Williamsburg. Located on Jamestown Road, it has made its niche locally, as well as with tourists who wish to see "the rest of Williamsburg." Many people come back to see the smiles of familiar staff, some of whom have been there thirty years. Whether one is hungry or not, the Chick is a good place to escape the current times for a few moments, smell revered Southern cuisine, and figure out where Biscuit will curl up next.

THE INN AT BURWELL PLACE
Oven Puff Pancakes

1 cup (1/2 percent) milk	1/4 teaspoon salt
1 egg	1 teaspoon vanilla extract
3 egg whites	1 tablespoon butter
1 cup all-purpose flour	(no substitution)
1 teaspoon sugar	

- Prepare the batter 30 minutes before baking if possible. Combine the milk, egg, egg whites, flour, sugar, salt, and vanilla extract in a bowl, and let stand for 30 minutes.
- Preheat the oven to 375°F. Heat the butter in a 10-inch skillet sprayed with vegetable cooking spray in the oven for 2 minutes, being careful to avoid burning the butter. Pour the batter into the skillet. Bake for approximately 30 minutes or until golden brown. Serve with sautéed apples, fresh fruit, or syrup, and sprinkle with confectioners' sugar. Cut into wedges and serve immediately.
- Makes 8 to 10 servings

This recipe was received courtesy of ALICE S. SHORTER, Regent of the Patrick Henry Chapter of the Virginia DAR, who is proud of her area. In turn, the recipe is generously shared by Cindi Lou MacMackin, innkeeper of the Inn at Burwell Place, a beautiful bed and breakfast in Salem. Set in a spacious mansion built in 1907 by Samuel H. McVitty, a local industrialist, the inn is on a summit overlooking Salem and the southwest Roanoke Valley. Restored to the glory of a bygone era, the mansion has been decorated by nationally acclaimed interior designer Lawrence Cummings. Antique walnut and cherry furnishings adorn the guestrooms.

NELLY CUSTIS'
Hoecakes

8 3/4 cups white cornmeal	Warm water
1 1/4 teaspoons active	1 egg
dry yeast	Shortening

- Mix together 4 cups of the cornmeal and the dry yeast in a large container, and stir in enough warm water (probably 3 to 4 cups) to give the mixture the consistency of pancake batter. Cover and set on the stove or counter overnight. In the morning, gradually add the remaining cornmeal, egg, and enough warm water to give the mixture the consistency of pancake batter. Cover and set aside for 15 to 20 minutes. Heat the shortening on a griddle or in a skillet until hot. Pour the batter by the spoonful onto the hot griddle. Stir the batter well between each batch. Cook until brown on one side. Turn the hoecake over, and brown the other side.
- Makes enough to easily feed a school class

MARY THOMPSON, of Mt. Vernon, shared this recipe.

Preservation of Virginia Antiquities

The Preservation of Virginia Antiquities has a list of many properties all over the state that may be of keen interest to the history-loving person who likes to explore. They are listed below. Other beautiful buildings and sites throughout Virginia are maintained by many other organizations, but this list is a great start to discovering our beautiful and historic Commonwealth.

AMHERST COUNTY
Gravesite of Sarah Winston
Syme Henry—1784
Clifford (804) 648-1889
Open year-round

BLACKSBURG
Smithfield Plantation—1774
Off 460 Bypass on Route 314
(540) 231-3947
Open April-October

CHARLOTTE COUNTY
Thomas Read's Clerk's Office—
c.1810
Charlotte Court House
(804) 542-5453
Open by appointment

Cub Creek Church Site—1738
(804) 648-1889
Open year-round

EASTERN SHORE
Debtor's Prison—1782
Accomac (757) 787-3436
Open by appointment

Hopkins and Brothers Store &
Steamship
Office—1840s and 1880s
Onancock (757) 787-3100
Open May-December

Eastville Courthouse
Buildings—1731 and 1814
Eastville (757) 678-0465 or
(757) 678-5755
Open year-round

Pear Valley—c. 1740
Northampton County
(804) 648-1889
Open by appointment

FREDERICKSBURG
Hugh Mercer Apothecary
Shop—mid-18th century
(540) 373-3362 or
(800) 678-4748
Open year-round

Rising Sun Tavern—c. 1760
(540) 371-1494 or
(800) 678-4748
Open year-round

Mary Washington House—
pre-1772
(540) 373-1569 or
(800) 678-4748
Open year-round

St. James' House—
late 18th century
(540) 373-1569 or
(800) 678-4748
Open by appointment

GLOUCESTER COUNTY
Walter Reed Birthplace—
pre-1850
(804) 693-3663
Open by appointment

Warner Hall Graveyard—
from 1674
(804) 693-6458
Open year-round

HANOVER
Scotchtown—c. 1719
Off Route 54, 11 miles
northwest of Ashland
(804) 227-3500
Open April-October

JAMESTOWN
Jamestown Island—1607
James City County
(757) 229-1733
Open year-round

PETERSBURG
Farmers Bank—1817
19 Bollingbrook Street
(800) 368-3595 or
(804) 733-2400
Open by appointment

RICHMOND
John Marshall House—1790
Ninth & Marshall Streets
(804) 648-7998
Open April-December (closed
Sundays and Mondays)

Old Stone House—1754
and Site of Edgar Allen Poe
Museum
1914 East Main Street
(804) 648-5523
Open year-round

Cole Digges House—c. 1800
204 West Franklin Street
(804) 648-1889
Open year-round, Monday-
Friday or by appointment

SMITHFIELD
Isle of Wight Courthouse—1750
(800) 365-9339 or
(804) 357-5182
Open year-round

SURRY COUNTY
Bacon's Castle—1665
Route 10
(757) 357-5976
Open March-November

Smith's Fort Plantation—c.1763
Route 31
(757) 294-3872

VIRGINIA BEACH
Cape Henry Lighthouse—1792
Fort Story off Route 60
(757) 422-9421
Open January-November

Lynnhaven House—1724
Wishart Road
(757) 460-1688
Open May-October

APVA
For the Preservation of
Virginia Antiquities
204 West Franklin Street
Richmond, Virginia 23220-5012
(804) 648-1889

CHAPTER THREE

Soups, Salads, and Splashes

Virginians love soups and stews, often called chowders. However, originally, the French word chaudiere really meant the pot in which the soup was cooked.

Soups

GOVERNOR MARK WARNER'S
"Creamless" Asparagus Soup

SOUP

1 tablespoon olive oil
3 tablespoons chopped
  leeks, white part only
2 tablespoons minced
  shallots
1 celery rib, chopped
1 medium carrot, peeled,
  chopped
1 teaspoon minced garlic
2 pounds thin asparagus, cut
  into 1 to 2-inch pieces,
  tips removed, reserved
  for garnish

6 cups chicken stock or
  vegetable broth
2 fresh bay leaves
1$^1/4$ teaspoons mustard seeds
$^3/4$ teaspoon kosher salt
$^1/4$ teaspoon ground white
  pepper
2 medium Yukon Gold
  potatoes, peeled, coarsely
  chopped
1 ounce sherry

GARNISH

1 tablespoon olive oil
8 to 10 shallots, peeled,
  cut into halves
4 ounces morel mushrooms,
  rinsed

Reserved asparagus tips
6 to 8 ounces jumbo lump
  crabmeat, shell bits
  removed

- To prepare the soup, heat the olive oil in a large saucepan over medium heat, and add the leeks, shallots, celery, carrots, and garlic. Sauté for 3 to 4 minutes. Add the asparagus, and cook for 4 to 5 minutes longer, stirring occasionally.
- Add the chicken stock, bay leaves, mustard seeds, salt, pepper, and potatoes, and mix well. Bring to a boil, reduce the heat, and simmer for approximately 20 minutes or until the asparagus is tender. Remove the bay leaves, and purée the soup in batches in a blender until smooth. Strain through a china cap strainer, and return the soup to the saucepan. Simmer over low heat. Stir in the sherry.
- To prepare the garnish, heat the olive oil in a medium sauté pan. Add the shallots, and cook until they begin to brown. Add the mushrooms, and cook until the mushrooms and shallots are tender. Blanch the asparagus tips in boiling water in a saucepan until crisp-tender. Add the mushrooms, shallots, asparagus tips, and crabmeat to the hot soup.
- Makes 6 to 8 servings

This recipe was shared by Virginia Governor MARK R. WARNER. See page 74 for more information on him.

A note about the recipe from Mark W. Herndon, Chief of the Executive Mansion of Virginia.

"This Asparagus Soup is a very "Virginia" recipe and is a healthier version of a cream-based soup with some twists thrown in, that being the blue crab from the Chesapeake Bay and morels, which are grown in abundance in the mountains of Southwest Virginia during the months of March and April. Additionally, I often obtain the asparagus from local farmers (particularly in the Northern Neck). The soup is perfect for any spring or summer luncheon or dinner party."

Colonial Williamsburg

*Enter the world of Virginia's yesteryears in
Colonial Williamsburg ...you can still hear
hoof beats on the street, expect and find
candles burning in the windows, smell the
aroma of homemade Sally Lunn bread, and
walk amid tailored, fragrant herb gardens...
hear the call of a colony striving to claim
identity in a world that was not ready for it to stand
as a new nation...here in the very taverns that
early patriots enjoyed are the authentic foods and
presentation so richly handed down as Virginia grew
from colony to Commonwealth....experiencing
Williamsburg leaves one understanding why George
and Martha Washington spent their honeymoon here!*

Colonial Williamsburg is the world's largest
outdoor living history museum. Once home
to the beginning of ideas of democracy and
independence for a new nation, this historic
town has been restored from the ground up.
Visitors follow the literal pathways that patriots
walked as they visit the revived town on 301
acres. With over 500 historic buildings, CW (as
locals amicably call Colonial Williamsburg)
offers American and many international visitors
a glimpse and taste of the Virginia Colony.

The Colonial Williamsburg Foundation's mission
statement is, *That the future may learn from the
past.* This is evident by the foundation's efforts
to preserve and restore the original town of
Williamsburg to the way it appeared in the 18th
century. It is also shown by the fact that the
foundation engages, informs, and inspires people
as they learn about the site, the events that
occurred there, and the diverse peoples that
lived and shaped our nation there.

After serving as the capital of Britain's largest
and most powerful colony, then being in the
spotlight as the seat of the Commonwealth's
government, Williamsburg became a quiet
country town after the decision to make
Richmond the capital city. The town survived
the Civil War, and life resumed as a small town
on the Virginia Peninsula. The location of old
foundations of forgotten buildings and buried
fragments of once brilliant architecture were
known only to a few as the years passed. Some of
the dwellings were still in use, but "modern-day"
1900's style buildings began to dot the prior
colonial village site, making it almost impossible
to see the town the patriots saw. In 1903,
Reverend Dr. W.A.R. Goodwin, rector of

the still-standing Bruton Parish Church,
walked the streets wistfully and dreamed
of restoring the historic town. John D.
Rockefeller Jr. decided to make the
restoration a reality by contributing funds
toward the stunning project in 1926. By
1934, when President Franklin D. Roosevelt
came to see the completion of the first phase
of work, he told the nation, "The atmosphere
of a whole glorious chapter in our history has
been recaptured."

Part of the splendid experience of visiting
Colonial Williamsburg is tasting the wonderful
culinary offerings throughout the site. One can
dine beside a warm, inviting fireplace in the
autumn or winter months or eat a fresh spring or
summer salad while looking out on a street with
townspeople dressed like those of yesterday
scurrying about amid the blooms. With so many
dining choices, visitors must rely on their instincts
to return for several distinctive menus from
colonial times.

Williamsburg had more taverns than the average
18th century town. It was regularly visited by
businessmen, government representatives, planters,
and other travelers as it served as the capital for
over eighty years. Demands for food and lodging
created lucrative business opportunities. Tavern
keepers posted bonds, and complied with the
regulations the town set for food prices and
prices for drinks and lodging. Some owners owned
more than one tavern. The owner of the famous
Raleigh Tavern also owned Weatherburn's
Tavern (the owner's namesake establishment).
At the Raleigh, important discussions and
opinions grew as men such as Patrick Henry,
George Washington, Thomas Jefferson, George
Wythe, and George Mason frequently met to
continue deliberations after leaving government
meetings in the Capitol. Students from The
College of William and Mary came by as well.

The 99-foot-wide Duke of Gloucester Street led
to other shops and taverns, which provided food
and shelter for Virginians as well. Storekeepers
stocked imported capers, olives, gooseberries,
currants, cheeses from England, and other
delicacies. Dinners in the taverns included
roasted, stewed, or fried meat, poultry, or fish
with seasonal vegetables and bread. The special
gatherings usually had a Virginia ham placed at
the top of the table with a large joint such as a

saddle of mutton or leg of lamb placed at the bottom. Platters of roast fowl went in the center as vegetables and "casseroles" appeared along the sides and corners of the presentation. Small dishes of pickles, sauces, and condiments dotted the table decoratively. The wines and ales were as plentiful as desserts of jellies, pies, cakes, "sweetmeats," syllabubs, tarts, and puddings. After several hours of feasting, fruits and nuts were lavishly served at evening's end!

Today, Colonial Williamsburg's functional taverns recreate the tastes, smells, and sounds that the townspeople experienced in colonial times. Careful attention to details and authentically reproduced furnishings enhance the foods served with the ambiance of the distinctive establishments. Tableware looks the part, as do the servers greeting guests.

CHOWNING'S TAVERN
Chowning's was the first tavern operated in Williamsburg. The interior is patterned after alehouses in England. Josiah Chowning (pronounced "chewning") ran his business on rented property. Common folk were welcome here. After eighteen months of operation, Josiah had to give up his enterprise; no one is certain why.

KING'S ARMS TAVERN
The King's Arms Tavern represents the upper strand of society in Williamsburg's past. Long favored by such notables as General Thomas Nelson, General Baron von Steuben, and General George Washington, the tavern was described as "where all the best people resorted." The owner of the Arms was a widow named Jane Vobe. When hostilities with Great Britain came about, the establishment began to be called "Mrs. Vobe's Tavern." Guests were more content with that!

CHRISTIANA CAMPBELL'S TAVERN
Mrs. Christiana Campbell, a lady with two small children, baby Ebenezer and toddler Molly, came home to Williamsburg from Petersburg after her husband died. She took up tavern keeping as her father, John Burdett, had done. George Washington frequented Christiana Campbell's as

he came to town for the Publick Times. Widow Campbell rented her property near the Capitol. When Richmond became the capital city, she retired from business.

SHIELD'S TAVERN
Shield's Tavern began with the vision of Jean Marot, the future father-in-law of James Shields, years before his daughter Anne would marry James. Jean bought property close to the Capitol and attracted a clientele to his tavern, which included leading citizens of the town and colony. After his sudden death in 1717, several years passed until Anne and her husband, James Shields, came into ownership of the establishment. When James died in 1750, Anne ran the tavern on her own until marrying competitor Henry Weatherburn, a recent widower. She and her five children then saw a rival tavern keeper become husband and stepfather respectively. Their businesses did very well!

OTHER COLONIAL WILLIAMSBURG DINING
Other dining experiences are offered at Colonial Williamsburg.

The Williamsburg Inn Regency Room offers savory foods with new American cuisine. Fabulous chefs plan award-winning menus. Coat and tie are required for dinner here.

The Williamsburg Lodge Bay Room provides strolling balladeers for dinnertime entertainment. Cuisine here includes the "Chesapeake Bay Feast," a favorite of locals on the Peninsula.

Each of Colonial Williamsburg's championship golf courses features a clubhouse with great selections for tasty meals and picturesque views. The Golden Horseshoe Gold and Green Courses offer trendy sandwiches and desserts daily.

THE
KING's ARMS

Cream of Peanut Soup

1/4 cup (1/2 stick) unsalted
  butter
1 medium onion, finely
  chopped
2 ribs celery, finely chopped
3 tablespoons flour

8 cups chicken stock
2 cups creamy peanut butter
1 3/4 cups light cream or
  half-and-half
Finely chopped salted
  peanuts for garnish

- Melt the butter in a large saucepan or soup pot over medium heat. Add the onion and celery, and cook for 3 to 5 minutes or until softened, stirring frequently. Stir in the flour, and cook for 2 minutes longer.
- Add the chicken stock (or low-sodium canned chicken stock) to the saucepan. Increase the heat to high. Bring to a boil, stirring constantly. Reduce the heat to medium, and cook for about 15 minutes or until slightly reduced and thickened, stirring frequently. Strain through a sieve set over a large bowl, pressing hard on the solids to extract as much flavor as possible.
- Return the soup to the saucepan. Whisk in the peanut butter and cream or half-and-half until smooth. Simmer over low heat for about 5 minutes or until serving temperature, whisking frequently. Do not boil. Serve warm, garnished with chopped peanuts.
- Makes 10 to 12 servings

THE KING'S ARMS TAVERN provided this recipe for us. Columbus took peanuts, native to South America, back to Europe, and then Portuguese slave traders introduced them to Africa. The legumes recrossed the Atlantic on slave ships. The peanut soup now served at the King's Arms Tavern is a Virginia tradition-a slight variation of a recipe developed by George Washington Carver in the early 1890s.

BEDFORD COUNTY

Bedford County was formed in 1753 from Albemarle and Lunenburg Counties. It was named in honor of the fourth duke of Bedford. It contains seven hundred ninety square miles and has a population of 60,371.

The county seat is Bedford. Poplar Forest, the estate of Thomas Jefferson, is located in this county, and it was from there that the future president of the United States wrote his book, *Notes on Virginia*. New London Academy, the oldest secondary school in Virginia still operating under its own charter, was established here in 1795.

MR. PEANUT LIVES IN SUFFOLK

Since Colonial times, peanuts have been grown in Virginia. Native to West Africa, the crop has been successful in our soil for nearly four hundred years. In fact, in the world market, the largest type of peanut is the Virginia peanut. How did the peanut establish itself as a quick snack for folks on the go? An Italian immigrant named Amadeo Obici came alone from Venice to stay with his uncle in Pennsylvania. He worked at a fruit stand that also offered roasted peanuts. Obici determined that he could take the product to the customers instead of waiting for them to come to him, so he invested in his own roaster and began to travel on a wagon selling peanuts. He was known as the "Peanut Man." He began to shell the peanuts, package them, salt them, skin them, and even cover them in chocolate! He began the Planters Nut and Chocolate Company in 1906.

Shipping peanuts from Virginia to Pennsylvania was expensive, so Obici moved to the peanuts. He based his operations in Suffolk and began to extend his business across the country. He offered a $5 First Prize in a 1916 contest for a trademark design. Anthony Gentile, a fourteen-year-old boy from Suffolk, won with his drawing of a peanut "man" with a smile and a cane. After some professional versions were drawn, "Mr. Peanut" was born!

Many collectible items began to appear with "Mr. Peanut" on them. There were dolls, glassware, napkins, and even the "Peanutmobile" to extend Planter's advertising. Suffolk became the "Peanut Capital of the World." Some of the other products were peanut butter and peanut brittle. Today, "Mr. Peanut" is very comfortable inside his modern Suffolk factory and world headquarters. Obici's beautiful mansion, Obici House, still stands today, and peanuts are, of course, served at festivities there!

Southern Peanut Soup

$1/4$ cup ($1/2$ stick) butter or margarine	1 quart plus 3 ounces milk
1 rib celery, chopped	$3/4$ cup peanut butter
1 onion, chopped	Dash of Worcestershire sauce
1 carrot, chopped	1 teaspoon sugar

- Melt the butter or margarine in a skillet, and add the celery, onions, and carrots. Sauté until the vegetables are soft. Heat the milk in a saucepan until hot, stirring occasionally. Add the sautéed vegetables, stirring to blend the ingredients.
- Strain the hot mixture through a sieve into a serving bowl, and add the peanut butter, stirring until smooth. Stir in Worcestershire sauce and sugar.
- Makes 6 to 8 servings

THE MIMSLYN INN shared this recipe. Situated on a sixteen-acre tract within close view of the Blue Ridge and Massanutten Mountains, and minutes from the George Washington National Forest, the Shenandoah National Park, and the Appalachian Trail, the Mimslyn Inn offers a beautiful vacation setting to guests and to the diners a wide choice of authentic Virginia foods prepared under exacting supervision and served graciously in a colonial atmosphere. Specialties include Southern Peanut Soup as served in western Virginia, Old Country Ham, and the Mimslyn's matchless Shenandoah Apple Pie. The Mimslyn's imposing brick building, built in 1930, is very much like an old Virginia estate with its huge white columns, winding staircase, circular driveway, and a beautiful setting surrounded by old boxwoods and formal gardens.

BLAND COUNTY

Bland County, named in honor of Richard Bland, an early activist against British rule, was formed in 1861 from Giles, Tazewell, and Wythe Counties. It contains three hundred sixty square miles and has a population of 6,871. The county seat is Bland.

Bland County is a rich producer of coal, and much of its territory lies within the Jefferson National Forest. William Elbert Munsey, a prominent nineteenth-century Methodist churchman, was born here in 1833.

ROWENA'S KITCHEN TIPS

Add a pinch of baking soda to your teapot while making tea, and your tea won't cloud. This works for iced tea, as well.

Williamsburg Inn
Rosemary-Scented Sweet Red Pepper Bisque

4 medium sprigs of fresh rosemary plus 6 small sprigs for garnish
2 medium sprigs of fresh sweet marjoram
3 tablespoons fruity olive oil
6 large red bell peppers, cut into $1/2$-inch strips
6 medium leeks, white part only, thinly sliced

2 large cloves garlic, pressed
$1/4$ teaspoon freshly ground black pepper
$2 1/2$ cups beef stock or canned beef broth
1 cup plus 2 tablespoons crème fraîche or sour cream, at room temperature
Salt

- Tie the medium sprigs of rosemary and the marjoram in a double thickness of cheesecloth. Wring lightly to release the volatile oils.
- Heat the olive oil in a large heavy saucepan over high heat for about 1 minute or until almost smoking. Add the pepper strips and cook, for about 2 minutes or until slightly softened, tossing occasionally. Add the leeks and garlic, and cook for 2 minutes longer, tossing occasionally. Stir in the herbs and the black pepper. Reduce the heat to low. Cook, covered tightly, for 1 hour or until a large amount of liquid has formed and the peppers are soft.
- Remove and discard the herbs. Add the vegetable mixture to a food processor or blender, and process until smooth. Press the puréed mixture through a sieve into a medium saucepan, and add the beef stock. Cook over moderate heat for 2 to 3 minutes or until just hot. Stir in $3/4$ cup of the crème fraîche or sour cream and season to taste with salt.
- Ladle the soup into heated soup bowls, and garnish each serving with 1 tablespoon of the crème fraîche or sour cream and a small rosemary sprig.
- Makes 6 servings

Chef de Cuisine GILE HASKINS of the Williamsburg Inn kindly shared this recipe.

ROWENA'S KITCHEN TIPS

One of my children's favorite breakfast treats was cinnamon toast. I always kept (and still do) a shaker full of cinnamon and sugar ready at all times.

MEET GOVERNOR MARK WARNER

Governor Mark R. Warner was elected Virginia's sixty-ninth governor in November 2001. He grew up in a family where he learned the values of hard work, faith, and family and the importance of a good education. He became the only member of his family to graduate from college and in addition earned a law degree from Harvard Law School in 1980. He started his first successful company in the fledgling cellular communications industry. He became a founding partner of Columbia Capital Corporation and has helped start more than 50 businesses that have grown to employ more than 15,000 workers. He also served as founding chair of the Virginia Health Care Foundation, which has provided health care to more than 425,000 underserved Virginians in rural and urban areas. He started a program that brings free computer training classes to houses of worship all across Virginia, called Tech Riders, and organized the Virginia High Tech Partnership to connect students at Virginia's five historically black colleges and universities with internships and jobs at leading high tech companies. He and his wife, Lisa Collis, have three daughters.

CANAL INNOVATOR WAS A VIRGINIAN

Canals were among the earliest expressions of American engineering ingenuity. As early as 1716, the Reverend James Maury had voiced the opinion that since the headwaters of rivers flowing eastward and westward in the Tidewater and Piedmont regions of Virginia were so close, there should be no reason why the streams could not be connected via canals. The James River and Kanawha Canal was proposed in the mid-1830s to connect the Atlantic Ocean at the mouth of the James with the Ohio River near the settlement of Point Pleasant. Although the canal was never completed along its entire proposed length, the eastern section was operating at near capacity by 1854, at which time two hundred boats of various sizes were being used. In July, 1842, the James River Canal was virtually destroyed by a severe flood that ravaged the James River valley. Embankments were destroyed in more than one hundred places, causing nearly fifty thousand dollars worth of damage. But, the canal survived and continued to operate almost to the end of the nineteenth century, when it was finally replaced by the railroad.

Williamsburg Lodge

Gingered Pumpkin Bisque with Maple

1¹/₂ cups walnut oil	2¹/₂ cups dark maple syrup
1 pound shallots, peeled, chopped	1 teaspoon cinnamon
1 pound onions, peeled, chopped	Spice bag of 1 tablespoon thyme, 8 bay leaves, 1 tablespoon black peppercorns, and 1 clove
2 ounces fresh gingerroot, peeled, chopped	4 ounces cider jelly
2 cups all-purpose flour	4 (16-ounce) cans solid-pack pumpkin
2 cups apple cider	1 quart heavy cream
1 gallon rich chicken stock	Salt and pepper, optional
1 tablespoon vanilla extract	

- Heat the walnut oil in a soup pot, and sauté the shallots, onions, and gingerroot until soft. Add enough of the flour to absorb the walnut oil, and cook, stirring frequently. Add the cider, and simmer until reduced by half. Stir in the chicken stock, and bring to a simmer. Whisk in the vanilla extract, maple syrup, cinnamon, spice bag, cider jelly, and pumpkin, stirring frequently to ensure the flour has dissolved and the bisque is of a smooth consistency.
- Remove and discard the spice bag. Process the mixture in a food processor until puréed and of a smooth consistency. Stir in the heavy cream, and adjust the seasonings with salt and pepper if necessary.
- The soup may be garnished with lightly sweetened whipped cream or a lemon-flavored crème fraîche, and it can be attractively served in a hollowed pumpkin or acorn squash. This recipe can be reduced easily by one-half or one-fourth.
- Makes 2¹/₂ gallons

Shared by CHEF BRIAN ASPELL of the Williamsburg Lodge.

BOTETOURT COUNTY

Botetourt County consists of three hundred sixty square miles and was established in 1769 from Augusta County. It was named after Norborne Berkeley, Baron de Botetourt (1717-1770), who served as Virginia's governor from 1768 till 1770. The county's latest census shows a population of 30,496. The county seat is Fincastle.

Judith Hancock, the wife of explorer William Clark, was born in her family's home, Santillane, located in this county. In 1851, the James River and Kanawha Canal reached the town of Buchanan and made it the region's western terminus for shipping

PROSPECT HILL PLANTATION INN
Virginia Bacon and Corn Chowder

6 ears fresh sweet corn
1 quart half-and-half
1/4 pound smoked bacon, chopped into small pieces
1 small yellow onion, finely chopped
2 ribs celery, finely chopped
2 cups (more or less) chicken broth
Salt and pepper
1/4 cup cornstarch for thickening, optional

- Cut the corn kernels from the cobs into a bowl, and reserve. Break the corn cobs into halves, and simmer in the half-and-half in a saucepan over low heat for approximately 1 hour.
- Sauté the bacon in a skillet over medium heat. Add the onion and celery, stirring constantly. Cook until the onions turn golden, being careful to not burn the bacon. Reduce the heat to low. Stir in the chicken stock, and simmer for 15 minutes. Remove and discard the corn cobs, reserving the half-and-half mixture. Stir the bacon mixture into the half-and-half mixture. Add the corn kernels, and simmer for 1 hour or longer.
- Adjust the seasonings with salt and pepper if necessary. If the soup needs to be thickened, combine the cornstarch, 1 teaspoon at a time, with water in a small bowl, stirring until smooth. Stir into the soup. Simmer for 30 minutes or until of the desired consistency.
- Makes 8 servings

Since this is a cream soup, never let the mixture come to a full boil or it will spill over or curdle. Remember that almost all soups taste even better if set aside (refrigerated for 5 to 6 days) and reheated slowly before serving.

BILL and MIREILLE SHEEHAN and their family, innkeepers since 1977 who live in Trevilians, Virginia, near Charlottesville, generously shared the recipe.

Prospect Hill, an authentic 18th century plantation just 15 miles east of Charlottesville, Virginia, offers twelve unique lodging rooms and suites in the 1732 manor house, as well as in the renovated original outbuildings such as the 1720 Overseer's Cottage, the 1796 Uncle Guy's Cottage, the 1699 Boy's Cabin, the 1850 Carriage House, the 1720 Summer Kitchen, and the 1874 Sanco Pansy's Cottage.

Nearby are the University of Virginia and the presidential homes of Thomas Jefferson, James Madison, and James Monroe. Civil War battlefields, wineries, Skyline Drive, and antique shopping are only minutes away.

ROWENA'S KITCHEN TIPS

If you have a tough piece of meat, rub it with baking soda or soak it in lemon or lime juice and let stand for several hours. This helps tenderize it. Just rinse it before cooking.

SYMBOLS, EMBLEMS, AND NICKNAMES

- The Virginia State Flower is the American dogwood (*Cornus florida*).

- The State Tree is also the American dogwood.

- The State Song is "Carry Me Back to Old Virginia," written in 1875 by James A. Bland, an African-American songwriter who originally called his song "Carry Me Back to Old Virginny."

- The State Bird is the Northern Cardinal (*Cardinalis cardinalis*).

- The State Dog is the American Foxhound, introduced into Virginia by George Washington and the breed from which all foxhounds in America are descended.

- The State Shell is the Oyster (*Crassostraea virginica*).

- The State Beverage is Milk.

- The State Boat is the Chesapeake Bay Deadrise, commonly used for oystering, fishing, and crabbing.

- The State Insect is the Tiger Swallowtail Butterfly (*Papilio glaucus linne*).

- The State Folk Dance is the Square Dance.

- The State Fish is the Brook Trout (*Salvelinus fontinalis*).

- The State Fossil is the *Chesapecten jeffersonius*, a bivalve mollusk that was the earliest fossil described from North America (1687).

- Some nicknames for Virginia are:
  The Old Dominion
  Mother of Presidents
  Mother of States
  The Cavalier State

- The State Motto is *Sic semper tyrannis* ("Thus always to tyrants").

Annie's Stew

1 (2- to 3-pound) whole chicken	1/2 cup sliced carrots
5 cups water	2 onions, chopped
1 or 2 (46-ounce) cans vegetable juice cocktail, such as V-8	1 (15^1/4-ounce) can corn, such as shoe peg corn
	1 (15^1/4-ounce) can lima beans
2 cups cubed potatoes	Sugar and black pepper

- Combine the chicken with the water in a large stock pot. Simmer for about 1 hour or until almost tender. Add the vegetable juice cocktail. Stir in the potatoes, carrots, onions, corn, and lima beans. Bring to a boil, and reduce the heat. Simmer for about 40 minutes or until the potatoes are tender. Remove the chicken from the mixture. Cut the meat from the chicken into large pieces when cool enough to handle, discarding the skin and bones. Return the meat to the stock pot. Season to taste with sugar and pepper.
- Note: Maintain a thin consistency if serving as a soup. For a hearty dish, simmer until thickened. Serve with biscuits or cornbread.
- Makes many servings

Annie's Stew, like all Virginia women, improves with age.

This recipe was taught by a Virginia mother to her daughter, GERRY HEMPEL DAVIS, who for seven years was a contributing correspondent on the Today Show, creating and presenting "on air" timely topics. She is the author of *Curves on the Highway: A Self Help Guide For Female Automobile Travelers*, *The Moving Experience: The First Upbeat Book On Moving*, and *The Today Show: An Anecdotal History*. Gerry resides in Virginia, and is currently working on books about grand and historic hotels.

Chicken Fiesta Soup

12 chicken tenders, about 1^1/2 pounds, cooked, chopped	2 (15-ounce) cans kidney beans, drained
4 (14^1/2-ounce) cans chicken broth	2 cups fresh or canned corn
	1 cup quick-cooking rice
2 cups salsa	Plain tortilla chips

- Combine the chicken, broth, salsa, beans, and corn in a large saucepan, and mix well. Bring to a boil. Reduce the heat, and simmer, uncovered, for 5 to 10 minutes. Stir in the rice, and remove from the heat. Let stand, covered, for 5 minutes. Serve with tortilla chips.
- Makes 6 to 8 servings

This soup recipe is shared by JULIA JENKINS LLOYD of Madison, a member of the Montpelier Chapter of the Virginia DAR.

WARRIQUE PLANTATION
Brunswick Stew

1 (6-pound) whole chicken
  or 2 (3-pound) broiler-
  fryers, cut into large pieces
2 to 3 quarts water
4 cups chopped fresh
  tomatoes, or 2 (16-ounce)
  cans chopped tomatoes
2 large onions, sliced

3 medium potatoes,
  chopped
2 cups small butter beans
4 cups fresh corn kernels, or
  2 (16-ounce) cans corn
1 tablespoon salt
1 teaspoon pepper
1 tablespoon sugar

- Combine the chicken with 3 quarts water for a thin stew or 2 quarts water for a thick stew in a large stock pot. Cook for about 2 hours or until the chicken is tender.
- Remove the chicken from the stock pot, reserving the broth. Cut the meat from the chicken into small pieces when cool enough to handle, discarding the skin and bones. Set the chicken aside.
- Add the tomatoes and onions to the broth, and simmer, uncovered, until the onions are tender. Stir in the potatoes and butter beans. Cook until the vegetables are tender. Add the chicken, corn, salt, pepper, and sugar during the last 15 minutes of cooking time. Adjust the amount of water accordingly if using canned vegetables with liquid.
- Makes 12 to 16 servings

In the early days, rabbit was the meat used in Brunswick Stew, but today everyone uses chicken. It is as delicious reheated as it is when first served.

Our wonderful family of six grown children enjoys Warrique Plantation as our weekend retreat. It is one of the six plantations located on the Blackwater River in Southampton County and was built from 1793 to the early 1800s by William Urquhart. He is believed to have come to Virginia from Scotland before 1750. When we entertain outside at a large gathering, we usually have an oyster roast with all the trimmings. When we have smaller groups of guests, I serve an old Virginia dinner, which consists of Brunswick stew, peach salad, ham biscuits, and dessert. That is why I would like to share my Brunswick stew recipe with you. It really came to me from Brunswick County, Virginia, which lays claim to the original Brunswick Stew.

From the recipes of JEAN R. HILLEGASS, a member of the Reverend Robert Hunt Chapter of the National Society Daughters of the American Colonists and the Great Bridge Chapter of the Virginia DAR.

EDGAR ALLAN POE

Although he was born in Boston and died in Baltimore, the great American writer, Edgar Allan Poe, has a strong connection with Virginia generally and with Richmond specifically. Born in 1809, Poe was orphaned two years later when his father and mother, both actors, died. He was befriended by a Richmond tobacco merchant named John Allan, and although he was never legally adopted by the Allan family, he took their name as part of his own. When he was six, Poe went to England and was provided with a good education for five years. Returning to Richmond, he completed his schooling there and later attended the University of Virginia.

When his foster father refused to send more money to Poe at the end of his first year at the University, the young man quit school, left home, and moved back to Boston where he soon published his first work, *Tamerlane and Other Poems*. The book was a flop; Poe joined the army for two years, then attended the U. S. Military Academy for six months before getting expelled for disobedience.

Poe eventually retuned to Richmond, where he edited a magazine, *The Southern Literary Messenger*. For the first time, he looked success in the eye, and during his tenure at the magazine, its circulation expanded seven-fold, primarily because of his own literary contributions.

When the Allans died, they failed to mention Poe in their will, so he remained poor, a condition that seemed to plague him for his entire short life. He married his fourteen-year-old cousin in 1836, and moved on to New York, then Philadelphia, publishing anything he could. A couple of high points in his career occurred with the publication of his story, "The Gold Bug," and with the release of his long poem, "The Raven." When his wife died in 1847, both his physical and mental health rapidly deteriorated. In 1849, he was found unconscious in Baltimore and died shortly thereafter on October 7. Today, the noted poet and writer is recognized as the progenitor of the modern-day detective novel.

Chicken Muddle

7 (4- to 5-pound) hens	10 to 15 pounds potatoes,
Shortening, such as Crisco,	cut into small pieces
for greasing	10 quarts butter beans
16 quarts tomatoes, cut up	7 quarts corn
4 pounds smoked side-meat	1 cup sugar
or bacon	Salt
3 (2-pound) bags carrots,	Black pepper
cut into small pieces	Red pepper
10 pounds onions, cut into	
small pieces	

- Combine the hens with enough water to cover in a large soup pot. Cook for approximately $1^1/2$ hours or until the hens are tender. Remove the hens from the soup pot, reserving the broth. Cut the meat from the hens when cool enough to handle, discarding the skin and bones.
- Grease a clean, large black pot with Crisco or shortening. Place the meat, reserved broth and tomatoes in the prepared soup pot. Fry the side-meat in a large skillet until crisp. Add the side-meat and drippings to the meat mixture, and mix well. Stir in the carrots and onions. Cook for 30 to 40 minutes.
- Add the potatoes, butter beans, and corn, and mix well. Simmer until the vegetables are tender. Add the sugar, salt, and pepper, and simmer until thickened.
- Stir! Stir! Stir! Cooking time is 6 to 8 hours.
- Makes 100 servings or 12 to 18 gallons

Chicken Muddle is a favorite in Emporia and Greensville County and is usually cooked by a group of men in a big, black, outdoor pot. It is sold as a fundraiser for church and civic groups. Few families are without several quarts in their freezer.

This recipe is compiled by LOU TULLOH from many recipes and several interviews. Lou is from Emporia and a member of the Hicksford Chapter of the Virginia DAR.

INN *at* OLD VIRGINIA

Quail and Apple Bisque

6 quail, partially boned
Salt and pepper
3 tablespoons olive oil
3 Granny Smith apples,
 peeled, cored, chopped,
 peelings reserved
2 tablespoons butter
3 medium carrots, peeled,
 chopped
3 ribs celery, chopped
2 green onions, chopped
2 cloves garlic, minced

^{1}/4 cup Chateau Monet
 plum or apricot liqueur
^{1}/2 cup tomato paste
1 quart chicken stock, heated
Bouquet garni of 1 sprig
 each of thyme, parsley,
 and basil or 1 bay leaf,
 and 6 peppercorns
Juice of 1 lemon and 1 lime
^{1}/2 cup heavy cream
3 tablespoons chopped fresh
 parsley

- Preheat the oven to 400°F. Season the quail with salt and pepper to taste. Heat the olive oil in a soup pan or braising pan over medium heat, and add the quail. Sauté until golden brown on both sides. Add the apple peelings, and cover. Place the soup pan in the oven for about 10 minutes.
- Remove the soup pan from the oven. Place the quail on a platter, discarding the apple peelings. Add the butter to the pan. Add the carrots, celery, onions, and garlic. Sauté until the onions are soft. Deglaze the pan with the plum liqueur, and add the tomato paste, apples, chicken stock, and bouquet garni. Simmer for about 45 minutes or until the vegetables are tender. Process the mixture in batches until puréed. Return the puréed mixture to the soup pan.
- Remove the meat from the quail, preserving the legs for garnish. Chop the quail meat, and add to the bisque. Squeeze the lemon and lime juice into the bisque, and add the cream gradually, stirring constantly. Ladle into soup bowls. Garnish each serving by crossing two legs of the quail on the side of the bowl, and sprinkle parsley around the edge.
- Makes 6 servings

This beautiful recipe from the Inn at Old Virginia is shared by Chef TRACY HINER at the bequest of Carolyn D. Bell, Regent of the Bell Manor Chapter of the Virginia DAR. Carolyn is proud to showcase the inn as representative of her city's best as the Queen City of Shenandoah.

The Inn at Old Virginia is located on twelve and one-half acres in historic Staunton, Virginia. Portions of the main house were constructed in the Civil War era on property owned by the Harmon family. Michael G. Harmon served as the Quartermaster of Staunton during the era. The main house has been renovated to include eleven rooms. The main dining area consists of an English glass conservatory that opens onto two brick patios to accommodate dinner seating during the many comfortable evenings in the Shenandoah. The rooms are uniquely decorated and bear the names of various Harmon family members and Civil War compatriots such as Stonewall Jackson and Jed Hotchkiss.

ASH LAWN-HIGHLAND

President James Monroe and his wife, Elizabeth Kortright Monroe, lived in an age when most people relied on their own land and farming skills to provide for their tables. The Monroes' Highland Plantation, in the Albemarle County foothills of Central Virginia, provided every staple of food from its thirty-five hundred acres for the Monroe family and for the thirty to forty slaves who lived and worked there. The fields yielded wheat and corn that was ground into flour at their own mill. Many orchards and vineyards provided their own fruits. Poultry, hogs, cattle, and sheep were plentiful on the property. Vegetables and herbs came from the garden. Rivers were close and brimmed with fish. Merchants in Virginia readily offered coffee, tea, sugar, and other "exotic" groceries. The Monroes were well prepared to dine and entertain.

James Monroe had purchased Highland in 1793 because of his friendship with Thomas Jefferson. As a neighbor, Jefferson sent gardeners from Monticello to start Monroe's orchards. The first guests at Highland were James and Dolley Madison. The Monroes had lived in Fredericksburg during the earlier years of their marriage. For forty-five years, they moved to wherever his public career required. When he was the U.S. Ambassador to France, they found themselves in the grand French society. But warned of food shortages in Revolutionary Paris, the Monroes took a supply of Virginia hams to France in 1794. Later, Monroe's two terms in the White House resulted in much entertaining.

A guest in their 1815 Washington townhouse noted:

The table wider than we have, and in the middle a larger, perhaps silver, waiter, with images . . . and vases filled with flowers, which made a very showy appearance as the candles were lighted when we went to the table. The dishes were silver and set round this waiter, the plates were handsome china, the forks silver, and so heavy I could hardly lift them to my mouth, dessert knives silver, and spoons very heavy.

The "waiter" was a mirrored center-piece decorated with silver, gilded candelabra, statues, and baskets for fruit or flowers. During their stay in Washington, the Monroes ordered another gilt "waiter," that still exists in the White House today.

The Monroes had planned to retire to Highland, but finances and poor health would not permit it. Today Ash Lawn - Highland is a five hundred thirty-five acre estate with the atmosphere of a working plantation. In 1974, Jay Winston Johns bequeathed the property to Monroe's alma mater, the College of William and Mary, "for the education of the general public."

Bedroom at Ashlawn (at right)

Brunswick Stew

- This stew is famed for its excellence throughout the State, and takes its name from the county where it originated and is found in perfection. Squirrel forms its basis, and hence it is especially the huntsman's dish, and seen most often during the early fall, when the squirrels throng and fatten in the corn-fields, and vegetables are still plentiful.
- For eight or ten persons allow four squirrels, skinned and well cleaned, cut them up into six pieces each, and as early in the morning as possible put them on the fire in a covered stewpan, with a seasoning of salt and pepper, both red and black, and an onion chopped up fine.
- After the meat has cooked for several hours withdraw it from the fire, and extract as many of the bones as it is practicable to do, then return it to the fire, adding some of every vegetable that you can get, except rice—there must be none of that. Especially see that there is a pint of green corn, cut from the cob, a quart of tomatoes, half a pint of Lima beans, a pint of Irish potatoes, one cucumber, one cymling [pattypan squash], one carrot, and a half a pint of okra. Cut them all up into small pieces, cover your stewpan up closely, and adding a good table-spoonful of butter, let the stew cook gently, without burning until dinner is to be dished, when it should have cooked until the ingredients of which it is made cannot be distinguished the one from the other. When done the gravy should be nearly absorbed. Serve in a regular plated stew-dish that is kept heated by an alcohol lamp, but if you have not this convenience, arrange the stew in the centre of a meat-dish and garnish with rings of carrot and springs of any green herb you fancy.
- A Brunswick stew may also be concocted in a similar fashion from a cold joint of mutton, beef, or veal, and is a popular dish whenever introduced. It has been served at gentlemen's dinner-parties instead of soup.

This recipe is still good with 2 chicks used for the squirrel, and a little Tabasco and Worcestershire sauce for seasoning. This "receipt" comes from the book of my great grandmother, Mary Stuart Smith, Virginia Cookery Book, copyright 1884. Mrs. Smith was a member of the Daughters of the American Revolution.

Submitted by MARY STUART COCKE STANLEY of Nancy Christian Fleming Chapter of the Virginia DAR.

MOUNT VERNON INN
Rabbit Stew

MARINADE
2 cups red wine
2 tablespoons olive oil
$^1/_4$ cup chopped parsley
$^1/_4$ cup chopped shallots

$^1/_2$ cup red wine vinegar
$1^1/_2$ teaspoons fresh thyme or
   $^1/_2$ teaspoon dried thyme
Freshly ground pepper

STEW
1 whole (approximately
   $2^1/_2$-pound) rabbit
2 cups chicken stock
1 cup flour
3 tablespoons olive oil

1 cup red wine
2 large carrots, shaped into
   small ovals
4 red bliss potatoes, shaped
   into small ovals

- To prepare the marinade, combine the wine, olive oil, parsley, shallots, wine vinegar, thyme, and pepper in a bowl, and mix well.
- To prepare the stew, bone the rabbit, and cut into $1^1/_2$-inch pieces. Place in the marinade in a bowl. Marinate, covered, in the refrigerator for 2 hours. Sauté the rabbit bones lightly in a skillet. Place the bones in a saucepan, add the chicken stock and $^1/_2$ cup of the marinade, and boil for 20 minutes. Strain through a sieve, reserving the stock.
- Coat the pieces of rabbit in the flour. Shake off the excess flour. Sauté the rabbit lightly in the olive oil in a skillet for about 5 minutes, turning frequently. Remove the rabbit from the skillet, add the red wine, and reduce the mixture slightly. Add 1 cup of the reserved stock. Return the rabbit to the skillet, and simmer for 20 minutes.
- Steam the carrots and potatoes in a steamer for 5 to 7 minutes or until crisp-tender. Arrange the potatoes and carrots on top of the stew in a serving dish or individual bowls.
- Makes 4 servings

This recipe was provided by ERIC K. SWANSON, general manager, The Mount Vernon Inn, Mount Vernon, Virginia.

BRUNSWICK COUNTY

Brunswick County was organized in 1720, and its lands were taken from Isle of Wight, Prince George, and Surry Counties. It was named for the Duchy of Brunswick-Luneburg, a German holding of King George I. Brunswick County covers five hundred fifty-seven square miles and contains a population of 18,419. The county seat is Lawrenceville.

Ebenezer Academy, Virginia's first Methodist school, was organized in Brunswick County in 1793 by the noted churchman, Bishop Francis Asbury. Governor Alexander Spotswood built Fort Christanna here in 1714 for protection from the Indians.

SAVING MT. VERNON

An Admiral of the British Navy during the War of 1812 did a favor for all Americans. Though citizens are not delighted that he was the one commanding the Naval Squadron that raided and burned Washington, D.C., he did make a gesture toward former President Washington's memory. That gesture turned into a tradition that led one to an idea: save Mt. Vernon.

Admiral Sir George Cockburn astonished Americans as his flagship, the *Sea Horse*, came down the Potomac River with the smoldering skies of Federal City behind him. When the ship approached the riverbank adjacent to the Mt. Vernon estate, the Admiral viewed the mansion directly. It was absolutely within range of his cannons, but instead he ordered the ship's loud bell to be tolled as she passed by.

Could it have been that the Admiral admired his deceased former foe George Washington so much that he graciously left the home intact? Washington had been laid to rest fifteen years earlier. Both of these men had fought during America's Revolution. This gesture stirred the hearts of many along the Potomac. Proud patriots began to toll their ship's bells when passing Mt. Vernon, regretting only that they did not first institute the tradition.

Forty years later, on a silvery moonlit evening, a steamboat passed by the same spot. The tolling-of-the-bell tradition had lived on. Mrs. Robert Cunningham of

South Carolina was present. Sadly, she saw a mansion with a sagging roof, peeling paint, broken pillars, and lawns in ruin. Congress and the Virginia Legislature had not declared funds to prevent what the Washington descendents had no funds to do. Therefore, the plantation was in disrepair.

The next morning, Mrs. Cunningham wrote a letter to her semi-invalid daughter who had been thrown from a horse a few years earlier at age sixteen, suffering a spinal injury. Her bright mind and spirit needed a cause. The mother saw an opportunity for her daughter to fulfill a mission that would make a difference. She asked her daughter, Ann, whether the women of the South could bind together to "rescue" Mt. Vernon. Ann Pamela Cunningham proceeded to organize and incorporate an association composed of a woman from each state, raise $200,000, and begin historic preservation in America by doing so!

Miss Cunningham from South Carolina enlisted Sarah Tracy from New York, and Edward Everett from Massachusetts, to assist. Due to their efforts and patriotism, the Mount Vernon Ladies' Association of the Union began in 1853, bought Mt. Vernon in 1858, and still holds ownership. In the association's infancy, the Civil War brought many battles and soldiers nearby as the war raged around it. Neither Union nor Confederate troops fired on Mt. Vernon. Today, Americans make pilgrimages to the site to honor the home of the "Father of Our Country."

He-Man Soup

2 (13- to 14-ounce) cans kidney beans	1/2 teaspoon minced garlic
2 (16-ounce) cans stewed tomatoes	1/2 teaspoon thyme
1 quart water	1/2 teaspoon seasoning salt
1 medium onion, chopped	1 pound hot sausage, browned, drained
1/2 teaspoon salt	1/2 cup chopped green pepper
1/2 teaspoon pepper	1 cup chopped potatoes

- Combine the kidney beans, tomatoes, water, onion, salt, pepper, garlic, thyme, and seasoning salt in a large pot, and simmer for 1 hour.
- Add the sausage, green pepper, and potatoes, and cook for approximately 30 minutes or until the potatoes are tender.
- Serve with hot bread for a wonderful cold-day meal. It's even better reheated the next day.
- Makes 8 to 10 servings

I have been a Virginia State Senator (D) for nineteen years. Originally the recipe was given to my wife by her very Republican aunt, Sharon Harless, from West Virginia. Unfortunately, cooking seems to lend itself better to bipartisanship than governing, since this recipe became mine after I adopted it for my annual Christmas party.

This recipe was shared by Virginia State Senator EDD HOUCK, born and raised in Virginia and now the Director of Student Services, Fredericksburg City Public Schools. Edd and his wife, Dana, have two grown children and live in Spotsylvania, Virginia.

BUCHANAN COUNTY

Buchanan County, named after President James Buchanan, was established in 1858 out of territory belonging to Russell and Tazewell Counties. It covers five hundred fourteen square miles, and its most recent population was 26,978. The county seat is Grundy.

The town of Grundy was named after Tennessee statesman, Felix Grundy (1777-1840), who was born in Berkeley County, Virginia, and who served as President Martin Van Buren's attorney general. Grundy was incorporated in 1876.

DID YOU KNOW THAT:

In 1860, on the eve of the War Between the States, Virginia had larger white, free Negro, and slave populations than any other Southern state?

THE SEA GULL PIER
Clam Chowder

2 pounds bacon, cut up
2 cups chopped onions
4 quarts chopped clams
5 (No. 10, 106-ounce) cans
   chopped potatoes
2 cups clam juice

$^1/_2$ cup chicken base
8 cups all-purpose flour
3 quarts water
6 bay leaves
3 tablespoons black pepper
Half-and-half

- Sauté the bacon and onions in a large skillet until golden brown. Transfer sautéed bacon and onions into a large stock pot. Add the clams, potatoes, clam juice, and chicken base, and mix well. Bring to a boil.
- Add a mixture of the flour and water. Cook until thickened, stirring constantly. Season with the bay leaves and black pepper, and serve with half-and-half to taste.
- Makes 100 servings

The recipe was submitted by THE SEA GULL PIER RESTAURANT, located on the award-winning Chesapeake Bay Bridge Tunnel and offering some of the Chesapeake Bay's finest seafood.

Fisherman's Chowder

$^1/_2$ pound (150-count)
   shrimp, peeled
1 (12-ounce) can
   mushrooms
2 (10$^3/_4$-ounce) cans cream
   of potato soup
1 (10$^3/_4$-ounce) can cream
   of celery soup

1 tablespoon garlic powder
$^1/_4$ pound lump or back-fin
   crabmeat
1 ($^1/_4$-ounce) bottle of hot
   sauce, such as Texas Pete's
1 pint half-and-half

- Steam or boil the shrimp in a saucepan, and let stand until cool. Combine the mushrooms, potato soup, celery soup, garlic powder, crabmeat, hot sauce, and half-and-half in a saucepan, and mix well. Add the shrimp. Heat to 140°F.. Serve and enjoy!
- Makes $^1/_2$ gallon

WILLIAM R. MILLER, III, president, Duck-In Restaurant, Virginia Beach, Virginia, generously contributed this recipe.

MEET YA AT THE SAND DUNE FOR LUNCH!

How many states have wild ponies running along an island shore munching American beach grass? The salty marsh grass is tasty, too...especially when you find fresh water from the loblolly pine forest to wash it down. Yes, this is the daily scene on Virginia's Assateague Island, home to the world-famous wild island ponies. If you plan to dine here as well, bring a picnic lunch . . . there's no commercialism on this beautiful National Seashore.

Virginians have been fascinated with the island and its ponies for centuries. *Assateague* is an American Indian word meaning "the marshy place across." Legends say horses have inhabited this barrier island off Virginia's Eastern Shore since the 1500's when a Spanish shipwreck occurred offshore. Sharing a border with Maryland, Assateague is today home to many animals, including great blue herons, horseshoe crabs, red foxes, turtles, sandpipers, egrets, butterflies, and even to snow geese in winter!

The "ponies" are actually hardy little horses that have weathered the island temperature extremes as they eat natural grasses found on the island. Well known to young Virginians (and to readers all over the world) is author Marguerite Henry's book *Misty of Chincoteague*. This delightful story explains much about life for the ponies, as they are associated with both islands. The Volunteer Fire Department on neighboring Chincoteague island actually owns the ponies. Thousands of visitors make the trek to witness the annual July "Pony Penning" when some of the herd is auctioned to raise department funds and to keep the number of ponies to a safe limit with regard to Assateague's survival. The firefighters actually round up the ponies on horseback and drive them into the small bay to Chincoteague for the sale. Thus, many folks call them *Chincoteague ponies*. Another year of island life begins again for those not auctioned as they are allowed to swim home.

Beautiful Assateague beach beckons from sunrise to sunset. The Assateague Lighthouse stands proudly for visitors to see as well. Its red and white stripes are a Virginia icon—now even represented on a state auto tag option. This true natural area is a very special place in America.

Golden Horseshoe Golf Club

Green Grill Chesapeake Crab, Corn, and Potato Chowder

13 ears whole corn, rinsed
3 quarts water
7 sprigs of fresh thyme, rinsed
7 Chesapeake bay leaves
3 cups apple wood-smoked bacon, sliced into lardons
3 cups chopped peeled onion
3 cups leeks, rinsed, sliced
3 cups sliced celery
3 cups sliced peeled carrot
1 1/2 quarts new potatoes, chopped
1/2 tablespoon cumin seeds, toasted, ground
3/4 teaspoon cayenne
1/2 tablespoon coriander seeds, toasted, ground
1 teaspoon black peppercorns, toasted, ground

1 teaspoon kosher salt
1 1/2 quarts Williamsburg Winery Governor's White Wine
1 1/2 quarts clam broth
3 red bell peppers, roasted, chopped
1 tablespoon chipotle chile canned in adobo sauce, seeded, minced
2/3 cup unsalted butter
1 1/3 cups all-purpose flour
1 1/2 quarts heavy cream
4 pounds blue jumbo crab, shell bits removed
Salt and pepper
1 1/3 cups finely chopped fresh parsley
1 1/3 cups finely chopped fresh cilantro

- Cut the corn kernels off the cobs, and set aside. Cut the corn cobs across. Combine the cobs with the water in a large soup pot. Remove the thyme leaves from the sprigs, and set aside. Place the thyme sprigs and bay leaves in the soup pot.
- Sauté the bacon lardons in a separate soup pot until crisp. Add the mire poix of onions, leeks, celery, carrots, and thyme leaves. Sauté for about 6 minutes or until the onions are tender; do not brown. Add the corn kernels, potatoes, corn cob stock, cumin seeds, cayenne, coriander seeds, peppercorns, kosher salt, wine, clam broth, bell peppers, and chipotle chile, and mix well.
- Melt the butter in a separate small pot, and stir in the flour to make a cooked-out roux. Whisk the roux into the chowder pot. Simmer for about 20 minutes or until the potatoes are tender. Remove the cobs. Add the cream and crabmeat. Season to taste with salt and pepper, and simmer for 2 minutes longer. Ladle into soup plates with chunks of ingredients sticking out of the broth. Sprinkle with the fresh herbs.
- Makes 72 servings

Green Grill Resort's Sous Chef, WILLIAM R. BERNIN, contributed this recipe.

Salads and Splashes

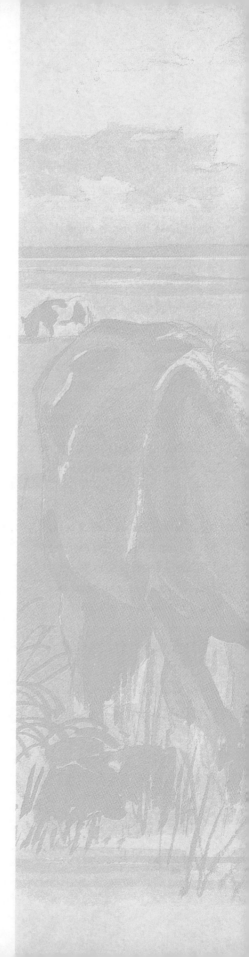

Aunt Kay's Salad

²/₃ cup sugar
1 (20-ounce) can
  crushed pineapple
  with juice
1 (3-ounce) package lemon
  gelatin

1 (8-ounce) package cream
  cheese, softened
1 cup chopped celery
1 cup chopped apples
1 cup chopped nuts
1 cup whipped topping

- Combine the sugar, pineapple, and pineapple juice in a saucepan. Bring to a boil over high heat. Boil for 3 minutes, stirring constantly. Add the gelatin, stirring until dissolved. Remove from the heat.
- Add the cream cheese, and mix well. Let stand until cool. Add the celery, apples, nuts, and whipped topping, and mix well. Spoon into a serving dish. Chill in the refrigerator until set.
- Makes 4 to 6 servings

This is a family favorite that is always a hit. It came from my Aunt Kay and is used by my mom, my wife, and daughters.

Virginia State Senator HARRY BLEVINS of the 14th Senatorial District, Chesapeake, Virginia, shared this recipe. Senator Blevins received his Masters degree from the University of Virginia and is a retired educator. He was a member of the House of Delegates from 1998 to 2001 and was elected to the Senate in 2001.

My Mother-in-Law's Fruit Salad

1 (10³/₄-ounce) can chunk
  pineapple
2 apples, chopped
2 bananas, sliced
Other fruit of choice

1 egg
1 cup sugar
1 tablespoon all-purpose
  flour
Juice of 1 lemon

- Drain the pineapple chunks, reserving the juice. Combine the pineapple chunks, apples, bananas, and any other fruit you desire in a large bowl, and mix well. Beat the egg and sugar in a medium bowl until light. Add the flour, and mix well. Heat the pineapple juice in a small saucepan. Add the egg mixture to the pineapple juice, and cook until thickened, stirring constantly. Squeeze in the lemon juice, and mix well. Pour the sauce over the fruit while hot. Toss to coat, and serve.
- Makes 4 to 6 servings

The recipe was submitted by MINA ANTLEY, who was born in 1913 and is one of the older members of the Louisa Court House Chapter of Virginia DAR.

Orange Salad

1 (20-ounce) can crushed
  pineapple
2 (3-ounce) packages
  orange gelatin

2 cups buttermilk
1 (8-ounce) container
  whipped topping, such as
  Cool Whip

- Bring the undrained pineapple to a boil in a saucepan over
  high heat. Add the gelatin, stirring until dissolved. Remove
  from the heat and cool slightly. Add the buttermilk and
  half the whipped topping, and mix well. Pour into a
  serving bowl. Chill until set. Spread the remaining
  whipped topping over the chilled salad.
- Makes 4 to 6 servings

So refreshing.

MILDRED S. GUSLER of Martinsville, a member of the
Patrick Henry Chapter of the Virginia DAR, sent this recipe.

WINETTE'S
Virginia Salad

1 (20-ounce) can pineapple
  slices in natural juice
1 (14.5-ounce) can peach
  halves, packed in syrup
1 head iceberg lettuce,
  rinsed, torn into pieces

1 cup mayonnaise, such as
  Duke's
2 cups shredded sharp
  cheddar cheese
Maraschino cherries,
  optional

- Drain the pineapple slices and peach halves, reserving
  the juice. Place a generous amount of lettuce on each of
  8 serving plates. Top each serving with 1 pineapple ring
  and 1 peach half, dome side up.
- Combine half the reserved juice and mayonnaise in a
  small mixing bowl. Whisk until the consistency of salad
  dressing, adding some of the reserved juice if necessary.
  Spoon approximately 4 tablespoons of the dressing over
  each serving. Sprinkle each serving with the desired amount
  of cheddar cheese. Top each with a cherry, if desired.
- Note: To save time, one bag of prepared shredded lettuce
  may be substituted for the head of lettuce.
- Makes 8 to 10 servings

*Several tearooms in Virginia have a variation of this recipe. The taste
changes with different brands of mayonnaise. Enjoy! —Winette*

ROWENA'S KITCHEN TIPS

Add 1 teaspoon of baking soda to your water
when cooking cauliflower to reduce cooking odor and
keep your cauliflower white.

BATTLE OF CHANCELLORSVILLE

May 1-5, 1863

Did you know that an army in the field
lives on its stomach? The soldier's lot in
the Civil War was hard tack, salted
meats, some corn and pork, grain, and
an occasional root vegetable—not very
appetizing, and nourishing only when
one could get enough of it. Can you
imagine where the food for an army
comes from? Once there's nothing
left to forage in the immediate area,
the "pickin's" become slim, with every
bit of food having to be brought
in and shipped overland. This was a
problem in the winter of 1862 and
the following spring as 130,000
Union Troops faced the 60,000-man
Confederate Army of Northern Virginia
across the Rappahannock River around
Fredericksburg. They had faced each
other since the Battle of Marye's
Heights at Fredericksburg Dec. 13,
1862, when Union forces had been
slaughtered trying in vain to penetrate

the southern defenses. The armies then settled back in defensive positions on either side of the river while the North looked for the energy to begin again.

In late April, Union forces crossed the river miles upstream and in a pincer movement moved down on General Robert E. Lee's Army while a flying army of 10,000 cavalry headed toward Richmond. This campaign, starting at Fredericksburg and the "Wilderness" more than twelve miles west, became known as the Battle of Chancellorsville and is often described as General Lee's greatest victory. His brilliant display of leadership gained victory over a force more than double its size, and again the Federals failed to destroy the Army of Northern Virginia or to capture Richmond.

BLACKBEARD'S
Salmagundi

1 head romaine, torn into bite-size pieces
1/2 head cabbage, shredded
1 (14-ounce) can hearts of palm, drained, coarsely chopped
1 pound grilled highly seasoned or marinated steak, cut into bite-size chunks
1 pound barbecued chicken or turkey, cut into bite-size chunks
16 ounces banana pepper rings, drained, sliced into halves
2 bunches scallions, cut into halves, sliced lengthwise
1 (4-ounce) bottle of capers, drained
2 ounces flat anchovies, drained, separated, cut into halves
12 ounces kalamata olives
4 ounces olive oil
Sea salt and coarsely ground pepper
6 to 8 hard-cooked eggs, thinly sliced

• Combine the romaine and cabbage in a bowl, and mix well. Arrange a bed of the mixture in a large salad bowl. Layer the hearts of palm, steak, chicken or turkey, pepper rings, scallions, capers, anchovies, and olives over the lettuce mixture. Drizzle with the olive oil. Season with the salt and pepper to taste, and toss well. Arrange the sliced eggs over the top, and serve with crusty bread.
• English ale or grög accompanies this meal well.
• Makes enough for 4 to 6 pirates

This recipe was provided by JOHN GLASS, a member of Blackbeard's Crew Reenactors, Hampton, Virginia.

BUCKINGHAM COUNTY

Buckingham County was established in 1761 from land belonging to Albemarle County. Its name derives from Buckinghamshire, England. The county covers five hundred eighty-four square miles and has a population of 15,623. The county seat is Buckingham.

Buckingham County is the site of Virginia's first college for women, the Female Collegiate Institute, established in 1837. The "father" of African-American history, Carter G. Woodson, was born in this county in 1875. He was the founder of the Association for the Study of Negro Life and History in 1915, and he launched the *Journal of Negro History* the following year.

ROWENA'S KITCHEN TIPS

Add fluff to your omelettes, pancakes, waffles, and mashed potatoes by adding a pinch of baking soda or soda water.

Craisin Salad

1 head red leaf lettuce, rinsed, torn into bite-size pieces
1 head green leaf lettuce, rinsed, torn into bite-size pieces
1 head iceberg lettuce, rinsed, torn into bite-size pieces
1 cup shredded mozzarella cheese
1 (6-ounce) package shredded Parmesan cheese
1 cup craisins (dried cranberries)
1 pound bacon, cooked, crumbled
1/2 cup sliced almonds
6 chicken breast halves, cooked, sliced
1/2 cup chopped sweet onion
1 cup sugar
2 teaspoons dry mustard
1/2 cup red wine vinegar
1 cup canola oil

- Combine the red leaf lettuce, green leaf lettuce, and iceberg lettuce in a large bowl, and mix well. Add the mozzarella cheese, Parmesan cheese, craisins, bacon, almonds, and chicken.
- Process the onion, sugar, dry mustard, and red wine vinegar in a blender until smooth, adding the canola oil gradually. Pour over the salad and toss to coat, or serve the dressing on the side.
- Makes 18 servings

This salad is especially good when the chicken and bacon are warm. Warm the chicken and bacon separately, and spoon the over the top of the greens.

JOYCE KIPPS, a member of the Montpelier Chapter of the Virginia DAR in Madison, Virginia, sent this recipe.

Carrot Jam Chicken Salad

1/2 cup Carrot Jam
1/2 cup mayonnaise
1/4 cup vinegar
2 tablespoons lemon juice
2 tablespoons ketchup
2 teaspoons soy sauce
1 1/2 cups cooked rice
2 cups chopped cooked chicken
1/2 cup chopped celery
1/4 cup chopped green onions
1/2 cup toasted almonds

- Combine the carrot jam, mayonnaise, vinegar, lemon juice, ketchup, and soy sauce in a medium bowl, and mix well. Combine the rice, chicken, celery, green onions, and almonds in a large bowl. Add the carrot jam mixture, and toss to combine. Chill, covered, in the refrigerator.
- Makes 6 to 8 servings

ROWENA'S, INC.

Three backyard fruit trees sparked what is today a thriving gourmet food business for Rowena Fullinwider, founder and president of Rowena's, Inc., in Norfolk, Virginia. It began modestly in Rowena's kitchen with gourmet holiday gifts for friends and neighbors. Soon her cakes, curds, and jams became a favored donation for fund raising at local charities. As word spread about the "Cake Lady," requests for Rowena's specialty foods exceeded the capabilities of her small kitchen.

After extensive planning and the renovation of an old warehouse, Rowena opened her gourmet manufacturing facility in May of 1983 with one full-time employee and a strong determination to succeed. That determination paid off. Since then, this facility has grown to house a beautiful tearoom, a gourmet gift shop, office facilities, and customer service for her mail-order catalog, as well as two spacious kitchens, and two warehouses. Rowena's employs twenty-five full-time employees and more than 100 part-time employees during the holidays.

Today, Rowena's is the creator and producer of wonderful pound cakes, special jams and curds, and sauces. Her products can be found in over 2,000 gourmet and gift shops in the United States. Rowena's has catalogs distributed across the nation for mail order, corporate and wholesale

Virginia's Finest

customers alike. Her products are also available on her website.

Rowena's has been featured in national publications such as *Ladies Home Journal, Gourmet, Bon Appetit, Southern Living*, and *Taste of Home*. Her products have been showcased on *Food Finds*, the *Today Show*, and *QVC*.

Rowena has authored two children's story/cookbooks, *The Adventures of Rowena and the Wonderful Jam and Jelly Factory* and *The Adventures of Rowena and Carrot Jam the Rabbit*, based in part on Rowena's childhood as a fun loving tomboy.

Rowena is always on the go! She and her supportive husband, Peter, tour the country sharing the wonders that she has invented. She is truly an ambassador for Virginia. (Many Virginia Governors think so!) You may wonder what she may come up with next, and then before you know it, you find it in a jar or as a new cake! Whether you tour the factory, sample her Carrot Jam, or read one of her children's books, you will soon realize that Rowena Fullinwider "truly takes the cake."

Rowena and her staff take personal responsibility to ensure that each customer and product receives a large measure of their finest ingredient: tender loving care. Although TLC is not listed on the label, Rowena's customers will tell you, "It's there."

Chicken Salad

6 cups chopped cooked white meat chicken	$^1/_4$ cup whole grain mustard
1 head celery, chopped	$1^1/_2$ cups mayonnaise
1 cup chopped pecans	1 tablespoon thyme
1 large white onion, chopped	1 tablespoon dill
	1 tablespoon garlic salt
$1^1/_2$ cups craisins (dried cranberries)	$^1/_2$ tablespoon white pepper
	$^1/_2$ tablespoon nutmeg
	1 teaspoon sea salt

- Combine the chicken, celery, pecans, onion, craisins, mustard, mayonnaise, thyme, dill, garlic salt, white pepper, nutmeg, and sea salt in a large bowl, and mix well. Serve over lettuce leaves, or spread on croissants as a sandwich.
- Makes 6 to 8 servings

ANITA DRISCOLL, café manager of Anderson's Showplace Cafe, Newport News, Virginia, contributed this recipe. The news from Newport News is that this premier and long-sought-after recipe is destined to become a favorite in your kitchen.

Hot Chicken Salad

7 cups chopped, cooled cooked chicken	$1^1/_2$ cups mayonnaise
3 cups chopped celery	Lemon juice
$1^1/_2$ (2-ounce) jars pimiento	Salt and pepper
2 (4-ounce) cans sliced mushrooms	6 slices Swiss cheese, cut into strips
1 cup slivered almonds	1 cup bread crumbs

- Preheat the oven to 350°F. Combine the chicken, celery, pimiento, mushrooms, almonds, and mayonnaise in a large bowl. Sprinkle with the lemon juice and salt and pepper to taste, and mix well. Spoon the mixture into a 9×13-inch baking dish. Arrange Swiss cheese strips over the top. Sprinkle with the bread crumbs. Bake for 30 minutes or until bubbly.
- Makes 14 to 18 servings

JOUETTE GRAHAM of the Royal Oak Chapter of the Virginia DAR in Smyth County, submitted this recipe.

Virginia Smoked Foods

Smoked Fish Salad

1 cup flaked, smoked white
   fish, such as mahi-mahi
$^1/_2$ cup chopped celery
$^1/_4$ cup mayonnaise
Lemon juice, optional

1 small onion, finely
   chopped, optional
2 tablespoons sour cream or
   cream cheese, or both,
   optional

- Combine the fish, celery, and mayonnaise in a bowl. Add
  the lemon juice, onion, and sour cream or cream cheese to
  taste if desired. Chill, covered, in the refrigerator. Garnish
  with sliced lemons, and serve with unsalted crackers.
- Makes 2 to 3 servings

*I first developed this recipe in the years I worked as a sailboat
captain in the Caribbean, and I would pick up smoked fish in
Florida. When I returned to Virginia Beach, I began to smoke my
own fish and opened a commercial smokehouse.*

**VIRGINIA AGRICULTURE
Virginia's Finest**

This recipe was contributed by KEITH GORE
at Beach Smokehouse, a family business in
operation twenty-two years. It smokes tuna,
mahi, and bluefish that are indigenous to our
waters, and it also smokes salmon. In addition
to fish, Beach Smokehouse also smokes whole turkeys,
turkey breasts, pork barbecue, and sausage. All of the
products are smoked with hickory and are truly delicious.

Pasta Tuna Salad

1 (12-ounce) can white
   tuna, drained, flaked
1 cup mayonnaise
1 cup shredded cheddar
   cheese

$^1/_4$ cup sweet relish
4 cups drained cooked pasta
Lettuce leaves, rinsed
1 tomato, sliced

- Combine the tuna, mayonnaise, cheese, and relish in a
  bowl, and mix well. Add the pasta, and mix well. Serve on
  a plate lined with lettuce leaves and sliced tomato. Serve
  warm or chilled.
- Makes 4 servings

This recipe was submitted by my daughter, ROWENA
POST, of Manassas, Virginia. She is the fourth generation
"Rowena" in our family and is a wonderful wife and stay-at-
home mother of whom I am very proud. —Rowena

ANDERSON'S SHOWPLACE CAFE

*People drive for miles to eat "Showplace
Chicken Salad" at Anderson's Showplace
Cafe. This fabulous home and garden
center houses a cozy tearoom atmosphere— well hidden inside!*

To the traveler passing by, Anderson's
Home and Garden Showplace in Newport
News looks appealing from the road, with
a large, well-landscaped brick building
hosting master greenhouses behind.
Whatever the season, a passerby would
find something appropriate on the exterior
that would be inviting. However, locals on
the Peninsula know that Anderson's is
not only a destination for plants and
décor needs. The Showplace Cafe, tucked
away inside, offers a wonderful menu of
fresh foods.

Newport News Shipyard employs many
people with varied hobbies and talents.
In the 1950's, many woods were
located along the city's Jefferson
Avenue that led many of them to work.
In 1953, Paul Anderson eyed a tract of
1.75 acres for sale beside the street.
Going back and forth to the Shipyard
daily, Paul would see those woods and
began to have a vision. His hobby was
growing plants in greenhouses such as
camellias, tomatoes, geraniums, and
African violets. He already had a pretty
steady side business growing the
plants at home. Paul finally bought the
tract of woods and began building
commercial sized greenhouses there.

Anderson's was accepted in the community so well that Paul quickly established a thriving wholesale business. He quit working at the Shipyard and concentrated on enlarging his enterprise. By 1972, with a steady stream of customers and generations of family shoppers across the Hampton Roads area, Paul sold his business to his son Clark. Clark immediately began to incorporate home décor and Virginia food items that homemakers liked to buy. The facility grew to encompass 6 acres alongside the now busy Jefferson Avenue.

Responding to customers' requests to "make a day of it" while shopping the vast grounds and buildings, the Anderson family opened their Cafe in 1998. The intimate, round marble-topped tables amid the kitchen and foods section of Anderson's beckoned to all. The dining fans began to spread the word about the gourmet lunches offering "fresh catch" Chesapeake Bay seafood and spectacular soups daily. When the Showplace Chicken Salad was introduced with its unique combination of seasonings and cranberries, it had to be made available to go by the pound! Today, customers go to this garden center to eat a fabulous meal and, oh, by the way, take home some African violets or a new holiday banner for their front door!

PARADISE NURSERY

Wild Rice Salad with Fresh Figs

3 cups uncooked wild rice
Water or broth
1 dozen firm, ripe fresh figs, chopped
1 cup chopped pecans
1/2 cup golden raisins, dried currants, or craisins
1 cup fresh or thawed frozen tiny peas

1/3 cup orange juice
1 tablespoon fig balsamic vinegar
1/4 cup light olive oil
2 tablespoons finely grated orange rind
1 teaspoon salt
Pepper

- Cook the wild rice according to package directions with water or broth, and drain well. Combine the wild rice with the figs, pecans, raisins, and peas in a large bowl. Stir the orange juice, balsamic vinegar, olive oil, and orange rind in a small bowl until combined. Drizzle the orange juice mixture over the wild rice. Stir to blend the flavors. Add the salt and pepper to taste, and mix well. Let stand for 2 hours.
- The flavors are best when served at room temperature.
- Makes 8 servings

The sweet flavor of fresh figs adds a gourmet touch to summer dishes. This is a favorite side dish to accompany grilled chicken and perhaps a green salad when we come in from the garden for a late supper on the porch. It is also wonderful for a luncheon.

Virginia's Finest

This rice dish was sent by ROB and SYBIL MAYS of Paradise Nursery, a small family-owned nursery in the farm country south of Virginia Beach. They specialize in growing fig trees and gourmet fruit varieties for the Mid-Atlantic region. The nursery sends fruit plants all over the country to customers who order through their website.

CAMPBELL COUNTY

Campbell County, formed from part of Bedford County in 1781, was named in honor of William Campbell, a hero of the Battle of Kings Mountain fought the previous year. It contains five hundred fifty-seven square miles and is home to 51,078 residents. The county seat is Rustburg.

The noted statesman and orator Patrick Henry (1736-1799) is buried at his last home place, Red Hill, located in this county. The term "lynch law" originated here, its origin dating to 1780, when Colonel Charles Lynch and others conducted vigilante court for local criminals.

RANDOLPH-MACON WOMAN'S COLLEGE
Salad Dressing

1/4 cup garlic juice	1 1/2 teaspoons paprika
3 quarts mayonnaise	3 tablespoons onion juice
1 1/2 quarts ketchup	1/4 cup lemon juice
1/4 cup prepared mustard	1 cup water
1 1/2 quarts chili sauce	3/4 cup Worcestershire sauce
3 tablespoons black pepper	

- Beat the garlic juice, mayonnaise, ketchup, mustard, chili sauce, pepper, paprika, onion juice, lemon juice, water, and Worcestershire in a mixing bowl until well blended. Serve over hearts of lettuce.
- Makes 2 gallons (enough for lots of young ladies)

This great-tasting dressing was received from the Randolph-Macon Women's College through MARY B. WHITE of Alexandria, Virginia. Mary is an alumna of the college and Regent of the John Alexander Chapter of the Virginia DAR. This recipe was printed in *Randolph-Macon Woman's College Recipes*, compiled and edited by Bobbye Mallory Hunter, Randolph-Macon Press.

It all started in the late 1800s, when one man had a novel idea to offer women the opportunity for higher education. The man was William Waugh Smith, then president of Randolph-Macon College (R-MC) in Ashland, Virginia. Getting no support from his trustees, Smith traveled across Virginia in search of a city open to the "radical" notion of a women's college. Lynchburg welcomed him with open arms. On September 14, 1893, Randolph-Macon Woman's College opened for its first session with 36 boarding students and 12 professors. Both Randolph-Macon College and Randolph-Macon Woman's College were named for John Randolph of Roanoke, Virginia, and Senator Nathaniel Macon of Warrenton, North Carolina. Both men were widely respected for their political roles in the early 19th century. R-MWC was founded under the charter of Randolph-Macon College, which was established 61 years before with the encouragement and financial support of the Methodist Church. Although R-MC and R-MWC established separate boards of trustees in 1953, both colleges have maintained their historic ties to the United Methodist Church. R-MWC's most famous alumna, Nobel Prize-winning author of *The Good Earth*, Pearl S. Buck, class of 1914, wrote, "We were very proud of our college. We still exulted when I was there in the knowledge that we were being taught what men were taught...We came out ready to use our heads and accustomed to work. I have always been glad of that." Building on a strong heritage of rigor and academic challenge in a close-knit community, Randolph-Macon Woman's College continues to prepare young women for *Vita Abundantior*, the life more abundant.

RANDOLPH-MACON COLLEGE

This is an interesting excerpt found on page 108 of *Randolph-Macon College: A Southern History 1825-1967* by Professor James Edward Scanton. The passage describes the cuisine served to students on the old Boynton, Virginia, campus during the Civil War, when the college attempted, unsuccessfully, to become a military school.

The food was terrible. For breakfast there was milk or coffee (but not both), starch (loaf bread and biscuit and either batter bread, waffles or muffins), and bacon or hash. 'Dinner' was bacon and greens, and 'one of the following kinds of meat, viz: beef, mutton, shoat, or fowle, with the vegetable of the season.' Supper was the same as breakfast without the meat, that is, mainly starch.

In the 1820s, the clergy of the Virginia Conference of the Methodist Church recognized the need to educate prospective clergymen. In 1830 the Virginia legislature approved a charter for Randolph-Macon College located in Boynton, Virginia, near the border of North Carolina. The names of John Randolph, a Virginia statesman, and Nathaniel Macon, a North Carolina statesman, were given to the college to dispel the notion that the school was to be only a sectarian one. Neither man was Methodist. The college was moved to Ashland, Virginia, in 1868 after the railroads to Boynton were destroyed during the Civil War. The students themselves raised most of the funds for the first major building constructed on the new campus. The 1899-1900 college catalog describes Ashland's location: "on the Richmond, Fredericksburg, Potomac Railroad, 16 miles north of Richmond, upon the most elevated plateau between that city and Fredericksburg, Virginia." The location was "distinguished for healthfulness and accessibility" because "severe pneumonia and violent fevers of the mountains and the malarial diseases of the Tidewater regions are comparatively unknown."

Today Randolph-Macon College is a private, co-educational college of the liberal arts and sciences and enrolls approximately 1,100 students.

THE APPLE HOUSE

Five-Star Broccoli and Yellow Squash Salad

1 (2-pound) package fresh broccoli florets
2 medium fresh yellow squash, sliced
1 small red onion, minced
1 (6-ounce) package golden raisins

4 cups mayonnaise
2 cups Old Virginia Apple Cider Vinegar
1 cup sugar or equivalent amount of sugar substitute
2 tablespoons black or white sesame seeds

- Combine the broccoli, squash, onion, and raisins in a large bowl, and toss. Whisk the mayonnaise, apple cider vinegar, and sugar in a separate bowl until smooth. Add to the broccoli mixture, and toss to mix. Sprinkle with the sesame seeds.
- For an interesting change, add Virginia peanuts or Virginia bacon pieces to this recipe.
- Makes 15 to 20 servings

A sweet salad with a great mix of wonderful Virginia vegetables, Virginia peanuts, Virginia bacon, and Virginia apple cider vinegar, this recipe is quite easy and quite good. It has a tendency to pull a meal together and makes a very nice presentation. It's really suited for any occasion. And, this salad keeps very well. Delicious!

This recipe is from the kitchen of THE APPLE HOUSE, the home of Alpenglow Sparkling Cider. It has been run by three generations of Virginians in the Shenandoah Valley since 1963 and has a gift shop with Virginia products as well as a popular restaurant.

CAROLINE COUNTY

Caroline, wife of King George II, lent her name to this county, formed in 1727 from parts of Essex, King and Queen, and King William Counties. The county covers five hundred twenty-nine square miles and contains 22,121 residents. Its county seat is Bowling Green.

John Lederer, an early explorer of the Blue Ridge Mountains, began his expedition from this county in 1670. Secretariat (1970-1989), the 1973 Triple Crown winner, was foaled and raised on Meadow Farm here, as were other champions, such as Riva Ridge, First Landing, and Hill Prince.

CHRISTY'S
Chinese Salad

DRESSING
1/2 cup red wine vinegar
1/2 cup light salad oil
1/2 cup sugar
2 tablespoons soy sauce

2 seasoning packets from
  oriental noodles, such as
  Ramen

SALAD
6 tablespoons (3/4 stick)
  butter or margarine
2 (3-ounce) packages
  oriental noodles, broken up
3/4 cup slivered almonds

3/4 cup sunflower seeds
1 head napa cabbage
1 bunch spring onions
1 (8-ounce) can sliced water
  chestnuts

- To prepare the dressing, combine the red wine vinegar, oil, sugar, soy sauce, and seasoning packets in a plastic container, and mix well. Chill, covered, in the refrigerator.
- To prepare the salad, preheat the oven to 350°F. Melt the butter or margarine in a small saucepan, and pour on a baking sheet, coating the surface. Arrange the noodles, almonds, and sunflower seeds on the prepared baking sheet, and coat with the melted butter. Toast in the oven until golden. Let stand until cool.
- Chop the cabbage horizontally with a sharp knife, and discard the core. Snip or finely chop the ends of the onions just to the white part of the stems. Combine the cabbage and onions in a large bowl. Add the noodle mixture and water chestnuts, and mix well.
- To serve, drizzle the dressing over the salad just before serving, and enjoy the compliments.
- Makes 8 to 12 servings

This recipe is from the family of CHRISTY JAAP, a great gal.

JEFFERY FAMILY'S
Corn Salad

2 (12-ounce) cans white or
  yellow whole kernel corn,
  drained, or fresh corn
  kernels, cooked
4 green onions, chopped

1 large tomato, chopped
2 tablespoons mayonnaise
1/2 teaspoon salt
1/2 teaspoon ground black
  pepper

- Combine the corn, green onions, and tomato in a bowl. Stir in the mayonnaise, salt, and pepper.
- Makes 8 servings

Great for covered-dish suppers or picnics.

TOM and WINETTE JEFFERY, and their children, Matthew, Brent, Allison, Daniel, and Trey of Poquoson, Virginia, shared this family favorite.

VIRGINIA TIMELINE

1700—Virginia's population approaches fifty-eight thousand people.

1716—Governor Alexander Spotswood and associates explore the vast region lying between the Blue Ridge and Allegheny Mountains.

1732—George Washington, first U.S. president (1789-1797), is born at Wakefield Plantation, located between the Potomac and the Rappahannock Rivers. His wife, Martha Dandridge, is born in New Kent County.

1743—Thomas Jefferson, third U.S. president (1801-1809), is born at Shadwell Plantation, located in present-day Albemarle County.

1751—James Madison, fourth U.S. president (1809-1817), is born at Port Conway in King George County.

1753—Governor Robert Dinwiddie sends Major George Washington to the French garrison, Fort Le Boeuf, located near Lake Erie, to demand the French evacuation of the upper Ohio River Valley.

1754—George Washington, now a lieutenant-colonel, surrenders to the French at Fort Necessity in Pennsylvania in what became the first battle of the French and Indian War.

Norwegian Coleslaw

SAUCE
4 cups sugar   1 cup water
2 cups white vinegar

VEGETABLES
1 tablespoon salt   4 carrots, shredded
2 pounds cabbage, shredded   1 large onion, chopped
2 green peppers, chopped   1 tablespoon celery seeds
1 bunch celery, chopped   1 tablespoon mustard seeds

- To prepare the sauce, combine the sugar, vinegar, and water in a large saucepan, stirring to dissolve the sugar. Bring to a boil over high heat. Boil for 5 minutes, stirring occasionally. Let stand until cool.
- To prepare the vegetables, sprinkle the salt over the cabbage in a large bowl. Let stand for 1 hour. Squeeze out the salt water using hands; do not rinse. Stir in the green peppers, celery, carrots, onion, celery seeds, and mustard seeds.
- To assemble, add the sauce to the vegetables, and mix well, stirring frequently for the first few hours. Store the coleslaw in covered containers in the refrigerator. It will keep indefinitely in the refrigerator.
- Makes 35 to 50 servings

A loving friend gave this to RUTH STEVENS many years ago. Ruth lives in Afton, Virginia, and she is Regent of the Albermarle Chapter of the Virginia DAR.

CARROLL COUNTY

Carroll County was established in 1842 from Grayson County. Its namesake is Charles Carroll, a Virginia signer of the Declaration of Independence. The county covers four hundred fifty-eight square miles and claims 29,245 residents. Its county seat is Hillsville.

Both the Blue Ridge Parkway and the New River intersect Carroll County. The first county court was held at Hillsville in 1842, with Judge A.W.C. Nowlin presiding.

CHARLES CITY COUNTY

Named for King Charles I, Charles City County was one of Virginia Colony's first eight shires. It was established in 1624, and its present-day size is one hundred eighty-eight square miles. Its population is 6,926. The county seat is Charles City.

William Henry Harrison (1773-1841) and John Tyler (1790-1862), ninth and tenth presidents of the United States, were both born in Charles City County. Thomas Jefferson was married to Martha Wayles Skelton here in 1772.

1755—British General Edward Braddock and his army leave Alexandria bound for Fort Duquesne at the forks of the Ohio River (today's Pittsburgh). Braddock is killed in action before his objective is achieved.

1758—James Monroe, fifth president of the United States (1817-1825), is born in Westmoreland County.

1763—The French and Indian War officially ends.

1773—William Henry Harrison, ninth U.S. president (1841), is born at Berkeley Plantation on the James River in Charles City County.

1775—Virginia's last royal governor, John Murray, fourth earl of Dunmore, flees Williamsburg, taking with him the last vestige of British rule in Virginia.

1776—Patrick Henry is elected the State of Virginia's first governor.

1779—Thomas Jefferson succeeds Patrick Henry as governor.

1780—Virginia's government is moved to Richmond, making the town on the James River the third and final capital.

Relish Salad

DRESSING

1 tablespoon water
$^{3}/_{4}$ cup vinegar
$^{1}/_{2}$ cup vegetable oil

$^{2}/_{3}$ cup sugar
$^{3}/_{4}$ teaspoon pepper

VEGETABLES

1 (15$^{1}/_{4}$-ounce) can white
  corn, drained
1 (15$^{1}/_{4}$-ounce) can yellow
  corn, drained
1 (15$^{1}/_{4}$-ounce) can French-
  style green beans, drained
1 (15$^{1}/_{4}$-ounce) can green
  peas, drained

1 (15$^{1}/_{4}$-ounce) can bean
  sprouts, drained
1 cup chopped onion
1 cup chopped green pepper
1 (4-ounce) jar pimiento

- To prepare the dressing, bring the water, vinegar, oil,
  sugar, and pepper to a boil in a saucepan over high heat.
  Boil until the sugar dissolves, stirring constantly. Let the
  mixture stand until cool.
- To prepare the vegetables, combine the white corn, yellow
  corn, green beans, green peas, bean sprouts, onion, green
  pepper and pimiento in a large bowl, and mix well.
- To assemble, drizzle the dressing over the vegetables, and
  toss to coat. Refrigerate, covered, for at least 24 hours
  before serving. This salad will keep several weeks in
  the refrigerator.
- Makes about 12 to 16 servings

CHERIE LINKO, a member of the Arlington House
Chapter of the Virginia DAR, sent this recipe.

CHARLOTTE COUNTY

Charlotte County was named in honor of Charlotte of
Mecklenburg-Strelitz, the wife of King George III. Formed in
1764 from part of Lunenburg County, it contains four hundred
ninety-six square miles and is home to 12,472 residents. Its
county seat is Charlotte Court House.

Thomas Jefferson's former friend and later critic John
Randolph lived at his estate, Roanoke Plantation, in this
county. John Randolph and Patrick Henry debated over
States' Rights here in 1799.

DID YOU KNOW THAT:

Shipbuilders in Newport News built more than four
hundred ships, amounting to nearly three and a half million
tons' burden, during World War II?

INTERESTING ITEMS TO REMEMBER

THE MOST IMPORTANT WORDS

- The six most important words in the
  English language: I admit I made
  a mistake.
- The five most important words: You
  did a good job.
- The four most important words:
  What is your opinion?
- The three most important words: If
  you please.
- The two most important words:
  Thank you.
- The one *most* important word: We.
- The one *least* important word: I.

A BIRTHDAY POEM

Monday's child is fair of face,
Tuesday's child is full of grace,
Wednesday's child is full of woe,
Thursday's child has far to go;
Friday's child is loving and giving,
Saturday's child works hard for
  a living;
But the child that is born on the
  Sabbath-day
Is bonny and blithe and good and gay.

—Brewer's Dictionary of
Phrase and Fable, 2nd revised
edition, London 1981

HOW ARTHUR CARVER "GINGERLY" MADE ALES

During the late 1800's, ginger ale was the most popular "soft drink" of the times in America. Some manufacturers used *capsicum* (a type of hot pepper) to flavor the ale, feigning the more expensive, true ginger root. Real ginger ale has a distinctive flavor and is appreciated by knowledgeable consumers. Arthur E. Carver, Sr. was wisely experimenting with extract of ginger root in the 1920's. Using cane sugar for sweetener, he devised a family "formula."

Today, the water used in manufacturing his label, Carver's Original Ginger Ale, originates in the Blue Ridge Mountains and is drawn from a 650-foot deep artesian well at the Northern Neck Bottling Company plant. Carver's Original is said to be the best in the country by many polls. Another brand that Arthur's company produced is called Northern Neck Ginger Ale. Both are sold today by special order or at retail in favored (and flavored) specialty stores in Virginia.

Spinach Salad with Strawberries and Blue Cheese

STRAWBERRY VINAIGRETTE

1 cup cider vinegar	1 cup fresh strawberries
2 teaspoons Dijon mustard	1 tablespoon salt
1 tablespoon honey	$1/2$ teaspoon white pepper
1 tablespoon chopped shallots	$2^1/2$ cups salad oil

- Combine the cider vinegar, mustard, honey, shallots, strawberries, salt, and white pepper in a food processor, and process until blended. Add the oil gradually with the food processor running. Store in a glass jar with a tight-fitting lid in the refrigerator. This keeps well for several weeks, and the recipe is easy to cut in half.
- Makes 1 quart

SALAD

2 pounds fresh spinach	1 cup crumbled blue cheese
$1^1/2$ cups quartered strawberries	$2^1/2$ cups Strawberry Vinaigrette
2 medium red onions, thinly sliced	

- Rinse the spinach, and tear into pieces into a large bowl. Add the strawberries, onions, and blue cheese. Drizzle the strawberry vinaigrette over the salad, and toss to coat.
- This is a very fresh salad with an unusual touch of using the strawberry vinaigrette.
- Makes 10 servings

The recipe is from the kitchen of GINGER VAN DE WATER, a hostess extraordinaire.

Ginger and Malcolm Van de Water have made Virginia their home for 26 years and find it to be perfect. They have been joined by four other relatives who visited and decided to make The Old Dominion their home; a new family hub has been formed. They live in a hundred-year-old home in Norfolk's historic Freemason district and spend weekends on the Corrotoman River. Ginger earned her doctorate at The College of William and Mary and is a clinical and school psychologist who has worked in public schools, Children's Hospital of the King's Daughters, and private practices focusing on children. Governor Gilmore appointed her to the Virginia Board of Medicine and the Virginia Board of Psychology.

DID YOU KNOW THAT:

Nancy Astor, a native Virginian, was elected the first woman member of the Parliament of Great Britain?

The
MARTHA WASHINGTON INN

Spinach and Potato Salad

2 cups chopped red potatoes	$1/4$ cup chopped country ham
$1/2$ cup mayonnaise	
$1/2$ cup sour cream	$1/2$ cup chopped onion
$1/2$ cup Creole mustard	$1/4$ cup chopped carrots
1 clove garlic, minced	$1/4$ cup chopped celery
1 tablespoon lemon juice	1 cup whole kernel corn
$1/2$ cup chopped fresh herbs	2 cups cleaned spinach
2 tablespoons butter	Salt and pepper

- Bring the potatoes and enough water to cover to a boil in a saucepan over high heat. Boil the potatoes until tender, and let stand to cool.
- Combine the mayonnaise, sour cream, Creole mustard, garlic, lemon juice, and herbs in a large bowl, and mix well. Place the butter and ham in a sauté pan. Add the onions, carrots, and celery, and sauté until the onions are soft. Add the corn, and cook for 1 minute longer. Let stand until cool.
- Add the potatoes to the mayonnaise mixture. Stir in the corn mixture and spinach, and season with salt and pepper to taste.
- Makes 4 to 6 servings

Thanks to THE MARTHA WASHINGTON INN, Abingdon, Virginia, for sharing this recipe.

CHESTERFIELD COUNTY

Chesterfield County, organized in 1749 from part of Henrico County, was named after noted statesman Philip Dormer Stanhope, the fourth earl of Chesterfield. It contains four hundred sixty-eight square miles and has a population of 259,903. The county seat is Chesterfield Court House.

The first iron furnace ever built in America was constructed in this county in 1619, but was soon destroyed by an Indian raid in 1622. Also, Virginia's first railroad—and America's second—originated in this county, beginning in 1831. The train was operated by mule and horse power.

CAPTAIN JOHN SMITH ON STARVATION

The first few years of Jamestown's existence were lean ones indeed. The colony was settled by so-called "gentlemen" from England, most of whom had no practical knowledge, skills, or experience in surviving in the wilderness of North America. Weather conditions during the period of colonization were less than ideal, as well; consequently, the village's inhabitants were forever on the verge of starvation and faced near-extinction on more than one occasion. Captain John Smith, the fourth president of the Jamestown Council, later described the horrible conditions in his book, *The Generall Historie of Virginia, New-England, and the Summer Isles*.

Though there be fish in the Sea, foules in the ayre, and Beasts in the woods, their bounds are so large, they so wilde, and we so weake and ignorant, we cannot much trouble them. . . . as for our Hogs, Hens,

Goats, Sheepe, Horse, or what lived, our commanders, officers and Salvages [Indians] daily consumed them, some small proportions sometimes we tasted, till all was devoured; then swords, armes, pieces, or any thing, wee traded with the Salvages, whose cruell fingers were so oft imbrewed in our blouds, that what by their crueltie, our Governours indiscretion, and the losse of our ships, of five hundred within six moneths . . . there remained not past sixtie men, women and children, most miserable and poore creatures; and those were preserved for the most part, by roots, herbes, acornes, walnuts, berries, now and then a little fish . . . . This was that time, which still to this day we called the starving time: it were too vile to say, and scarce to be beleeved, what we endured.

CONGRESSMAN OWEN PICKETT'S
Summer Garden Tomato Salad

2 tomatoes, chopped
1 cucumber, chopped
1 sweet onion, chopped
1 green pepper, chopped
3/4 cup olive oil
1/3 to 1/2 cup vinegar
3 to 4 cloves fresh garlic, minced

1/4 teaspoon freshly ground basil
1/4 teaspoon freshly ground parsley
1/4 teaspoon freshly ground oregano
Salt and pepper

- Combine the tomatoes, cucumber, onion, and green pepper in a medium bowl. Combine the olive oil, vinegar, garlic, basil, parsley, oregano, salt and pepper to taste in a jar. Shake, tighly covered, until well blended. Pour the dressing over the vegetables, and toss to coat. Refrigerate, covered, for 1 hour or longer, stirring frequently.
- Makes approximately 4 servings

Former Congressman OWEN PICKETT generously provided this recipe. The elder statesman is a much respected and admired Virginia gentleman, who served for fourteen years in the Virginia House of Delegates, followed by fourteen years as the Hampton Roads Representative in the U.S. Congress before retiring to the practice of law in Virginia Beach.

CLARKE COUNTY

Clarke County was named in honor of George Rogers Clark of Revolutionary War fame, the older brother of explorer William Clark. Formed from part of Frederick County in 1836, it contains one hundred seventy-one square miles, and its population is 12,652. The county seat is Berryville.

During the late 1860s and early 1870s, the first wireless signals in history originated in Clarke County, sent into space by kites and copper wires. George Washington's adopted daughter, Nelly Custis, and General Daniel Morgan both lived at one time in this county.

CRAIG COUNTY

Craig County was formed in 1851 from several counties that are now part of West Virginia. Named for Robert Craig, a U.S. congressman, its area is three hundred thirty-three square miles, and its population is 5,091. Its county seat is New Castle.

Craig County sits astride the Great Eastern Divide, where water on the western slopes eventually flow into the Gulf of Mexico, while those on the eastern slopes flow into the Atlantic Ocean. Much of Craig County lies within Jefferson National Forest.

How Michie Came to Have His Tavern

Most Virginians have heard of Michie Tavern, and certainly Virginians of the past frequently made trails to this popular establishment, which has remained part of the Commonwealth's ongoing history. As Virginia grew and transport routes changed, the Michie was moved to the road more traveled—and still remains a highlight.

MICHIE TAVERN
ca. 1784

Michie Tavern, a Virginia Historic Landmark, is one of the oldest homesteads remaining in Virginia. Time and the forces of Mother Nature have been good to this structure, and by way of grace, hard work, and much love, it now stands well preserved on a mountain in Charlottesville, near Thomas Jefferson's beloved Monticello. "The Museum," rich in folklore and history, offers visitors a glimpse into the past, and "The Ordinary" still serves hot meals to weary travelers.

Corporal William Michie (pronounced "mick-ee") was at Valley Forge in 1777 when an urgent message came for him to return home. Leaving behind the winter encampment, Michie began the tedious journey to Virginia, only to learn upon his arrival that his ailing father had passed on. Young William's father, "Scotch" John Michie, had bequeathed a large parcel of land to his son. The site was the original 1735 land grant to Major John Henry, father of the famous Patrick Henry. John Michie had purchased the land in1746 and had eventually also obtained the rest of Major Henry's holdings in Albemarle County. The Blue Ridge Mountains surround this region, and because it was so highly populated with deer, the site was called Buck Mountain. There was a creek with the same name nearby, and the fields were watered by a natural spring. It was an ideal place for the cultivation of wheat and tobacco. Here, William Michie settled into what he thought was to be a quiet, settled, sturdy cabin on the side of a road.

The Buck Mountain Road led to the county courthouse and became a popular stagecoach route. Taverns were a scarcity on roads not much more than Indian paths. A ten-mile journey was a full day's travel. Michie's cabin became a welcome site to those traveling and knocking on his door. "Strangers," as travelers were known, were welcomed by Michie. He provided food and shelter, often giving up his own bed. Michie simply shared what he had and enjoyed the diverse company.

As the visits became more frequent, he decided to open a tavern. He hired a carpenter, gave him precise three-story plans that included a large foyer and a parlor for gentlemen. A chamber for ladies would be built with more elaborate decor. The upstairs Long Room or Ballroom would serve as additional sleeping quarters on busy nights, and a wonderful kitchen was built as Michie realized that meals were his main sales.

Michie Tavern became known for its ham, bacon, fish, fowl, dried venison, Indian or wheaten bread, and eggs. Milk and cheese were kept in the Spring House adjacent to the kitchen. Other service buildings were the smokehouse, outhouse or "necessary," well, and barn. In time, the tavern became so popular that a post office and makeshift school were located there. The Ballroom became a place for Sunday worship until the Buck Mountain Church was constructed.

Michie Tavern had some rules, which included: *No More Than Four to Sleep in One Bed; No Boots to Be Worn in Bed; and, No Beer Allowed in Kitchen.*

Sharing beds was commonplace among travelers due to the lack of availability and the need for warmth. When "Publick Times" were occurring in Williamsburg, many travelers came along Buck Mountain Road. Seeing a need for expansion, Michie began to connect his buildings into a larger structure.

In 1811, Michie died, leaving the tavern to his son, William Jr. The property remained in the family until 1910. When new highways were established, few people passed by the tavern, making it finally a quiet place. By 1927, a local businesswoman, Mrs. Mark Henderson, expressed an interest to relocate the Michie nearby. She was confident that the structure could house her vast collection of antiques and be a museum. A pioneer activist in historic preservation, Henderson had the tavern painstakingly dismantled, numbered, and moved seventeen miles by horse and wagon to be reconstructed one-half mile from Monticello at the ascent of Carter's Mountain. Little did she know that her efforts would one day lead to Michie Tavern's becoming designated as a Virginia Historic Landmark. Today's "Strangers" can still smell the good warm foods and sit by the fire to rest and reflect upon Michie's times.

CHAPTER FOUR

Meat, Poultry,
and
Seafood Entrées

*"The Groaning Board" was a board used
like we use a buffet today, so heavy with food that the
weight of it made the board groan.*

Meats

Beef Kapama

1/4 cup (1/2 stick) butter or margarine
2 1/2 pounds stew beef, cut into bite-size pieces
1 (8-ounce) can tomato sauce
1 (14-ounce) can whole tomatoes, or to taste

Several slices orange peel
1 bay leaf
1 cinnamon stick
1/2 cup water
1 clove garlic
Salt and pepper to taste

- Melt the butter or margarine in a large skillet. Add the beef, and cook until browned.
- Remove the beef, and place in a deep heavy pot. Add the tomato sauce, tomatoes, orange peel, bay leaf, cinnamon stick, water, garlic clove, and salt and pepper to taste, and mix well. Cook over low heat for about 2 hours or until the beef is tender.
- Serve with noodles or macaroni.
- Note: This recipe can be stretched and stretched as you can see by the story below.
- Makes 6 servings

This Greek recipe does have a connection to the State of Virginia inasmuch as the Virginia Opera, based in Norfolk, triggered its preparation in a wild and memorable way. As a board member of the opera, I developed the custom of inviting the cast and a few friends over for a post-opera dinner after an occasional performance. One such dinner was scheduled for a Friday night, and I had already prepared the Beef Kapama, set up the buffet table, cut a salad, and gone with my husband to see the first two acts of the production. During the first intermission we overheard a perfect stranger say to her companion, "There's a party after the opera at 1316 Graydon Avenue." OUR ADDRESS. Terrified, we left the theater, tires screeching, and went straight to the supermarket to buy a few more pounds of noodles and a few cold cuts. It was too late to make more kapama, because that has to simmer for several hours. After the opera, people began to arrive—first in dribbles, then in groups of ten or more, until I had to put out every dish in the house and send my husband to the store three times for bags of noodles, mushrooms, butter, and lettuce. The crowd ate like locusts, pound after pound of food, and occasionally we would send someone out for a few gallons of wine to deaden the pain. This recipe serves six, and we hope for your sake that you won't have to stretch it to loaves and fishes proportions. Kapama, by the way, is pronounced kapaMA, with the accent on the last syllable, just the way baklava is supposed to be pronounced. The dish can also be made with stewing lamb or chicken.

This recipe was submitted by HOPE MIHILAP who, when not dishing up Beef Kapama for the crowds, is a national award-winning humorist who lives in Norfolk, Virginia. She has received the Mark Twain Award for Humor and the Speaker Hall of Fame Award from the National Speakers Association. She is the author of an autobiography, *Where There's Hope, There's Laughter.*

Montpelier

Enter the world of James and Dolley Madison as you travel to Montpelier in Orange County. Here the "Father of the Constitution" was raised after being born at his maternal grandparents' home near Fredericksburg. In 1771, James graduated from Princeton and within three years entered politics, beginning four decades of service to his country. His bride was Dolley Payne Todd, a gentle woman of Quaker birth raised at the Virginia home Scotchtown.

Recalling a romance that lasted until death, one wistfully reads Dolley Payne Todd's diary of thoughts and letters through her years with her "Jemmy," as she affectionately called James Madison or in later years as First Lady, admitting fear of the British troops as they approached Washington, D.C., while she scampered about the "President's House" rescuing important Cabinet papers, silver urns, velvet drapery and the famous portrait of George Washington that she was determined the British would not have.

One also remembers how James Madison came to be the man to suggest the Articles of Confederation were not strong enough to keep individual states from "clashing," or how he addressed the need for stronger currency in the young nation. He took it upon himself to study books describing strengths and weaknesses of other governments. Along with George Mason, he helped develop the "Virginia Plan" at the Constitutional Convention. Madison kept

a word-by-word account of the Convention debates to preserve it for America's future generations. This led to his being considered the "Father of the Constitution" twenty-two years before he became the nation's fourth President.

Knowing about James and Dolley's contributions to the United States, Virginia is proud to claim this unselfish couple. What was life at Montpelier like? What were their White House years like before Washington was attacked? Food played an important role; Dolley's fame as a hostess resulted in her being the first woman addressed as "First Lady." Used to being a splendid hostess at home, Dolley had been a stand-in First Lady for Thomas Jefferson's presidential functions before her husband's tenure of office. She enjoyed being hostess of the President's House (as the White House was then called). She defined the formal and ceremonial roles of the president's wife. She also symbolized gracious entertaining, fashion, and hospitality and served as a trusting listener to several presidents in her older years.

President Madison liked a Round of Beef with rich garlic gravy served with a boiled cabbage. He also liked ham with his boiled cabbage. A favorite dessert was heavily spiced Upside Down Apple Cake with brown sugar. And then there was ice cream! Unfortunately, no recipes of the Round of Beef or Upside Down Apple Cake survive.

The Madisons' guests often wrote about the abundance of fine wines and punches available for consumption at Montpelier.

Rarely have I drunk finer wine.

—John Latrobe, August 1832

Like Jefferson and Monroe, Madison collected wines from around the world, often sending special orders with his friends when they went overseas on diplomatic missions. The wine of choice at Montpelier seems to have been Madeira, which is a fortified wine made on Madeira, one of a group of Portuguese islands off the coast of Morocco.

Volunteers recently working on a cookbook entitled *Montpelier Hospitality* undertook a painstaking effort to track down recipes that were used by Dolley herself. "After pouring [sic] through old cookbooks, journals, and letters in search of truly authentic recipes, we found that very few, if any, survive," the cookbook committee notes in its introduction. The committee found many recipes attributed to Dolley—a reflection of her status, more than 150 years after her death, as America's premier hostess. Dolley's recipe for Soft Gingerbread, for instance, is said to be preserved in White House files, but a check with the White House curator turned up no Dolley recipes at all! That's not surprising; during the War of 1812, while Madison was President, as the British burned the President's House, Dolley lost all her own property, including her recipes. Recipes that appear in one cookbook as an "Old Virginia" favorite turn up in later books as a "Dolley Specialty."

In the days when Lafayette and his entourage toured America, visiting distinguished Americans (such as Washington, Jefferson, and Andrew Jackson) in 1824, Dolley served her famous Harvest Home Supper.

Copious research by the Montpelier staff led to the careful choices made with regard to color, rug selections, furniture placement, wall and window treatments, as well as the selection of foods and beverages. All research by the Montpelier staff indicates that the Madisons loved to entertain at Montpelier and also at the President's House in Federal City. They entertained on a regular (and some might say exhausting) basis!

After their tenure in politics, Dolley wrote on March 25, 1815:

Home at Montpelier—and peace. Mr. Madison's family home is a true Garden of Eden. I have missed the quiet beauty of Montpelier more than I realized. Indeed, this is the first real vacation we have had in years.

At her funeral, President Zachary Taylor (another Virginian), eulogized, "She will never be forgotten because she truly was our First Lady for a half-century."

James Madison: Builder of the Nation

James Madison expressed concern about the state of world affairs when he took office the first time. At his inauguration on March 4, 1809—in a speech that could well have derived from today's newspaper headlines—he declared, "The present condition of the world is indeed without a parallel, and that of our own country full of difficulties." Continuing, he said, "The pressure of these, too, is the more severely felt because they have fallen upon us at a moment when the national prosperity being at a height not before attained, the contrast resulting from the change has been rendered the more striking. Under the benign influence of our republican institutions, and the maintenance of peace with all nations whilst so many of them were engaged in bloody and wasteful wars, the fruits of a just policy were enjoyed in an unrivaled growth of our faculties and resources . . . ."

Madison was a force behind the convening of the Constitutional Convention of 1787, and along with other pro-ratification members of the Continental Congress, he successfully defended the Constitution against a strong anti-ratification element. While serving in the U. S. House of Representatives in 1789-97, he was also instrumental in framing and gaining support for the passage of the Bill of Rights.

Beef Wine-O

1 pound stew beef, cut up
1 (10³/4-ounce) can cream
of golden mushroom soup

¹/2 cup cooking sherry
1 (1.3-ounce) package
onion soup mix

- Preheat the oven to 300°F. Combine the beef, mushroom soup, sherry, and soup mix in a 2-quart casserole dish and mix well. Bake, covered, for 3 hours.
- Makes 4 servings

The recipe was contributed by MARY PHARR, a member of the Freedom Hill Chapter in McLean, in honor of her grandmother, Virginia J. Pharr from Yorktown, past Regent of the Comte de Grasse Chapter of the Virginia DAR, who passed away in 2002.

Gourmet Beef

¹/4 cup soy sauce
1 tablespoon lemon juice
1 teaspoon sugar
¹/2 teaspoon ground ginger
1 clove garlic, crushed
6 (1-inch-thick) slices beef
tenderloin

Butter or margarine
1 cup sliced fresh
mushrooms
¹/2 cup thinly sliced onion

- Combine the soy sauce, lemon juice, sugar, ginger, garlic in a medium bowl, and mix well. Add the beef tenderloin. Marinate, covered, in the refrigerator for ¹/2 hour, turning frequently.
- Drain the beef tenderloins, reserving the marinade. Melt the butter or margarine in a medium skillet, and sauté the beef for 5 minutes on each side. Remove the beef tenderloin to a hot platter, and keep warm. Add the mushrooms and onion to the skillet, and sauté until the onion is soft. Add the reserved marinade, and bring to a boil. Pour over the beef tenderloin.
- Makes 6 servings

Flank steak is also wonderful marinated in this sauce. I would then broil the flank steaks.

From the kitchen of ORIANA and FRANK HARGROVE. Delegate Frank D. Hargrove, Sr., a busy Virginia businessman and community activist, has, for over 20 years, served the Commonwealth of Virginia in the Virginia House of Delegates from Hanover County, the 55th Legislative District.

DID YOU KNOW THAT:

The Cape Henry Lighthouse in Virginia Beach, completed in 1792, is the oldest such structure in the country?

LYNCHBURG'S SEVEN HILLS

Any visitor to Lynchburg is awed by the beauty of its views. Called the City of Seven Hills, a distinction shared with Rome, Italy, Lynchburg offers views of these seven "ladies":

- Diamond Hill and White Rock Hill have names that reflect their geographic surroundings.
- College Hill is named for a pre-Civil War military school that became a hospital during the war.
- Federal Hill is named for the former Federal Hotel.
- Daniel's Hill is named in honor of Judge William Daniel Jr., who owned the Point of Honor property.
- Garland Hill was named in honor of a prominent lawyer from the city's early days, Sam Garland Jr.
- Franklin Hill honors the patriot Benjamin Franklin.

DIJON TOMATO CREAM SAUCE

To prepare the sauce, add 1 teaspoon chopped garlic to a warm sauté pan over medium heat. Let stand for about 1 minute, and add 1 sliced fresh Roma tomato, 3 ounces white wine, a pinch of dry basil, and 3 ounces fresh or canned chicken broth. Cook for several minutes or until the liquid is reduced. Add 2 teaspoons Dijon mustard, a dash of white pepper, and 4 ounces heavy cream, and cook until slightly thickened and reduced.

Filet Mignon Medallions Stuffed with Crab Imperial

CRAB IMPERIAL

1 egg	3 dashes of white pepper
1 teaspoon Dijon mustard	3 dashes of Tabasco sauce
1 teaspoon chopped garlic	3 tablespoons mayonnaise
1 tablespoon sugar	1/4 cup grated Parmesan
1/2 teaspoon Old Bay Seasoning	cheese
1 tablespoon freshly squeezed lemon juice	1 (8-ounce) can back-fin crabmeat, shell bits removed

MEDALLIONS

Filet mignon, cut into 3-ounce medallions	Salt and pepper
Flour for coating	2 ounces olive oil

ASSEMBLY

Dijon Tomato Cream Sauce (at left)	Chopped fresh parsley for garnish
Sprigs of fresh chives	

- To prepare the Crab Imperial, combine the egg, Dijon mustard, garlic, sugar, Old Bay seasoning, lemon juice, white pepper, Tabasco sauce, and mayonnaise in a mixing bowl, and whisk until blended. Fold in the Parmesan cheese. Stir in the crabmeat. Refrigerate, covered, for 1 hour for the flavors to blend. Note: Add bread crumbs to firm up the mixture if desired. Jumbo lump crabmeat can be substituted for the back-fin crabmeat.
- To prepare the medallions, sprinkle the medallions lightly with flour, and salt and pepper to taste. Heat the olive oil in a medium sauté pan over medium heat. Add the medallions, and sauté until lightly browned. Remove the medallions to a serving platter. Top the medallions with a heaping scoop of the Crab Imperial. Place in a preheated oven on the broiler setting, and broil for a few minutes or until lightly browned.
- To serve, spoon Dijon Tomato Cream Sauce into the center of each serving plate, and top with 2 stuffed medallions. Garnish with chives and parsley.
- Makes 2 to 3 servings

In July of 1890, the firm of White Star Mills was created for manufacturing flour. The principal brand of flour, Melrose, was a staple in southern kitchens for the entire life of the mill. The mill operated successfully every year until 1963. Now this turn-of-the-century flour mill is The Mill Street Grill, offering a cozy atmosphere and specializing in barbecued ribs, grilled steaks, and seafood.

We received this recipe through the efforts of JANE SHERMAN and WHITNEY DEITZ, Regent and treasurer of the Colonel Thomas Hughart Chapter of the Virginia DAR in Staunton, Virginia.

Grilled Filet Mignon with Sweet Potato Hash, Spicy Peanut Sauce, and Wilted Collards

FILET MIGNONS

2 tablespoons finely
  chopped spring onions
2 tablespoons minced
  gingerroot

2 tablespoons minced garlic
6 ounces peanut oil
6 filet mignons
Salt and pepper

PEANUT SAUCE

4 ounces creamy peanut
  butter
3 ounces lime juice
3 ounces peanut oil
2 ounces honey
1 tablespoon minced spring
  onion

2 tablespoons minced fresh
  gingerroot
2 teaspoons minced garlic
$1/2$ teaspoon cayenne
Salt and pepper

ASSEMBLY

Wilted Collards (at right)
Sweet Potato Hash
  (at right)

Chopped peanuts
Spring onions, finely
  chopped

- To prepare the filet mignons, combine the onions, gingerroot, garlic and peanut oil in a bowl, and mix well. Place the filets in the marinade. Marinate, covered, in the refrigerator for 3 hours. Drain the filets, discarding the marinade. Season with salt and pepper. Grill or sauté the filets in a skillet until of the desired doneness. Let stand for a few minutes, and slice into servings.
- To prepare the peanut sauce, blend the peanut butter, lime juice, peanut oil, honey, onion, gingerroot, garlic, cayenne, and salt and pepper to taste in a bowl until of a smooth consistency.
- To serve, drizzle the peanut sauce on a plate in any desired pattern. Arrange the collards loosely in a ring in the center of the plate. Spoon the sweet potato hash into the center of the collards. Arrange the sliced filets over the sweet potato hash, and garnish with peanuts and spring onions.
- Makes 6 servings

Shared by EILEEN PERNA THOMASSON,, who is not only a fabulous and creative cook, but is also the hardworking Chair of the Virginia Opera Guild. She is a true lover of the arts.

Virginia Opera

PETER MARK
ARTISTIC DIRECTOR

SING FOR YOUR SUPPER

The Story of Virginia Opera and
Many Years of Beautiful Music

Wonderful food and glorious music come together in a powerful duet at Virginia Opera. Virginia Opera has been host to an array of gala parties, balls, and social events in which delicious meals have played a starring role over the years. Food has also had a significant impact in raising funds to support this most complex art form. Maestro Peter Mark would agree that Virginia Opera lovers love great music and great food. In its supporting role to Virginia Opera Association, the Opera Guild uses the skills of its volunteer cooks to welcome singers to Virginia in our Artist Outreach Program by providing dinner for the cast of Principals of every opera and by cooking for Guild nights and fundraisers. Many years ago, the Guild used to cater a meal for the entire cast of an opera. The menu was always an attempt to stay in tune with the theme of each opera. During Thea Musgrave's *A Woman Called Moses*, the diva who was singing the role of Harriet Tubman was seen to eat the ham biscuits and watermelon pickle provided just before stepping onto the stage to sing in the world premiere. Southern food was her inspiration.

FUN FACTS IN HISTORY

Pork was hard to get and expensive. When special visitors came, a host who could, put out the bacon to show off. Thus, it became a sign of wealth if a man could "bring home the bacon." The family would then share some of that bacon with their guests, and all would sit around and "chew the fat."

People ate mostly vegetables and grain. Meat was a rare commodity and usually went into the big kettle that always hung over the fire. The family would eat the stew during the evening meal, leaving the leftovers in the pot to get cold overnight. The next day, they would start the fire again and add what they had available that day. Often some of the food in this pot would be there quite a while—hence the rhyme, "Peas porridge hot, peas porridge cold, peas porridge in the pot nine days old."

Sweet Potato Hash

3 medium sweet potatoes, cubed
Peanut oil
Salt and pepper
1 yellow onion, chopped
1/4 cup (1/2 stick) butter or margarine
1 red bell pepper, chopped
1 yellow bell pepper, chopped
1 tablespoon nutmeg
1 teaspoon cinnamon
2 tablespoons brown sugar

- Place the sweet potato cubes in a baking pan. Drizzle with peanut oil. Season with salt and pepper, and roast in a 400°F oven until fork tender.
- Caramelize the onion in the butter or margarine in a large saucepan, and add the red and yellow peppers. Season with salt and pepper to taste. Add the roasted sweet potato cubes, and mix well. Sprinkle with the nutmeg, cinnamon, and brown sugar. Reheat at serving time. Adjust seasoning with salt and pepper if necessary.
- Makes 6 servings

Wilted Collards

6 strips bacon, chopped
1 tablespoon minced garlic
2 bunches collards or turnip greens, chopped or torn
1 lemon
Salt and pepper

- Sauté the bacon in a large frying pan until crisp. Add the minced garlic, and sweat until fragrant. Toss the collards into the drippings, and sauté until the collards are just wilted. Squeeze the lemon juice over the collards just before serving. Season with salt and pepper.
- Makes 6 servings

CULPEPER COUNTY

Culpeper County was named in honor of Thomas Culpeper (1635-1689), Virginia's governor from 1677 till 1683, or at least for his family. It was organized in 1749 out of land belonging to Orange County. It covers three hundred eighty-four square miles, its population is 34,262, and its county seat is Culpeper.

Robert E. Lee's Army of Northern Virginia gathered in Culpeper County in early June 1863 in preparation for the march to Gettysburg. The George Washington Carver Regional High School was chartered in this county in 1948 with the mission to fulfill the learning needs of black students in a four-county area.

Barbecued Ribs

1 cup mayonnaise	¹/₂ teaspoon black pepper
¹/₄ cup (2 ounces) sherry	3 tablespoons brown sugar
¹/₄ cup (2 ounces) soy sauce	³/₄ cup (6 ounces) pineapple
1 teaspoon chili powder	juice, or any fruit juice
1 teaspoon ground ginger	4 teaspoons white vinegar
1 teaspoon salt	1 teaspoon onion juice, or
2 garlic cloves, crushed	1 small onion, finely
2 tablespoons	chopped
Worcestershire sauce	¹/₂ teaspoon oregano
2 teaspoons prepared	¹/₂ teaspoon celery salt
horseradish	Approximately 6 to
1 teaspoon dry mustard	7 pounds of beef or
2 tablespoons tomato paste	pork ribs

- Preheat the oven to 500°F. Combine the mayonnaise, sherry, soy sauce, chili powder, ginger, salt, garlic, Worcestershire sauce, horseradish, dry mustard, tomato paste, pepper, brown sugar, pineapple juice, white vinegar, onion juice or onion, oregano, and celery salt in a large bowl, and mix well. This makes a scant 3 cups.
- Place the ribs in a baking pan. Bake for 30 minutes or until the fat has been rendered, discarding the drippings. Reduce the heat to 300°F. Bake for 2 hours, basting with the sauce every 30 minutes.
- Makes approximately 12 servings

The
MARTHA WASHINGTON INN

Grilled Strip Steak with Sorghum Cured Onions

2 sweet onions, peeled, cut into halves vertically	1 cup veal stock, or 1 can beef broth
2 tablespoons sorghum	4 New York strip steaks
2 ounces bourbon	

- Preheat the oven to 350°F. Place the onion halves in an ovenproof dish, and drizzle with the sorghum and bourbon. Fill the dish with the stock ¹/₂ to ²/₃ the height of the onions. Bake, covered with foil, for 1 hour. Grill the strip steaks. Place the steaks on individual serving plates. Top each serving with an onion half and the sauce.
- Makes 4 servings

This recipe came to us from THE MARTHA WASHINGTON INN, Abingdon, Virginia.

Long before the first settlers arrived at Jamestown in 1607, the Indians had been curing venison and fish, which were plentiful in the forest and rivers. The taste of salt-cured and smoked meat was different from the sun-dried method the settlers knew in their native England.

The settlers soon brought hogs, which were left to forage New World vegetation, including nuts and acorns. By 1608, the colonists were keeping their hogs on an island five miles below the Jamestown settlement. The island soon became know as Hog Island, as it is today, over three centuries later. In 1652, Surry County was formed, encompassing Hog Island and much other land across the James River from Jamestown.

These early colonists soon developed a process of rubbing pork with salt obtained from evaporating seawater and then smoking it over hickory and oak fires before allowing the meat to stand for a time. The salt preserved the meat, while the smoking and aging enhanced the flavor.

When other crops failed or tobacco prices fell, there were always hams to trade. Thus, Virginia hams were exported to England from Surry.

For generations, ham curing has been a seasonal event for Virginia farmers. Hogs were killed in the winter and their meat packed in cure while weather was cool enough to keep it from spoiling. The meat was then rinsed and hung to dry and smoke during the remaining cool months. With luck, it would endure the high temperatures of summer to age properly.

Many people receive a Virginia ham as a gift, the highest compliment anyone could pay you! Unfortunately, many of these hams have been discarded by recipients because of the presence of mold on the ham. This is a normal characteristic and is formed during the curing process by a reaction of moisture from the ham with heat and humidity in the air. Simply wash it in hot water and scrub off the mold with a stiff brush. Until you are ready to cook your ham, keep it in a cool, dry place.

Credit: S. Wallace Edwards and Sons of Surry, Virginia.

FORMER LT. GOVERNOR AND MRS. JOHN HAGER'S
Veal Stroganoff

1^1/$_2$ pounds boneless veal, cubed	1 small onion, chopped
1 tablespoon oil	1 tablespoon all-purpose flour
1 tablespoon butter or margarine	^{1}/$_3$ cup chicken stock
Juice of 1 lemon	^{3}/$_4$ cup sour cream
^{1}/$_2$ pound sliced mushrooms	^{1}/$_2$ teaspoon salt
	^{1}/$_8$ teaspoon pepper

- Preheat oven to 300°F. Cook the veal in the oil and butter or margarine in a medium skillet until browned, stirring frequently. Squeeze the fresh lemon juice over the mushrooms in a bowl, and let stand for a few minutes.
- Note: The lemon juice adds zest to the veal, and prevents the mushrooms from darkening.
- Place the veal in an 8×8-inch ovenproof dish. Sauté the onion and mushrooms in the drippings in the skillet until tender. Remove from the heat, and stir in the flour, stock, sour cream, and salt and pepper to taste. Pour over the veal. Bake, covered, for 1 hour.
- This recipe is delicious served with rice or noodles.
- Makes 4 servings

This is a dish that can be served morning, noon, or night. It holds well if your dinner is running late.

The recipe is shared by MAGGIE HAGER from Richmond, an incredible woman of great energy and thoughtfulness, and a great hostess.

CUMBERLAND COUNTY

Cumberland County was established in 1749 out of Goochland County. It was named in honor of William Augustus, Duke of Cumberland, and son of King George II. It covers two hundred ninety-three square miles. The population is 9,017, and the county seat is Cumberland.

The nation's first publicly approved declaration of independence from Great Britain was issued in this county on April 22, 1776, at the home of Carter Henry Harrison. The famed Revolutionary War general, Baron Friedrich von Steuben, campaigned in this county during the summer of 1781.

DID YOU KNOW THAT:

Prehistoric Indian remains dating back nearly fifteen thousand years have been discovered near Saltville along the Virginia-Tennessee-North Carolina border?

RAMONA'S
Beefy Pasta Casserole

1 onion, chopped
1 clove garlic, chopped, or
  garlic powder to taste
Red pepper
1 pound ground beef
Salt and pepper
$1/2$ teaspoon sugar
1 (8-ounce) can tomato
  sauce
1 (6-ounce) can tomato
  paste

1 (32-ounce) jar meat-flavor
  pasta sauce
1 (12-ounce) package shells
  and cheese, such as Kraft
1 ($5^1/2$-ounce) bag potato
  chips, crushed, or
  1 (6-ounce) can onion
  rings

- Sauté the onion, garlic, and red pepper to taste in a saucepan. Add the ground beef, salt and pepper to taste, and sugar, mixing well. Cover the saucepan until the mixture begins to cook. Remove the cover, and cook until the juices are reduced, stirring frequently. Add the tomato sauce, tomato paste, and pasta sauce, and mix well. Reduce the heat. Simmer for 30 minutes.
- Prepare the shells and cheese according to the package directions in a saucepan. Combine with the sauce mixture, and spoon into a 2-quart casserole dish. Top with the potato chips or canned onion rings, and bake at 350°F for 20 minutes or until browned.
- Makes 6 servings

Ramona created this for family and friends and gave it, as friends do, to me.

This was provided by JENNIE PALACIOS of the Great Bridge Chapter of the Virginia DAR. The family home of Jennie Palacios is the Stone House built by Peter Gose around 1812. It was purchased by his niece and her husband, Thomas and Anna Gose Peery, and remained in the Peery family for many years. There is a legend that the house is haunted by the sound of a baby crying.

DICKENSON COUNTY

Dickenson County was formed in 1880 from Buchanan, Russell, and Wise Counties. It is named in honor of William J. Dickenson, a delegate to the General Assembly at the time. Its size is three hundred twenty-five square miles, and its population is 16,395. The county seat is Clintwood.

"Fighting" Dick Colley, who moved here from the Clinch River region in 1816, was the first permanent resident in present-day Dickenson County. The advent of the railroad to the county in 1915 started an economic boom with the exploitation of timber and mineral resources in the area.

AFRICAN-AMERICAN MEMBERS OF THE

Alfred W. Harris
House of Delegates, 1881-1888
A lawyer who began his practice in Petersburg in 1882, he lived in Dinwiddie County and was elected from that county to the legislature

William W. Evans
Petersburg
A barber and lawyer who owned real estate in Petersburg

Nathaniel M. Griggs
Prince Edward County
A jeweler and deputy collector of Internal Revenue

John H. Robinson
Elizabeth City County
A teacher and lawyer, as well as deacon and clerk of the Queen Street Baptist Church

VIRGINIA GENERAL ASSEMBLY 1887-1888

Caesar Perkins

Buckingham County

A brick mason, brick maker, farmer, storekeeper, and minister

William H. Ash

Nottoway County

A teacher-turned-politician who spent his last years as a professor

Britton Baskerville Jr.

Mecklenburg County

A teacher and farmer who also served as a superintendent of Sunday school at Bloom Hill Baptist Church

Goodman Brown

Surry County

A Navy cabin boy aboard the *USS Maratanza* who reportedly served the U.S. Army in a civilian capacity before turning to politics and, later, to farming

Hurricane Casserole

5 or 6 medium-size zucchini, peeled, cut lengthwise into fourths
2 to 3 tablespoons butter or margarine
1 pound ground beef
1 large onion, finely chopped
Salt and pepper
$1/2$ to 1 teaspoon fines herbes
$1/2$ cup grated cheddar cheese
4 to 5 medium tomatoes, sliced

- Preheat the oven to 350°F. Fry the zucchini in the butter or margarine in a large skillet until tender and browned. Place in a container, and set aside.
- Add the ground beef and onion to the skillet. Season with salt and pepper to taste. Cook until the ground beef is browned and the onion is soft, stirring until crumbly. Add the fines herbes, and mix well.
- Layer the zucchini and the ground beef mixture in a buttered 9×12-inch baking, beginning with the zucchini. Sprinkle with the cheese. Top with the tomatoes and season with salt and pepper to taste. Bake for 30 minutes or until the tomatoes are tender.
- Makes 10 to 12 servings

We named this dish "Hurricane Casserole" because it fed us when Hurricane Bonnie came through Norfolk in 1996. The power was out in our little neighborhood for two days, but our gas stove worked. We tripled the recipe and invited hungry neighbors in for a feast. Complement the casserole with soda biscuits, and you have an easy delicious meal. Dinner parties allow me to share my travel experiences with my "Virginia family and friends." I love mixing recipes for a global meal.

ELAINE KENNEDY is a Virginian by choice, and she is passionate about her adopted state. Having lived and traveled extensively in the USA and abroad, Elaine found her home in Tidewater.

DINWIDDIE COUNTY

Dinwiddie County was organized in 1752 out of land belonging to Prince George County. Named in honor of Governor Robert Dinwiddie (1692-1770), the county covers five hundred twenty-one square miles. Its population is 24,533, and the county seat is Dinwiddie.

Mexican War hero General Winfield Scott was born in Dinwiddie County in 1786 and practiced law here for several years. Confederate General A.P. Hill was killed here on April 2, 1865, when he accidentally encountered Union troops on their way to Petersburg.

SENATOR GEORGE ALLEN'S
Lasagna

SAUCE

1/4 cup olive oil	1 can water
1 large onion, finely chopped	1 tablespoon oregano
2 large cloves garlic, minced	1 1/2 tablespoons basil
2 large cans tomatoes, coarsely chopped	1 bay leaf
	1 teaspoon garlic powder
1 (12-ounce) can tomato paste	2 teaspoons sugar
	1 1/2 teaspoons salt
	Pepper

FILLING AND ASSEMBLY

1/4 cup olive oil	1/2 pound mozzarella cheese, chopped
1 large onion, chopped	
1 clove garlic, minced	1/2 cup grated Romano cheese
1 1/2 pounds ground beef	
1 1/2 pounds Italian sausage	1/2 cup grated Parmesan cheese
1 pound sliced mushrooms, optional	
2 eggs, beaten	1 (16-ounce) package lasagna noodles, parboiled
Salt and pepper	

- To prepare the sauce, heat the olive oil in a medium skillet, and sauté the onions and garlic until soft. Combine the tomatoes, tomato paste, water, oregano, basil, bay leaf, garlic powder, sugar, salt, and pepper to taste in a large pot, and mix well. Add the sautéed onion and garlic mixture. Simmer for several hours or until smooth and thickened. The sauce should be prepared several hours before assembling the dish.
- To prepare the filling, preheat the oven to 350°F. Heat the olive oil in a large skillet, and sauté the onions until soft. Add the garlic, ground beef, sausage, and mushrooms, if desired, and cook until the ground beef and sausage are browned and the mushrooms are tender, stirring frequently. Stir in the eggs. Season with the salt and pepper to taste.
- To assemble the lasagna, toss the cheeses together in a medium bowl. Spread a small amount of the sauce in the bottom of a 9×13-inch baking pan. Layer with the noodles, filling, sauce, and cheeses. Repeat the process, ending with the noodles. Spread the remaining sauce over the noodles, and top with the remaining cheeses. Bake for 1 hour or until bubbly.
- Makes approximately 12 servings

SENATOR GEORGE ALLEN shares this recipe, which he says is his all-time favorite dish. Senator Allen, Virginia's 67th governor from 1994 to 1998, began his public service in 1982 as a member of Virginia's House of Delegates, representing the seat once held by Thomas Jefferson, his ideological and philosophical inspiration. Now he serves Virginia as the 51st senator and as deputy whip for the 107th Congress. He is the son of George Allen, the popular coach of the Washington Redskins.

PREPARATION OF COUNTRY HAM, 1674

To eat ye ham in perfection, steep it in half milk and half water for thirty-six hours, and then having brought fresh water to a boil, put ye ham therein and let simmer, not boil, for four or five hours according to size of ye ham...simmering brings out ye salt and boiling drives it in.

Virginia ham was very esteemed in the Virginia Colony. Sir William Gooch (Lieutenant Governor of Virginia from 1727 to 1749) sent hams to his brothers, the Bishop of Norwich and to the Bishop of Salisbury, London, and Bangor.

This very old recipe was written on the fly-leaf of the Bible owned by the first William Byrd of Westover (1674). It is printed in the *Williamsburg Art of Cookery* copyright December, 1938, by Mrs. Helen Bullock of Blair Kitchen in Williamsburg, Virginia.

This recipe has been used and truly is delicious. It is graciously shared by CARMEL LONGLEY, Regent of the Shenandoah River Chapter of the Virginia DAR.

VIRGINIA STAGE COMPANY

The Wells Theatre was opened on August 26, 1913, by Jack and Otto Wells. That first year, Maude Adams flew across the stage as Peter Pan, and Wells presented Ben-Hur complete with teams of horses on treadmills. Fred and Adele Astaire, Will Rogers, Billie Burke, John Drew, John Phillips Sousa, and Dorothy Gish all appeared on the Wells stage. In 1916, Wells installed a movie screen, and by the beginning of World War II, burlesque had joined the repertory. In the 1960s the Wells Theatre became an X-rated movie house, its backstage area converted into The Jamaican Room, a notorious gin mill and brothel. Virginia Stage Company moved into the Wells Theatre in 1979 and, in 1986 completed a $3.5 million restoration, resulting in this Beaux-Arts gem's designation as a National Historic Landmark.

Everyday Meatloaf

MEATLOAF

2 eggs
3/4 cup milk
2/3 cup fine dried bread crumbs
2 tablespoons chopped onion
3/4 teaspoon salt

Dash of pepper
1/2 teaspoon crushed dried sage
1 1/2 pounds ground beef, or a combination of ground beef, ground veal, and ground pork

TOPPING

1/4 cup ketchup
2 tablespoons brown sugar

1 teaspoon dry mustard
1 teaspoon lemon juice

- To prepare the meatloaf, preheat the oven to 350°F. Combine the eggs, milk, bread crumbs, onion, salt, pepper, sage, and ground beef in a large bowl, and mix well. Shape into a loaf, and place in a shallow baking pan. Bake for 1 hour.
- To prepare the topping, combine the ketchup, brown sugar, dry mustard, and lemon juice in a small bowl, and mix well.
- Spoon the topping over the meatloaf, and bake for 15 minutes longer.
- Makes 6 servings

THE VIRGINIA STAGE COMPANY at the Wells Theatre, Norfolk, and their community partners and volunteers, The Virginia Stage Associates, shared this recipe. The latter are vitally important, as they are responsible for preparing the "Matinee Meal" on Saturdays. Those "Matinee Meals" take place in between the afternoon and evening performances when there isn't enough time for a dinner break, so volunteers bring their specialties, providing salads, main dishes, veggies, bread, and dessert for each meal, which serves cast, crew, and box-office staff. It seems that even the most sophisticated and worldly stage palates enjoy home-style food once in a while, so here is one recipe in that category which has been enthusiastically received each time it is served (that means no leftovers).

VIRGINIA
STAGE
COMPANY
at the Wells Theatre

Williamsburg Lodge
Mushroom-Crusted Loin of Lamb

1 tablespoon canola oil
2 loins of lamb, boned
Salt and freshly ground
   black pepper
1 teaspoon finely chopped
   fresh rosemary

¹/₂ cup whole grain mustard,
   such as Pommery
1 cup finely chopped
   assorted dried mushrooms

- Preheat the oven to 375°F. Heat the canola oil in an iron skillet. Season the lamb loins with salt and pepper to taste, and rosemary. Sear the loins in the hot oil for 1 minute on each side.
- Remove the loins from the skillet, and let stand until cool. Brush the loins with the mustard, adding a thin coating. Press a thin coating of the mushrooms onto the loins, and place on a sheet roasting pan. Roast for 8 to 10 minutes. Let stand before slicing.
- Makes 6 to 8 servings

CHEF BRIAN ASPELL graciously provided this recipe.

Poli

1 pound bacon, cut up
2 white onions, chopped
1¹/₂ cups cooked white rice

1 (6-ounce) can tomato
   paste
Salt and black pepper

- Fry the bacon in a heavy-duty saucepan until almost crisp. Add the onions, and stir. Drain the bacon drippings. Remove the bacon and onions to an electric frying pan. Add the rice, and stir in the tomato paste, blending well. Season with salt and pepper to taste. Keep warm on a low heat.
- Makes 6 to 8 servings

This is one of my favorites from childhood. It is a great main course for a quick supper. Tastes wonderful when accompanied with a fresh salad. I really don't know where the name came from, but the recipe has a Spanish flavor.

Shared by our daughter, MARY FRANCIS BELLMAN, who was raised in Virginia. After a career in international publishing, she is now a stay-at-home mom taking care of twins. She loves to recreate her favorite foods from childhood for her own children. —Rowena

LA PETITE TEAROOM

As she stood to leave the table, daintily pushing her chair, she looked around to others having luncheon at La Petite and proclaimed softly, "That's the best cup of tea I've ever had in America!"

—An English tourist

In June 1999, the first tearoom in modern-day Williamsburg opened at Williamsburg Antique Mall. Her Scottish heritage (the Fraser Clan) shining, Jean Reitmeyer articulated her goal with her logo: *Great food for people with great taste!* Reitmeyer uses the best quality ingredients in all of her cooking and baking. She insists on what she calls "divine" presentation, as well.

Shortly after opening La Petite, Reitmeyer and her staff served their original "Jamestown Surry Chowder," a recipe dedicated to the honor of the Jamestown women of 1619. Mrs. Edwards, from the famous Edwards Ham family in Surry, tasted it and took a sample to her son at their business headquarters. Soon to follow was "Yorktown Chowder." Reitmeyer now mass produces the chowders for Edwards, Ukrop's Grocers, and more!

Eventually, six different chowders will be available. Reitmeyer gives 50 percent of the proceeds from the chowders and the tearoom's unique cookbook to support a farm for autistic adults who have lost their parents.

Favorite dishes served in La Petite Tearoom include Scottish Cream Scones, McGinty's Shortbread, Irish Bailey's Cream Mousse, Scottish Egg Salad, Scottish Chicken Salad, and Irish Potato Soup. A sampler plate is available with tea sandwiches on skewers. The soup of the day is always tasty. And the tea is always "divine."

Reitmeyer feels fortunate to be in Virginia. She lives where the original Belle Farm of Williamsburg used to be. The beautiful cow pasture and farm was so close to the College of William and Mary that the cows with their tinkling bells would wander about the campus nudging the students affectionately.

Jean hugs all visitors to her tearoom before they leave. From bright-eyed children to lady cookbook authors to male motorcycle enthusiasts—everyone gets hugged!

— Winette, a regular customer

Ham and Asparagus Crêpes

1 cup milk
2 eggs, beaten
2 tablespoons oil
$^1/_2$ cup plus 3 tablespoons all-purpose flour
1 teaspoon baking powder
$^1/_2$ teaspoon salt
3 tablespoons butter or margarine
1 jar sliced mushrooms, drained
$^3/_4$ cup water
$^1/_4$ cup white wine
2 teaspoons instant chicken bouillon
$^1/_3$ cup half-and-half
$^1/_4$ cup shredded cheddar cheese
1 tablespoon chopped chives
8 to 16 slices ham
8 slices Swiss cheese
1 bunch asparagus, steamed crisp-tender

- Combine the milk, eggs, and oil in a large mixing bowl. Stir in $^1/_2$ cup of the flour, baking powder, and salt. Pour the mixture into a shallow bowl, and dip a crêpe maker into the batter until the surface is covered. Cook until lightly browned, but still pliable. This can also be done in a skillet. Add the batter to a greased skillet, and tilt the skillet to make a circle. Brown for 1 minute, and turn and brown the other side. These crêpes can be frozen with wax paper between each one. Store the crêpes in a tightly sealed container if preparing ahead of time.
- Melt the butter or margarine in a medium saucepan, and sauté the mushrooms. Stir in 3 tablespoons of the flour. Add the water and wine gradually, stirring constantly. Stir in the bouillon, half-and-half, cheese, and chives. Cook over medium heat until thickened, stirring constantly.
- Preheat the oven to 350°F. Place 1 or 2 slices of the ham, 1 slice of the Swiss cheese, and 3 to 4 asparagus spears on each crêpe, and roll up. Place the crêpes, seam side down, in a 9×13-inch baking dish. Spoon the sauce over the crêpes. Bake for 30 minutes. This is a great dinner or brunch dish.
- Makes 4 servings

I have been making this recipe for the past twenty-five years. I can't remember how I came across the original, but over the years I have added or changed ingredients to come up with this version. This was always a "grown up" dinner, because our daughters didn't like asparagus; but they loved when I made it, because I would make extra crêpes with cinnamon and sugar and fold them in pockets for them. You can make the crêpes from scratch, as we have done here, or buy prepared ones at the grocery store. (Sara Moulton from the Food TV network even condones using store bought ones.) My husband, Major General Jack Holbein, USAF, and I are privileged to live in one of the lovely homes from the Jamestown exposition now owned by the Navy. These homes were built by the various states in 1907. We live in the West Virginia House East. Some of the original buildings have become two-family residences. My husband is currently the Chief of Staff of Joint Forces Command, and we love this area so much, we've decided to retire here.

This recipe was sent to us by PAULA HOLBEIN.

GRANDMOTHER HARRELL'S
Kettle Method for Preparing Whole, Aged Virginia Hams

1 Virginia ham   Sugar
Water   Whole cloves

- Rinse the ham thoroughly in warm water. Soak in cold water overnight. Bring enough water to cover the ham to a boil in a large pot or ham boiler. Place the ham, skin side up, in the boiling water. Reduce the heat to low, and simmer, covered, for about 20 to 25 minutes per pound or until until tender. Note: The protruding bone on the back side will separate from the meat.
- Remove the ham from the pot, and remove the skin. Place the ham, fat side up, in a baking pan. Add 1 cup of water. Rub the ham with the sugar. Stud the fat at intervals with whole cloves.
- Bake at 300°F for about 30 minutes or until until browned. Remove the ham to a serving platter. Let the ham pot liquor stand until cool, and skim the grease, refrigerating for future seasoning. Serve with cabbage cooked in the remaining ham broth if desired.
- Makes a variable number of servings, depending on the size of the ham. Plan on 1/2-pound servings per person.

This recipe is from *The Ham Book* written by MONETTE and ROBERT HARRELL. They are ham experts from ham country in Suffolk, Virginia, where Bob's family has been in the ham packing business since 1898. Monette Harrell, a home economist and teacher, has collected every kind of recipe for using ham, even the leftovers and the hambone.

THE PLEASURES OF "POT LIQUOR"

"Pot liquor" is a Southern institution with origins far back in the earliest days of our region's past. "Pot liquor" was not of as humble origin as its name implies. During occasions which demanded "big dinners," a whole ham, or possibly two, were placed in a big pot of water and suspended from the chimney crane over the fire. When the meat was partly cooked, cabbages were added, and later peeled potatoes were placed in the pot, and when these vegetables were partly cooked, corn meal dumplings were added, and after all were sufficiently cooked together, they were taken out and a handful of corn meal was sprinkled over the pot liquor and allowed to cook a few minutes. The pot liquor was thus seasoned with juicy, fat ham, scraps of the cabbages, potatoes, and corn meal dumplings, and thickened with corn meal. It needed no other seasoning, and was superior in flavor and strength of nourishment to many soups of the present day cooking.

—from *Life in Old Virginia,* by James J. McDonald, published in 1907.

S. WALLACE EDWARDS AND SONS, INC.

Rich mahogany-colored Virginia hams, slowly smoked over hickory fires, carefully aged to perfection, scented with hickory, and sliced paper-thin, have been the centerpiece of banquet tables and festive celebrations in Virginia for centuries. It's part of our proud history. Since 1926 three generations—grandfather, father, and son of the Edwards family—have held true to this special Virginia curing process and have continued a tradition of exceptional taste. It's a tradition as old as Virginia itself. When the first settlers landed in Jamestown in 1607, they discovered that the Indians had perfected a method of curing and smoking their meats. The settlers soon began keeping their own hogs on a small island below Jamestown called Hog Island, now a part of Surry County, Virginia. They followed the Indian ways of hand curing their meat and slowly smoking it over

Virginia's Finest

hickory fires to bring out its full succulent flavor. It was in 1926 that S. Wallace Edwards, the young captain of the Jamestown-Surry ferryboat, first served a ham sandwich to one of his passengers. The ham had been cured on the family farm. So quickly did the demand grow that the young captain began curing and selling this ham on a full-time basis. Soon he was supplying nearby country stores and gracious manor homes. As word of the "Edwards' ham" spread, he began shipping his products throughout the country. The flavor and texture of Edwards' hams have received the highest awards. The Edwards family even had the honor of demonstrating the art of curing at a Smithsonian Institution Folklife Festival.

Today S. Wallace Edwards & Sons remains a family endeavor following the same curing method handed down by their grandfather. The Edwards' family smokehouses are located in Surry, close to the spot where the Indians first taught the colonists the secret of bringing out the full flavor in meats.

Elegant Ham-Chicken Divan

3 (10-ounce) packages frozen broccoli spears, thawed, or fresh broccoli spears, partially cooked, drained
6 chicken breasts, cooked, shredded
8 thin slices cooked Edwards Virginia ham
1 cup mayonnaise
2 (10³/4-ounce) cans cream of chicken soup
1 tablespoon Worcestershire sauce
2 tablespoons lemon juice
1/2 teaspoon sage
1 cup grated sharp cheddar cheese
1 cup seasoned bread crumbs

• Preheat the oven to 350°F. Layer the broccoli and chicken in a buttered 9×13-inch casserole dish. Cover with the ham slices. Mix the mayonnaise, soup, Worcestershire sauce, lemon juice, and sage in a large bowl. Spoon over the layers. Sprinkle the cheese and bread crumbs over the sauce. Bake for 20 minutes or until bubbly.
• Makes 6 servings

This recipe was sent by SAM EDWARDS of S. Wallace Edwards and Sons, Inc., producers of fine Virginia hams, bacon, and sausage in Surry, Virginia.

La Petite Tea Room
& Antiques
Great Food For People With Great Taste

Old Southern Pork Cake

1/2 cup boiling water
1/4 pound salt pork, minced
2 cups flour
1/2 teaspoon baking soda
1 teaspoon cinnamon
1/2 teaspoon allspice
1/4 teaspoon nutmeg
1/4 teaspoon ground cloves
1/2 cup raisins
1/2 cup currants
2 ounces chopped citron
1 egg, beaten
1/2 cup sugar
1/2 cup molasses

• Pour the boiling water over the pork in a bowl, and let stand for 10 minutes. Preheat the oven to 300°F. Sift the flour, baking soda, cinnamon, allspice, nutmeg, and cloves together into a bowl. Add the raisins, currants, and citron to the dry ingredients, and mix well. Beat the egg, sugar, and molasses in a separate bowl, and add to the soaking pork. Stir in the fruit mixture gradually.
• Spoon the batter into a greased loaf pan lined with greased waxed paper. Bake for 1¹/2 to 1³/4 hours or until the cake tests done.
• Makes approximately 6 to 8 servings

This recipe, a specialty of the restaurant, was given by JEAN REITMEYER, La Petite Tea Room, Williamsburg, Virginia.

Italian Gravy

2 (28-ounce) cans tomato purée
1 (6-ounce) can tomato paste
1 quart chicken or beef stock
2 cups dry red wine
1/4 cup olive oil
2 medium yellow onions, chopped
6 large cloves garlic, pressed
2 ribs celery, chopped
1/2 cup chopped parsley
1/2 pound chopped mushrooms
1 tablespoon oregano, or 1/2 cup minced fresh oregano
1 tablespoon basil, or 1/2 cup minced fresh basil
1 teaspoon freshly ground pepper
2 bay leaves
1 pound pork neck bones
Salt

- Combine the tomato purée, tomato paste, stock, and red wine in a large pot. Heat the olive oil in a large frying pan. Add the onions, garlic, celery, and parsley, and sauté until tender. Add the sautéed vegetables, mushrooms, oregano, basil, pepper, bay leaves, pork neck bones, and salt to taste to the tomato mixture.
- Bring to a slow boil, and reduce the heat. Simmer, partially covered, for 2 hours, stirring frequently. Remove the bones from the pork, and skim the fat if desired. Store in a covered container for up to a week in the refrigerator or freeze. Use in any dish where a tomato sauce is needed.
- Makes about 3 quarts

This favorite Earley family recipe was adapted from The Frugal Gourmet. *After a full day at work, chopping vegetables and creating a sauce has been a healthy form of relaxation for Mark. Besides, we can double the recipe, divide it into portions, freeze it, and pull it out for any pasta dish.*

MARK L. EARLEY is a native of Chesapeake, Virginia. He practiced law there for fifteen years in the firm of Tavss, Fletcher, Earley, and King. For ten years, he served as a Virginia state senator and then as attorney general from 1997-2001. Mark is now president and CEO of Prison Fellowship Ministries in Reston, Virginia. Mark and his wife, Cynthia, reside in Loudoun County with their six children.

DID YOU KNOW THAT:

No Americans were involved in the important naval engagement fought off the coast of Cape Henry during the last days of the Revolutionary War (September 5, 1781)? The battle pitted British and French fleets, and the French victory ensured the American defeat of the British at Yorktown later in the month.

THE SMITHFIELD INN

Traditions of the first two hundred fifty years

In 1752, the Town of Smithfield was chartered by Captain Arthur Smith with some families anxious to build homes the first year. On lot number 7, on the north side of Main Street, Henry Woodley of Four Square Plantation built a brick home. In 1758, Woodley sold it to William Rand, the contractor who had built the courthouse on the adjoining lot. The next year, Rand began operating the site as a tavern. So began the ongoing innkeeping tradition as the Inn began offering hospitality to travelers who came by sailing vessel or the stage coach as it passed through on the way from Norfolk to Richmond. Later, visitors arrived by steamboat, motor vehicles, and air.

In an advertisement in the *Virginia Gazette* of Williamsburg in 1766, Rand offered to lease the Inn, giving the following description: "a spacious Brick House, upwards of 50 ft. in length, with 4 rooms below and 3 above, and a good cellar under the same in three apartments," adjoining the courthouse in the town of Smithfield. At that time, the building was a story-and-a half, with dormer windows, and a chimney at each end. After Rand's death, the Inn was leased to Richard Taylor, originator of the Gaming House on the property. In 1792, the heirs of William Rand sold the property to Mallory Todd, who then leased the Inn to various occupants. By the time of the Civil War, the structure had fallen into a dilapidated state.

Remodeling began in 1870, and soon the Reverend F.A. Meade took residence there.

A four-decade tradition began in 1922 as Daniel Webster Sykes and his wife purchased the property to begin the Sykes Inn. Folks came from miles away to see the profusion of flowers in the backyard and the exquisitely decorated parlors, and to taste the great southern dishes, such as hot biscuits, corn bread, fried chicken, smothered tenderloin, bowls of vegetables, apple cobbler, and lemon chess pie. Lines of people overcrowded the lobby, porch, and sidewalk awaiting the greatest delicacy of all: Smithfield ham.

The Sykes Inn was given the highest rating in the *Duncan Hines Directory of Fine Eating Places* for years as patrons such as John D. Rockefeller Jr. made a pilgrimage to the eighteenth-century door. Valued employee Margaret Reese Tynes helped the Sykes family carry on with Inn traditions. After Mrs. Sykes retired in 1968, several owners ran the Inn. Today, it is owned and operated by Smithfield Foods, Incorporated, and Joseph Luter III (family of Mrs. Sykes). In 1993, major renovations and additions became part of the Inn. Overnight guests and visiting diners witness the elegance and charm of the historic site as they taste the menu, which now offers a southern slant with a European twist.

Baby-Back Pork Ribs

1 full rack baby-back pork ribs	12 ounces Virginia Gentleman Bourbon BBQ Sauce

- Preheat the oven to 250°F. Wrap the ribs in foil. Bake for 3 to 4 hours, depending on the size of the ribs. Remove the ribs from the juice to a new piece of foil. Slather the ribs with the barbecue sauce. At this point you have two choices: (1) Place the ribs in the oven, and broil, uncovered, for 5 to 10 minutes, or (2) place the ribs on a hot charcoal grill for 10 minutes (which is more difficult to do since the meat is falling off the bone); I like the grill top to be down, but either works. Remove the ribs to a platter.
- Makes approximately 2 servings

Virginia's Finest

This wonderful recipe was sent to us by TIM ASHMAN, president of Ashman Manufacturing and Distribution Company. The company manufactures over 250 specialty products, which include sauces, marinades, dry blends, salad dressings, and the list goes on. Ashman has been in business fifteen years after starting out with one product, its House London Broil Sauce. The company manufactures for large and small businesses, and its specialty is gourmet sauces.

Peanut-Crusted Pork with Bourbon Mushroom Cream

1 pound pork loin, cut into $^{1}/_{4}$-inch slices	$1^{1}/_{2}$ cups sliced shiitake mushrooms
2 cups salted peanuts, chopped	1 tablespoon chopped garlic
$^{1}/_{4}$ cup canola oil	3 tablespoons to $^{1}/_{4}$ cup sugar
$1^{1}/_{2}$ cups sliced button mushrooms	$^{1}/_{2}$ cup bourbon
	2 cups heavy cream

- Preheat the oven to 350°F. Coat 1 side of the pork with the peanuts, and place, peanut side up, in an oiled baking pan. Bake for about 5 minutes or until done. Heat the oil in a medium saucepan over medium heat, and add the mushrooms and garlic. Cook for about 4 minutes. Stir in the sugar, and remove from the heat. Add the bourbon, and cook for 3 minutes. Stir in the heavy cream, and reduce the heat. Cook until the sauce thickens, stirring frequently. Spoon over the pork.
- Makes 4 to 6 servings

BETTY THOMAS, Smithfield Inn, Smithfield, Virginia, sent in this delicious recipe. It's a favorite at the Inn.

FORMER GOVERNOR GERALD L. BALILE'S

Asian Marinated Pork Tenderloin with Cantaloupe Salsa

PORK

1 tablespoon minced fresh cilantro	1 tablespoon Thai red chili sauce
2 cloves garlic, minced	4 teaspoons grated fresh gingerroot
1/4 cup white or red wine	
2 tablespoons soy sauce	1/4 teaspoon freshly ground black pepper
2 tablespoons molasses	
1 tablespoon Asian sesame oil	2 (8-ounce) pork tenderloins, trimmed
1 tablespoon Thai black bean garlic paste	

CANTALOUPE SALSA

1/4 cantaloupe, finely chopped	1 jalapeño pepper, minced
2 tablespoons minced onion	Dash of lime juice
	Dash of salt

- To prepare the pork tenderloins, combine the cilantro, garlic, wine, soy sauce, molasses, sesame oil, black bean garlic paste, red chili sauce, gingerroot, and black pepper in a large bowl, and mix well. Add the pork, turning to coat. Refrigerate, covered with plastic wrap, for at least 2 hours or up to 10 hours, turning the pork tenderloins occasionally.
- Preheat the oven to 375°F. Drain the pork tenderloins, discarding the marinade. Place pork tenderloins in a roasting pan, and bake for 1 hour or until a meat thermometer inserted in the thickest portion of the tenderloin registers 140°F. Let stand for 10 minutes, and cut into thin slices.
- To prepare the cantaloupe salsa, combine the cantaloupe, onion, jalapeño pepper, lime juice, and salt in a medium bowl, and mix well. Serve the salsa on the side as an accompaniment to the pork.
- Makes 3 to 4 servings

I have been long impressed during my international travels with the understated elegance of Asian design, decorating, and culinary offerings. This recipe comes from one of those memorable trips.

This recipe was graciously shared by the HONORABLE GERALD L. BALILES, former governor of Virginia. Governor Baliles was graduated from Wesleyan University with a Bachelor of Arts degree in government in 1963 and from the University of Virginia with a degree in law in 1967. A partner in his law firm, he became first the attorney general in 1982, then governor of Virginia from 1986 to 1990. He remains active in Virginia, national, and international law, focusing on aviation, trade, and transportation law with Hunton and Williams of Richmond. He serves on many boards and commissions as well.

PREHISTORIC SETTLEMENT OF VIRGINIA

The enigmatic question of just how and when the Western Hemisphere was populated by prehistoric ancestors of the American Indian has recently been the subject of a renewed scrutiny by anthropologists and archaeologists. For years, it has been generally accepted that the first waves of migrants crossed the Bering Land Bridge from Siberia some ten thousand or so years ago, that they traveled southward through today's Alaska and Canada, and that they entered the present-day United States along an ice-free corridor into the western part of the country. From there, it was supposed that various bands of the prehistoric wanderers spread out and eventually populated North and South America. This logic was based upon a 1937 discovery near Clovis, New Mexico, which placed man-made spear points *in situ* with Ice Age mammoth remains. Through various methods of dating, the remains of so-called "Clovis Man" were determined to be around ten thousand years old. It was further supposed that the Clovis culture represented the very first appearance of man in the New World.

Pork Tenderloin

$^{1}/_{2}$ cup soy sauce	2 tablespoons brown sugar
$^{1}/_{2}$ cup catsup	1 clove garlic, crushed
$^{1}/_{2}$ cup white wine	1 pork tenderloin

- Preheat the oven to 350°F. Combine the soy sauce, catsup, wine, brown sugar, and garlic in a medium bowl, and mix well. Place the pork tenderloin in a baking pan on a low oven rack. Coat with the soy sauce mixture. Cook for about 30 minutes or until done.
- May add a jar of baby food peaches or apricots if desired.
- Makes variable number of servings, depending on the size of the tenderloin. Plan on $^{1}/_{2}$-pound servings per person.

Jean MacArthur, the wife of General Douglas MacArthur, loved pork, so I often served it when I entertained for her. And her favorite dessert was pecan pie. The first time that she came for dinner, she spotted Fortaleza, our Filipino steward, in the kitchen. She immediately went over and sat on a stool and munched carrots while he was preparing to serve dinner.

This recipe is from the collection of IRENE ANDERSON. Major General Norman Anderson was executive director of The MacArthur Memorial in Norfolk, Virginia, and he and his wife entertained Mrs. MacArthur frequently.

Following relief from command in Korea by President Truman on April 11, 1951, General MacArthur toured the United States, accepting the accolades of many cities. Norfolk chose to honor the general's mother, Norfolk native Mary Pinkney Hardy MacArthur, by creating a park near the site of her home, Riveredge, in the Berkley section of the city. On November 19, 1951, the general and his family were on hand to dedicate the park. The general was touched by this tribute, and he never forgot it. He yearned to return to his ancestral home, Norfolk. He was scheduled to attend the dedication of the MacArthur Memorial May 30, 1964. He died just weeks short of that date. He and his wife were laid to rest in the rotunda of the Memorial.

DID YOU KNOW THAT:

From 1934 till 1958, when the oversight was corrected by law, Virginia had no state executive officers for about a half-day during each inaugural year? The discrepancy occurred because outgoing officers left their jobs on the day before the newly elected officials were sworn in.

Recently, this entire scenario has been questioned. Archaeological sites in several parts of both North and South America—two of them located in Virginia—have been discovered, and intense, on-going investigation of these sites suggest that they predate the Clovis culture. Cactus Hill, located along the Nottoway River, has been investigated by members of the National Geographic Society and the Archaeological Society of Virginia, and evidences of human habitation there have been determined to date to between 15,000 and 17,000 years ago. Similar remains at Saltville, located in southwestern Virginia, date to around 14,500 years ago.

Clearly, these two Virginia sites suggest that man has inhabited the New World for thousands of years longer than once supposed. And, because new research shows that the so-called "ice-free corridor" was not really ice-free during these early times, another pathway to the interior of North and South America has been suggested—via watercraft southward along the Pacific Rim.

Fran's Fast Pasta Dinner

2 to 3 tablespoons olive oil	1 (12-ounce) package
3 Italian sausages or	specialty- flavored
3 chicken breasts,	pasta, preferably Pasta
cut into bite-size pieces	Valente Garlic Parsley
1 onion, sliced, or 1 red bell	Fettuccine or Tomato
pepper, julienned, or both	Basil Fettuccine
1 package frozen broccoli,	Salt and pepper
peas, or cauliflower	Grated Parmesan cheese or
1 cup water or chicken stock	feta cheese

- Heat the olive oil in a medium pan over medium heat until warm. Add the meat and onion or bell pepper. Cook for about 10 minutes or until the meat is completely cooked, stirring frequently. Place the frozen vegetables on the meat, and pour the water or chicken stock over the vegetables. Steam, covered, for 2 minutes or until the vegetables are tender.
- Cook the pasta in boiling salted water in a large pot for about 3 to 4 minutes. Drain the pasta in a colander. Place the pasta in a serving bowl, and spoon the meat and vegetables over the top. Season with salt and pepper to taste. Sprinkle with the grated Parmesan cheese or feta cheese, and toss gently.
- Makes 4 to 6 servings

This is my favorite for a fast meal. One night my children were hungry, and we were running late. I only had plain pasta in my house, and while I waited 20 minutes for the pasta to cook, I knew right then and there that "never again" would I run out of Pasta Valente at home. This is my any-pasta dinner in 20 minutes. Sometimes I use canned artichoke hearts, onions, and chicken. I use what I have in the cupboard. You may cook on high to create color, or you may cover and steam. I do what I need to do to get dinner on the table. I cover and steam if the children need my attention. Otherwise I cook on high to give the meat color.

Virginia's Finest

FRAN VALENTE began Pasta Valente in 1982. Her daughter Mary Ann joined the company a few years later. Together they make over 100 different, all-natural pasta and sauce products available in specialty stores across the country. Mrs. Valente raised five children on pasta and now is raising fifteen grandchildren on it. It's only natural she would want to share her secrets with you.

DID YOU KNOW THAT:

Aaron Burr, the former vice president of the United States, was acquitted of treason charges at Richmond (September 1, 1807)?

THE LANE COMPANY'S "HOPE CHESTS"

John and Edward Lane Sr. started the famous cedar chest company in 1912 in a tiny town called Altavista near Lynchburg. It was famous throughout the United States for seals so tight that it prevented moths from doing damage to anything within. They even offered a mothproof insurance policy. They were truly "Hope Chests," designed to protect very special heirlooms and often were a gift for a newly married couple.

During the Great Depression, the Lanes went to great lengths to pay their workers when money and orders were almost nonexistent. Their country, as well as their community, were important to them, and during World War II, they made ammunition boxes — but never collected the money owed them by the federal government.

The Lane family sold their company to Furniture Brands International in 1988. In September 2001, the last Lane chest was manufactured in Altavista. They are now made in China, but the Lanes still take pride in the company's American and Virginian roots.

—*The Virginian-Pilot*, July 25, 2002

NORFOLK STATE UNIVERSITY

Norfolk State University was founded in 1935. The college came to life in the midst of the Depression, providing a setting in which youth of the region could give expression to their hopes and aspirations. Today, more than 7,000 students take courses at Norfolk State University. The University is proud to be one of the largest, predominately African-American institutions in Virginia.

Jambalaya

$1/4$ cup vegetable oil
1 to 2 tablespoons all-purpose flour
1 medium onion, peeled, chopped
$1/2$ medium bell pepper, seeded, chopped
$1/2$ pound seasoning ham chunks, chopped
$1/2$ pound smoked sausage, cut into $1/2$-inch slices
$1/8$ cup water
1 pound hot sausage
3 pounds medium to large shrimp, peeled, deveined
Salt and pepper
3 tablespoons seasoning salt, such as Lawry's
1 (8-ounce) can tomato sauce
1 (16-ounce) can chopped tomatoes
8 cups boiling water
6 cloves garlic, peeled, chopped
1 bunch green onions, rinsed, chopped
1 tablespoon dried thyme
2 dried whole bay leaves
3 tablespoons minced parsley
1 (32-ounce) package white rice, such as Uncle Ben's

- Heat the oil in a large Dutch oven over low heat. Add the flour, and stir to make a smooth light brown roux about the color of caramel custard. Add the onion and bell pepper, simmering until the onion and bell pepper are soft. Add the ham chunks and smoked sausage, and simmer until heated through.
- Combine $1/8$ cup water and the hot sausage in a skillet, pricking the sausage in several places to allow the juices to flow into the skillet. Cook, covered, until the hot sausage is almost done, turning once. Remove the hot sausage from the skillet, and cut into $1/2$-inch slices, reserving the juices in the skillet. Place the shrimp in the skillet with the reserved sausage liquid, and season with salt and pepper to taste and the seasoning salt. Simmer until the shrimp are tender and turn pink. Do not overcook.
- Add the tomato sauce and undrained tomatoes to the Dutch oven. Stir in the boiling water, garlic, shrimp, hot sausage, green onions, thyme, and bay leaves. Bring the mixture to a low boil over medium heat, and add the parsley and additional salt and pepper if necessary. Add the rice, folding slowly in from the bottom of the Dutch oven. Cook, covered, for 45 minutes or until the rice is tender and a small amount of the liquid remains, folding from the bottom of the Dutch oven to keep the ingredients from sticking after about 30 minutes. Note: Folding the ingredients from the bottom of the Dutch oven helps to evenly distribute the ingredients through the fluffing rice and allows the steam to be evenly distributed.
- Makes 10 to 14 servings

This is a wonderful dish for Mardi Gras company, especially when served with red beans on the side and some fried chicken.

The recipe is shared by MARIE McDEMMOND, a native of New Orleans, Louisiana, where members of her family were in the catering business. She is president of Norfolk State University in Norfolk, Virginia. She is the mother of two adult sons and believes strongly in community and young people.

MARTINETTE FAMILY 'S
Sunday Spaghetti Gravy

2 (14.5-ounce) cans peeled whole tomatoes
3 large cloves garlic
1 medium onion, peeled, cut into quarters
$1/2$ teaspoon salt
$1/2$ teaspoon black pepper
$1/2$ teaspoon sugar
1 teaspoon dried oregano
1 (28-ounce) can tomato purée

1 (28-ounce) can water
2 bay leaves
$1/4$ cup grated Parmesan cheese
1 loaf Italian bread, optional
Browned sausage, browned meatballs or ground beef, crabmeat in season, optional

- Process the tomatoes, garlic, onion, salt, pepper, sugar, and oregano in a blender until of a smooth consistency. Pour the tomato mixture into a large pot, and add the tomato purée and water. Bring to a boil over high heat. Boil for 15 minutes or until there is no pink foam, stirring frequently. Reduce the heat to low. Add the bay leaves and cheese, and simmer for at least 1 hour. Add the meats if desired, and simmer until heated through.
- Note: The longer the sauce simmers, the better the flavors blend.
- Makes 12 servings

SAM MARTINETTE is a lifelong resident of Norfolk and Hampton Roads. He managed restaurants during the formation of the Ghent Restaurant District in the 1970s, and his popular weekly newspaper column on restaurants was widely read from 1988 to 2001.

ESSEX COUNTY

Essex County was most likely named for the county of the same name in England. It was organized in 1692 from the original Rappahannock County. Covering two hundred fifty-eight square miles, its population is 9,989, and its county seat is Tappahannock.

Essex County was the site of the two primary towns of the local Portobago Indians, as well as the location of "Appamatuck," referred to by Captain John Smith in his writings. Fort Lowery, a Confederate post built for the defense of Fredericksburg, was built in this county.

ROWENA'S KITCHEN TIPS

Add a very small amount of lemon juice or vinegar while cooking vegetables to prevent them from discoloring. This also sharpens the taste.

SPAGHETTI "GRAVY"

The following suggestion is optional, but recommended: use the heel of a loaf of Italian bread, or white bread if you must dip the bread to sample the gravy .... I mean sauce. I know foodies cringe hearing the word gravy substituted for sauce in connection with pasta, and I'll admit I no longer refer to spaghetti gravy and have long since learned that there are many sauces for the various forms of pasta. But it wasn't always that way.

Growing up as an Italian-American child in the Norfolk of the early 1950s, I was keenly aware of something different about my father's side of the family. His many brothers and sisters always seemed to have more life than the quiet Scottish-English ancestors my mother claimed. The fact that there were thirteen children at my father's dinner table when he was a child no doubt raised the decibel level of discourse, even for a simple request such as passing the butter.

There was no mistaking the affection shared among those first generation American siblings, and the central point for the spreading of gossip or family history was Sunday lunch. That generation had already marched head first into the American melting pot, having anglicized the Italian name Martignetti to Martinette following the family's migration south from North End Boston to New Jersey, then to Virginia, where my grandfather worked as a carpenter during World War I. Only one of my dad's generation spoke fluent Italian, a language I later studied at Old Dominion University, paying good money to learn the basics of the tongue of my ancestors. I have always been fascinated by films portraying the Italian neighborhoods of the Northeast, because my family worked hard just to be Americans. Today we all blend in, and certainly times have changed for the better in many ways, but one constant remains.

My mother learned to cook the family gravy from her Italian mother-in-law. My wife, Julie, learned from my mother. So, even if my children, Nick, Jake, and Amy groan, "not pasta again." on Sunday, you can bet there will be a pot of gravy bubbling on the stove and bread nearby.

—Sam Martinette

Tomato Black Bean Dinner with Tomato Salsa

3 fresh tomatoes, chopped
2 green onions, chopped
1 tablespoon balsamic vinegar
Salt and pepper
1 medium onion, chopped
1 large clove garlic, minced
2 tablespoons olive oil
1/2 pound kielbasa, cut into small cubes
2 (16-ounce) cans black beans, rinsed, drained
1 teaspoon cumin
1 tablespoon chopped cilantro
1 large tomato, chopped
Sour cream, optional

- Combine the tomatoes, green onions, balsamic vinegar, and salt and pepper to taste in a bowl, and set aside.
- Sauté the onion and garlic in the olive oil in a medium saucepan until soft. Add the kielbasa, beans, cumin, and cilantro, and mix well. Cook for 8 to 10 minutes.
- Stir in the tomato, and cook until heated through. Serve the beans with 1 tablespoon of the fresh salsa and, if desired, a dollop of sour cream.
- Makes approximately 6 servings

During one of our pledge drives, the local public television station, WHRO in Norfolk, asked the community to submit tomato recipes for a "T is for Tomato" cook-off. It was a great year for our tomatoes, and Bob was continually trying out new recipes. We finally decided on this recipe to send to the station. WHRO called and asked us to cook on TV. Now Jacques and Julia we were not, but we had a wonderful time with the "T is for Tomato" and our friends pledged for WHRO.

The recipe is shared by BEVERLEY and BOB PARRISH.

FAIRFAX COUNTY

Fairfax County was organized in1742 from Loudoun and Prince William Counties. Named for Lord Thomas Fairfax, owner of the Northern Neck, it contains four hundred seventeen square miles and is home to 969,749 residents. The county seat is Fairfax.

George Washington's Mount Vernon estate, built in 1743 by his brother, Lawrence, is located in this county, as is Washington's other plantation, Woodlawn. The Union Army's southern defense lines protecting Washington, D.C., ran through much of Fairfax County.

Thanksgiving Day

By Rowena Tyler Morrel

Raised on my grandfather's farm in Central Virginia in the 1940s, I learned country ways of living that had been practiced there since the 1880s. We farmed with mules and horses and raised all of our food except the game we hunted in season. Thanksgiving did not provide the usual fare because area sportsmen came to hunt and feast on famous Tyler's Brunswick Stew. For the men, this daylong hunt was part of the good life. For Mamma Tyler, my grandmother, and my mother, it was an opportunity to purge our food storage, making way for fresh game and hog killing that would follow in a few days.

Before Thanksgiving, my mother and grandmother went through the food storage, selecting meats and vegetables that should be used to make way for fresh game and pork. We did not have electricity until 1950, so meats were preserved by smoking or canning and some premium beef and pork were stored in a frozen food locker in a nearby town. Typically, vegetables and game that had been canned the year before were earmarked for this stew. Two days before Thanksgiving, an array of foods were brought to the kitchen.

Quarts of butter beans, corn, and string beans; rabbit and squirrel; half-gallon jars of tomatoes; stored potatoes, onions, and a few turnips came from the cellar. Smoked ham hocks came from the smokehouse. By dawn on Thanksgiving Day, everything was simmering in a very large cast-iron pot over an open fire in the yard. The stew was ready by late morning, and hunters helped themselves throughout the day. Cornbread was baked and served in large cast-iron skillets. It's hard to say how many people were served, but I know that we had twenty tin plates; it was my job to see that clean plates and spoons were always available.

I found this handwritten list of ingredients, no preparation notes or quantities, in the back of Mamma Tyler's cookbook in the late 1950s, labeled Tyler's Brunswick Stew. In the mid-1960s, I asked my mother to try to reconstruct the procedure. Here's the recipe for Tyler's Brunswick Stew, which I have developed and used for many years.

MAMMA TYLER'S LIST:

10 quarts of butter beans
10 quarts of corn
5 quarts of string beans
4 quarts of canned squirrel
2 quarts of canned rabbit
10 half-gallons of tomatoes
Bushel of potatoes, onions, and turnips
6 ham hocks
Venison hindquarter or 10 pounds of beef shank
Water and stock to make 25 to 30 gallons
Handful of herbs, salt, and black pepper

I know that this list was just a guideline because the objective was to use what we had.

MOTHER'S PREPARATION REMARKS:

Ham hocks were scrubbed and soaked in water for several days, then boiled until they fell apart, skinned, boned, lean pulled and put back into stock. Skins were roasted until crisp, chopped and left out to sprinkle on top of the stew.

Venison was covered with bacon and slow roasted without liquid. What you were after was the roasted flavor. If you had to add water to get it to be very tender, you added it after the browning. It was cut in small pieces and added to the pot, along with the pan juices. Beef shanks were treated the same way. The roasting and browning were important to the flavor of the stew.

We used twice as many potatoes as we did onions and just a few turnips. Potatoes were scrubbed and peeled only when necessary. Turnips were peeled. All were rough chopped.

Before light on Thanksgiving morning, a fire was built outside and the kettle was heated.

All of the canned food went in the hot kettle and was allowed to slow boil for a half-hour before the prepared and canned meats were added. This took about an hour in the cold open air. The ham and venison were chopped, pulled, and added to the pot with stock and juices available. When this had simmered awhile, the raw vegetables were added.

Salt and black pepper were added with each ingredient. But a lot of salt was used in canning, so you had to be careful with the salt. The herbs grew at the back door. We just pulled a handful that always contained parsley, rosemary, sage, and thyme and threw them in the pot.

—Blanche Tyler

Rowena's Tyler Brunswick Stew

Backs and front legs of 1 squirrel and
   1 rabbit (hind legs are reserved for a
   more elegant fare)
2 chicken backs and wings (2 legs may be
   substituted for rabbit and squirrel)
About 2 pounds venison or beef stew meat,
   cut into 1-inch pieces
1 country-cured ham hock, or $1^1/_3$ pounds
   country-cured ham
$^1/_4$ cup plus 2 tablespoons bacon drippings or
   cooking oil
6 large potatoes, scrubbed, cut into
   1-inch pieces
3 large onions, peeled, coarsely chopped
1 large turnip, peeled, cut into 1-inch pieces
1 quart home-canned or frozen butter beans
1 quart canned or frozen corn
1 pint home-canned or frozen green beans
4 quarts canned tomatoes
Parsley, sage, rosemary, and thyme, finely
   chopped
Salt and pepper to taste
2 quarts water or stock

Choose a large heavy kettle that will eventually hold 4 gallons of stew. Boil ham hock until it falls apart. Pull the lean meat, and reserve the stock. Parboil the chicken, squirrel, and rabbit in water to cover; add salt, pepper and sage; cool and pull the meat from the bones. Sauté venison or beef stew meat in bacon drippings in a large heavy pot until browned on all sides, add half the chopped onions, add 2 quarts of the stock. Cover and simmer until tender. Meanwhile, peel and chop the fresh vegetables; assemble the frozen or canned vegetables and the herbs. Pour the vegetables into the simmering pot; increase the heat until all is simmering. Remove the lid; add fresh herbs, and simmer for 1 hour. Cool and refrigerate for a day. This stew is always better the second day.

My father said that my stew is better than that made years ago. I think he is prejudiced — and I think he is right. I have given more care to developing flavors during the various cooking stages. But Tyler Farm is certainly the genesis of my Brunswick stew. On occasion, I have prepared the various cooking stages in my kitchen and simmered the last hour on an open fire outdoors. On Thanksgiving Day 1996, my husband and I prepared my recipe on an open fire for our hunting friends who were kind enough to contribute game bagged earlier in the season. It was a huge success.

Microwave Hints

- **Gravy:** Brown flour in butter or fat from roast or meat in flat glass dish, add liquid—milk or water—mix, and cook 2 minutes or so at 50 percent heat. You will have no lumps.
- **Ears of fresh corn:** Wrap each ear in wax paper, and heat for 3 minutes (per ear) on high.
- **Chocolate:** Put squares of unsweetened chocolate or chocolate chips in a glass dish on high for 1 to 2 minutes and stir.
- **Roast chicken:** Put one small (2- to 3-pound) chicken in a covered glass dish on high for 28 minutes. The chicken will be brown from the fat in the skin, and the meat will be moist and tender.
- **Freshen nuts, chips, or crackers:** Place them on a paper towel in the microwave for no more than 60 seconds on high; remove and let stand for 2 minutes to dry, and they are ready to eat.
- **Hot pastrami and cheese sandwiches:** Put mustard on frozen bread slices; add pastrami and cheese. Lay a paper towel over the sandwich, and heat on high for 2 minutes.
- **Hot chocolate:** Add cocoa to cold milk, and place marshmallows on top. Cover loosely with a paper towel, and heat 2 minutes.

Shared by BOBBI WRIGHT, a Navy wife who was known in Northern Virginia for her fun and elegant entertaining and for being a really special and super-creative teacher of young children.

Poultry

Miss Annette's
Chicken and Chips Casserole

1¹/4 cups chopped celery
¹/2 cup sliced mushrooms
2 tablespoons butter
3 cups cooked chicken
1 (10³/4-ounce) can cream
    of chicken soup, diluted
    with ¹/4 cup milk

1 cup sour cream
³/4 cup mayonnaise
1 cup slivered almonds
¹/4 teaspoon salt
1 cup shredded sharp
    cheddar cheese
¹/2 cup crushed potato chips

- Preheat the oven to 375°F. Sauté the celery and mushrooms in the butter in a saucepan until tender. Add the chicken, soup mixture, sour cream, mayonnaise, almonds, and salt, and mix well. Spoon into 9×13-inch baking dish. Sprinkle with the cheese, and top with the potato chips. Bake for 35 minutes.
- Makes 6 to 8 servings

JIM and ANNETTE MOORE, Tabb (York County), Virginia, friends of Winette Jeffery, shared this recipe.

Chinese Chicken

2 cups cubed cooked
    chicken
1 cup chopped celery
1 cup cooked rice
³/4 cup mayonnaise
1 cup sliced fresh
    mushrooms
1 teaspoon chopped onion
1 teaspoon lemon juice

1 teaspoon salt
1 (10³/4-ounce) can cream
    of chicken soup
4 ounces slivered water
    chestnuts, drained
¹/2 cup (1 stick) butter or
    margarine
¹/2 cup slivered almonds
1 cup cornflakes

- Preheat the oven to 350°F. Combine the chicken, celery, rice, mayonnaise, mushrooms, onion, lemon juice, salt, soup, and water chestnuts in a 2-quart casserole dish, and mix well. Melt the butter in a saucepan, and stir in the almonds and cornflakes. Cook for a few minutes. Sprinkle over the top of the casserole. Bake for 35 minutes.
- Makes 6 to 8 servings

This is a great party dish.

This recipe came from *Virginia Hospitality* and was shared by SAMANTHA BISHOP, president of the Junior League of Hampton Roads.

DID YOU KNOW THAT:

The Compleat Housewife, released in Williamsburg in 1742, was the first cookbook ever published in America?

Chicken and Dumplings

5 pounds whole chicken
3 ribs celery, chopped
1 large onion, chopped
6 cubes chicken bouillon
2 teaspoons dried tarragon
$1/2$ teaspoon poultry
  seasoning
$1/4$ teaspoon pepper
$1/2$ teaspoon salt
5 quarts water
5 (7.5-ounce) cans
  refrigerated biscuits
Flour

• Rinse the chicken, and place in a large stockpot with the celery, onion, bouillon, tarragon, poultry seasoning, pepper, salt, and water. Bring to a boil, and reduce the heat. Simmer, covered, for $1^1/2$ hours or until the chicken is tender. Remove the chicken from the broth and let stand to cool. Remove the meat from the bones, and shred, discarding the skin and bones. Skim the fat from the broth, and strain the broth into a large pot.
• Roll each biscuit approximately $1/8$ inch thick on a well-floured board, making sure each side of the biscuit is lightly dusted with flour. Cut each round into $1/2$-inch strips. Return the broth to a slow boil. Add the dumplings a few at a time, stirring until all are mixed in. Simmer, covered, for 20 minutes or until the dumplings are tender. Add the shredded chicken, and simmer until the chicken is heated through. Add additional broth if the mixture becomes too thick. Ladle into serving bowls.
• Makes 12 to 16 servings

This Archers' family favorite came from Sandy's grandmother in Virginia Beach.

SANDY and BOB ARCHER live in Salem. Bob is president of The Blue Ridge Beverage Company, which dates back to the post prohibition era, when it was founded in 1938 as a small wholesaler of beer and soft drinks. Since 1958, the company has been under direct ownership and management of the Archer family. It now is one of the largest wholesale beverage distributors in Virginia. Bob also has worked diligently for business in Virginia and was chairman of the governor's Small Business Advisory Board for years-a chairmanship to which I succeeded him. —Rowena

FAUQUIER COUNTY

Fauquier County was formed in 1759 from land originally belonging to Prince William County. Named in honor of Frances Fauquier (1703-1768), the governor of Virginia from 1758 until his death, the county contains six hundred sixty-six square miles. The population is 55,139, and the county seat is Warrenton.

Chief Justice of the U.S. Supreme Court John Marshall (1755-1835) was born in this county. Much of the action during the Campaign of Second Manassas in August 1862, also occurred here.

THE STORY OF JAMESTOWN SETTLEMENT

JAMESTOWN SETTLEMENT

The story of America's beginnings—from the first permanent English settlement in 1607 to the decisive Revolutionary War victory in 1781—is told at Jamestown Settlement and Yorktown Victory Center. Administered by the Jamestown-Yorktown Foundation, which is an educational agency of the Commonwealth of Virginia, Jamestown Settlement and Yorktown Victory Center are accredited by the American Association of Museums. Each offers a distinctive rendering of America's beginnings.

Jamestown Settlement is a living-history museum of seventeenth-century Virginia. It is located directly beside Historic Jamestowne, administered by the Association for the Preservation of Virginia Antiquities and by the National Park Service.

The film *Jamestown: The Beginning* provides an overview of the colony's first years. Gallery exhibits detail social, political, and economic conditions that motivated exploration of the New World, describe the land and lifestyle of the people who inhabited coastal Virginia when the settlers arrived, and trace the first one hundred years of the colony.

Chicken and Yellow Rice

1 chicken, cut into pieces, rinsed	1 large green bell pepper, cut into bite-size pieces
Water	2 (5-ounce) bags yellow
Salt	rice, such as Mahatma
1/4 cup vegetable oil	4 cups chicken stock
1 large onion, sliced, cut into thin strips	

- Place the chicken in a large pan, and cover with cold water. Add salt to taste, and bring to a boil. Cook until the chicken is tender. Cut the meat from the chicken into small pieces when cool enough to handle, discarding the skin and bones. Reserve the chicken stock.
- Heat the vegetable oil in a skillet, and add the onion and green pepper. Sauté until soft.
- Cook the rice, covered, in 4 cups of the chicken stock in a medium saucepan for about 20 minutes. Add the sautéed onion and green pepper, and chicken to the rice, and cook for 5 to 10 minutes longer. Remove the saucepan from the heat, and let the mixture stand for a few minutes.
- Makes 6 to 8 servings

This is one of my family's and friends' favorite dishes. Serve with seasoned black beans (I use canned ones and season them with a little bacon grease and pepper), your favorite salad, and hot bread. Enjoy!

This recipe comes from the kitchen of GLORIA BUNTING, a one-person, caring committee for all those in need, and president of Quality Camera and Photo Imaging, Inc., which has been in the historic Ghent section of Norfolk, Virginia, for forty years.

FLOYD COUNTY

Floyd County was formed in 1831 from land in Montgomery County. Named for John Floyd (1783-1837), Virginia's governor from 1830 to 1834, the county contains three hundred seventy-six square miles. Its population is 13,874, and its county seat is Floyd.

The town of Floyd was originally called Jacksonville in honor of Andrew Jackson, the president of the United States at the time. Admiral Robley D. Evans, noted for his Spanish-American War service, was born in this county.

DID YOU KNOW THAT:

The first commercially profitable agricultural product grown by Virginians was tobacco?

A functioning replica of James Fort is recreated in the triangular palisade, with three bulwarks at the corners. Recreated wattle and daub houses with thatched roofs and three public buildings are within the walls. A church, an armory, and a storehouse are represented. Visitors may grind corn, steer with a whipstaff or tiller, try on armor, and climb into a dugout canoe. Close by is the short path to the James River where actual replicas of the *Susan Constant*, *Godspeed*, and *Discovery* are anchored in the water. Conditions of shipboard living are available for visitors to witness and explore.

The Powhatan Indian Village replica extends welcome with "yehakins"—houses—used for sleeping and storage. The houses are made of sapling frames covered with reed mats. A ceremonial-dance circle, garden, hide-tanning area, and fields are also represented. Historical interpreters discuss and demonstrate the Powhatan way of life. They grow and prepare food, process animal hides, make tools and pottery, and weave natural fibers into cordage. Hands-on experiences are available daily. The foundation suggests that the original Historic Jamestowne be visited as well.

Poulet a l'Oriental

CHICKEN

1 whole (approximately 4-pound) chicken, skin removed	4 cinnamon sticks
	10 cardamom seeds
	1 tablespoon salt
1 medium yellow or white onion, chopped	Pinch of black pepper
	12 cups water
5 ribs celery, cut into 1-inch pieces	

RICE AND GROUND BEEF

3 cups basmati rice	2 tablespoons butter or margarine
Warm water	
1 pound lean ground beef	6 cups chicken broth
	1 teaspoon salt

NUT AND RAISIN TOPPING

1 tablespoon butter or margarine	$1/4$ cup pine nuts
	$1/4$ cup golden raisins
$1/4$ cup sliced almonds	

- To prepare the chicken, place the chicken in a large stockpot with the onion, celery, cinnamon sticks, cardamom seeds, salt, pepper, and water. Simmer for about 1 hour or until the chicken is cooked through. Remove the chicken from the stockpot, and let stand. Remove and discard the bones when the chicken is cool enough to handle. Strain the broth into a separate large container. Remove and discard the cinnamon sticks and cardamom seeds. Combine the onions, celery, and chicken in a bowl, and refrigerate. Place the broth in the refrigerator, and cool until the fat rises to the top. Skim the fat with a spoon.
- To prepare the rice and ground beef, rinse the rice thoroughly in warm water, and drain in a colander. Soak the rice in warm water in a large pot for 15 minutes, and drain. Sauté the ground beef in 1 tablespoon of the butter or margarine in a large skillet. Add the rice, and sauté, stirring for 15 to 20 seconds. Add the broth and salt, stirring well. Pour the mixture into a pot, and bring to a boil. Boil until the broth recedes from the surface. Turn off the heat, and let stand, covered, for 15 minutes. Spread the mixture onto a baking sheet to let some of the heat dissipate and to stop the cooking process. Return the warm mixture to the pot, fluff with a fork, and mix in the remaining butter.
- To prepare the topping, melt the butter or margarine in a medium skillet, and sauté the almonds, pine nuts, and raisins until golden brown.
- To serve, heat the chicken in a small amount of the broth. Place the rice on a platter, and top with the chicken. Spoon the nuts and raisins over the chicken and rice. Serve with plain yogurt.
- Makes approximately 12 servings

This recipe is from GEORGE W. AZAR, the president of Azar's Natural Foods, Inc., of Virginia Beach.

AZAR'S NATURAL FOODS, INC.

Along with his son-in-law, Tony Saady, George W. Azar operates Azar's Market and Café and produces a complete line of Lebanese, Middle Eastern, and Mediterranean products. Azar's hummus, tabouli, couscous, pestos, stuffed grape leaves, and other dips and spreads are widely available in grocery and defense commissary stores.

He opened his business in Virginia Beach quite by happenstance. He and his wife, Laila, were owners of a restaurant in New Hampshire. They decided to sell the business and take a long-deserved vacation visiting friends and relatives in Florida. While making a stop in New York City, someone broke into his car and attempted to steal it. The ignition was fouled, and he was able to drive the car only by using a knife for a key. That lasted until he got to Virginia Beach, where he had friends. Then the car died. George looked over the area and liked what he saw. He bought a house the next week and called his children in Massachusetts to tell them they were moving to Virginia. Asked why he made such a bold move, he says, "I liked the idea of shoveling sand rather than snow."

Virginia's Finest

VIRGINIA'S INDEPENDENT CITIES

Virginia is unique among the fifty states in its establishment and maintenance of independent cities. An independent city is a political entity that, in most cases, is geographically located within the physical boundaries of a particular county, yet maintains its own political and administrative independence.

Until 1892, a special act by the Virginia General Assembly was required to create an independent city. Since then, such status can be bestowed by petitioning the circuit court. Most of the Commonwealth's larger communities are independent cities. In the case of Chesapeake, Hampton, Newport News, Suffolk, and Virginia Beach, the city has expanded its territorial limits to completely absorb the county in which it was originally located.

Virginia's forty-one independent cities:

Alexandria	Manassas
Bedford	Manassas Park
Bristol	Martinsville
Buena Vista	Newport News
Charlottesville	Norfolk
Chesapeake	Norton
Clifton Forge	Petersburg
Colonial Heights	Poquoson
Covington	Portsmouth
Danville	Radford
Emporia	Richmond
Fairfax	Roanoke
Falls Church	Salem
Franklin	South Boston
Fredericksburg	Staunton
Galax	Suffolk
Hampton	Virginia Beach
Harrisonburg	Waynesboro
Hopewell	Williamsburg
Lexington	Winchester
Lynchburg	

Cheesy Chicken

1/2 cup (1 stick) butter or margarine	1/4 cup finely grated Parmesan cheese
1 clove garlic, pressed	1 teaspoon salt
1 cup fine dried bread crumbs	1/8 teaspoon pepper
1/2 cup finely grated sharp cheddar cheese	4 boneless skinless chicken breasts

- Preheat the oven to 350°F. Combine the butter or margarine and garlic in a small saucepan. Heat until the butter or margarine melts. Combine the bread crumbs, cheeses, salt, and pepper in a medium bowl, and mix well.
- Dip the chicken breasts into the butter mixture, and coat with the bread crumb mixture. Place in a shallow 9×9-inch baking pan. Tuck the sides of each chicken breast under to form a roll.
- Pour the remaining butter mixture over the chicken, and bake, uncovered, for 1 hour.
- Makes 4 servings

This recipe is so easy. It can be made early in the day and then refrigerated until you are ready to heat it. I love serving this when we have company. I always get a lot of compliments.

Virginia State SENATOR RUSS POTTS and his wife, EMILY, submitted this recipe. Senator Potts was raised in Winchester, Virginia. In 1982, he founded Russ Potts Productions, Inc., which has promoted more sporting events than any other entity in North America. It was in 1991 that he was first elected to the Virginia Senate, 27th District, which represents a constituency of almost 200,000.

FLUVANNA COUNTY

Fluvanna County was organized in 1777 from land belonging to Albemarle County. Its name is Latin for Anne's River, after Queen Anne of England. It contains two hundred eighty-five square miles. The population is 20,047, and the county seat is Palmyra.

In the early 1600s, a Monacan Indian village flourished in this county before its inhabitants were defeated and forced to evacuate the area by the Iroquois tribe. "Texas Jack" Omohundro, a Confederate scout with General J.E.B. Stuart and later a noted protégé of "Buffalo Bill" Cody, was born here in 1846.

DID YOU KNOW THAT:

The Pentagon contains three times the floor space as the Empire State Building?

Chicken and Crabmeat in Sun-Dried Tomato Sauce

1 (8.5-ounce) jar julienne-style marinated sun-dried tomatoes
1 tablespoon butter or margarine
1 medium clove garlic, minced
1 (10½-ounce) can fat-free and 50% less sodium chicken broth
1 pint light or heavy cream
3 boneless skinless chicken breasts

Salt and freshly ground pepper
2 tablespoons vegetable oil or olive oil
2 tablespoons chopped fresh basil or 2 teaspoons dried basil
1 (6-ounce) can jumbo lump crabmeat
1 (6-ounce) can white crabmeat
1 (8-ounce) package spaghetti, prepared

- Strain the sun-dried tomatoes, and rinse. Pat lightly with a paper towel. Snip the tomatoes into bite-size pieces, or process in a mini chopper until slightly chopped.
- Melt the butter or margarine in a large saucepan over low heat. Add the garlic, and cook for 30 seconds. Stir in ¾ cup of the broth and the tomatoes, and bring to a boil. Simmer, uncovered, over medium heat for 10 minutes. Add the cream, and bring to a boil, stirring constantly. Simmer over medium heat until the sauce is thick enough to coat the back of a spoon.
- Sprinkle the chicken with salt and pepper to taste. Heat the oil in a large skillet, and add the chicken. Cook just until the chicken is no longer pink inside. Remove to a plate, cover, and keep warm.
- Drain the skillet, discarding the fat. Add the remaining broth, and bring to a boil, stirring the pan juices. Boil to reduce slightly, and add the pan juices to the tomato sauce. Stir in the basil and crabmeat, and remove from the heat.
- Slice the chicken breasts diagonally, and place over the pasta in a serving dish. Pour the sauce over the chicken and pasta.
- Makes 6 servings

This dish is even better the next day.

From LARRY BLY, chef of the popular television cooking show, *Cookin' Cheap* in the Roanoke Valley. It is one of America's longest running cooking shows. With a sense of humor and tongue in cheek, Bly makes this a show you would really enjoy. Be sure you check out the Cook Sisters, those sweet aunties named Sister and Toots.

DID YOU KNOW THAT:

Both the Revolutionary War and the War Between the States ended in Virginia (at Yorktown and at Appomattox Court House, respectively)?

YORKTOWN VICTORY CENTER

The story of America's beginnings look to the decisive Revolutionary War victory at Yorktown in 1781. The Jamestown-Yorktown Foundation is dedicated to administering the Yorktown Victory Center to educate the public about Yorktown's role as the site of the climactic battle in which Washington and Rochambeau had the British army trapped along the shores of the York River. The allied armies had all the land escapes blocked. The French Navy blockaded escape by sea. Cornwallis had no option but to surrender to the combined forces. Visiting the center today complements a visit to the actual battlefield and town.

The Yorktown Victory Center chronicles the struggle for independence from the beginnings of colonial unrest to the formation of the new nation. Exhibits and living-history programs relate the experiences of ordinary men and women of the era. The center is adjacent to Colonial National Historic Park, which encompasses Yorktown Battlefield. It is twelve miles from Williamsburg at the opposite end of Colonial Parkway from Jamestown.

YORKTOWN
VICTORY CENTER

An open-air walkway leads visitors to indoor exhibits that chronicle events leading to the American Colonies' declaring independence from Great Britain. The Witnesses to Revolution Gallery presents stories of a representative group of ten individuals of the era. Another area tells how Yorktown became the setting for the decisive battle of the Revolution. The British ship *Betsy* is highlighted as one scuttled or lost in the York River during the siege of Yorktown. The film entitled *A Time of Revolution* takes visitors to an encampment at night during the siege. In an outdoor recreated Continental Army encampment, historical interpreters describe and depict the daily life of a company of American soldiers during the last year of the war. A recreated 1780s farm shows how many Americans lived in the decade following the military end of the Revolution. A Children's Kaleidoscope discovery room offers youngsters opportunities for participatory activities, while adults have an in-depth resource area available.

Chicken Forever Easy

1 (1-ounce) package dried onion soup mix
1 package (approximately 3½ ounces) minute rice
4 chicken breasts

1 (10¾-ounce) can cream of chicken soup
¼ cup sherry or wine
Water

- Preheat the oven to 375°F. Grease the inside of an 8×8-inch casserole dish (or a 9×13-casserole dish if the recipe is doubled) with butter or margarine, or spray with nonstick cooking spray, such as Pam.
- Sprinkle the onion soup mixture over the bottom of the dish. Spread a thin layer of the rice over the onion soup mix. Place the chicken breasts on top. Note: The chicken breasts will be more moist if the skin and bones are not removed.
- Spread the soup over the top. Add the sherry or wine to the soup can, and fill with water. Pour the mixture over the casserole. Bake for 1 hour.
- Makes 4 servings

The casserole will be brown and bubbly. Perfect for our family, even after 44 years of marriage. Aunt Virginia Gant, longtime Arlington resident and wife of Dr. Landon Gant, gave us this recipe when we came to Virginia in 1961.

The family of FRANCES REDMON, a true lover of the arts, who serves as a commissioner for the Virginia Commission for the Arts in Alexandria, Virginia, submitted this recipe.

Chicken Supreme

6 thin slices baked country ham, Smithfield ham, or small package chipped beef
3 slices bacon, cut into halves
6 chicken breasts, boned

1 cup sour cream
1 (10¾-ounce) can cream of mushroom soup
¾ cup grated sharp cheese
2 to 3 tablespoons parsley flakes

- Preheat the oven to 300°F. Line a 8×12-inch dish with the ham slices or chipped beef. Wrap 1 bacon half around each chicken breast. Place over the ham or beef layer.
- Combine the sour cream and soup in a medium bowl, and mix well., Pour over the chicken. Bake, covered, for 2 hours. Top with the cheese and parsley flakes.
- Makes 6 servings

This recipe is from the kitchen of FRANCES POWELL, a member of the Falls Church Chapter of the Virginia DAR.

THE HOTEL ROANOKE AND CONFERENCE CENTER
Chicken Penne with Mushrooms

8 ounces chicken breasts,
cut into strips
2 tablespoons olive oil
1 clove garlic, minced
1 small shallot, minced
3 ounces (about ½ cup)
sliced mushrooms

1 roasted red pepper, sliced
3 ounces Marsala wine
2 cups cooked penne pasta
Salt and pepper
2 to 3 tablespoons butter
Grated Parmesan cheese

- Sauté the chicken in the olive oil in a hot skillet for
  2 minutes. Stir in the garlic, shallots, and mushrooms.
  Cook for 1 minute longer.
- Add the roasted red pepper and wine, and mix well. Cook
  until the wine is reduce by half, and add the pasta. Season
  with salt and pepper to taste. Cook until the wine has
  been reduced to about 1 or 2 teaspoons.
- Add the butter. Remove from the heat, and stir until the
  butter is melted. Adjust the seasonings if necessary.
  Sprinkle with Parmesan cheese to taste.
- Makes 2 to 3 servings

From the kitchen of CHEF BILLIE RAPER, executive chef
at The Hotel Roanoke. Chef Raper, born in Richmond,
Virginia, started cooking at a very young age alongside his
mother. After serving an apprenticeship at Kingsmill Resort
and Colonial Williamsburg, he started at The Hotel Roanoke
and Conference Center in 1995. He is now executive chef.

The Hotel Roanoke, built in 1882, is nestled in the heart of
the spectacular Blue Ridge Mountains in southwest Virginia.
Throughout its history, The Hotel Roanoke has charmed
guests with a rich heritage of service, style, and sophistication,
and surrounded them with the warmest of traditional
Southern hospitality. The hotel has recently been restored to
its rich, nineteenth century elegance and is listed in the
National Register of Historic Places.

FRANKLIN COUNTY

Named in honor of Benjamin Franklin, Franklin County
was organized in 1785 from Bedford and Henry
Counties. The county consists of six hundred ninety-seven
square miles and is home to 47,286 residents. The
county seat is Rocky Mount.

The "Unreconstructed Rebel," General Jubal Early, was born
here in 1816 and went on to participate in more battles during
the War Between the States than any other general officer.
The noted humanitarian and educator Booker T. Washington
was born in a slave cabin in this county in 1856.

THE FIRST COWS IN AMERICA

America's first Jersey cow lived in Middle Plantation.

Indications are that the early Jamestown
settlers had cows on Jamestown Island
as early as 1611. Ships that brought
provisions and women to the fort made
room for the cows, as milk provided
necessary nutrition. But which breeds
were brought to the New World is not
certain until a few years later. Newer
American settlements such as Plymoth
(1620) might have fared better had they
been fortunate enough to have milk in
their diet.

The island of Jersey in England was
known for its small, docile cows that
could produce "rich milk;" enough milk
to produce a pound of butter a day. For
centuries, the Jersey cow was known
for having a head like a fawn, a soft eye,
an elegant crumpled horn, small ears, a
clean neck and throat, fine bones, and a
fine tail. It was as a family cow that the
Jersey first crossed the Atlantic Ocean
to America.

Our Famous Fried Chicken

Fresh boneless chicken breasts, based on number of guests
Salted water
2 cups all-purpose flour
1 tablespoon salt
1 teaspoon white pepper
1 teaspoon black pepper
2 to 4 cups equal amounts of butter or margarine and shortening

- Soak the chicken breasts in salted water to cover in a large pot for several hours in the refrigerator, draining and changing the water every hour.
- Cut each chicken breast into 3 or 4 small pieces. Combine the flour, salt, white pepper, and black pepper in a bowl or baking dish, and mix well. Place generous amounts of the butter or margarine and shortening in a large skillet (preferably cast-iron). Heat to about 350°F or until very hot. Coat the chicken pieces in the flour mixture, and place in the prepared skillet. Cook, covered, for about 5 to 7 minutes, and turn. Cook, covered, until the chicken pieces are golden brown. Remove to a platter lined with paper towels. Serve on an attractive platter, and garnish as desired.
- Makes approximately 1 chicken breast for each lady and 2 chicken breasts for each man

This recipe has been closely guarded in our family for generations. We hope you will enjoy it as much as we do.

The recipe is shared by TOM JOHNSON, the director of weddings and events at the Norfolk Waterside Marriott in Norfolk, Virginia. He started catering at the age of fifteen and has catered over 2,900 weddings to date. He also gives back constantly to his community and is an amazingly creative person.

George and Susanna Poingdestre emigrated to America in 1657. They settled on a farm in Middle Plantation (later called Williamsburg), Virginia. George had been determined to bring several cows from his ancestral home, Swan Farm, on the island of Jersey.

English sea captains were agreeable to bringing cows across the ocean because they considered cows "part of families." This was true especially when their own wives and children accompanied them on a voyage. They made a "floating home" aboard their ships, and thus provided milk for their families. Sometimes, after reaching America, the captains would sell or give away a cow.

The Poingdestre family has the first such recorded "cow-crossing" on record. This led the way to Virginia's (and America's) dairies of today.

FREDERICK COUNTY

Containing four hundred thirty-five square miles, Frederick County was organized in 1738 out of Orange County. Named for the father of King George III, its population is 59,209, and its county seat is Winchester.

Winchester was the site of three separate battles during the War Between the States. Pulitzer Prize-winning novelist Willa Cather was born in this county in 1873 and resided here for the first ten years of her life.

DID YOU KNOW THAT:

British General Edward Braddock's headquarters during the early days of the French and Indian War were in the Carlyle House in Alexandria?

Ham-and-Peanut-Stuffed Chicken Breasts with Cider Sauce and Apple Garnish

STUFFING

1/2 cup roasted unsalted peanuts
1 tablespoon unsalted butter, softened
1/4 cup heavy cream
1/4 cup unseasoned bread crumbs

1/4 teaspoon salt
1/8 teaspoon freshly ground black pepper
1/8 teaspoon ground nutmeg
1/8 teaspoon cayenne

CHICKEN

8 boneless skinless chicken breast halves
1/8 pound Smithfield ham, thinly sliced
2 medium yellow onions, peeled, coarsely chopped
1 large carrot, peeled, coarsely chopped

1 large apple, peeled, cored, coarsely chopped
1/4 cup plus 1 tablespoon unsalted butter
1 1/2 cups unpasteurized fresh apple cider
3 tablespoons cider vinegar

APPLE GARNISH

3 tablespoons unsalted butter
1 unpeeled medium apple, cored, sliced 1/4 inch thick

2 to 3 tablespoons sugar

- To prepare the stuffing, process the peanuts in a food processor or blender until finely ground. Add the butter, and process until smooth. Add the cream, bread crumbs, salt, pepper, nutmeg, and cayenne, and process until well blended.
- To prepare the chicken and sauce, preheat the oven to 375°F. Place each chicken breast half between sheets of waxed paper, and flatten with a mallet, the flat side of a cleaver, or a rolling pin to a thickness of about 1/2 inch. Place the chicken, smooth side down, on a work surface, discarding the waxed paper. Lay 1 ham slice over each breast half. Spread approximately 3 teaspoons of the stuffing on top of the ham. Roll each chicken breast from the narrowest end into a neat, plump shape, tucking the edges in. Secure with wooden picks. Scatter the onions, carrot, and apple in a baking dish large enough for the rolled breasts to fit snugly, and mix well. Place the chicken rolls on top of the mixture. Melt 1/4 cup of the butter in a small saucepan, and brush over the chicken rolls. Bake, uncovered, in the center of the oven for 30 minutes, turning and basting twice at 10-minute intervals.
- Bring the cider and vinegar to a boil in a small saucepan over high heat. Boil until reduced to 6 tablespoons, and set aside. Remove the chicken breasts to a warm platter, and cover with foil. Combine the onions, carrot, apple, and any juices from the baking pan in a food processor. Add the cider reduction, and process until smooth. Press

PEANUTS HIGH ON LIST OF CASH CROPS

Since the 1840s, when the first commercial crop was harvested in Sussex County, peanuts have been popular in the Commonwealth. With nearly three thousand farms and almost one hundred thousand acres devoted to the crop, peanuts, indeed, hold a special place in the hearts of Virginia and Virginians. After the boll weevil severely reduced the South's cotton-growing ability in the early 1900s, the peanut picked up the slack and rapidly became an important cash crop across the region. Today, Virginia produces nearly one-third billion pounds annually, representing between 6 to 8 percent of the nation's total crop.

Four varieties of peanuts are grown in the United States: Runner, Spanish, Valencia, and Virginia. True to its name, the Virginia peanut grows best in south-eastern Virginia and northeastern North Carolina. Virginia peanuts are known for their large kernels and are widely distributed as "snack" nuts. In addition to the fine eating provided by the kernels, peanut shells and skins are used in a variety of nonfood products, including face creams, paint, explosives, kitty litter, and axle grease.

MARY PEAKE AND THE EMANCIPATION OAK

African-American heritage in Virginia reaches back to Jamestown days. Through the decades of early Virginia, schooling for African Americans was not provided unless some plantation owner allowed it on his premises. One who recognized need for educating both free and enslaved African Americans during the War Between the States was Hampton resident Mary Peake. As a free-born woman of color, Peake began some of the first organized programs available to teach free and enslaved African Americans to read and write.

She ignored statutes forbidding African Americans an education and began teaching classes near a large oak tree in Hampton on September 17, 1861. On January 1, 1863, President Abraham Lincoln issued the Emancipation Proclamation, freeing the enslaved people of the Confederacy. The proclamation was officially read in Hampton under the large oak tree by Mary's school.

Today the Emancipation Oak is a significant landmark of African-American history. Hampton University (formerly Hampton Normal and Agricultural Institute), which owns the site, was created in 1868 to educate newly freed African Americans there. The city of Hampton also has a public school called the Mary Peake Center, which serves as a Gifted Education Magnet for upper elementary grade children.

the mixture through a sieve into a medium saucepan over low heat, and whisk in the remaining butter. Keep warm.
- To prepare the apple garnish, heat the butter in a large heavy skillet. Coat 1 side of each apple slice in the sugar, and place, sugared side down, in the hot butter. Cook over medium-high heat for 4 to 5 minutes or until deep golden brown. Sprinkle the remaining sugar over the apples, turn, and brown the other side. Add any juices from the chicken to the sauce, and reheat if necessary.
- To serve, cut each chicken breast roll into $1/4$-inch to 1-inch slices, discarding the wooden picks. Divide the sauce evenly among 4 serving plates. Place the chicken slices on top of the sauce in an overlapping pattern, and garnish with 2 or 3 apple slices.
- Makes 4 servings

This recipe was kindly shared by WILLIAM J. HENNESSEY, director of The Chrysler Museum in Norfolk, Virginia. The Chrysler Museum is named for Walter P. Chrysler, who married a Norfolk girl, Jean Outland. Today it is known as one of America's great fine-art museums, housing many of Walter Chrysler's collections in addition to many other collections. It is noted for its world-class glass collection that spans from early Egyptian times to the present day.

L and T Chicken

$1/4$ cup ($1/2$ stick) butter or margarine	4 large chicken breasts
$1/4$ cup chopped onion	1 cup honey
1 (7-ounce) can sliced mushrooms	$1 1/2$ tablespoons (or more) lemon juice, or to taste
4 slices bread, cut into small cubes	Hot cooked wild rice

- Preheat the oven to 350°F. Melt the butter in a skillet, and sauté the onion until soft. Add the mushrooms and bread cubes, and sauté until heated through. Lift up the skin from the chicken to form a pocket in each chicken breast, and stuff with the mixture. Place the stuffed chicken breasts in a baking pan, and bake for 15 minutes.
- Combine the honey and lemon juice in a small bowl, and mix well. Pour over the chicken, and bake for 30 minutes longer or until the skin is browned, basting with the sauce several times. Serve on a bed of wild rice, with or without sauce.
- Makes 4 servings

This is a recipe given to me at Lord and Taylor by a co-worker many years ago. It soon became a family favorite. Very easy.

The recipe is from the collection of Rowena's sister, JOAN MAROULIS, who had the privilege of being born in Norfolk, Virginia, at what is now Norfolk Sentara.

Lemon Cajun Barbecue Sauce for Chicken

1 cup olive oil	1/2 teaspoon thyme
1/2 cup lemon juice	6 to 8 fresh cloves garlic
1 tablespoon salt	1 to 2 tablespoons Cajun
1 teaspoon paprika	seasoning, or to taste
2 teaspoons basil	Chicken or (beef)
1 large onion, chopped	

- Blend the olive oil, lemon juice, salt, paprika, basil, onion, thyme, garlic, and Cajun seasoning in a blender, and pour over the chicken or beef. Marinate, covered, in the refrigerator for 4 to 8 hours. Grill the meat over hot coals, or bake in the oven, until cooked through.
- Store any leftovers in freezer bags, or freeze the uncooked meat in the barbecue sauce for future use. If freezing for future use, place 4 split boned chicken breasts or 1 flank steak in a 1-quart freezer bag. Add 1/4 to 1/2 cup sauce.
- Makes enough sauce for 4 to 6 bags of chicken or (beef)

My son Shelly and I made the marinated chicken and beef packages to freeze for his college use. The Cajun seasoning adds a little zip, but you can leave it out, and it's still delicious. YUM!

This is from the kitchen of ALLYN JONES, our loving daughter, world traveler, and fabulous nutritional cook in Vienna, Virginia. Allyn has sent three boys through Virginia Universities with her stay-at-home business, which focuses on the family through preservation of each family's photo memorabilia, most usually found piled in shoe boxes or closets. She is a senior director of Creative Memories, which is the source of ideas, tools, materials, and business structure that she transmits through fun and instructive home classes and workshops. —Rowena

GILES COUNTY

Giles County was formed in 1806 from parts of Monroe (now in West Virginia), Montgomery, and Tazewell Counties. It was named for William B. Giles (1762-1830), who served as Virginia's governor from 1827 till 1830. The county contains three hundred sixty-nine square miles, and its population is 16,657. The county seat is Pearisburg.

Adventurer Abraham Wood explored present-day Giles County in 1654. Indian captive Mary Ingles was discovered here by early settler Adam Harmon after she escaped from her captors in 1755.

SHARING GRACE

Too often our holidays are marred by spending too much time in the kitchen. After years of spending hours working instead of visiting with family and friends, I developed a dinner that is delicious but is quick to fix. (See page 174 for Rowena's "Fast" Holiday Menu.) Often other people like to bring things, a corn pudding, steamed broccoli, spinach pie, or whatever they choose. I welcome it all. Holidays are about family and friends and sharing.

Dinner starts with a special grace with all of us standing, holding hands, and completing the circle of love and thanksgiving. We sit at one table with lots of extensions that starts at one end of the dining room and extends into the hallway. I always set the table the day before or even two days before. When the food is ready to be served, I put all the dishes on a separate table in the hallway. One of the men helps my husband with carving the turkey and two or three of the gals serve the rest of the dishes so all does not get too cold. I excuse myself and go into the kitchen to make the gravy at the last minute so it is hot. We sit around the table and talk two to three hours taking a respite between dinner and dessert. As you can imagine, it's a very special time!

—Rowena

THE BARTER THEATER

During the Depression when actors and actresses were starving in New York City, Robert Porterfield acquired an old church building and, with the help of Lady Aster and using the interior of the Empire Theater, created the "Barter Theater." Farmers brought chickens, eggs, and produce as barter to see professional acting. Before the beginning of each performance, Porterfield would say, "If you like us, talk about us. If you don't like us, keep your mouth shut." The Barter Theater is now the State Theater of Virginia (people must have talked about it).

Timeless Chicken

1 (10³/4-ounce) can cream of mushroom soup
1 cup sour cream
8 to 10 fresh or frozen chicken breast halves
Paprika
8 to 10 thin slices Virginia ham
¹/2 cup dry sherry
1 (4-ounce) can mushrooms, drained

- Preheat the oven to 350°F. Combine the soup and sour cream in a medium mixing bowl, and mix well. Spoon a small amount of the mixture over the bottom of a 9×13-inch baking dish or casserole dish, spreading to cover.
- Sprinkle the chicken breasts with paprika to taste. Wrap 1 ham slice around each chicken breast. Place in the baking dish in a single layer. Add the sherry and mushrooms to the remaining soup mixture, and mix well. Pour over the chicken. Bake for 1 to 1¹/2 hours or until bubbly and crusty around the sides.
- Makes 8 to 10 servings

Say Virginia, and I think ham. (Yes, I do cook my own Virginia ham, but not everyone has the time or inclination these days.) Say Virginia, and I think home cooking. (Once again, not everyone has the time or inclination to do true home cooking these days.) That's what makes this old-fashioned recipe that incorporates Virginia ham a real staple at my house for company dinners. Timeless Chicken has been a favorite recipe of mine ever since I was young bride back in the 1960s. Most people have forgotten about it these days. They seem to prefer steaks on the grill or poached salmon. But I assure you that when you serve this dish along with a wild rice side dish, there won't be a morsel left.

This recipe is from a really terrific lady, EMYL JENKINS, who is a resident of Danville, Virginia, and author of many books, including *From Storebought to Homemade*, the first place cookbook winner of the Virginia Women's Competition and the National Federation of Press Women's Competition, 2002.

JOHN SEVIER'S
Braised Doves

Salt and pepper the doves, and dredge them in flour or a combination of flour and cornmeal. Heat some fat in a heavy pan, such as a Dutch oven. Brown the birds quickly on both sides. Remove most of the fat, add a small amount of water, cover, and simmer 1 hour over low heat. Serve hot.

Reprinted from *Miss Daisy Celebrates Tennessee* © 1995 by Daisy King, James A. Crutchfield, and Winette Sparkman, with permission.

Seafood

THE OAKS VICTORIAN INN
Pasta Soufflé with Baked Salmon in Dill Sauce

SOUFFLÉ

1 cup heavy cream	2 tablespoons minced fresh
1/3 cup freshly grated	basil
Parmesan cheese	Pinch of red pepper flakes
1/3 cup gorgonzola cheese,	Dash of salt
grated	1/4 teaspoon nutmeg
4 eggs, slightly beaten	Angel hair pasta

SALMON

20 fresh aparagus spears	Vegetable oil
Salt	1 (20-ounce) salmon fillet
Almonds	Light seasoned salt

DILL SAUCE

1 tablespoon butter	Salt
1 tablespoon flour	2 cups skim milk
1 tablespoon minced fresh	2 egg yolks
dill, or 1 teaspoon dried	Juice of 1/2 lemon, or
Pinch of red pepper flakes	to taste

- To prepare the soufflé, combine the cream, cheeses, eggs, basil, red pepper flakes, salt, and nutmeg in a bowl, whisking to blend. Spray ten ramekins with nonstick vegetable cooking spray, and place in 1 inch of water bath in a baking pan. Preheat the oven to 400°F. Cook the pasta in boiling, salted water until just tender, about 3 minutes. Rinse in cold water, and drain thoroughly. Fill the ramekins about half full with the pasta. Divide the cream mixture among the ramekins. Bake until light brown and puffed.
- Note: The soufflés must be served immediately, so the salmon and asparagus need to be prepared ahead.
- To prepare the salmon, cook the asparagus in salted water until just tender. Drain. Toast almonds that have been sprayed with vegetable oil and lightly salted until lightly browned. Bake the salmon in a 450°F oven until opaque. Do not overcook. Can be warmed when ready to serve. Sprinkle with seasoned salt to taste. Cut in 10 equal portions.
- To prepare the sauce, combine the butter and flour in the top of a double boiler, whisking until the butter has melted. Whisk in the dill, red pepper, salt, and milk, and cook until slightly thickened. Beat the egg yolks and lemon juice in a bowl, and add to the hot mixture, whisking constantly. Cook to the consistency of syrup. Adjust the seasonings.
- To serve, cover warmed plates with the dill sauce. Unmold the soufflé in the center. Top with the salmon, and add more sauce on the salmon. Place two asparagus spears on the side, and garnish with toasted almonds, a tiny lemon sliver, and snipped fresh parsley. Serve with corn mini-muffins and a crisp green salad.
- Makes 4 to 6 servings

The OAKS VICTORIAN INN, Christiansburg, Virginia, provided this recipe.

The Homes of Woodrow Wilson

America's twenty-eighth President enjoyed life as a boy in the small town of Staunton near the Blue Ridge Mountains. His home, The Manse, was built in 1846, in a Greek Revival style. After his presidency, he would live in Washington D.C. in a house on S Street. Woodrow and his wife, Edith, were both Virginia natives!

Born on December 28, 1856 in The Manse of Staunton, Thomas Woodrow Wilson was the third child of Joseph Ruggles Wilson and Janet Woodrow Wilson. Young Tommy (as he was then called) grew up in a deeply religious and educated family. He attended Davidson College in North Carolina and then proceeded to graduate from Princeton. Later, he attended the University of Virginia Law School before finally enrolling at John Hopkins University for graduate studies.

In 1883, Woodrow Wilson married the former Ellen Louise Axson, a very quiet, personable lady

from Georgia. Their three daughters joined them as the Wilsons moved into the White House in 1913. Ellen's "Afternoon Teas" were thought to be simple, yet beautiful, as she presided at functions as First Lady. Mrs. Elizabeth Jaffray, the Wilson family cook, became the executive housekeeper. She planned exquisite menus for the Wilson administrative dinners, as Ellen became ill and then died while the President was in office.

In time, President Wilson met Edith Bolling Galt of Wytheville, Virginia. She was a descendent of Pocahontas and had ancestors from Williamsburg. They were married, but the new First Lady did not "entertain" as the impact of World War I was evident in all American homes—including the White House. She experienced some heatless evenings and simple meals while the nation was at war. Edith went to Europe with her husband as needed and saw many national leaders and American troops along the way.

After the war, the first people actually to be entertained at a White House garden party tea were 800 convalescing sick and wounded soldiers from Walter Reed and Naval Hospitals. It was one of the most unique and informal parties ever gathered under the trees of the historic south lawn! The guests arrived by ambulances, army transports, limousines, and any means possible to assemble in the great "back yard." The U.S. Marine Band played the Star-Spangled Banner as all who could stand, did so. As Woodrow and Edith mingled around the crowd, the President assisted as host first hand. He personally served many of the soldiers as he took plates of food to those in wheelchairs or on cots. One Private took the President's picture as he was "doing K.P." President Wilson had a big smile on his face.

Near the end of his presidency, the Wilsons bought a red brick Georgian-style house on S Street in Washington, D.C. in 1921. On their fifth wedding anniversary, Woodrow followed a Scottish custom by presenting Edith with a piece of sod from the garden and the key to the front door as they moved in.

Three years later, Wilson died, leaving Edith as resident in the home for forty more years. She had wonderful recipes and entertained privately. She once had a luncheon in honor of First Lady Jacqueline Kennedy in 1961. Invitations were sent to eight other guests, including the Governor of Virginia's wife, Mrs. J. Lindsay Almond, who was driven up from Richmond. Mrs. Wilson and Mrs. Kennedy received guests in the second floor drawing room. The menu included: Terrapin Stew, Quail Wild Rice, Asparagus, and Fresh Strawberries.

Edith Wilson had hosted such an event for Mamie Eisenhower eight years earlier. As Jacqueline Kennedy left the Wilson House to go on an Easter holiday with Caroline and John Jr., she graciously smiled at Mrs. Wilson at the open door. 88-year old Edith shyly waved; duly staying out of photographers' views as the new First Lady said good-bye.

Today, the Wilson House is open to the public as a historic house museum. Edith bequeathed the property to the National Trust for Historic Preservation after her death, which occurred in 1961. The Manse is also open as one of the few original Presidential birthplaces in America. These homes pay tribute to Virginia's son, Woodrow Wilson, an American President who truly pursued world peace and security. His influence is still present today.

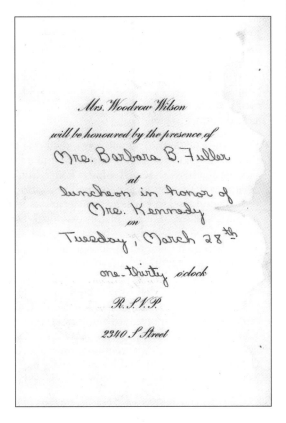

Woodrow Wilson's Legacy

In order to shorten the war in Europe and to bring Germany and Austria-Hungary to the negotiating table, President Woodrow Wilson developed his now-famous "Fourteen Points." Announced in a speech delivered on January 8, 1918, the points were requirements that were essential for nations to meet in order for peace to be achieved. Both major Axis powers agreed to the premise of the points, but when actual peace negotiations began in Paris in early 1919, much of the context of Wilson's logic was compromised by Italy, Japan, Great Britain, and France. Wilson returned to Washington facing certain failure to obtain Senate approval either

for the proposed peace treaty or for his other "pet" project, the creation of a League of Nations, which was the forerunner to today's United Nations. Facing continued opposition in the Senate, Wilson decided to take his arguments to the people. The president collapsed on September 25, 1919 while on this mission. He remained an invalid until his death in 1924. Ironically, despite Wilson's Herculean efforts—which no doubt contributed to the failure of his health—neither the Versailles Treaty, which officially ended World War One, nor consent for U. S. participation in the League of Nations ever received the Senate's approval.

Salmon Mousse

2 (14³/₄-ounce) cans red
  salmon
2 tablespoons unflavored
  gelatin
¹/₄ cup lemon juice
¹/₃ cup mayonnaise
¹/₂ cup sour cream
¹/₂ teaspoon nutmeg, freshly
  grated nutmeg is preferred

1 teaspoon salt
¹/₄ teaspoon freshly ground
  pepper
³/₄ cup heavy cream, stiffly
  beaten
Fresh dill, optional
1 lemon, cut into wedges,
  optional

- Drain the salmon into a small bowl, reserving the liquid.
  Remove the skin and bones, and flake into a large bowl.
  Add ¹/₂ cup of the reserved salmon liquid. Soften the
  gelatin in the lemon juice in a small bowl. Bring 1 cup of
  the salmon liquid to a boil in a saucepan. Add the gelatin
  mixture, and stir until completely dissolved. Let stand
  until cool. Note: Water may be added to the salmon liquid
  before boiling if there is not enough liquid.
- Combine the salmon, gelatin mixture, mayonnaise, sour
  cream, nutmeg, salt, and pepper, mixing gently but
  completely. Fold in the stiffly beaten cream. Spoon the
  mousse carefully into a ring mold or 6-cup loaf pan that
  has been oiled or sprayed with nonstick vegetable spray.
  Refrigerate, covered, until set.
- To serve, invert the salmon mousse onto a serving tray.
  Garnish with fresh dill and lemon wedges if desired.
- Makes approximately 12 servings

*This is my absolute favorite. Enjoy with crackers or sliced
fresh cucumbers.*

This was sent by Virginia State Senator, LINDA T. "TODDY"
PULLER, a 1998 "Distinguished Alumni Award" recipient
from Mary Washington College, who has served her state
since 1991. She was elected to the Virginia House of
Delegates for the 44th District at that time. She then ran,
and was elected, in 1999 to the Virginia Senate 36th
District, which includes portions of Fairfax County and
Prince William County.

GLOUCESTER COUNTY

Gloucester County was organized in 1651 from
York County. Named after the county of the same name in
England, it contains two hundred twenty-three square miles.
Its population is 34,780, and the county seat is Gloucester.

Walter Reed (1851-1902), the U.S. army physician who
discovered that yellow fever was transmitted by the
mosquito, was born in this county. Robert Russa Moton,
founder of the Urban League and an advisor to five
U.S. presidents, died here in 1940, at his home Holly Knoll.

THE VIRGINIA COMET

How many times has Halley's Comet
blazed across Virginia's night skies?
In recorded history, only five or six
occasions. Native Americans surely saw
it in prior times over the water that they
called *Tschiswapeki* (Great Shellfish Bay)
in the Algonquin language, or later
Chesapioke (Great Saltwater), a variant
of the name. Perhaps the Spanish
explorers from La Florida on one of their
Bahia de Santa Maria (The Bay of the
Mother of God) attempts at settlement
saw it in the 1500s.

In the winter of 1606, as the Virginia
Company of London associates prepared
three ships for a venture over the
Atlantic Ocean to that same bay,
Halley's Comet was flashing its
presence again. Perhaps the men were
thoughtful about this brilliance in the

sky and the luck it could bring finding gold in the New World. There's a chance some saw it as providence for absolutely being dedicated to the journey and the new crop productions they could establish for sales in England. Others may have seen it as a direction for pursuing the goal of spreading Christianity to new peoples in the new land. Certainly, they hoped to fare better than their countrymen had earlier with the lost Roanoke Colony.

As the *Susan Constant*, *Godspeed*, and *Discovery* were readied, Captain Christopher Newport, his three crews, and one hundred five men were heading on a voyage under a comet's night sky to fulfill a destiny that would change the world. Where would their first footsteps fall? Wherever it was to be, they had already named the land—it would be called *Virginia*.

Salmon Teriyaki

1/2 cup firmly packed brown sugar	2 tablespoons fresh lemon juice
1/4 cup soy sauce	4 salmon steaks
1/4 cup water	Lemon slices

- Heat the brown sugar, soy sauce, water, and lemon juice in a medium to large skillet that is large enough to hold the salmon steaks snugly. Boil, uncovered, until the sugar is melted, stirring occasionally.
- Add the salmon steaks, and reduce the heat. Simmer the steaks, covered, for 5 to 6 minutes per side. Remove the steaks to a platter, and keep warm. Boil the sauce for about 4 minutes or until thickened. Serve the salmon steaks drizzled with the sauce, and garnished with lemon slices.
- For a barbecue grill, prepare the sauce as directed above. Marinate the steaks in the sauce for 10 minutes. Cook on a well-oiled barbecue grill over medium heat for about 4 to 5 minutes per side.
- Makes 4 servings

NORMA DOREY, the owner of Changes and City Spa in Norfolk, Virginia, shared this recipe. She is a brilliant and creative businesswoman who is greatly admired and has created a beautiful, caring environment in her very successful business.

GOOCHLAND COUNTY

Goochland County was organized in 1727 from lands that were part of Henrico County. Named for Sir William Gooch (1681-1751), Virginia's governor from 1727 till 1749, the county covers two hundred eighty-seven square miles. Goochland County has a population of 16,863. The county seat is Goochland.

Goochland County was the site of an early French Huguenot settlement that flourished from about 1699. Thomas Jefferson's grandfather, Isham Randolph, built his plantation, Dungeness, in this county in 1730.

DID YOU KNOW THAT:

The Rotunda of the Virginia State Capitol in Richmond houses the only full-length statue of George Washington made during his lifetime? It was sculpted in marble by the French artist Jean Antoine Houdon and placed in the Capitol in 1796.

DELAWARE HOUSE
Stuffed Salmon

¹/₂ whole salmon	1 cup crumbled feta cheese
4 cloves garlic, minced	¹/₄ cup chopped fresh basil
4 shallots, chopped	Salt and pepper
2 cups thinly sliced shiitake mushrooms	1 lemon, cut into halves
¹/₄ cup olive oil	2 tablespoons soy sauce
	Fresh dill for garnish

- Preheat the oven to 375°F. Clean the salmon, and remove the skin. Slice the salmon carefully lengthwise to create 2 equal fillets. Place in a container. Chill, covered, in the refrigerator for 1 hour.
- Sauté the garlic and shallots in 2 tablespoons of the olive oil in a medium skillet for about 2 minutes. Add the mushrooms and additional olive oil to prevent the mushrooms from sticking. Sauté until the mushrooms are tender. Add the feta cheese and basil, and mix well. Turn off the heat, and let the filling stand to cool.
- Brush a roasting pan with the remaining olive oil. Place the salmon on the roasting pan, and season lightly with salt and pepper to taste. Spread the cooled filling on the cut side of 1 fillet. Top with the remaining fillet. Sprinkle with lemon juice and soy sauce. Roast for 20 to 25 minutes. Garnish with fresh dill.
- Makes several servings depending on the size of the salmon

Absolutely one of the most elegant and delicious dishes that one can serve.

KATHY GROSSENBACHER is president of the Dolphin Scholarship Foundation, started in 1961. This very active organization is supported by donations and fund-raising activities of submariners and their wives. It provides undergraduate college scholarships for the children of past and present members of the U. S. Submarine Force, officers and enlisted. Kathy interestingly lives in the Delaware House on the Naval Base in Norfolk, Virginia. It is part of the Jamestown Exposition, one of the largest national events of the early twentieth century. The Exposition in 1907 commemorated the 300th anniversary of the settlement of Jamestown.

DID YOU KNOW THAT:

During the War Between the States, the First Maryland Regiment, USA and the First Maryland Regiment, CSA went head-to-head with each other near Front Royal on May 23, 1862? The Confederates, part of the command of General "Stonewall" Jackson, took the day.

THE SHAD PLANKING

The Shad Planking has evolved into a tradition among many Virginians. Held each April by the Wakefield Ruritan Club for over fifty years, it is a favorite meeting and greeting event for local and state politicians, as well as many friends and citizens who have attended year after year.

It originated with the American Indians, who cooked fresh shad on planks each spring on an open fire. Now Ruritan volunteers do exactly that. The four- to six-pound shad is split and nailed in pairs to washed oak planks. Then each plank is placed along the long open pit with the fish facing away from the fire. After a few hours the planks are turned

with the shad now facing the fire for several more hours. Then it is time to baste with "Dr. Nettle's Secret Sauce." This spicy sauce adds flavor and moisture to the shad. There is nothing like this shad, especially when served with the Ruritan's deep-fried roe, cole slaw, cornbread, baked beans, and fried fish fillets. Over twenty-five hundred people attend this wonderful event each year; it is the Wakefield Ruritan's most important and popular fund-raising event.

FORMER CONGRESSMAN AND
MRS. WILLIAM WHITEHURST'S
Baked Shad Roe

Bacon slices   1 set shad roe per person

- Preheat the oven to 400°F. Divide the bacon slices lengthwise, and place a slice under each half of the shad roe set. Cut some of the bacon into very small pieces, and sprinkle over the shad roe. Bake for 25 to 30 minutes or just until done.
- Makes 1 set of shad roe per person

Fortunately, I already knew how to cook (I even spent a summer prior to our wedding at the Fanny Farmer Cooking School in Boston), but as a transplanted Virginian, I've learned to appreciate Virginia food, and I'm happy to share some of my Virginia-oriented recipes.

From the kitchen of JANIE WHITEHURST, the wife, and in her words, true partner of Bill Whitehurst, an esteemed Congressman of eighteen years from the Second District of Virginia. Janie is also the author of a cookbook and what she calls her survival manual, *The Other Side of the House.*

While a young junior at Wheaton College in Massachusetts, Janie met a young sailor from Norfolk, Virginia, at a New Year's Eve dance at Otis Field near Cape Cod. Neither of them could ever have imagined where the next fifty-six years would take them—from the classrooms to the United States Congress and back to the classrooms. They had no idea that their mutual careers would take them around the world and give them the opportunity to meet famous people, but more important, to serve the constituents of the Second District of Virginia.

GRAYSON COUNTY

Grayson County was formed in 1792 from Wythe County and named in honor of William Grayson (1740-1790), one of the first U.S. senators from Virginia. It consists of four hundred twenty-five square miles, and its population is 17,917. Its county seat is Independence.

Grayson County was home to some of the first musicians, including Henry Whitter, to record in New York City in 1928, thus inaugurating today's country music industry. Among other popular musicians who resided here were Kelly Harrell and E.V. "Pop" Stoneman.

Ring of Shad Roe

SHAD ROE
2 sets fresh shad roe
2 to 3 lemon slices
1 tablespoon capers
1 packet unflavored gelatin

$1^1/_2$ cups chicken broth
Watercress, optional
Cucumber slices, optional

SAUCE
$^3/_4$ cup mayonnaise
$^1/_4$ cup sour cream

Lime juice

- To prepare the shad roe, poach the shad roe gently with the lemon slices in water in a medium skillet for about 10 to 12 minutes. Drain, and let stand to cool.
- Remove as much of the shad roe membrane as possible. Separate the roe carefully with a fork. Add the capers, and pack in a ring mold. Dissolve the gelatin in the chicken broth in a bowl, and pour over the shad roe. Chill in the refrigerator. Unmold the shad roe, and fill the center with watercress and slices of cucumber, if desired.
- To prepare the sauce, mix the mayonnaise, sour cream, and lime juice to taste in a serving bowl. Serve with the shad roe.
- Note: Shad roe has a short season, but many fish markets freeze it and sell it for many months after the season.
- Makes 6 first courses or hors d'oeuvres for a crowd

My husband, Senator Edward Breeden, was in the group that went to invite the Queen of England to come for the 350th Virginia celebration. She and Prince Philip joined us. Later, the Jamestown Foundation presented a handsome statue of Captain John Smith to the City of London. It is in the charming little park next to the Christopher Wren Church, St. Mary-le-Bow. I visited it recently, and there is a café in the crypt of the church called The Place Below. The late Queen Mother and our colorful Virginian Lady Astor were present at the presentation and attended a luncheon hosted by the Lord Mayor at his official residence, Mansion Hall. I lived and worked in Williamsburg and used to go to Jamestown, often trying to visualize what men could get in those small boats when they set out for a new land. We are much in their debt. I am sure they had shad and shad roe from our Virginia waters, and so I chose this shad roe ring, which we served on official, and many non-official occasions, in Williamsburg.

This recipe was provided by VIRGINIA BREEDEN.

GREENE COUNTY

Greene County was formed from Orange County in 1838 and named for General Nathanael Greene of Revolutionary War fame. It contains one hundred fifty-five square miles and has a population of 15,244. The county seat is Stanardsville.

Greene County was the site of settlement for the Rucker family, who were descendants of early French Huguenot residents of the region. The western part of this county lies among the Blue Ridge Mountains.

THE BIRTH OF THE LIBRARY OF CONGRESS

In 1800, with the delivery of about nine hundred books and maps purchased in England with a $5,000 appropriation from the United States Congress, the renowned Library of Congress was founded. When the British burned Washington, D. C. in 1814, most of the library was destroyed, but former president Thomas Jefferson sold his collection of books to the Nation at cost for the establishment of a new library. Housed in the Capitol building, the library grew steadily until December, 1851, when once again fire struck the collection. Two-thirds of Jefferson's books were destroyed as well as thousands of other valuable tomes. The Library of Congress finally acquired its own building in 1897, where it continued to grow (with the addition of two more buildings in the twentieth century) to become one of the world's largest and most famous archives.

THE HOMESTEAD, 1776

The Homestead has been renowned for superb cuisine, gracious service, and elegant accommodations for over two centuries. Since 1766, twenty Presidents of the United States have made the resort their home away from home, including Thomas Jefferson, James Madison, and Woodrow Wilson, who enjoyed both great golf and fine cuisine on his honeymoon. Today this historic symbol of Virginia hospitality is complemented by three championship golf courses, equestrian activities, fly fishing, tennis, mountain biking, indoor and outdoor pools, falconry, miles of scenic walking trails, trap, skeet, and English sporting clays, and, of course, the internationally celebrated natural mineral baths, hydrotherapy treatments, and massages in the Homestead Spa.

A traditional Homestead favorite, Sautéed Mountain Trout is a simple and delicious way to prepare any delicate fish to protect its flavor. Use only fresh trout—ours come from nearby Allegheny streams. If you have a rushing mountain stream nearby and can catch your own, your reward will be doubled.

Sautéed Mountain Trout Homestead

6 (10- to 12-ounce) fresh trout	Salt and freshly ground white pepper
Juice of 3 lemons	1 cup all-purpose flour
1/2 cup canned or peeled fresh grapes, 4 to 5 grapes per serving	1/4 to 1/2 cup peanut oil
	6 tablespoons butter
1/3 cup blanched sliced almonds	1 tablespoon chopped fresh parsley
1/2 cup half-and-half	Sprigs of fresh parsley or dill
	6 lemon wedges

- Rinse each trout thoroughly under cold running water, and butterfly using a boning knife. Split the trout open along the belly, leaving the halves attached along the back, and carefully remove the entrails, bones (including the backbone), head, and gills. Do not remove the skin. Trim away about 1/4 inch along the belly flaps.
- Squeeze the lemons into a bowl. Drain the grapes, and toast the almonds, if desired. Preheat the oven to 250°F if toasting the almonds. Arrange the almonds on a pan, and toast until golden brown. Remove from the oven.
- Pour the half-and-half into a small bowl. Season with salt and pepper to taste. Spread the flour on waxed paper or a plate, and, dip each fillet carefully into the cream, coating both sides. Let any excess cream drip off, and place the fillets on the flour. Pat the fillets lightly into the flour, and turn over. Coat the other side in the flour, shaking off the excess flour gently. Note: Do this just before sautéing the fillets, or otherwise they will be pasty.
- Pour the oil into a sauté pan over high heat to a depth of 1/8 inch, and heat until hot. Place the trout into the oil, skin side up, being careful not to crowd the pan. Cook the fillets in separate batches as necessary, changing the oil after the first two. Reduce the heat to medium high when the trout begins to sizzle, and sauté for 3 minutes. Turn over the fillets, and, after the sizzling begins, sauté for 2 minutes. Drain on paper towels, and place on a warm serving platter or plates.
- Pour the oil from the pan, and wipe clean. Add the butter, and place over medium heat. Shake the pan gently, swirling the butter around until melted and light golden brown. Add the lemon juice immediately to prevent the butter from browning any further. Note: The butter at this stage is called "beurre noisette" and has a nutlike flavor. Stir in the chopped parsley, almonds, and grapes. Pour over the the fish. Garnish with sprigs of parsley or dill and lemon wedges, and serve immediately.
- Makes 6 servings

This recipe was created by CHEF ALBERT SCHNARWYLER, who is retired now. The recipe is still used by CHEF JOSEF SCHELCH.

Grilled Tuna and Grilled Potatoes

4 Idaho potatoes, unpeeled
1 cup vegetable oil
1/4 cup plus 1 tablespoon
  fresh lemon juice
8 (6-ounce) tuna fillets,
  about 1/4 inch thick
Salt and pepper
1/4 cup plus 2 tablespoons
  cider vinegar
4 teaspoons Dijon mustard
1/2 teaspoon salt
1/4 teaspoon ground pepper
1 1/2 cups olive oil
1 small onion, thinly sliced

2 teaspoons minced basil
2 teaspoons minced thyme
1/2 tablespoon minced garlic
2 anchovies, minced
1 pound green beans,
  trimmed
4 medium tomatoes, peeled,
  cut into 8 wedges each
2 medium heads red leaf
  lettuce, rinsed, dried
64 Mediterranean black
  olives
2 tablespoons chopped fresh
  chives

- Cook the potatoes in boiling salted water to cover in a saucepan for 35 minutes. Rinse under cold running water until cool. Drain and refrigerate for 1 hour. Cut each potato into eight 1/4-inch-thick slices, discarding the end slices. Place the potato slices on plastic wrap-lined baking sheets. Cover with plastic wrap, and refrigerate.
- Combine 1/2 cup of the vegetable oil and 2 tablespoons of the lemon juice in a bowl, and coat the tuna fillets. Season with salt and pepper to taste. Refrigerate each fillet individually wrapped in plastic wrap. Whisk the vinegar, remaining lemon juice, Dijon mustard, salt, and black pepper in a stainless steel bowl. Add the olive oil gradually in a slow steady stream, whisking constantly until the oil has been incorporated. Stir in the onion, basil, thyme, garlic, and anchovies. Refrigerate, covered with plastic wrap.
- Blanch the green beans in 2 quarts boiling salted water in a saucepan for 2 to 2 1/2 minutes or until tender but still crunchy. Drain the beans, and plunge into ice water. Remove from the ice water, and drain well.
- Arrange 4 tomato wedges evenly spaced round the outside edge of each of eight 10-inch plates. Place a bed of red leaf lettuce leaves in the center of each plate. Sprinkle some green beans over each bed of lettuce. Place 2 olives between each tomato wedge on each plate. Preheat the oven to 225°F. Brush the potatoes on both sides with the remaining vegetable oil. Season with salt and pepper to taste. Grill over medium-hot coals for 2 to 2 1/2 minutes or until slightly charred on each side. Remove to a baking sheet, and place in the oven. Season the tuna fillets with salt and pepper. Grill over medium-hot coals for 1 1/2 minutes on each side.
- Stir the dressing, mixing well. Drizzle 6 tablespoons of the dressing over each serving. Place a warm potato slice next to each tomato wedge on each plate. Place a grilled tuna fillet in the center of each plate. Sprinkle the chives over the tuna fillet, and serve immediately.
- Makes 8 servings

Marcel Desaulniers and his partner, John Curtis, opened The Trellis Restaurant in 1980. The world-famous success of the restaurant led Marcel to publish his first book, *The Trellis Cookbook*, in 1988. He has since published seven more cookbooks. As an award-winning executive chef, he is a much-sought-after teacher and celebrated television personality whose life has always revolved around mouthwatering food.

This wonderful recipe was shared by CHEF MARCEL DESAULNIERS from *The Trellis Cookbook, Expanded Edition.*

THE CARTER FAMILY

Sometimes hailed as country music's "first" family, the famous Carters had their beginning in southwestern Virginia in 1915 when the group's patriarch, A. P. Carter, married Sara Dougherty. When Maybelle Addington joined the pair after marrying A. P.'s brother in 1926, the trio began recording in a makeshift studio in Bristol. Before long, their sound spread across the country, and when they released "Wildwood Flower" in 1928, the single sold more than a million copies. Although A. P. and Sara divorced in 1936, Maybelle's three daughters—June, Helen, and Anita—soon joined the group and were influential in its continued success. June eventually married Johnny Cash, and she, along with her mother and sisters, appeared regularly on Cash's national TV shows of the mid-1960s. The Carter Family was inducted into the Country Music Hall of Fame in 1970.

Jamaican Escoveiched Fish

Fish without many bones, dressed	$^1/_8$ cup oil for frying
1 to 2 teaspoons salt	1 white onion, chopped
1 to 2 teaspoons pepper	4 pimiento seeds
	1 cup white vinegar

- Season the fish with the salt and pepper. Fry the fish on both sides in the oil in a skillet. Drain on a paper towel.
- Simmer the onion and pimiento seeds in the white vinegar in a saucepan for about 3 minutes or until the onions are soft. Place the fish on a serving plate, and spoon the onion mixture over the fish. Pour the vinegar over the entire dish.
- Makes several servings depending on the size of the fish

I was born in Jamaica, so I thought your readers might want a 'different' sort of recipe.

This recipe was sent by Virginia delegate to the General Assembly WINSOME EARLE SEARS, representing parts of Norfolk and Chesapeake. She was born in Jamaica, and came to the United States when she was six years old. Raised in New York City, she graduated meritoriously from high school. She enlisted in the United States Marine Corps at the age of 19, holding various leadership positions in the Marine Corps, and became a U.S. citizen one year later. In 1999 she was the first black Republican woman elected to the Virginia General Assembly, the first female veteran elected to the Virginia General Assembly, and the first foreign-born woman elected to the Virginia General Assembly. She is deeply involved in, and committed to, her community.

GREENSVILLE COUNTY

When it was formed in 1780 from Brunswick County, Greensville County was most likely named in honor of Sir Richard Grenville, who settled Roanoke Island for the English in 1585. The county contains three hundred seven square miles and 11,560 residents. Its county seat is Emporia.

Greensville County is the site of Homestead, the plantation of James Mason, a Revolutionary War figure. During the last days of the Revolution, in May 1781, British cavalry officer Banastre Tarleton marched through Greensville County causing much havoc along the way.

DID YOU KNOW THAT:

Thomas Jefferson's personal library provided the basis from which today's Library of Congress grew?

CHIEF HOLLOWAY'S
Clam Fritters

25 chowder clams, chopped, juice reserved	Salt and pepper
1 large white onion, chopped	Dash of Tabasco sauce
	1 1/2 cups pancake flour
	1 cup cornmeal

- Combine the clams, clam juice, onion, salt and pepper to taste, Tabasco sauce, flour, and cornmeal in a bowl, and mix well. Fry as you would a pancake.
- Makes 6 to 8 servings

This is the recipe of CHIEF JACKIE W. HOLLOWAY, a 40-year veteran of the Poquoson Volunteer Fire Department, Poquoson, Virginia.

BLACKBEARD'S
Crabmeat Casserole

1 egg	1 pound crabmeat
2 tablespoons mayonnaise	4 slices bread, finely crumbled
1 tablespoon dry mustard	1/2 cup hot milk
Dash of Tabasco sauce	Bread crumbs for topping
1 tablespoon minced onion, optional	1 teaspoon paprika
2 tablespoons Worcestershire sauce	Butter or margarine

- Preheat the oven to 350°F. Beat the egg in a large bowl until light and frothy. Add the mayonnaise, dry mustard, Tabasco sauce, onion, if desired, Worcestershire sauce, crabmeat, and bread crumbs. Blend thoroughly, and add the milk. Pour into a casserole dish. Top with the bread crumbs and paprika. Dot with butter or margarine. Bake until brown and bubbly, about 30 minutes.
- Makes 6 servings

This recipe was submitted by JANE POLONSKY of the Virginia DAR Chapter in Hampton, where Blackbeard the pirate made history by ravaging the coastline.

HOW TO HOST A CLAMBAKE

At a clambake, shellfish are roasted over coals in a pit dug on the beach. You can also use a covered barbecue. Be sure you set out the clam knives so diners can finish opening up the shellfish. You need:

Burlap or fishnet, optional
5 dozen fresh clams, well scrubbed
Tangy cocktail sauce
Seafood butter with herbs

Pit method: Soak the burlap or fishnet in water to cover while preparing the fire. Dig a shallow pit in the beach sand. Line with flat rocks, bricks or seashells. Now build the fire in the pit. Let it burn down to coals; then place a large metal grill over the coals. Arrange the clams on the grill. Top with the wet net and seaweed, if available. Roast until the shells begin to open, about 15 minutes. Remove the shellfish from the grill using kitchen gloves. Serve with sauces.

Barbecue method: Prepare a barbecue grill (set on low heat). Place the clams on the grill rack. Cover and cook until shells begin to open, about 15 minutes. Remove to a platter and serve with sauces. This method is also used for roasting oysters, which is also very popular in Virginia.

Makes 12 servings

—Blue Crab Bay Company

CHESAPEAKE BAY BLUE CRABS

Crabs and Virginia's gourmets go back a long way. John White, the artist-governor of the ill-fated Roanoke Colony—the first English attempt to settle Virginia in the 1580s—left a painting of a crab, and his associate, Thomas Hariot, in his book *New Found Land of Virginia*, published in 1588, described the species to his readers. The Commonwealth's favorite species— blue crabs—are found along the Atlantic seaboard from Nova Scotia all the way to Argentina. None make better eating, however, than the ones native to the Chesapeake Bay. Today, the Chesapeake blue crab is a much-sought-after delicacy that is enjoyed in a wide variety of dishes, including salads and gumbo.

Crab Casserole "Full Measure"

1 pound crabmeat	1 egg
2 tablespoons chopped parsley	1/2 to 3/4 cup mayonnaise
2 tablespoons chopped onion	1/4 cup sherry
2 teaspoons mustard	Dash of Tabasco sauce
1 tablespoon Worcestershire sauce	Seasoned croutons, such as Pepperidge Farm
	Shredded cheddar cheese

- Preheat the oven to 350°F. Combine the crabmeat, parsley, onion, mustard, Worcestershire sauce, egg, mayonnaise, sherry, and Tabasco sauce in a bowl, and mix well. Spoon into a serving dish, and top with the croutons and cheese. Bake until heated through and the cheese is lightly browned.
- Makes 4 to 6 servings

The recipe was provided by MRS. PHILIP PAYNE of Pungoteague, Virginia, a member of Eastern Shore of Virginia Historical Society.

Eastern Shore Crab Cakes

2 eggs	1 tablespoon mayonnaise
1 tablespoon Worcestershire sauce	2 tablespoons cracker meal
2 tablespoons minced parsley	1 pound white crabmeat
2 teaspoons Old Bay Seasoning	2 teaspoons olive oil
2 teaspoons prepared mustard	2 teaspoons butter or margarine

- Combine the eggs, Worcestershire sauce, parsley, Old Bay Seasoning, prepared mustard, mayonnaise, and cracker meal in a large bowl. Add the crabmeat carefully so as not to disturb the "beautiful crab lump", and blend gently. Shape the crab mixture into crab cakes. Cook the crab cakes in a mixture of the olive oil and butter or margarine in a medium skillet for about 3 minutes or until the crab cakes are heated through and browned.
- Makes 4 crab cakes

This is a typical eastern shore dish that totally everyone truly loves. Crab is delicious any way you eat it, as crab cakes, as crab salad, or just plain with your fingers.

The recipe is shared by TATA KELLAM, who owned Mr. Greenjeans. She is married to Lucius J. Kellam III, and they live in the 1820 Kellam House on the eastern shore of Virginia. Grandchildren and crabbing are two of their most fun-filled interests. Cooking crabs in a big pot of water with some Old Bay Seasoning, a little vinegar, beer, and a little hot sauce is a real event. A table covered with newspaper and a big pile of crabs is the best kind of party.

SENATOR JOHN WARNER'S
Norfolk Crab Cakes

Fresh onions, preferably 2 types for variety of flavor and texture, chopped
Fresh butter
Green bell peppers, chopped
Bread crumbs (or mix with a little cornmeal)
Fresh Chesapeake Bay blue crabmeat (important that crabs come from the Virginia side of the bay)
Eggs
Black pepper
Heavy cream

- Melt the butter in a medium skillet, and precook the onions, taking care not to lose firmness of texture. Also, slightly sauté the chopped green peppers to release full flavor.
- Note: Precooking the onions and peppers, then adding bread crumbs or mixing with a little cornmeal, if used, at the end of this step reduces the amount of further cooking to which the crabmeat is subjected. As you know, crabmeat is packaged fully cooked and further heat diminishes its quality, a mistake most cooks make. Mix the crab, eggs, cooked onions and green peppers, bread crumbs, and black pepper.
- Note: Another mistake is adding salt. Don't try to improve on nature. If the eater wants to add salt, then let him "eat cake" instead. Add sufficient cream to blend the mixture lightly. Now you are ready to cook the mixture. First, let's precook the butter. It might surprise you to learn that butter tastes better, is more digestible, and browns the outside of cake more quickly if heated slowly until you see a slight browning of the solids from the butter in the bottom of your pan. Now quickly add the hand-molded crab cake before your butter begins to burn. This takes skillful timing, and once mastered, elevates you to chef. If you have done a proper job of precooking ingredients (less the crabmeat), allowing this mixture to achieve room temperature, and preparing the butter, the rest is easy. Add the crab cake, no more than $1/2$ to $3/4$ inch thick. A thicker crab cake will tend to overcook on the outside while properly cooking the inside. Got it! By now you have had enough of the recipe, especially the advice. Two last hints: The less you have to cook the crab cake, the better, for you are preserving the "seasoning of the sea" and one of nature's finest gifts. When it's done, get it out of the pan, and don't let it soak up excess butter. Good luck, and thank you for making the effort to join me in this venture.
- Makes as many crab cakes as you have time and energy to make

Chef's Note: This is a creative recipe and the precise measurements, preparation of the mix, and cooking variables are trade secrets known only to the chef. Traditional crab cakes are those made with a mix of the ingredients recommended above and amounts to suit the chef's particular taste.

This marvelous recipe was sent by SENATOR JOHN W. WARNER, senior senator from Virginia.

VIRGINIA'S SENIOR SENATOR

Senator John W. Warner is serving his fifth term in the United States Senate. Prior to his service in the Senate, he served Presidential appointments as Under Secretary of the Navy, Secretary of the Navy, and as administrator of the American Revolution Bicentennial Administration. He is one of just four elected officials in Virginia's political history to have won five or more statewide elections. Senator Warner is the senior Republican member of the Armed Services Committee and also serves on the Environment and Public Works, Health, Education, Labor and Pensions, and Rules and Administration Committees.

THE ORDEAL OF WARS AT ENDVIEW PLANTATION

Built in 1769 by Colonel William Harwood, Jr., a signer of the Virginia Resolves, this Georgian-styled wooden farmhouse has experienced the ordeal of three wars. Endview was used as a muster site on September 28, 1781 by Major General Thomas Nelson, Jr.'s Virginia Militia enroute to the climatic siege of Yorktown. During the War of 1812, the plantation was a training ground for the 115th Virginia Militia. By the outbreak of the Civil War, Endview has passed to Dr. Humphrey Harwood Curtis. Curtis became captain of the Warwick Beauregards, Co. H, 32nd Virginia Infantry Regiment. The home was used as a Confederate hospital during the April 5 to May 3, 1862 siege of the Yorktown-Warwick River Line and then by the Union army following the May 5, 1862 Battle of Williamsburg. This beautiful house has been restored to its 1862 appearance and now operates as a historic house museum interpreting Civil War themes.

—John V. Quarstein, Director
The Virginia War Museum

Mammaw's Steamed Crabs

- First of all, the best crabs in the world are the ones you catch yourself. That's a whole 'nother story though, about catching crabs. But now that you have the crabs, about a bushel, fill the bathtub half full of water and dump them in. Now you can see what you have. Don't take too long to get the pot and stove ready or the crabs will drown for lack of oxygen.
- Get a big pot with a tray inside the bottom to keep crabs out of the fluids. Remember you're steaming them, not boiling them.
- Fill the pot to the top with crabs; be careful, they'll cut your fingers with their sharp claws. Maybe use some tongs or heavy gloves.
- Into the pot, pour one 12-ounce can of beer, 2 spoonfuls of Old Bay Seasoning, 6 ounces of vinegar and fill to the bottom of the raised tray with water. [Somehow my grandmother always had a can of beer around, although I never saw her drink one.]
- Fill the pot with crabs. Pour some more Old Bay on top of the crabs (but don't let them jump out of the pot). Turn on the heat and steam 'em up. Stay close by because when it starts getting hot in the pot, the crabs may try to push the top off and jump out.
- When they've just turned red, they're done.
- Spread out some newspapers on the table and pour the crabs (not the sauce) out. Have some large handled butter knives or small wooden mallets to help (with breaking the shells). Maybe some melted butter in bowls and a few piles of Old Bay Seasoning out on the table. Some people like crackers to go with their coca colas or beer.
- Now, picking and eating them crabs is another story too . . .

The recipe is from Delegate THELMA DRAKE and husband, TED, in Hampton Roads, in the tidal waters of the Chesapeake Bay in southeastern Virginia. This recipe was passed down from Ted's grandmother, Mollie Elsie Flora Sawyer. "Mammaw" and Ted's four brothers and sisters caught, cooked, and ate crabs from 1960 to 1970 in East Ghent and Ocean View in Norfolk, Virginia.

The Honorable Thelma Drake serves Virginia and her community of Norfolk in many ways. She was elected to the House of Delegates in 1995 from the 87th District in Norfolk, the first woman of her party elected from Norfolk. She is a strong and respected leader in the House. She is also a leading regional realtor, and with her other civic achievements and participation, she was awarded honors as the 1997 Outstanding Professional Woman of Hampton Roads, the 2000 YMCA Legislator of the Year, and the 2000 Virginia Commissioner of Revenue Legislator of the Year.

DID YOU KNOW THAT:

Silk culture in America had its beginnings in Virginia?

RED FOX INN
Crab Cakes

3 eggs
3/4 to 1 cup mayonnaise
1/2 cup minced onions
1/2 cup minced celery
1 to 1 1/2 cups bread crumbs
1/4 cup lemon juice
2 tablespoons Old Bay
  Seasoning

3 tablespoons
  Worcestershire sauce
1 teaspoon black pepper
2 pounds fresh lump
  crabmeat
Oil for frying

- Combine the eggs, mayonnaise, onions, celery, bread crumbs, lemon juice, Old Bay Seasoning, Worcestershire sauce, and black pepper in a large bowl, and mix well. Add the crabmeat, and toss lightly. Shape into patties, and broil or fry in shallow oil in a frying pan.
- Makes 8 servings

The RED FOX INN, which is among the most award-winning bed and breakfasts nationwide, has maintained its romantic country inn charm since 1728. Halfway between Alexandria and the frontier town of Winchester, Virginia, Joseph Chinn built a tavern out of fieldstone in 1728. Mr. Chinn's Ordinary, as it came to be called, became a popular stopping point for traveling colonists such as young George Washington. In 1787, the area was sold for $2.50 an acre to the newly chartered town of Middleburg, which grew in reputation as the foremost area for fox hunting, thorough-bred breeding, and horse racing. During the Civil War, the inn served as both a headquarters and hospital for the Confederacy. The pine service bar, still in use today, was made from the field operating table by an Army surgeon in General John Stuart's Cavalry. In 1937 the inn acquired the name it bears today, The Red Fox Inn. It has maintained a goal of providing guests with good food, romantic accommodations, and pleasant service.

HALIFAX COUNTY

Halifax County was organized in 1752 out of Lunenburg County. It was named after George Montague Dunk, the Earl of Halifax. The county contains eight hundred fourteen square miles and provides home to 37,355 residents. The county seat is Halifax.

President George Washington visited the town of Halifax on June 4, 1791, when he toured the southern states. The Reverend Charles A. Dresser, the minister who married Mary Todd and Abraham Lincoln in Springfield, Illinois, in 1842, once lived in this county.

THE APPALACHIAN TRAIL

The Appalachian Trail is a 2,015 mile-long footpath that stretches through fourteen states along the crest of the Appalachian Mountains, from Springer Mountain, Georgia, to Mount Katahdin, Maine. Almost twenty-five per cent of the Trail's mileage is contained within Virginia, entering the state in the south near Damascus and exiting in the north several miles beyond Front Royal. The Trail had its beginnings in 1921 when Benton MacKaye sat down with two associates and described to them his dream of creating "a trail that would run in a wilderness belt from one of the highest mountains in New England to one of the highest in the South." Later in the year, MacKaye published an article entitled *An Appalachian Trail, A Project in Regional Planning*, in the *Journal of the American Institute of Architects (AIA)*.

Work began soon thereafter, with the first sections of the Trail being cleared in New York and New Jersey. The first meeting of the coordinating organ, the Appalachian Trail Conference, convened in Washington, D. C. in 1925, and by the time of its second meeting three years later, about five hundred miles of pathway had been opened to hikers. The entire length of the Trail was opened to the public in August, 1937.

In 1968, the National Trails System Act was enacted which guarantees federal protection for the Trail. Today, tens of thousands of hikers make their ways along the Appalachian Trail, if not over its entire length, at least over part of it. In 1953, the noted naturalist, John Kieran, wrote the following words which are as applicable to Trail hikers today as they were a half-century ago.

Take to the woods on windy days. It's quieter there. Keep your ears open. You can always hear more birds than you can see. Keep your eyes open. There are flowers in bloom through most months of the year, and trees are as interesting even in early spring as they are in summer. . . .Take the sun over your shoulder for the best views. Avoid slippery footing as you would the plague, and don't sit on damp ground. Keep walking.

TRAVIS HOUSE
Escalloped Oysters

1 cup (2 sticks) butter or salad oil	1 green bell pepper, chopped
1 cup all-purpose flour	$^1/_2$ clove garlic, minced
1$^1/_2$ teaspoons paprika	1 tablespoon lemon juice
$^1/_2$ teaspoon salt	1 tablespoon Worcestershire sauce
$^1/_4$ teaspoon black pepper	1 quart oysters
Dash of cayenne	$^1/_4$ cup cracker crumbs
2 onions, chopped	

- Preheat the oven to 400°F. Heat the butter or salad oil in a saucepan until hot. Remove saucepan from the heat, and add the flour, stirring until smooth. Return to the heat, and cook for 5 minutes or until light brown, stirring constantly.
- Add the paprika, salt, pepper, and cayenne, and mix well. Remove the saucepan from the heat, and add the onions, green pepper, and garlic. Cool for 5 minutes, stirring constantly, and add the lemon juice, Worcestershire sauce, and oysters with liquid, mixing well.
- Pour into a 2-quart baking dish, and sprinkle with the cracker crumbs. Bake for 30 minutes.
- Makes 4 to 6 servings

The Travis House, a gracious 1765 dwelling, was renovated and moved to the heart of the famous Colonial Williamsburg, and once it was used as a restaurant.

FRANCES PONS from Surry, Virginia, a past Regent of the Williamsburg Chapter of the Virginia DAR, submitted this recipe. Source: *The Ford Treasury of Famous Recipes from Famous Eating Places* by The Ford Motor Company (1946-1950).

HANOVER COUNTY

Hanover County was formed from New Kent County in 1720. Named after King George I, who once was the elector of Hanover, Germany, the county contains five hundred twelve square miles. Its population is 86,320, and the county seat is Hanover.

The famed American statesmen Henry Clay (1777-1852) and Patrick Henry (1736-1799) were born in this county. The Seven Days' Battle during the War Between the States was fought here during June and July 1862

DID YOU KNOW THAT:

The College of William and Mary in Williamsburg is the second oldest institute of higher learning in the United States?

Christiana Campbell's

TAVERN

Oyster Fritters with Dipping Sauce

DIPPING SAUCE

2 tablespoons (or more) prepared horseradish, drained

³/4 cup ketchup
³/4 cup mayonnaise

OYSTER FRITTERS

¹/4 cup plus 2 tablespoons flour
²/3 cup lukewarm water
2 tablespoons vegetable oil
1 tablespoon finely chopped fresh parsley
2 egg whites, stiffly beaten

Vegetable oil for frying
24 medium oysters, shucked, drained
Flour for coating
Salt and freshly ground black pepper
Lemon wedges for garnish

- To prepare the sauce, combine the horseradish, ketchup, and mayonnaise in a small bowl, and mix well. Chill, covered, in the refrigerator until ready to serve.
- To prepare the fritters, combine ¹/4 cup plus 2 tablespoons flour, water, oil, and parsley in a large bowl, whisking until smooth. Stir about ¹/4 of the egg whites into the mixture to lighten. Fold in the remaining egg whites gently.
- Fill an electric deep-fat fryer or a large skillet with enough oil to measure 1 to 1¹/2 inches deep. Heat to 375°F. Coat the oysters with flour, and dip into the batter. Place the oysters in the hot oil, and fry for 1 to 2 minutes or until golden brown, turning frequently. Sprinkle with salt and pepper to taste.
- Drain well on paper towels, and serve warm with the dipping sauce. Garnish with lemon wedges.
- Makes 4 servings

Since 1607, when Captains John Smith and Christopher Newport landed in Jamestown and found an abundance of oysters "lying thick as stones", oysters have been a staple of the Virginia diet. The oysters are left whole in the butter to keep their juicy shape and creamy texture. The dipping sauce that accompanies this dish is reminiscent of the creamy cocktail sauce made with tomato ketchup mixed with mayonnaise and horseradish. An early recipe for tomato ketchup appeared in the Virginia Housewife *in 1824.*

This recipe was given to us by CHRISTIANA CAMPBELL'S TAVERN.

DID YOU KNOW THAT:

Arlington National Cemetery occupies the site of Mrs. Robert E. Lee's family home place?

HISTORY OF THE DAR

In October 1875, a group of patriots in California formed a group called the Sons of the Revolution Sires. In 1883, the Sons of the Revolution organized in New York. As it happened, some of the SAR Societies permitted women and some did not. But at its general meeting in April 1890, the Sons of the American Revolution made the decision to completely exclude women. Much publicity and media attention ensued, and in October 1890, eighteen ladies and four gentlemen met in Washington, D.C., for the purpose of founding the Daughters of the American Revolution. Any woman over the age of eighteen who is lineally descended from a man or woman who, with unfailing loyalty, aided the cause for independence in military or public service is eligible for membership.

Thus, it was chartered by the U.S. Congress and each year reports to that assembly of the DAR. The first President General (1890-1892), Caroline Scott Harrison, was the wife of President Benjamin Harrison. There are currently more than two hundred twenty thousand members in over three thousand one

hundred chapters in the United States and other countries. Echoing George Washington's farewell address, the DAR bylaws state the organization's objectives:

To perpetuate the memory and spirit of the men and women who achieved American independence . . . to promote . . . institutions for the general diffusion of knowledge . . . and to cherish, maintain, and extend the institution of American freedom; to foster true patriotism and love of country, and to aid in securing for mankind all blessings of liberty.

The chief goals of the DAR are to preserve American history and to promote appreciation of its heritage; to lead and promote good citizenship among immigrants to the United States; and to foster education for the future by supporting schools and colleges and providing scholarships and loans for underprivileged youth.

—A Century of Service: The Story of the DAR by Ann Arnold Hunter, an Honorary Regent of Virginia and a member of the Narrow Passage Chapter

Perfect Fried Oysters

BATTER
2 eggs
²/₃ cup milk
1 teaspoon salt

1 teaspoon baking soda
1 cup all-purpose flour

CRACKER MEAL MIXTURE
3 cups all-purpose flour
1 teaspoon baking soda
1 teaspoon salt

1 teaspoon baking powder
2 cups cracker crumbs
1 cup vegetable oil

OYSTERS
1 quart fresh oysters

1 teaspoon salt

- To prepare the batter, beat the eggs in a medium bowl. Add the milk, salt, baking soda, and flour, and beat well.
- To prepare the cracker meal mixture, combine the flour, baking soda, salt, baking powder, and cracker crumbs in a large bowl, and mix well.
- To prepare the oysters, drain the oysters, and remove the shell bits. Sprinkle the salt over the oysters. Drop 8 to 10 oysters at a time into the batter, and coat completely. Remove each oyster from the batter, shaking off the excess. Coat the bottom of a large frying pan with ¹/₂ inch of the vegetable oil, and heat. Roll the battered oysters in the cracker meal mixture until completely coated. Drop the oysters carefully into medium hot oil. Fry the oysters quickly, turning once. Do not overcook.
- Makes approximately 4 to 6 servings depending on your passion for oysters

The two-coating process is the secret to this recipe's success. Flounder is also delicious cooked this way.

This recipe is shared by JULIE PLUNKETT, one of the most organized and enthusiastic ladies I have ever known. She creates partnerships between businesses and the non-profit sector and donates much of her consulting services to over thirty non-profit organizations. In addition she has coordinated such prestigious events as the U.S. Open Tennis Tournament, the Memorial Golf Tournament, and the Gold Cup Steeplechase, as well as the inaugurations of three U.S. Presidents. —Rowena

DID YOU KNOW THAT:

The first Greek-letter society to be organized in America, Phi Beta Kappa, was established at the College of William and Mary in Williamsburg (1776)? The society's charter encouraged both men and women to pursue "scholarship in the liberal arts and sciences."

Old Virginia Ham-Wrapped Sea Scallops

$^1/_2$ cup (1 stick) butter or margarine, melted
2 pounds large sea scallops
2 teaspoons coarsely ground pepper
1 tablespoon Italian seasoning

1 (12-ounce) package center-cut and end slices Edward's Hickory Smoked Dry Cured Country Style Virginia Ham
Wooden picks

- Brush the melted butter or margarine over the scallops. Season the scallops generously with the pepper and Italian seasoning.
- Cut the ham into $^1/_4$ to $^1/_2$-inch strips, each long enough to wrap around a scallop. Wrap a ham strip around each scallop. Secure with a wooden pick. Place in a broiler pan.
- Broil on a lower rack of the oven for about 5 to 7 minutes on each side or until the scallops are done.
- Makes 5 to 6 servings

Suggested side dishes are chopped spinach greens and candied sweet potatoes. Top the meal off with a warm apple crisp smothered in French vanilla ice cream. My family enjoys good Southern cooking, which I learned to love growing up in southeast Virginia. When I prepare meals, the recipe is only the rough outline. The rest is the joy of experimentation. The scallops and ham were one of my kitchen creations that became a big hit the moment I set the dish down on the table.

AMY WATERS YARSINSKE, a native of Norfolk, Virginia, and noted author and historian, submitted this recipe. As a professional writer and former intelligence officer in the Naval Reserve, Amy Waters Yarsinke has published over two dozen books and has been nominated for the Pulitzer Prize for Journalism for her six-part series on Scott Speicher, written with Lon Wagner for the *Virginian-Pilot*.

HENRICO COUNTY

Henrico County was one of Virginia's original shires, organized in 1634. Named in honor of Henry, Prince of Wales, and the oldest son of King James I, the county contains two hundred eighty square miles, and the population is 262,300. The county seat is Richmond.

Confederate General J.E.B. Stuart was mortally wounded on May 11, 1864, at Yellow Tavern north of Richmond. Virginia Estelle Randolph (1874-1958) was born into slavery in this county and went on to become one of Virginia's foremost educators.

VIRGINIA TIMELINE

1781—The old Governor's Palace at Williamsburg, being used as a hospital for American troops, burns to the ground. The British, under the command of Lord Cornwallis, surrender to General George Washington at Yorktown, thus effectively ending the Revolutionary War.

1784—Zachary Taylor, twelfth U.S. president (1849-1850), is born in Orange County.

1787—The Northwest Ordinance is passed to provide for the administration of that part of Virginia that was ceded to the federal government three years earlier. The territory is later organized into the states of Ohio, Indiana, Illinois, Michigan, and Wisconsin.

1788—Virginia becomes the tenth state to ratify the U.S. Constitution.

1789—George Washington is inaugurated first president of the United States.

1790—John Tyler, tenth U.S. president (1841-1845), is born at Greenway Plantation in Charles City County. His wife, Letitia Christian (Tyler), is born at Cedar Grove Plantation in New Kent County.

1792—The capitol building at Richmond is completed. Virginia relinquishes its lands south of the Ohio River, and the new state of Kentucky is organized.

1799—George Washington dies at Mount Vernon.

1802—Martha Washington dies at Mount Vernon.

1803—President Thomas Jefferson appoints his personal secretary, Virginia-born Meriwether Lewis, to head up an expedition to explore the newly purchased Louisiana Territory.

1814—British soldiers burn Washington, D.C., in the War of 1812.

1825—The University of Virginia opens its doors for the first time to students.

1831—In Southampton County, a group of slaves led by one of their own, Nat Turner, revolts. Sixty people are killed in the ensuing violence.

1834—The *Southern Literary Messenger* is founded in Richmond; the magazine's most eminent editor will be Edgar Allan Poe.

1846—Zachary Taylor and Winfield Scott, both natives of Virginia, command the American armies in the Mexican-American War.

1851—The James River and Kanawha Canal, connecting Richmond with Buchanan, opens for use.

THE BLUE HIPPO

Drunken Coconut Shrimp "Martini" with Ginger-Scented Tomato Chutney

SHRIMP

1 teaspoon baking powder	12 large shrimp
1 cup all-purpose flour	12 ounces sweetened
1 (12-ounce) bottle of beer	coconut
2 tablespoons Cajun seasoning	4 cups peanut oil

CHUTNEY

1 tablespoon butter	$1/4$ cup firmly packed light
2 tablespoons minced gingerroot	brown sugar
2 cloves garlic, minced	1 teaspoon ground cumin
$1/4$ cup apple cider vinegar	$1/4$ teaspoon cayenne
1 cinnamon stick	$1/8$ teaspoon ground cloves
3 (5-ounce) cans chopped peeled tomatoes with juice	$1/4$ cup honey
	Salt and freshly ground pepper

- To prepare the shrimp, combine the baking powder, flour, beer, and Cajun seasoning in a bowl, and mix well. Let stand for 10 minutes. Place the shrimp in the batter, coating evenly. Roll the shrimp in the sweetened coconut until coated. Heat the peanut oil in a large saucepan to 360°F. Cook the shrimp in the hot oil for about 3 to 4 minutes. Remove the shrimp with a slotted spoon to a plate lined with paper towels. Season with salt and pepper to taste.
- To prepare the chutney, melt the butter in a saucepan over moderately high heat. Add the gingerroot and garlic, and cook until fragrant, stirring contantly. Add the vinegar and cinnamon stick, and cook for about 1 minute or until reduced to a glaze. Stir in the tomatoes, brown sugar, cumin, cayenne, and cloves. Reduce the heat to low, and cook for 45 minutes or until the liquid has evaporated, stirring occasionally. Remove and discard the cinnamon stick. Stir in the honey, and season with salt and pepper to taste. Place the mixture in a food processor, and process until smooth.
- To serve, divide the chutney among 4 martini glasses. Hang 3 shrimp from each of the martini glasses. Garnish with fresh edible orchids and other fresh edible flowers.
- Makes 4 servings

CHAD MARTIN, chef, The Blue Hippo, Norfolk, kindly shared this wonderful recipe.

DID YOU KNOW THAT:

Although John Smith is the man most often associated with the success of the Jamestown settlement, he was actually the fourth leader of the colony and only served as chief executive for one year?

Shrimp Potpie

$^{1}/_{4}$ cup plus 2 tablespoons
  ($^{3}/_{4}$ stick) butter or
  margarine
1 cup chopped onions
$^{1}/_{2}$ cup chopped celery
$^{1}/_{4}$ cup plus 2 tablespoons
  all-purpose flour
3 cups seafood stock or
  chicken stock
1 cup milk
Salt and freshly ground
  white pepper

2 cups blanched chopped
  potatoes
1 cup blanched chopped
  carrots
1 cup sweet peas
1 cup chopped baked ham
1 pound shrimp or lobster
  meat, cooked, chopped
$^{1}/_{2}$ to 1 cup water
2 Basic Savory Piecrusts
  (page 169)

- Preheat the oven to 375°F. Grease a 9×13-inch glass baking dish. Melt the butter or margarine in a large sauté pan. Add the onions and celery, and sauté for 2 minutes. Stir in the flour, and cook for about 3 to 4 minutes for a blond roux (white sauce). Add the stock, and mix well. Bring to a boil, and reduce the heat. Simmer for 8 to 10 minutes or until the sauce starts to thicken. Stir in the milk, and cook for 4 minutes. Season with salt and pepper to taste. Remove from the heat. Stir in the potatoes, carrots, peas, ham, and shrimp or lobster. Combine the filling thoroughly. Add a small amount of water to thin the filling if too thick. Fit 1 of the Basic Savory Piecrust into the prepared baking dish.
- Pour the filling into the piecrust. Place the remaining Basic Savory Piecrust over the top of the filling. Tuck the overlapping piecrust carefully into the dish, forming a thick edge. Crimp the edges of the piecrust, and place the dish on a baking sheet. Cut several slits in the top of the piecrust using a sharp knife. Place in the oven, and bake for about 25 to 30 minutes or until the piecrust is golden brown and crisp. Remove from the oven, and let stand for 5 minutes before serving.
- Makes 4 servings

This recipe was sent by KATHY BYRON. She is a member of the Virginia House of Delegates, 22nd District, first elected in 1997, and represents all of Campbell County and part of Bedford County. Married for 28 years to Jack Byron, Kathy is the mother of three children and has three grandchildren.

DID YOU KNOW THAT:

George Washington surrendered his command in the first battle he ever fought (at Fort Necessity in the backwoods of Pennsylvania on July 4, 1754)? The battle is considered to be the first conflict in the French and Indian War, and it occurred exactly twenty-two years before the Declaration of Independence was signed.

THE JEFFERSON HOTEL IN RICHMOND

Since 1895, the Jefferson Hotel has been recognized by discerning visitors and guests as one of America's grandest hotels. Located in the heart of Richmond's historic Franklin Street district, the hotel boasts two hundred seventy-four luxurious guest rooms and suites that feature fifty-seven distinctive styles. Tastefully decorated with mahogany pieces, heavy draperies, and refined art work, the hotel has welcomed guests from Charlton Heston to Frank Sinatra to Elvis Presley. Live alligators used to slither around in a pit in the lobby, which has been renovated to accentuate its magnificent sweeping staircase—similar to the one in the movie, *Gone With the Wind*. Presidents Coolidge, Harrison, Reagan, Franklin D. Roosevelt, Theodore (Teddy) Roosevelt, McKinley, Taft, Truman, and Wilson have all stayed at the Jefferson.

The Jefferson's restaurant, Lemaire, is named for Etienne Lemaire, who served as maître d'hôtel to Thomas Jefferson from 1794 through the end of his presidency. Jefferson was known for his appreciation of fine wines, and Lemaire is widely credited for introducing the fine art of cooking with wines to America. Jefferson was also known for his fondness for meals prepared with light sauces, garden-fresh herbs, and creative uses for the region's abundant variety of ingredients. That spirit has inspired Lemaire's menu, which features only fresh ingredients and home-grown herbs. Chefs prepare light sauces, smoked items, breads, and magnificent desserts. The restaurant is located in what used to be the original ladies' parlors of the hundred-year-old plus hotel. Seven dining areas provide historic ambiance for fine dining.

Overlooking an engaging view of the Rotunda's hustle and bustle, T.J.'s offers classic but less formal dining at the Jefferson. Superior luncheons are served here as Richmond natives fill the restaurant. Night dining is a culinary adventure, with late-night fare and cocktails also available. The superb Sunday Champagne Brunch is served in the hotel's Rotunda, and many visitors take advantage of the traditional Afternoon Tea served in the Palm Court area of the establishment.

The Jefferson is a national historic landmark and a charter member of Historic Hotels of America. It has been completely renovated to enhance the original beauty of its distinct architecture. Reminiscent of a more gracious era, the Jefferson enjoys a legendary reputation for warm and friendly service, providing the finest Virginian hospitality.

Basic Savory Piecrust

3¹/₄ cups all-purpose flour	1¹/₂ cups cold lard or solid vegetable shortening
1 teaspoon salt	4 to 5 tablespoons ice water

- To prepare the piecrust dough, combine the flour and salt in a bowl. Add the lard or shortening, and work in with the hands until the mixture resembles coarse crumbs. Add the water, 1 tablespoon at a time, and work in with the hands, adding just enough water to make a smooth ball of dough. Refrigerate, wrapped in plastic wrap, for at least 30 minutes. Remove the dough from the refrigerator, and place on a lightly floured surface. Cut the dough into 2 equal portions, and wrap each portion in plastic wrap. Chill in the refrigerator.
- To prepare a piecrust, roll out 1 portion of the dough on a floured surface into a square about 14 inches in diameter and ¹/₈ inch thick. Fold the dough square gently into halves and then into halves again to prevent tearing. Repeat this process for the remaining piecrust.
- Makes 2 piecrusts

Shrimp Scampi and Tomatoes

1 tablespoon butter or margarine	¹/₄ cup chopped fresh basil
¹/₄ cup olive oil	1 cup chopped fresh tomatoes
¹/₂ cup chopped onion	1 tablespoon lemon zest
4 to 5 cloves garlic, chopped	Salt and freshly ground pepper
1 pound medium-to-large, shelled deveined shrimp	Cooked vermicelli or angel hair pasta
¹/₄ cup dry white wine	Parmesan cheese
2 tablespoons lemon juice	
¹/₄ cup chopped fresh parsley	

- Melt the butter or margarine in a large skillet. Add the onion and garlic, and sauté for 10 minutes. Add the shrimp. Sauté until the shrimp turn pink. Remove the shrimp, and keep warm.
- Add the wine, lemon juice, parsley, and basil to the skillet, and simmer for 2 to 3 minutes. Stir in the tomatoes, and return the shrimp to the skillet. Add the lemon zest and the salt and pepper to taste, and mix well. Cook until heated through.
- Serve over the vermicelli or angel hair pasta, and sprinkle with the Parmesan cheese.
- Makes 6 to 8 servings

LINDA GEER of Virginia Beach, who has a passion for elegant food and the art of its preparation, shared this recipe.

BLUE CRAB BAY

Bloody Mary Shrimp and Pasta

1 pound fettuccine or other
  pasta
1 pound fresh shrimp,
  peeled, deveined
3 cloves garlic, crushed
1/4 cup olive oil

1 cup Sting Ray Bloody
  Mary Mixer
2 tablespoons freshly
  chopped parsley
1/4 cup grated Parmesan
  cheese

- Cook the pasta according to package directions in a large pot. Drain, and keep warm.
- Sauté the shrimp with the garlic in the olive oil in a large skillet for about 3 to 5 minutes or until the shrimp turns pink. Add to the pasta, and top with Sting Ray Bloody Mary Mixer.
- Garnish with the parsley and Parmesan cheese. Serve with a fresh garden salad and bread.
- Note: Provide a little extra Sting Ray Mixer in a small creamer for guests who enjoy extra zing.
- Makes approximately 4 servings

We never realized what a great cooking ingredient our Sting Ray Bloody Mary Mixer with Clam Juice was until a customer called and told us she served it as a chilled soup with sour cream and chives when unexpected guests arrived. It was a hit.

Virginia's Finest

This recipe was sent by PAM BAREFOOT, president and founder of Blue Crab Bay Company. It was in 1985 that Pamela Barefoot imagined a company that would put tastes of the Chesapeake Bay region on the map, be a protector of the environment, and provide stimulating and fun employment for citizens of her rural community. Surrounding herself with food offerings from the Chesapeake, a functioning stove, a list of contacts, and boatloads of imagination and determination, Barefoot went to work. Her first brand, Blue Crab Bay Company, featured original products like seasonings for crab dip and gift packs wrapped in weathered fishnet with seashells. Today the corporate culture of Pam's company, Bay Beyond, Inc., continues to demonstrate a strong commitment to the environment and its rural eastern shore community. Each year, employees energetically plan and execute charity events. As an example, in 1998 the Blue Crabbers Relay for Life Team raised more than $35,000 to benefit the American Cancer Society. The company supports various organizations including The Chesapeake Bay Foundation, Citizens for a Better Eastern Shore, The Nature Conservancy, the Barrier Island Center, and the United Way of Virginia's Eastern Shore.

DID YOU KNOW THAT:

Zachary Taylor was the first U.S. president who had
never before held elective office?

FRANCIS BAILY ON NORFOLK HOSPITALITY

As part of an extended American visit, Francis Baily, a young Englishman who in later life would become a founder and four-times president of Great Britain's world-renowned Royal Astronomical Society, paused in Norfolk during mid-February 1796. Baily's memoir of his adventures, *Journal of a Tour in Unsettled Parts of North America in 1796 & 1797*, was published posthumously in 1856. In the book, Baily reveals that room and board in Norfolk, which included breakfast

JOURNAL

OF A

TOUR IN UNSETTLED PARTS

OF

NORTH AMERICA

IN 1796 & 1797.

BY THE LATE

FRANCIS BAILY, F.R.S.,

PRESIDENT OF THE ROYAL ASTRONOMICAL SOCIETY.

With a Memoir of the Author.

LONDON:
BAILY BROTHERS, ROYAL EXCHANGE BUILDINGS.
MDCCCLVI.

and dinner, but no supper, cost one dollar per day. He describes a typical Norfolk breakfast:

Their breakfasts consist of beefsteaks, sausages, stewed veal, fried ham, eggs, coffee and tea, and a dish, or rather a cake peculiar to the southern states, made out of the meal of Indian corn, and called hoe-cake, of which the inhabitants are very fond. Its taste I do not dislike when buttered and eaten with eggs, though to many it is disagreeable: it is simply a mixture of Indian meal and water, and baked on an iron plate over the fire.

Horseradish and Dill Shrimp Croquettes

2 cups cooked salad shrimp	$1/2$ cup minced celery
$1/2$ teaspoon Old Bay Seasoning	Pinch of cayenne
1 teaspoon dill weed	1 tablespoon minced parsley
1 tablespoon horseradish	2 eggs, beaten
$1/2$ cup chopped tomatoes	1 to $1^1/3$ cups bread crumbs
	Oil for frying, optional

- Mix the shrimp, Old Bay Seasoning, dill weed, horseradish, tomatoes, celery, cayenne, parsley, and eggs. Fold in the bread crumbs, and shape into small patties. Deep-fry or bake at 350°F for approximately 25 minutes or until golden brown.
- Makes 6 to 8 croquettes

Thanks to the PAINTED LADY TEA ROOM in Norfolk, Virginia, for sending this recipe.

Rémoulade Sauce for Cold Shrimp

1 small clove garlic, minced	1 teaspoon prepared mustard
1 hard-cooked egg, minced	1 teaspoon prepared horseradish
1 tablespoon minced green onion	1 cup mayonnaise
1 tablespoon minced parsley	

- Mix all the ingredients in a medium bowl. Serve with fresh shrimp or crab. Note: The recipe can be doubled.
- Makes 1 to 2 cups

The recipe is shared by the staff of CHRIST AND SAINT LUKE'S EPISCOPAL CHURCH, one of the signature buildings of Norfolk. It is listed as a Historic Virginia Landmark and is generally considered to be the finest example of 20th century Gothic Revival design between Washington, D.C., and Atlanta, Georgia. The mother church of South Hampton Roads Episcopal churches, it descended directly from the "Congregation of Christians of South Hampton Roads," which was organized in 1637. However, this is the fourth building in the congregation's long and illustrious career. As Norfolk began to develop the neighborhood of Ghent, the church elected to follow its people out of the old downtown center to the present location on West Olney Road and Stockley Gardens. This structure was completed and opened on Christmas Day, 1910. A 130-foot bell tower rises from the southwest corner of the long narrow building, which has a traditional gable roof. The nave is 150 feet long, and 55 feet high with seating for about 800 persons. Indiana limestone lines the interior and provides trim for the exterior. Ample stone carvings and other stylistically appropriate ornamentation adorn the exterior of the building. The old 1,218-pound G-tone bell was moved from the third church building to this location, and it hangs in the tower today.

Crêpes à la Mer

CRÊPES

1 cup cold water
1 cup cold milk
4 eggs
1/2 teaspoon salt

2 cups sifted all-purpose flour
1/4 cup (1/2 stick) butter,
  melted
Peanut oil for brushing pan

- Combine the water, milk, eggs, and salt in a blender. Add the flour and butter. Process, covered, for 1 minute at high speed until well blended, using a rubber scraper to push down bits of flour from the sides of the blender container. Process 2 to 3 seconds longer. Refrigerate, covered, for at least 2 hours. The batter should resemble a light cream, and coat a wooden spoon. Note: Thin with milk or water, adding 1 spoonful at a time, if the batter is too thick.
- Brush a 6 1/2 to 7-inch crêpe pan with peanut oil using a pastry brush. (Repeat process after each crêpe.) Place the pan over moderately high heat. Pour about 1/4 cup of batter into the center of the pan, and tilt from side to side, covering the bottom of the pan evenly. Move the pan back and forth after 60 to 80 seconds to loosen the crêpe. Turn over the crêpe with a spatula. Bake for about 30 seconds. Invert the pan over a plate to remove the crêpe. Place waxed paper between each crêpe, and keep warm until serving time.
- Makes 18 crêpes

SEAFOOD FILLING

3 tablespoons butter or
  margarine
25 or 30 fresh mushrooms,
  cleaned, sliced
Peanut oil, optional
8 to 10 ounces shrimp,
  cooked, shelled, deveined
12 to 16 ounces scallops

Crabmeat, if available
1 teaspoon parsley
1 teaspoon tarragon
3/4 to 1 cup sherry
2 tablespoons all-purpose
  flour
1 cup cold water
Crêpes

- To prepare the filling, melt 2 tablespoons of the butter or margarine in a large skillet over low heat, and sauté the mushrooms for 3 to 4 minutes. Remove from the skillet.
- Cut the seafood into 1/2-inch-long pieces. Melt the remaining butter or margarine, or peanut oil if desired, in the skillet. Add the seafood, parsley and tarragon, and sauté. Pour 1/2 cup of the sherry over the seafood, and remove from the heat. Combine the flour and cold water in a bowl until smooth, adding the water a little at a time, and stirring after each addition. Stir just enough of flour mixture into the seafood to thicken. Cook slowly, stirring constantly.
- Spoon some of the seafood mixture onto the center of the lighter side of a crêpe. Roll 1 side over the filling, and then the other. Place in a buttered 9×13-inch baking dish. Keep warm. Combine the sautéed mushrooms, remaining flour mixture, and remaining sherry in a pan, and mix well. Heat and serve as a sauce with the seafood crêpes.
- Makes 18 servings

ANNE CARICO, a member of the Botetourt County Chapter of the Virginia DAR, sent this recipe.

CHINCOTEAGUE ISLAND SEAFOOD LINGUINE

This recipe comes from the family of WANDA THORNTON, who, since 1963, has lived on Chincoteague Island, famous for its wild Chincoteague ponies. She has served as a member of the Chincoteague Town Council and is currently a member of the Accomak County Board of Supervisors. Wanda enjoys cooking, especially Chincoteague food. The recipe is one that has been handed down in her family for years.

Heat 1 tablespoon olive oil in a large nonstick skillet. Add 7 thinly sliced scallions and 3 minced cloves of garlic. Cook for 2 to 3 minutes or until the scallions are softened, stirring constantly. Add 1/2 cup peeled cooked shrimp, 1/2 cup crabmeat, 3 tablespoons dry white wine, 1 tablespoon lemon juice, 1/4 teaspoon crushed pepper, 1/4 teaspoon thyme, and 1/4 teaspoon salt. Cook for about 3 minutes or until heated through, stirring constantly. Keep warm.

Prepare 1 pound of linguine in a large pot as directed on the package. Drain, and place in a large serving bowl. Top with the seafood mixture, and serve.

Make 4 servings

VISITING KINGSMILL

Kingsmill Resort is made up of four plantations, Kingsmill Plantation, Littleton Plantation, Utopia Plantation, and Tutter's Neck Plantation. Five generations of the Burwell family have owned Kingsmill Plantations. Edward Burwell, a London merchant, was a founding member of The Virginia Company, which landed at present day Jamestown in May 1607 with the first colonists. The most prominent feature of the Kingsmill Plantation was the grand manor house built by Edward Burwell's son, Lewis Burwell III, in 1736. The foundation, kitchen, and one other outside building still exist on the property.

KINGSMILL
Seafood Paella

TOMATO SAFFRON BROTH

2 tablespoons olive oil
2 cloves garlic, minced
2 shallots, chopped
1 medium yellow onion, chopped
1 leek, chopped

1 fennel bulb, minced
Pinch of saffron
4 ounces white wine
1 (16-ounce) can stewed tomatoes
1 (12-ounce) can clam juice

SAFFRON RICE

1/4 cup olive oil
1 yellow onion, chopped
Pinch of saffron

2 cups parboiled white rice
4 cups vegetable stock, fish stock, or chicken stock

ASSEMBLY

16 clams, cleaned
16 mussels, cleaned
1 ounce fresh tarragon, chopped

1 ounce fresh parsley, minced

- To prepare the tomato saffron broth, combine the olive oil, garlic, shallots, onion, leek, and fennel in a saucepan over medium heat. Sweat (sauté) until soft, and add the saffron, stirring to distribute the threads evenly. Deglaze the saucepan with the white wine, allowing the saffron to bloom. Add the tomatoes and clam juice, and mix well. Simmer for 20 minutes to blend the flavors.
- To prepare the saffron rice, combine the olive oil, onion, and saffron in a saucepan over medium heat, and cook gradually until the saffron bleeds into the onion. Add the rice, stirring to coat. Stir in the stock, and cover. Increase the heat. Bring the mixture to a boil. Reduce the heat to a simmer. Cook for 12 to 15 minutes or until a small amount of liquid remains in the saucepan. Turn off the heat, and steam the rice for 5 minutes, keeping the pot covered. Note: Seasoned water can be used if stock is not available.
- To assemble, place the clams and mussels in a paella pan or a large sauté pan over high heat, and add the tomato saffron broth to steam open the clams and mussels. Fold in the saffron rice, and sprinkle with the tarragon and parsley.
- Makes 4 to 6 servings

This recipe was made possible by ANNE TREVARTHEN, past Regent of the Williamsburg Chapter of the Virginia DAR and with permission of BRENT E. WERTH, director of culinary operations and executive chef of Kingsmill Resort.

DID YOU KNOW THAT:

John Colter, often called America's first mountain man and the discoverer of the region that became Yellowstone National Park, was born near Staunton around 1774?

Rowena's "Fast" Holiday Menu

Please read through the entire process because preparing as instructed is essential to keeping the time under an hour. Have on hand: 1 defrosted or fresh turkey (approximately 14 to 20 pounds), 3 to 4 days in the refrigerator; 1 can or jar of your favorite cranberry sauce; and 1 half-gallon vanilla ice cream.

STUFFING

1/2 cup (1 stick) butter or margarine	2 to 3 tablespoons poultry seasoning
4 to 6 large onions, chopped	1 (16-ounce) package crumbled herb-seasoned stuffing mix
1 bunch celery, chopped	1/4 to 1/2 cup green or red pepper jelly
1/3 cup chopped fresh parsley	

- Melt the butter or margarine in a large heavy skillet, and add onions and celery. Cook until soft. Add a small amount of water towards the end, if needed. Cook until the liquid is reduced. Stir in the parsley and poultry seasoning. Add the herb stuffing, and mix well. Stir in 1/4 cup pepper jelly. Add additional poultry seasoning or pepper jelly, if desired.

While the onions and celery are cooking in the step above, start cooking the bacon in:

AUNT SALLY'S SCHNITZEL BEANS

1 pound bacon, cut up	1 (14 1/2-ounce) can cut green beans, drained
1 cup sugar	2 large onions, chopped
1/2 cup vinegar	
1 (50-ounce) can cut green beans, drained	

- Cook the bacon in an extra heavy pot, until almost crisp, and drain Add the sugar, vinegar, and green beans, and mix well. Cook until the mixture is bubbly. Add the onions, and turn off burner, leaving the pot on the burner.

While the onions, celery, and bacon are cooking in the step above, drain the fruit for:

CURRIED FRUIT

1 (29-ounce) can each yellow cling peach halves and pear halves	1 (11-ounce) can mandarin orange sections
1 (15 1/4-ounce) can each pineapple chunks and apricot halves,	1/2 cup raisins
	1/3 cup butter or margarine, melted
1 (16-ounce) can grapefruit sections	3/4 cup firmly packed brown sugar
	2 teaspoons curry powder

- Preheat the oven to 375 degrees F. Arrange the peaches and pears in a 9×13-inch aluminum pan. Add the pineapple, apricots, grapefruit and mandarin oranges. Scatter the raisins over the top. Melt butter or margarine in a small saucepan. Stir in in the brown sugar and curry powder. Pour over the fruit. Bake for 1 hour.
- Place the dish on the stove burner over medium heat, if too much liquid remains, and cook until the liquid is reduced. Note: This recipe can be made several days in advance and refrigerated. You may substitute dried cranberries for the raisins and sweet prepared mustard for the curry powder. Leftovers can be frozen.

The stuffing is ready, the green beans are sitting on top of the stove, and the fruit is in the oven. Now it's time to rinse and stuff the turkey. Be sure to remove the paper bag that contains the gizzard and neck from the turkey. And while a wonderful helper is rinsing out the turkey, make the:

QUICK AND EASY SWEET POTATOES

1 (20-ounce) can sweet potatoes	1/2 cup Rowena's Carrot Jam, or
1/2 cup firmly packed brown sugar	2 to 3 shredded carrots

- Drain the sweet potatoes, reserving half the syrup. Combine the sweet potatoes, syrup, brown sugar, and Carrot Jam or carrots in a heavy saucepan, stirring gently. Cook over medium heat until the liquid is thickened and reduced.

By the time you finish stuffing the turkey, the sweet potatoes should be finished. I rub the turkey with olive oil, and cook according to directions.

You now have: Your turkey stuffed and in the oven. Green beans ready and on the stove. Curried Fruit finished and in the oven. Sweet Potatoes are ready on top of the stove.

Be sure you have a can of cranberries or cranberry sauce in the refrigerator. I get up early to do all this so I can have the kitchen to myself. In order to do it quickly, you need to concentrate. By the time I need help with the turkey, people are up and wandering around.

All desserts are made the day before. I also have a container of good vanilla ice cream in the freezer. Remove the carton and place the ice cream in a champagne bucket to serve with dessert. It's pretty and festive!

Thanksgiving dinner is ready! —Rowena

Vegetables and Other Super Side Dishes

The colonists noticed when they were hunting cranes that the birds ate red berries, which they named "crane berries." The word eventually became what we know today as cranberries.

Vegetables

Southeast Asian Vegetables and Noodles

4 ounces uncooked
vermicelli, broken into
2-inch pieces
1 cup chicken broth
1 (1-pound) package frozen
mixed vegetables, thawed
1 teaspoon minced garlic
1 teaspoon finely chopped
jalapeño or ¼ teaspoon
crushed red pepper flakes

1 teaspoon grated gingerroot
2 tablespoons dry sherry
¼ teaspoon salt
2 tablespoons sesame oil
½ cup diagonally sliced
green onions for garnish
¼ cup dry-roasted unsalted
peanuts for garnish

- Combine the vermicelli and chicken broth in a large skillet. Bring to a boil over medium-high heat. Reduce the heat, and simmer, covered, for 5 minutes, stirring occasionally. Add the vegetables.
- Combine the garlic, jalapeño or red pepper flakes, gingerroot, sherry, salt, and sesame oil in a small bowl, and mix well. Stir into the vermicelli mixture. Increase the heat to medium, and cook, covered, for 7 to 9 minutes longer or until the vermicelli is tender and the vegetables are crisp-tender, stirring occasionally. Sprinkle with the green onions and peanuts.
- Variation: To prepare as an entrée, add cooked chicken (jungle fowl to the Burmese) or shrimp.
- Makes approximately 4 (1-cup) servings

I have traveled extensively in Southeast Asia. I am an avid bird watcher and this area of the world is renown for its birdlife, including wild jungle fowl known to us as the chicken. It is also renown for delicious, low-calorie dishes like this one.

This recipe is from H. MORGAN GRIFFITH, who was elected Majority leader of the Virginia House of Delegates in 2002. He was first elected delegate in 1994 from the 8th District, which includes parts of the County of Roanoke and the city of Salem. The Boy Scouts rank high in his wide range of interests.

HENRY COUNTY

Henry County was organized in 1776 from Pittsylvania County. Named in honor of famed Virginia statesman and governor Patrick Henry (1736-1799), the county contains four hundred forty-four square miles. The population is 57,930, and the county seat is Martinsville.

While surveying the boundary line between Virginia and North Carolina in 1728, William Byrd and his party camped in present-day Henry County. Major John Redd, an early settler and veteran of the Battle at Yorktown in 1781, lived here.

Roasted Vegetables

1½ to 2 pounds potatoes, cut into 1-inch cubes
1 pound carrots, cut into 1-inch pieces
1 quart Brussels sprouts
1 pound asparagus, trimmed
1 pound green beans, trimmed

Florets of 1 large bunch broccoli
Florets of 1 large head cauliflower
1 large onion, cut into quarters
Cloves of 1 large head garlic
3 to 4 tablespoons olive oil
Salt and pepper

- Preheat the oven to 400°F. Place 2 or 3 of the vegetables, the onion, and garlic cloves in a 9×13-inch baking pan. Drizzle with the olive oil. Season with salt and pepper to taste, and toss. Bake for about 45 minutes for potatoes, carrots, or Brussels sprouts. Asparagus, beans, broccoli, and cauliflower need less time.
- Makes 8 to 10 servings

The recipe is shared by JOAN PLACE, my friend and general manager of Rowena's, Inc., who has perfected the roasted vegetable. Her rule—use as few ingredients as possible—is also her motto. You may use only one vegetable if you want to stay within the three-ingredients rule, but you can mix more. Joan also uses kosher salt, but this is not necessary; table salt will do. She does not count salt and pepper in the "big three."

Joan is a direct descendent of Henry Clay, who was born in Hanover County, Virginia and ran for President in 1844. Her grandmother's name was Alpheous Clay and her family received their land under a land grant from England in the early 1700's. —Rowena

HIGHLAND COUNTY

Highland County was formed in 1847 from parts of Bath and Pendleton Counties. Its name derives from its altitude among the Blue Ridge Mountains. The county contains four hundred twenty-two square miles, and its population is 2,536. The county seat is Monterey.

Fort George, a French and Indian War post, and Fort Edward Johnson, a Confederate structure, were both located in this county. Confederate General "Stonewall" Jackson and Union General John Charles Fremont pitted their wits against each other near McDowell in May 1862.

DID YOU KNOW THAT:

Near Fort Myer in September, 1908, Orville Wright carried the world's first aircraft passenger on a flight that lasted just over six minutes?

THREE DIAMOND DINING ON CHINCOTEAGUE

April Stillson and her sister, Lisa Smith, had big dreams in 1985 as they spied a former fast food restaurant site available "on the road to Assateague." Anyone familiar with Chincoteague Island and Assateague Island off Virginia's Eastern Shore knows that there is only one road connecting the two by bridge. Knowing their customers would not "get lost" was a plus. Also, they wanted to have a restaurant near the noncommercialized beach offered on Assateague's National Seashore. They rehired all of the employees from the former McDuffy's and then proceeded to open with the same name on April Fool's Day. They did well the first year, then found out that McDonald's was building closer to the beach "on the road to Assateague."

Their proposed plans to upscale had to be immediate in order to make their dining experience distinctive, so Dad came to the rescue! Everyone knew their Dad, A.J., would make the difference, and he did. As an architect and designer, their father brought plans and fabrics right over. Plans for a twenty-seat lounge and an upgrade to the inside dining room were put in place. The name the sisters chose for the establishment was A.J.'s ... on the Creek. A screened porch of the renovated restaurant beside a small stream provides guests with wonderful views of egrets, blue herons, and occasionally an island opossum.

With proud dad, A.J., looking on, today the restaurant flourishes with such dishes as fresh grilled local fish, sautéed seafood pastas, and veal. Locals say A.J.'s offers "the best steaks in town." Wonderful wines, great atmosphere, and the superb quality of the food have earned the establishment a Three Diamond rating. Lisa and April have a local crowd every week and hope that tourists try their restaurant when they are on Chincoteague Island. After all, it's easy to find . . . it's "on the road to Assateague!"

A.J.'s On The Creek
Deep-Fried Artichoke Hearts

1/2 cup mayonnaise	1/2 cup milk
2 to 3 tablespoons horseradish, well drained	1 egg
1 tablespoon Dijon mustard	1 can whole artichokes in water, drained, cut into
1 1/2 teaspoons Worcestershire sauce	halves
Oil for deep-frying	Flour for dusting
	3/4 cup panko bread crumbs

- Combine the mayonnaise, horseradish, Dijon mustard, and Worcestershire sauce in a small bowl, and mix well.
- Heat oil in a deep fryer to 350°F. Combine the milk and egg in a bowl, and mix well. Dust the artichoke halves in the flour, and dip in the egg mixture. Coat with the bread crumbs. Let the artichokes stand in the bread crumbs for 1 to 2 minutes to ensure the breading adheres. Fry for 3 to 4 minutes until the artichokes are light golden brown. Drain on paper towels. Serve with the horseradish sauce.
- Makes 2 to 3 servings

The recipe was provided by APRIL B. STILLSON, owner and chef, A.J.'s On The Creek Restaurant, Chincoteague, Virginia.

Asparagus Casserole

1 (15-ounce) can asparagus	2 hard-cooked eggs, chopped
1/2 cup milk	1/2 cup grated sharp cheese
1 tablespoon (or more) all-purpose flour	Cracker crumbs
Salt and pepper	Parmesan cheese
	1/4 cup (1/2 stick) butter or margarine

- Drain the asparagus, reserving 1/2 cup of the juice. Combine the asparagus juice, milk, flour, and salt and pepper to taste in a medium saucepan, and mix well. Cook over low heat until slightly thickened, stirring frequently.
- Note: One cup asparagus juice can be substituted for 1/2 cup milk and 1/2 cup asparagus juice.
- Preheat the oven to 325°F. Place the asparagus in the bottom of a 9×9-inch casserole dish. Cover with the eggs, cheese, and cream sauce mixture. Sprinkle with enough cracker crumbs and Parmesan cheese to cover the mixture, and dot with butter or margarine. Bake for 25 minutes. Leftovers can be refrigerated and reheated.
- Makes 4 to 6 servings

This recipe was sent by ALICE BIRDSEYE of the Virginia Frontier Chapter of the Virginia DAR.

HALFWAY HOUSE
Beets in Orange Sauce

8 to 10 beets, cooked and
  sliced
1 small onion, grated
1 tablespoon vinegar
3 tablespoons sugar

1 tablespoon butter or
  margarine, melted
Juice and grated rind of
  1 orange
Salt

- Combine the beets, onion, vinegar, sugar, butter or margarine, orange juice and rind, and salt in a saucepan, and mix well. Simmer, tightly covered, for 15 minutes.
- Makes 10 to 12 servings depending on the size of the beets

The recipe was submitted by FRANCES PONS from Surry, Virginia, a past Regent of the Williamsburg Chapter of the Virginia DAR. Credit for the recipe goes to *The Ford Treasury of Famous Recipes from Famous Eating Places* by The Ford Motor Company (1946-1950).

This historic restaurant acquired its name because it was just halfway on the stagecoach route between Petersburg and Richmond. It was built in 1760 on a grant of land from George II of England. Famous guests read like a page from your history book—Washington, Lafayette, and Patrick Henry to name a few. It is no longer operating as a restaurant.

Sauerkraut Shenandoah

4 (14-ounce) cans
  sauerkraut
1 medium onion, chopped
2 tart unpeeled apples,
  chopped

1/2 to 3/4 teaspoon red
  pepper or cayenne, or
  to taste
6 small pork chops

- Preheat the oven to 200°F. Combine the undrained sauerkraut, onion, apples, and red pepper or cayenne in a large bowl, and mix well. Spoon into a 2 1/2 to 3-quart baking dish. Place the pork chops on the top. Cook, tightly covered with foil, for at least 12 hours. Remove the bone from the chops, and stir the meat into the sauerkraut mixture.
- Makes approximately 10 servings

This is a recipe from my side of the family, the Peers. I grew up in the Shenandoah Valley (Woodstock), and it is typical of the table fare of the Valley's early German settlers. This dish is definitely for the adult palate; our children won't touch it. However, all the adult Fraims love it, and we always serve it at our holiday family gatherings because it goes great with a traditional turkey, dressing, and gravy dinner.

From the family of BETH PEER FRAIM. Beth is the wife of Paul Fraim, the creative, hardworking mayor of Norfolk, Virginia.

BILL JANIS' "UNCLE JIMMY"

I served for eleven years in the U.S. Navy. For much of that time I was at sea in submarines and destroyers. Rose Ann and I moved seven times in eleven years. We were stationed all over the South and finished my Navy service in Tidewater, where we bought our first home in Chesapeake and lived for five years. Along the way we had the pleasure of trying many different styles of Southern cooking. Along the way we picked up this recipe. It became very popular when we served it at our post-game oyster roasts when we still played the Oyster Bowl in Norfolk.

Uncle Jimmy was not really my uncle. My father, Robert, served with James Luwisch in the United States Marine Corps in the '50s. Jimmy hailed from Jefferson Parish, Louisiana, where he still lives today with his bride of many years, Aunt Connie, or "Con Con." Uncle Jimmy is larger than life. His voice, no matter what the subject matter, has a lyrical aspect that mesmerizes its listeners regardless of their age.

Although they were not related by blood, marriage, or adoption, Uncle Jimmy and my dad were closer than any brothers. The Marine Corp has a way of doing that. As children, Dad would pile us in the car and drive for many hours to go see Uncle Jimmy and Aunt Connie. Uncle Jimmy taught us to catch crawfish (and copperheads!) with cow brains, a piece of wire, a long pole, and a little Cajun ingenuity. He showed us how to beg for doubloons from the Crewe of Bacchus. He introduced us to the joys of mudbugs, beignets, fried mirlitons, and chicory coffee. On wash day, the pot would boil slowly on the stove and fill the Luwisch home with the heavenly elixir of Con Con's cooking. You can have your haute cuisine; I'll settle for supper at Uncle Jimmy's. This recipe, which I picked up during my long service in the United States Navy, is a modest tribute to my father and Uncle Jimmy and the brotherhood that they shared. *Laissez le bon temps rouler!*

UNCLE JIMMY'S
World Famous Red Beans and Rice

1 pound large, dried red kidney beans	3 pints water
1 pound salt pork, smoked kielbasa, or andouille sausage	3 carrots, sliced
	3 sprigs of parsley
	1 bay leaf
1 teaspoon oil	Pinch of powdered thyme
1 tablespoon all-purpose flour	Pinch of sage
	2 ribs celery with leaves, chopped
1 large onion, chopped	Salt and pepper
5 beef bouillon cubes	Hot cooked rice

- Soak the beans in cold water to cover in a large pot for 8 to 10 hours or until the skins split and shrivel. Drain the water.
- Slice the meat into thin rounds or cubes. Brown the meat in the oil in a medium skillet. Remove the meat from the skillet. Stir in the flour, and brown slightly, stirring constantly. Add the onion, and cook for 3 minutes.
- Dissolve the bouillon cubes in the water in a large pot. Add the beans, carrots, and meat, and mix well. Cook over low heat for 1 hour, stirring frequently. Add the parsley, bay leaf, thyme, sage, celery, and salt and pepper to taste, and mix well. Cook over low heat for 1¹/₂ hours or until the gravy is thickened and dark, stirring frequently to prevent scorching.
- Serve with hot cooked rice.
- Makes 12 to 15 servings

Cooking slowly provides an ideal opportunity for the cook to taste the savory mixture. Remember, Rome wasn't built in a day; patience is a virtue. The longer you cook these beans, the better.

BILL JANIS is a member of the Virginia House of Delegates from the 56th District, which includes the counties of Goochland, part of Henrico, and Louisa.

ISLE OF WIGHT COUNTY

Isle of Wight County was originally named Warrascoyack County when it was established as one of Virginia's first shires in 1634. The name was changed in 1637 and honors the Isle of Wight off the coast of England. It contains three hundred fourteen square miles. The population is 29,728, and the county seat is Isle of Wight.

Local Indians killed about fifty early settlers in this region in March 1622. One of the oldest, if not the oldest, churches in America, St. Luke's, dating from 1632, is located in Isle of Wight County.

Copper Carrot Pennies

2 pounds large carrots,
  thinly sliced
1 rib celery, thinly sliced
1/4 cup vegetable oil
2/3 cup vinegar
1 cup sugar
1 teaspoon prepared
  mustard
1 teaspoon Worcestershire
  sauce

1 (10³/4-ounce) can
  condensed tomato soup
1 onion, chopped
1 green onion, chopped
1 red bell pepper, chopped
1 yellow bell pepper,
  chopped

- Boil the carrots and celery in a large saucepan for 5 minutes or until crisp-tender, and drain.
- Combine the oil, vinegar, sugar, mustard, Worcestershire sauce, and soup in a small saucepan, and mix well. Bring to a boil, stirring frequently.
- Combine the carrots and celery with the onion, green onion, and peppers in a large bowl. Add sauce mixture, and mix well. Marinate, covered, in the refrigerator for at least 24 to 36 hours, stirring at least two times.
- Spoon the carrot mixture into small airtight containers, and store in the refrigerator for up to two months.
- Makes 6 to 8 servings

I have eaten my grandmother's carrots since I was a child, but I added red and yellow peppers and celery when I started to make them. My grandmother, Marion Olney Brownson, moved from Ohio to Richmond, Virginia. She belonged to the DAR for more than fifty years, and because of her keen interest, her mother, my mother, my sister, and I became DAR members. Before my grandmother died at age ninety-one, four generations of our family belonged to the DAR.

MARION W. LUNNEMAN, Regent of the Virginia Frontier Chapter of the Virginia DAR, generously contributed this recipe.

JAMES CITY COUNTY

James City County was one of Virginia's original eight shires, established in 1634. Named after the first permanent English settlement in the New World, Jamestown, it contains one hundred sixty-four square miles, and its population is 48,102. The county seat is Williamsburg.

James City County was the site of the arrival, in 1619, of the first Africans in the future United States, an event that predicated slavery in America. The early plantations, Martin's Hundred, which also dates from 1619, and Carter's Grove, the 1751 mansion of Carter Burwell, are both located here.

ROBERT BEVERLY ON INDIAN AGRICULTURE

Robert Beverly has been called Virginia's first historian. Born in 1673, he was educated in England, but soon returned to his native shores to run a large plantation located in Gloucester County. His love of history led him to write a book entitled *The History and Present State of Virginia*, published in London in 1705. In describing the agricultural products of the American Indian tribes that lived throughout Virginia, Beverly wrote:

[O]ur Natives had originally amongst them, Indian Corn, Peas, Beans, Potatoes, and Tobacco. This Indian

Corn was the Staff of Food, upon which the Indians did ever depend; for when Sickness, bad Weather, War, or any other ill Accident kept them from Hunting, Fishing and Fowling; this, with the Addition of some Peas, Beans, and such other Fruits of the Earth, as were thenin Season, was the Families Dependance, and the Support of their Women and Children.

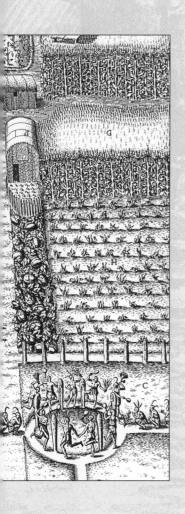

Carrots in Mustard Glaze

2 pounds carrots, peeled, sliced
Boiling water
3 tablespoons butter or margarine
1/3 cup firmly packed light brown sugar

3 tablespoons prepared mustard
1 to 2 tablespoons chopped parsley

- Combine the carrots and enough boiling water to measure 1 inch in a saucepan. Simmer, covered, for 20 minutes or until tender; drain.
- Combine the butter or margarine, brown sugar, and the mustard in a small saucepan. Heat until the butter melts and the sugar dissolves, stirring constantly. Cook for 3 minutes longer.
- Pour the glaze over the carrots, and toss gently. Heat for several minutes, and garnish with the parsley.
- Makes 4 servings

As a career woman all my adult life, the fact that someone asked me for a cooking recipe sort of brings me back to earth. We all have to eat, and we all love to eat good things no matter what we do for a living. I believe that cooking well has as many attributes as anything else we do in life.

The recipe is from the kitchen of LEE MILTEER of Virginia Beach, a very special person and one of North America's most highly regarded human-potential speakers and executive coaches. She is the author of *Success is an Inside Job* plus other books and audio and videotapes.

THE SMITHFIELD INN

Corn Custard

2 teaspoons cornstarch
1/2 cup sugar
2 large eggs
12 ounces heavy cream

1 (16-ounce) can cream-style corn
1/4 cup (1/2 stick) butter, melted

- Preheat the oven to 400°F. Combine the cornstarch with the sugar in a bowl, and beat in the eggs, 1 at a time. Stir in the cream and corn. Spoon into a buttered 8×8-inch or 6×9-inch pan or ovenproof dish. Pour the melted butter on top. Bake for 50 minutes or until the custard has set but still jiggles, or until a straw inserted in the center comes out clean.
- Note: Baking in a water bath helps to prevent the custard from becoming too dry.
- Makes 4 to 6 servings

This recipe was generously contributed by BETTY THOMAS of The Smithfield Inn, Smithfield, Virginia.

Nannie's Fried Corn

3 to 4 slices bacon
12 (or more) ears of corn,
   shucked, silks removed

1 tablespoon sugar
Salt and pepper
2 tablespoons butter

- Fry the bacon in a skillet until crisp. Drain on a paper towel, and crumble, reserving the drippings.
- Cut the cap from each ear of corn using a sharp knife, and barely slice the tops of each kernel into a large bowl. Scrape the remaining corn from the cob with a blunt knife into the bowl. Add the corn to the bacon drippings in the hot skillet, and stir in the sugar, mixing well. Cook the corn, stirring frequently.
- Add salt and pepper to taste, and the butter, mixing well. Cook until the corn is thickened and browned. Turn with a spatula so that the corn stays together, and brown the other side.
- Remove the corn to a warm platter when well browned. Top with the crumbled bacon. Eat and enjoy while it's hot.
- Makes 6 to 8 servings

The secret to making this recipe is using a large, black iron skillet. My grandmother "Nannie," Linnie Elizabeth Osborne Collins, had a large family of six children, and she often made this fried corn during the summer, using corn from the garden, which her husband, Dr. William English Collins, planted each spring. It was a family favorite and has passed down in the family through four generations—children, grandchildren, great-grandchildren and great-great-grandchildren. It is such a family favorite that some of the children have wished for a platter of Nannie's Fried Corn made especially on their birthday.

The recipe comes from CLARLYN HAMILTON BYCHOK of the Chesapeake Chapter of the Virginia DAR.

KING AND QUEEN COUNTY

King and Queen County was established in 1691 from part of New Kent County. It name honors King William III and Queen Mary of England. It contains three hundred twenty square miles. Its population is 6,630, and the county seat is King and Queen Courthouse.

The famous Clark family, of whom George Rogers and William were members, originally lived in King and Queen County before moving west. A servants' plot for freedom that occurred in this county in 1663 is the basis for the novel *Prisoners of Hope* by Mary Johnston.

VIRGINIA'S GOURMET CHIPS

Edward Cohen was a native of Washington D.C., whose family came from southwestern Virginia. His father, Wally, had long family ties in Wise County. Edward's daughter, Sarah Cohen, says her father was a "meat and potatoes" man; it was his love of potatoes that inspired him to raise the crop in Northwestern Virginia and go into the gourmet potato chip business. Edward and his wife, Fritzi, already owned the Tabard Inn in the District and they had earlier established the Tabard Farm in Reliance to supply organic produce to some of D.C.'s finest restaurants with fresh tomatoes, eggplant, beets, lettuces, and other vegetables.

Edward set up business along Highway 11 in Middletown. He experimented with potato chips first in 1985 when he "chipped" 40,000 pounds of organic Kennebec potatoes. Daughter Sarah says the business was "young, clueless, broke, and full of dreams" at that time, but people raved about the chips and Route 11 Chips were born!

The plant uses vintage 1960's equipment to clean, peel, and slice one ton of potatoes daily. The gourmet chips are cooked using 110 gallons of peanut oil blended with high monounsaturated sunflower oil for their distinctive texture and taste. This kettle cooking distinguishes the chips from other brand's mass-frying techniques.

As President of Route 11 Potato Chips, Sarah Cohen is pleased to be in the specialty market. Her factory hosts a retail store that tourists strive to visit on the way to Winchester, the childhood home of Patsy Cline. Visitors can watch the potato chip process and buy the chips along with the company's line of dips. She is also pleased that her chips are well known in Williams-Sonoma stores as well as local small markets. "Fritos considers us a mere flea," says Sarah, but her smile is wide for she knows her business fills its own niche.

Route 11 offers such favorites as Lightly Salted Potato Chips, Chesapeake Crab Potato Chips, Mama Zuma's Revenge Chips, Tabard Farm Yukon Golds, and chips that include sweet potatoes, yuccas, carrots, parsnips, taro roots, purple potatoes, and beets! These are sent across the country to folks that cannot come to Virginia to get them. In the potato chip world, all roads lead to Route 11!

Tobacco Farmer's Corn Pudding

1 (15.25-ounce) can cream-style corn	1/2 cup sugar
1 egg	3/4 cup milk
3 tablespoons all-purpose flour	Butter or margarine

- Preheat the oven to 350°F to 400°F. Combine the corn, egg, flour, sugar, and milk in a medium bowl, and mix well. Pour the mixture into a greased 9×9-inch casserole dish. Dot the top with butter or margarine. Bake for approximately 30 minutes or until set.
- Makes 4 servings

You may need substantially more for farmhands.

SUE CAVIN of Rose Hill, Virginia, who is Regent of the Major George Gibson Chapter of the Virginia DAR, sent this recipe. Rose Hill lies in Lee County, the last county before Kentucky and Tennessee in southwest Virginia. This is tobacco country, and this recipe has been handed down through the generations as a very satisfying meal for hardworking farmhands stripping tobacco in the fall. An interesting facet of Sue Cavin's lineage as a DAR is that one line of her ancestry leads back to a participant in the Revolution, Charles Vincent, who is documented as a "Patriot". This meant that if an individual had conviction against violence, he could support the military effort with full honor by providing corn or other supplies for the army.

TIPS ON COOKING CORN

Betty Fussell, in her book *Crazy for Corn* (Harper/Perennial, 1995), gives us these hints:

Keeping the husk tightly closed keeps corn at maximum freshness. In fact, it is best to cook corn on the cob with the husks on.

GRILLING: Grill corn (do not soak first) so that the husks char a bit on the outside or grill it without the husks directly over the heat. This gives it wonderful flavor and intensifies its sweetness.

ROASTING: Roast your corn in the husk in a 450-degree to 500-degree Fahrenheit oven for 6 to 8 minutes. This produces a wonderfully hot piece of corn.

MICROWAVE: For just two or three pieces of corn, cook them with the husks on at the highest setting for 6 minutes. The corn is wonderfully hot, and husk is easy to remove.

Slice corn into wheels. Your children and grandchildren will love it!

Yummy Corn Casserole

1 (15-ounce) can cream-
   style corn
1 (15-ounce) can whole
   kernel corn
1 package Mexican-style
   cornbread mix, such as
   Martha White

2 eggs, beaten
$1/2$ cup oil
1 onion, finely chopped
$1/2$ pound mild Mexican
   processed cheese, such as
   Velveeta, grated

- Preheat the oven to 375°F. Combine the cream-style corn, undrained whole kernel corn, cornbread mix, eggs, oil, onion, and cheese, and mix well. Pour into a $2^1/2$-quart casserole dish. Bake, uncovered, for approximately 45 minutes.
- Makes 8 to 10 servings

This is an old family recipe that my family today loves with any kind of beef or chicken. Before the days of mixes, the cornbread ingredients were mixed together with some peppers and spices added for flavor. Today, the cornbread mix makes this a very easy dish for a large group or hungry family. It can be made ahead of time and stored in the refrigerator until it is time to bake. My son-in-law believes this dish is the best thing to happen to corn since the cob.

KITTY HOWARD has been a resident of Virginia for more than thirty years. She is an excellent cook who loves to entertain in the gracious Southern style, and she specializes in dishes that are easy to make for a large crowd. Kitty lives in northern Virginia with John, her husband of more than fifty-five years, who still loves to eat her cooking. John has been playing golf with my husband for more than thirty years. —Rowena

KING GEORGE COUNTY

King George County was organized in 1720 from part of Richmond County and was named in honor of King George I. The county contains one hundred eighty square miles, and the population is 16,803. The county seat is King George.

James Madison (1751-1836), fourth president of the United States, was born in King George County. On April 23, 1865, John Wilkes Booth, President Abraham Lincoln's assassin, stopped at Dr. Richard Stuart's home in this county seeking medical attention.

THANK YOU, GEORGE WYTHE

No man ever left behind him a character more venerated than George Wythe. His virtue was of the purest tint; his integrity inflexible, and his justice exact; of warm patriotism, and, devoted as he was to liberty, and the natural and equal rights of man, he might truly be called the Cato of his country.

— Thomas Jefferson

In 1726, George Wythe was born at Chesterville in what was formerly called Elizabeth City County. The plantation and home was situated on the present NASA Langley Research Center and Langley AFB in Hampton. His father Thomas, a planter, died soon after George was born. His mother, Margaret Walker Wythe, was determined to instill a love of learning in George. She taught him Latin and Greek. He read law with his uncle, Stephen Dewey. After Mrs. Wythe passed away, George grew up under the guardianship of his older brother, Thomas. In 1746, George began practicing law in Elizabeth City County. In 1747, he married Ann Lewis.

The York County bar admitted George in 1748. Ann Wythe died on August 8. By 1754, the widower was elected to the House of Burgesses. Living in Williamsburg, he met and married Elizabeth Taliaferro, the daughter of Richard Taliaferro, who built the George Wythe House. Their only child died in infancy.

Through his years in Williamsburg, George achieved accreditation by the

Stuffed Eggplant

1 eggplant
1/2 pound ground beef
1 rib celery, finely chopped
3 small green onions, finely chopped
2 sprigs of parsley, finely chopped
Salt and pepper
1/4 cup crushed cornflakes
Grated cheese, optional

- Preheat the oven to 350°F. Boil the eggplant in water to cover in a large saucepan for 12 minutes. Slice the top from the eggplant, and cut lengthwise into halves. Scoop out the inside of the eggplant, leaving about 1/2 inch around the edges, and reserve the pulp.
- Combine the ground beef, celery, onion, parsley, salt and pepper to taste, and eggplant pulp in a large bowl, and mix well. Stuff each half of the eggplant with the ground beef mixture. Top with the cornflakes, and sprinkle with the cheese if desired. Bake for 1 hour.
- Makes 2 servings

This serves two and is a meal in itself, but I usually serve a salad with it.

This recipe was from the kitchen of ELIZABETH BETTY M. STYLES in the *Cherry Hill Cookbook*. Betty actually wrote the introduction for that cookbook in 1976 as a member of the Falls Church Chapter of the Virginia DAR. Cherry Hill Farm in Falls Church, Virginia, is a historical farm complex adjacent to the City Hall. Earliest records date back to 1729, when Thomas Lord Fairfax granted 248 acres to John Trammel. The present house and barn, built around 1840, are the earliest documented structures on the land. Ownership passed through a number of hands until 1870, when Joseph S. Riley bought the property. His son willed it to the University of Virginia in 1941. The city of Falls Church bought Cherry Hill in 1956 and renovated it as a major Bicentennial project.

KING WILLIAM COUNTY

King William County was formed in 1701 from part of King and Queen County. Its namesake is King William III. The county contains two hundred sixty-three square miles and has a population of 13,146. The county seat is King William.

The Pamunkey and Mattapony Indian tribes, both part of Chief Powhatan's confederacy in the early 1600s, have reservations in this county. Declaration of Independence signer Carter Braxton lived here.

colonial supreme court. He served in the House of Burgesses from the mid-1750s until 1775, as a delegate and as a clerk. Later, he served as Mayor of Williamsburg, then sat on the board of visitors of the College of William and Mary. During these years, he also instructed young scholars interested in legal studies, including Thomas Jefferson. The two began a lifelong friendship.

George Wythe opposed the Stamp Act and was one of the first to express the idea of a separate nation. He believed that Virginia's Declaration of Rights, written by George Mason, included African Americans among the "all men" born free and equally independent. In 1779, Thomas Jefferson and others created the first chair of law in a U.S. institution of higher learning at the College of William and Mary. George was appointed to fill it. Two of his pupils were John Marshall and James Monroe. By 1791, chancery duties called George to Richmond. Still learning (he taught himself Hebrew) and teaching (private lessons for Henry Clay), he died under mysterious circumstances. His grandnephew, George Wythe Sweeney, was accused of forgery of his uncle's accounts and poisoning him. A grand jury indicted Sweeney for murder, but he went free because of circumstantial evidence.

Our nation owes thanks to this Virginian who touched so many lives. His influence on the patriots and lawmakers in our country's infant stages is unsurpassed.

Golden Horseshoe Golf Club
Gold Grill's "The Fairway"

6 pounds onions, cut into 48 slices	1¹/₂ pounds provolone, cut into 24 thin slices
6 pounds eggplant, peeled, cut into 48 slices	6 pounds roasted sweet red pepper, cut into 48 slices
¹/₃ cup minced garlic	6 pounds tomato, cut into 48 slices
1¹/₂ cups pesto	1¹/₂ pounds mozzarella, cut into 24 thin slices
24 (6-inch) Italian bread loaves, sliced into halves lengthwise, toasted	48 fresh basil leaves

- Arrange the onion and eggplant slices in a single layer on lightly oiled sheet pans. Spread the garlic over the onions. Bake at 400°F for 20 minutes or until tender. Spread about 1 tablespoon pesto on 1 side of 24 bread halves.
- Place 1 provolone slice, 2 roasted pepper slices, 2 eggplant slices, 2 tomato slices, 2 onion slices, 1 mozzarella slice, and 2 basil leaves over each pesto side. Top with the remaining bread halves.
- Makes 24 sandwiches

The recipe was given to us by Gold Grill Resort in Williamsburg by sous chef WILLIAM R. BERNING.

Marinated Onions

2 or 3 Vidalia onions or other yellow onions, peeled, sliced into ¹/₂-inch slices	1 teaspoon pepper
	¹/₂ teaspoon sugar
	1 cup virgin olive oil
1 teaspoon salt	1 cup (more or less) white vinegar

- Place the onions into a jar with a tight-fitting lid. Add the salt, pepper, and sugar. Pour in the olive oil, and add enough vinegar to fill the jar. Store, tightly covered, in the refrigerator overnight or longer, inverting the jar twice daily.
- Makes approximately 1 quart

This recipe is from the collection of MINETTE COOPER, who has been involved with Young Audiences of Virginia since 1963. Young Audiences of Virginia, a statewide nonprofit organization, strives to keep the arts a basic part of education. Young Audiences believes the arts can be the creative means to reach the non-traditional learners in a class, to create the project that turns a group of children and educators into a community, to break down cultural barriers, to build relationships, and to teach the whole child.

POKE SALIT

The following excerpt was written in 1939 by Emory L. Hamilton of Wise, a small town in southwestern Virginia. The information was gathered for the Virginia office of the Federal Writers' Project, part of President Franklin D. Roosevelt's Works Progress Administration. It is reproduced from *Pigsfoot Jelly & Persimmon Beer*, edited by Charles L. Perdue Jr.

A very unusual food dish that is prepared in the Cumberland mountain section and one that is quite widely used here is that of fried Poke, from the pokeweed . . . . This dish is sometimes called "dry land fish" due to its slight fishy taste. Early in the spring after the new shoots or sprouts have come from the roots they are gathered while still young and tender, peeled, sliced and parboiled for about ten minutes. Then they are taken from the hot water, rolled in corn meal, salted and peppered to taste and then fried in deep fat until very brown.

These tender poke shoots are also gathered and prepared like asparagus. . . . The young shoots when prepared look very much like asparagus tips. It is also gathered while tender and used as greens.

Many of the mountain wives gather these tender shoots in the spring and can them for winter use. For canning they are peeled, sliced and parboiled until tender. Then taken from the water placed in the jars and covered with scalding water, with either a small amount of salt or acid being added to each jar.

MICHIE TAVERN
Black-Eyed Peas

1 pound fresh black-eyed peas, rinsed
1 ham hock, or 1 slice salt pork
1 teaspoon seasoning salt
$1/2$ teaspoon garlic salt
1 teaspoon pepper
1 tablespoon butter

- Combine the peas and ham hock or salt pork with enough water to cover in a large pot. Cook for 50 minutes or until the peas are tender. Add the seasoning salt, garlic salt, pepper, and butter, and mix gently.
- Makes 4 to 6 servings

This recipe comes from MICHIE TAVERN, Charlottesville, Virginia.

New Potatoes and Broccoli with Red Currant Glaze

2 pounds new potatoes, cut into halves
3 tablespoons olive oil
10 ounces broccoli florets
2 red onions, cut into wedges
2 tablespoons red currant jelly
Salt and pepper

- Boil the potatoes in water to cover in a large pot for 15 minutes or until tender, and drain.
- Heat the olive oil in a large wok or frying pan. Stir-fry the broccoli and red onions for 5 minutes or until softened. Toss in the potatoes, and cook until golden. Stir in the red currant jelly, and season with salt and pepper to taste. Cook for 1 to 2 minutes or until the onions are caramelized, and the potatoes are hot.
- Makes 8 to 10 servings

This is wonderful served with roast leg of lamb.

BRENDA MCNEIL GRAVES, a member of the Montpelier Chapter of the Virginia DAR in Madison, Virginia, sent this recipe.

Thomas Jefferson's
Poplar Forest

Horseradish Mashed Potatoes

2 to 3 pounds baking
   potatoes, peeled, cut into
   chunks
$^1/_3$ cup butter or margarine
$^3/_4$ cup half-and-half
$^3/_4$ teaspoon salt

$^1/_4$ teaspoon pepper
1 to 2 tablespoons freshly
   grated horseradish, or
2 to 4 tablespoons
   prepared horseradish

• Cook the potatoes in boiling water to cover in a large
saucepan over medium-high heat for 20 minutes or until
tender, and drain. Beat the potatoes at medium speed until
whipped. Add the butter or margarine, half-and-half, salt,
pepper, and horseradish. Beat until fluffy.
• Makes 6 to 8 servings

JOAN KILGOR GUMPRICH, Regent of the Poplar Forest
Chapter of the Virginia DAR, shares this recipe.

LANCASTER COUNTY

When it was organized in 1651 from Northumberland and
York Counties, Lancaster County was named after Lancaster,
England. It contains one hundred thirty square miles and is
home to 11,567 residents. The county seat is Lancaster.

Mary Ball, the mother of George Washington, was born
in this county circa 1707. Henrietta Hall (1817-1844), who
became the first American woman to perform missionary
work in China, was also born here.

LEE COUNTY

Lee County, formed in 1792 from Russell County, was
named in honor of Henry "Lighthorse Harry" Lee, hero of the
Revolution and an early Virginia governor. It contains
four hundred forty-six square miles. The population is
23,589, and the county seat is Jonesville.

Daniel Boone's son, James, was killed by Indians in Lee
County. Within a one-square-mile area here, three men who
in later life were elected to the U.S. Congress—
James B. Richmond, Campbell Slemp, and Campbell
Bascom Slemp—were born.

POPLAR FOREST

Thomas Jefferson designed Poplar Forest
as his year-round retreat. Building began
on the octagonal house in 1806, and
Jefferson called the Bedford County
plantation "the most valuable of my
possessions." The house and grounds
underwent many changes after leaving
the Jefferson family in 1826. In 1984, the
nonprofit corporation for Jefferson's
Poplar Forest rescued the site.
Restorations of the exterior of the house
were completed in 1998. Some interior
structural restoration work has been
done. Currently, Jefferson's "Wing of
Offices," or service rooms, is being
reconstructed, including an elaborate
kitchen with a large fireplace, oven, set
kettle, and three stew pots. Awarding-
winning restoration and archaeology
continue.

THE PAINTED LADY TEA ROOM

Bill and Patty Hoover have transformed four turn-of-the-century Victorian homes into a Historic Ghent landmark that has quickly established itself as a *must* for locals and out-of-town guests. With its five original fireplaces, handmade pub bar, white baby grand piano, white table cloths, and walls an art gallery would envy, the Painted Lady has earned its reputation as the "Most Romantic Restaurant" in Norfolk.

As a Victorian Tea Room by day and upscale, fine-dining restaurant by night, the Painted Lady serves foods in an ambiance that is warm, comfortable, and refined without being "stuffy." The tea menu includes freshly made scones with Devonshire cream, assorted finger sandwiches, heavenly home-made pastries, and chocolate-covered strawberries. A special Teddy Bear Tea is available for children.

The Painted Lady also serves She Crab Soup, Free Range Chicken, and Steak Crêpes. Considering which dessert to partake of is the pleasant problem at the end of the meal. There are flaming coffees and flambé desserts prepared tableside. A favorite is the original Banoffee Pie.

This restaurant has received Norfolk's "Best Fine Dining" Award by the *Virginian Pilot* for many years.

The
Painted Lady

Coriander Champagne Mashed Potatoes

8 medium all-purpose potatoes, peeled, cut into quarters
2 tablespoons unsalted butter
1/2 cup heavy cream, scalded
2 teaspoons ground coriander
1/3 to 1/2 cup Champagne
Salt and pepper

- Combine the potatoes with enough cold water to cover in a saucepan. Bring to a boil. Simmer for 15 to 20 minutes or until the potatoes are tender when pierced with a fork. Drain, and return to low heat.
- Add the butter, cream, coriander, and Champagne. Mash the potatoes with a potato masher or fork. Remove to a warm bowl, and whip with a fork or whisk until light and fluffy. Season with salt and pepper to taste.
- Makes about 5 cups

BILL and PATTY HOOVER, of The Painted Lady Tea Room, graciously shared this recipe.

LOUDOUN COUNTY

Loudoun County was organized from Fairfax County in 1757. Its namesake is John Campbell, fourth Earl of Loudoun (1705-1782), a Virginia governor (1756-1759) and British army commander during the French and Indian War. Its size is five hundred nineteen square miles, and its population is 169,599. The county seat is Leesburg.

Charles Fenton Mercer (1778-1858), a liberal statesman and early advocate for the Liberian colonization of free blacks, was born here, as well as Julia Beckwith Neale, Stonewall Jackson's mother (1798-1831).

Twice-Baked Potatoes

6 large baking potatoes
1/2 cup (1 stick) butter or margarine, sliced into tablespoons

Salt and pepper
1 cup sour cream
1 cup milk
Paprika

- Preheat the oven to 350°F. Bake the potatoes for 1 1/4 hours. Remove from the oven, and cut into halves lengthwise.
- Place the butter or margarine in a large bowl. Scoop out the hot potato pulp, being careful not to tear the skins. Reserve the potato skins.
- Combine the hot potato pulp with the butter or margarine in the bowl, and mash with a hand masher. Season with salt and pepper to taste. Stir in the sour cream. Add the milk, stirring until of the desired consistency.
- Spoon the potato mixture into the reserved skins, and place on a shallow baking pan. Sprinkle with the paprika, and bake for 15 minutes.
- Makes 6 servings

This recipe was sent by Virginia state senator FRANK WAGNER. Besides golf and swimming, one of Senator Wagner's favorite pastimes is cooking. As his wife, Susan, states, *He loves to create the mess, but he is hard to find after dinner*. Senator Wagner was first elected to the Senate of Virginia in 2000. Prior to that election, he served in the House of Delegates for nine years. Senator Wagner, his wife, and their four daughters reside in the city of Virginia Beach.

Mrs. K's Spinach Bread

2 (10-ounce) packages chopped spinach, thawed, reserve liquid
6 slices white bread, cut in 1/4-inch cubes
1/4 cup (1/2 stick) butter or margarine
1/4 cup olive oil
1 cup milk

6 eggs, beaten
1 onion, minced
1 teaspoon garlic powder
2 teaspoons herb seasonings, such as basil and thyme
1 teaspoon MSG
1 teaspoon pepper
2/3 cup Parmesan cheese
1/2 to 1 teaspoon paprika

- Preheat the oven to 350°F. Combine the spinach, bread cubes, butter or margarine, olive oil, milk, eggs, onion, garlic powder, herb seasonings, MSG, pepper, and Parmesan cheese in a large bow, and mix well. Spoon the mixture into an 8×12-inch or 9×13-inch baking pan. Sprinkle with the paprika. Bake for 35 to 45 minutes. Let stand until cool. Cut into small squares for appetizers or into larger squares to serve with a meal. Note: May be frozen.
- Makes approximately 12 servings

Given to us by Mrs. K's brother, JOE MCKENZIE, a naval officer, golfer, and the man who built Rowena's Wonderful Jam and Jelly Factory in Norfolk. This was her favorite recipe.

MRS. K

Mrs. K, loved by all at Georgetown University, was a professor of nutrition for thirty-three years and a clinical dietitian in the School of Nursing. She was both president of the Washington, D.C., Dietetic Association and the National Association of Dietitians.

She also received presidential awards in 1985 at Queens College and Georgetown University. In1981, the Marian McKenzie Scholarship program was established in her name for students in nursing and dietetics.

THE SETTLEMENT OF JAMESTOWN

On May 14, 1607, a little more than a century after Columbus died, a group of 105 English "gentlemen" landed upon the shores of Virginia and quickly organized a village that they called Jamestown, the first permanent English settlement in the New World. The site they chose was ill-suited for human habitation, and the surrounding marshes and swamps were infested with mosquitoes. One of the first orders of the day was the construction of a fort, which they named "James Fort," in honor of the ruling monarch of England, King James I. Jamestown fell into disrepair toward the end of the seventeenth century when the capital of Virginia was moved from there to Williamsburg. Portions of the fort, long thought to have vanished into the nearby bay, have recently been discovered by archaeologists and are currently in the process of being excavated.

Squash Casserole

4 to 6 medium yellow squash, rinsed, sliced	6 to 7 slices American cheese, torn into small pieces
1 cup boiling water	Milk
1 medium onion, chopped	1 roll butter crackers, such
Dash of black pepper	as Ritz, crushed
1 egg, beaten	
1/2 cup (1 stick) butter or margarine	

- Preheat the oven to 350°F. Combine the squash and boiling water in a medium saucepan. Cook the squash until tender, and reduce to medium heat. Do not drain. Add the onion, pepper, and egg, and mix well.
- Place pats of the butter or margarine in the bottom of a baking dish. Sprinkle some of the cheese over the butter. Add half the squash mixture with liquid to the dish. Stir a small amount of milk into the squash mixture if too dry.
- Layer pats of butter and cheese over the squash mixture. Sprinkle with some of the cracker crumbs.
- Add the remaining squash mixture. Arrange pats of the remaining butter over the squash mixture. Top with the remaining cheese. Sprinkle with the remaining cracker crumbs. Bake for 25 to 30 minutes.
- Makes approximately 6 servings

This is absolutely delicious and a big favorite when fresh squash is used, especially when it is in season. You really can't stop eating it, and it's even better the next day.

The recipe is from the kitchen of COO FITZPATRICK, a dear friend and neighbor, who has cooked for many in her lifetime. Her husband, Bill Fitzpatrick, was the executive editor for Landmark Communications, and they have a very interesting life. —Rowena

LOUISA COUNTY

Louisa County was formed in 1742 from part of Hanover County. Named for King George II's daughter, Queen Louisa of Denmark, it contains five hundred sixteen square miles. Its population is 25,627, and the county seat is Louisa.

Patrick Henry had his political beginnings in this county, which he represented in the House of Burgesses from 1765 to 1768. From a tavern located here, Jack Jouett rode to Charlottesville to warn government officials of the approaching British cavalry during the Revolution.

DID YOU KNOW THAT:

The first newspaper to be published in Virginia was the *Virginia Gazette*, printed in Williamsburg beginning in 1736?

Eastern Shore Sweet Potato Casserole

CASSEROLE
3 cups mashed, cooked
   peeled sweet potatoes
1/2 cup (1 stick) butter

1/2 cup sugar
2 eggs, beaten
1 teaspoon vanilla extract

TOPPING
1 cup sugar
1/2 cup flour

1/3 stick butter, melted
1 cup chopped pecans

- Preheat the oven to 350°F. Combine the sweet potatoes, butter, sugar, eggs, and vanilla extract in a bowl, and mix well. Spoon into a casserole dish. Combine the sugar, flour, butter, and pecans, and mix well. Set aside. Bake for 30 minutes, sprinkling the topping over the sweet potato mixture after the first 20 minutes of cooking time.
- Makes approximately 6 servings

This recipe was provided by CONNIE and RICK KELLAM, Exmore, Virginia, members of Eastern Shore of Virginia Historical Society.

Franklin Sweet Potato Pudding

2 large sweet potatoes,
   peeled, grated
2 tablespoons all-purpose
   flour
2 teaspoons baking powder
1 cup buttermilk
1/2 cup (1 stick) butter,
   melted

2/3 cup firmly packed brown
   sugar
2/3 cup sugar
1/2 teaspoon salt
1 cup milk
Generous dash of nutmeg
1 egg, beaten

- Preheat the oven to 350°F. Combine the sweet potatoes and the flour in a large bowl, and mix well.
- Dissolve the baking powder in the buttermilk. Stir the buttermilk mixture into the sweet potato mixture, and add the butter, brown sugar, sugar, salt, milk, nutmeg, and egg, and mix well.
- Spoon the pudding mixture into a buttered 2-quart casserole dish. Bake for 1 hour or until the pudding thickens, stirring frequently to mix the crusted top into the pudding.
- Note: White sweet potatoes may be used in this recipe.
- Makes about 2 quarts

A vegetable dish perfect for poultry, pork, or wild game-a favorite at holiday time.

This recipe has passed through four generations of BILL PERDUE'S family, which has ties to Franklin County, Virginia.

HAYMAN SWEET POTATOES

The sandy shoals of Virginia's Eastern Shore conjure images of watermen harvesting blue crabs and trucks laden with field-grown tomatoes. A lesser known but immensely popular gastronomic treasure from this ecologically significant region is the heirloom Hayman potato.

Described by various food writers as "lowly but noble," "homely but sweet," and "ugly, pale, and green after baking," this obscure delicacy is currently grown on a handful of the Shore's small farms.

Hayman sweet potatoes are true sweet potatoes, but of a somewhat primitive nature. They are of the same genus (*Ipomoea*) and species (*batatas*) as the orange-skinned and -fleshed sweet potatoes with which you are familiar.

The Hayman has a grayish white skin and flesh, not unlike an Irish potato. White, that is, until it is cooked. During cooking, the flesh goes from white to gray to green and often several variations of these colors. It is somewhat ugly, but when baked, the Hayman is transformed into the sweetest, softest, most moist and delicious sweet potato you have ever eaten. This is due to the Hayman's ability to convert its starches into sugars during cooking.

Columbus did more than discover the New World. He discovered many new fruits and vegetables the people of the Old

World had never seen or tasted. Among those was the sweet potato, which he discovered on what is now the island of Cuba. In all likelihood, the sweet potato he discovered was very similar to the Hayman and not the orange-fleshed ones typically found in today's supermarkets. According to legend, the Hayman was brought to the early colonies by a sea captain named Allan Hayman in the early nineteenth century.

Since the skin of the Hayman sweet potato is almost never eaten, it is best to peel the skin before serving. Once peeled, they may be served hot or cold. Place a pat of butter or margarine on top or cover with gravy and enjoy the best sweet potatoes you and your family have ever eaten.

The Hayman is usually baked, but it can be boiled, fried, candied, used in pies and breads, and prepared any other way you would fix sweet potatoes. But the true character and flavor of the Hayman is at its best when it is baked. Rub lightly with cooking oil, and place on a baking sheet. Bake at 350°F for about 55 minutes or until soft. The next step is very important. Remove the sweet potatoes from the oven and place in a pyrex dish; cover with a damp tea towel, and let stand for 15 to 20 minutes. This helps separate the skin from the flesh. The skin of the Hayman is not usually eaten. Remember, the flesh of the Hayman sweet potato turns green after it is cooked.

WOODLAWN PLANTATION
Sweet Potato Soufflé

4 pounds sweet potatoes, cooked, peeled, or 3 (18-ounce) cans sweet potatoes, drained
1/2 cup (1 stick) unsalted butter, melted
6 egg yolks

1/4 cup sugar or firmly packed brown sugar
1/2 teaspoon salt
1 teaspoon ground ginger
1/2 cup whole milk
Grated rind of 1 lemon
6 egg whites

- Preheat the oven to 325°F. Beat the sweet potatoes in a mixing bowl until smooth. Add the butter, and beat well. Beat in the egg yolks until well blended and smooth. Add the sugar, salt, ginger, milk, and lemon rind, and beat well. Beat the egg whites in a bowl until stiff, but not dry. Fold into the sweet potato mixture. Spoon into a buttered 2-quart soufflé dish and bake for 1 hour. Serve immediately.
- Makes 4 to 6 servings

ROSALYN BELLIS, First Vice Regent of the Nelly Custis Chapter of the Virginia DAR, provided this recipe with permission from Ross G. Randall, director, Woodlawn Plantation.

Erin Baked Tomatoes

1 (28-ounce) can and 1 (14 1/2-ounce) can premium-quality whole tomatoes
1 medium onion, sliced

1/4 cup sugar
Salt and pepper
1/2 cup (1 stick) butter, no substitution

- Preheat the oven to 375°F. Place the undrained tomatoes in an iron skillet, and cover with the onions. Sprinkle with the sugar, and salt and pepper to taste. Do not stir. Place the butter in the center of the skillet over the onions. Bake, uncovered, for 1 1/2 hours or until the liquid is reduced by half and is somewhat syrupy.
- Makes 6 servings

This recipe is shared by MELBA and WILLIAM TRENARY, who own Erin, a plantation home built circa 1840 by David Funsten and his wife, Margaret Meade. Funsten was a member of the Virginia Assembly, a Confederate colonel, and Virginia representative in the Confederate Congress. Erin, a Virginia Historic Landmark several miles north of Front Royal, is a wonderful example of a three-part Greek Revival plantation house with a sweeping spiral staircase, semicircular hall, and handsome woodwork. It has been in the Trenary family for sixty-five years, and it is the private residence of family members Sue and John Murray. She is a member of the Front Royal Chapter of the Virginia DAR.

MICHIE TAVERN
Stewed Tomatoes and Murphy's Biscuits

MURPHY'S BISCUITS

2 cups self-rising flour
1/4 teaspoon salt

3 tablespoons shortening
2/3 cup whole milk

- Preheat the oven to 450°F. Sift the flour and salt together in a bowl. Add the shortening, and stir in the milk quickly with a fork to make a light and fluffy, but not sticky, dough. Knead approximately 10 times or until the dough is smooth. Roll out the dough on a lightly floured board. Cut the biscuits 1/2 inch thick. Place on a greased baking sheet. Bake for 8 to 10 minutes.
- Makes 10 to 12 biscuits

STEWED TOMATOES

4 cups canned tomatoes,
  cut into quarters
1/2 cup sugar

2 tablespoons butter, melted
Salt and pepper
6 Murphy's Biscuits

- Combine the tomatoes, sugar, butter, and salt and pepper to taste in a saucepan, and mix well. Crumble the biscuits into the tomato mixture. Cook, covered, over medium heat for 15 minutes.
- Makes 6 servings

MICHIE TAVERN of Charlottesville shared this recipe.

MOUNT VERNON INN
Tomato Cobbler

1/2 cup olive oil
48 plum tomatoes or
  36 beefsteak tomatoes,
  cut into halves, seeded
Salt and pepper
4 1/2 cups biscuit mix

1 tablespoon plus
  1 teaspoon dried basil
2 teaspoons dried oregano
2 teaspoons dried parsley
1 1/3 cups milk
Flour for dusting

- Preheat the oven to 350°F. Brush baking sheets with the olive oil. Place the tomatoes face down, and brush lightly with the olive oil. Season with the salt and pepper to taste, and bake for 45 minutes, turning once. Chop the tomatoes coarsely, and divide among twelve (12-ounce) soufflé cups. Combine the biscuit mix and herbs in a bowl, and add the milk, stirring just until moistened. Divide the dough into 12 portions, and dust with flour. Shape into thin patties the size of the soufflé cups. Top the tomatoes with the biscuit patties, and bake for 15 minutes or until golden brown.
- Makes 12 servings

ERIC R. SWANSON, general manager, The Mount Vernon Inn, Mount Vernon, Virginia, sent this recipe.

WOODLAWN PLANTATION

Given to Eleanor (Nelly) Custis by her step-grandfather, George Washington, and her grandmother, Martha, Woodlawn Plantation flourished under the direction of the new bride and her husband, Major Lawrence Lewis (George Washington's favorite nephew). Because she was reared at neighboring Mt. Vernon after her father's (Jacky Custis) death during the Revolutionary War, Nelly naturally was used to being a young lady in a Virginia manor house.

At Woodlawn, the arts of cookery and domestic management were paramount. Nelly was proud to please the Washingtons as she took over as mistress of a plantation. She and her husband moved into the newly built home in 1803. The house was about seven miles south of Alexandria. Their 2,000-acre platation eventually included a gristmill and distillery, and agriculture and livestock were important daily operations. Fresh fish, crabs, oysters, and turtles were readily available from Dogue Creek, which flowed into the nearby Potomac River. Since Alexandria was close, foodstuffs from merchants were handy as well. Nelly found beautiful fine china, table linens, crystal, and silver in cargo carried by ships which regularly arrived from Europe to the port.

The Lewises had eight children, of whom four survived infancy or early childhood. Nelly often shared remedies with her family using the "receipts" that Martha Washington had given her. Her guests were fed fabulous meals and were then entertained by the harpsichord and guitar played by family members. Through the years, Nelly's expertise with foods and management shone. Grandmother Martha had prepared her well to truly represent a Virginia wife.

FORMER LT. GOVERNOR AND MRS. JOHN HAGER'S
Hanover County Tomato Pie

1 (9-inch) frozen piecrust
7 tomatoes, sliced, drained
1/2 teaspoon salt
1/2 teaspoon pepper
1/3 to 1/2 cup sugar, or enough to sprinkle each layer
1 tablespoon all-purpose flour
1 cup mayonnaise
1 (3-ounce) package shredded Parmesan cheese

- Preheat the oven to 350°F. Line the piecrust with foil, and fill with pie weights, dried beans, or rice. Bake for 5 minutes, and remove the weights. Bake for 4 to 5 minutes longer. Layer the tomato slices in the piecrust, sprinkling each layer evenly with sugar, salt, and pepper. Sprinkle the top layer with flour. Combine the mayonnaise and cheese in a bowl, and mix well. Spread evenly over the tomatoes. Bake for 30 minutes.
- Makes 8 servings

Since we grow parsley, chives, and basil in pots at our kitchen door, I always add these fresh herbs to the pie before baking.

MAGGIE HAGER has graciously shared The Hanover County Tomato Pie recipe with us. The Hanover County Tomato Festival is held every year in August in Mechanicsville, Virginia. The "Hanover tomato" is famous throughout Virginia as being the most delicious of all tomatoes. During one of former Lieutenant Governor John and Maggie Hager's many visits to the festival, they were greeted by members of the Black Creek Fire Department Ladies Auxiliary, who generously gave them a copy of their *1998 Tomato Cookbook* in which appeared Sandra Blake's recipe for Hanover County Tomato Pie. While John was Lieutenant Governor, Maggie entertained more than 600 ladies for lunch in their home. Her luncheon menu began with refreshments served with homemade pecan cheese biscuits followed by: Homemade Chicken Tetrazzini, Sally Lunn Bread, Hanover County Tomato Pie, Crème Brûlée with Raspberry Sauce, Mixed Green Salad, and Coffee.

John and Maggie Hager believe in the people of Virginia, and they know personally that the best work is accomplished at the community level. While John was campaigning for lieutenant governor, he carried out what he called "Rolling through Virginia" from July to Labor Day, 1997. He visited every locality and jurisdiction in Virginia, meeting and talking with the people in those areas, reaching out to all types of individuals and groups. Their message and spirit of doing good things for the people were widely recognized and appreciated, and many friendships were made that have lasted through the years. John now works as Homeland Security Director for the Commonwealth. A special involvement of the Hagers is the 400-year celebration of Jamestown 2007. John is a member of the executive committee and steering committee of this major event.

Side Dishes

Apple Fritters

1 cup all-purpose flour
1¹/₂ teaspoons baking powder
¹/₂ teaspoon salt
1 egg, beaten
¹/₂ cup milk
1 tablespoon margarine, melted

1 tablespoon sugar
1 cup chopped peeled tart apples
Hot oil for deep frying (365°F to 375°F)
Confectioners' sugar for dusting

• Combine the flour, baking powder, and salt in a medium bowl, and mix well. Combine the egg, milk, margarine, and sugar in a large bowl, and mix well. Stir in the dry mixture. Add additional milk gradually until the batter is of the desired consistency if the batter is too thick. Stir in the apples.
• Drop by spoonfuls into hot oil, and deep-fry for 5 minutes or until done. Drain, and dust with confectioners' sugar.
• Makes 8 to 10 servings

MARY FRANCES WYKOWSKI from Virginia Beach, Regent of the Lynnhaven Parish Chapter of the Virginia DAR, submitted this recipe.

Sam Houston's Apple Relish

14 large apples, peeled, cored
1 large bunch celery
6 red bell peppers, seeded

6 green bell peppers, seeded
12 onions, peeled
1 quart vinegar
6 cups sugar

• Process the apples, celery, peppers, and onions through a food chopper. Combine with the vinegar and sugar, and boil for about 15 minutes. Can and seal.
• Makes 8 to 10 pints

Mr. Houston's favorite relish recipe was handed down from the *Sam Houston Schoolhouse Cookbook*. The recipe is reprinted from *Miss Daisy Celebrates Tennessee*, ©1995 by Daisy King, James A. Crutchfield, and Winette Sparkman, with permission.

LUNENBURG COUNTY

Formed in 1746 from Brunswick County, Lunenburg County derived its name from Brunswick-Lunenburg, a German duchy ruled by King George II. The county contains four hundred thirty square miles, and its population is 13,146. The county seat is Lunenburg.

Early physician and minister James Craig lived here until he was taken prisoner by the British army during the Revolution. The British cavalryman Tarleton operated extensively in this county.

ROWENA'S
Banana Chutney

3 cups sugar
2 cups cider vinegar
1/4 cup chopped crystallized
  ginger
1 tablespoon curry powder
1 teaspoon salt
1 cup golden raisins

1 pound onions, chopped
2 (8-ounce) packages
  chopped dates
6 ripe bananas, peeled,
  sliced (approximately
  4 cups)

- Combine the sugar, cider vinegar, ginger, curry powder,
  and salt in a heavy saucepan. Add the raisins, onions,
  dates, and bananas, and bring to a boil. Reduce the heat.
  Simmer for 15 minutes or until thickened. Spoon into
  8 half-pint jars. Store, covered, in the refrigerator. Can also
  be frozen in jars.
- Makes 8 cups

*So easy, and terrific with lamb or any curry dish. This recipe was
a real favorite of my mother, Mary Jane Gotshall, one of the
most loving cooks I have ever known. —Rowena*

Cranberry Chutney

1 cup water
3/4 cup sugar
1 (12-ounce) package fresh
  or frozen cranberries
1 cup chopped peeled apple
1/2 cup cider vinegar

1/2 cup raisins
1/2 teaspoon ground
  cinnamon
1/4 teaspoon ground ginger
1/4 teaspoon ground allspice
1/8 teaspoon ground cloves

- Combine the water and sugar in a medium saucepan, and
  bring to a boil over medium heat. Add the cranberries,
  apple, cider vinegar, raisins, cinnamon, ginger, allspice,
  and cloves, and mix well. Bring to a boil, and reduce heat
  to low. Simmer gently for 10 minutes, stirring frequently.
- Pour cranberry mixture into a mixing bowl. Place plastic
  wrap directly on the surface of the cranberry mixture. Cool
  to room temperature and serve, or refrigerate, covered.
  Bring to room temperature before serving.
- Makes 2 2/3 cups

*This is wonderful with all poultry dishes. It keeps well in the
refrigerator.*

This recipe was shared by BARBARA L. SEGAR, Regent of
the Leedstown Resolution Chapter of the Virginia DAR.

ROWENA'S KITCHEN TIPS

I always put a skewer through the center of potatoes
when I am baking. The skewer conducts heat and guarantees
the center of the potato is completely done.

VIRGINIA IS FAMOUS FOR ITS APPLES

Name a variety of apple, and chances
are good that it's successfully grown
somewhere in Virginia. Red Delicious,
Golden Delicious, Rome, Stayman, Gala,
Winesap, York, Granny Smith, Jonathan,
Fuji, and Ginger Gold— they're all
harvested from Commonwealth orchards.
Although apples are popularly grown all
across Virginia, the best commercial
areas lie among the Blue Ridge
Mountains and within the Shenandoah
and Roanoke Valleys.

Today, in Virginia, about two hundred
fifty commercial orchards, covering
some eighteen thousand acres, produce
nearly ten million bushels of apples
annually, valued at nearly $250 million.
Harvest time, depending upon the
variety of apple, runs from July through
early November.

PULLING THE TRIGGER: FRENCH- INDIAN WAR

During the fall and winter of 1753, Major George Washington of the Virginia militia, under authority of Royal Governor Robert Dinwiddie, made a trip to French-occupied Fort Le Boeuf, located near the Pennsylvania-New York border. There, he presented the governor's demand that the French immediately evacuate the Ohio River valley. The French commandant flatly refused the order. After returning to Virginia and spending the winter there, Washington, now sporting the rank of lieutenant-colonel, was given a second assignment. Amid rumors of a large French army moving south out of Canada, he was ordered to cut a road through the Virginia, Maryland, and Pennsylvania wilderness to accommodate his own militia, as well as any British military forces that might arrive later. The road would be used to march troops toward the upper Ohio River valley to confront the French. Washington and his men left Alexandria, Virginia on April 2, 1754. Washington's ambush attack on a small French military contingent later in the spring, and his subsequent surrender at the Great Meadows in July, were the contributing factors to the beginning of the French and Indian War in North America.

Baked Fresh Pears

5 ripe pears, peeled, cut into halves, stems and seeds removed	5 tablespoons honey Ground nutmeg Slivers of butter or margarine
5 tablespoons thawed orange juice concentrate	

- Preheat the oven to 350°F. Combine the pears with enough cold water to cover in a large saucepan. Bring to a boil. Cook until the pears are slightly tender. Place the pears, cavity side up, in an 8×8-inch baking dish sprayed with oil.
- Combine the orange juice concentrate and honey in a bowl, and mix well. Drizzle over the pears. Sprinkle with the nutmeg, and place the slivers of butter or margarine in the pear cavities. Bake for 35 minutes.
- Makes 10 servings

The recipe was generously provided from their family recipes by innkeepers JIM and BECKY ELLIS, who host the lovely and historic Overhome Bed and Breakfast in Hardy, Virginia, ten miles from Roanoke. Overhome is a pre-Civil War home (c.1840) with tall ceilings and great windows with rooms decorated with antiques and collectibles and working fireplaces. It is located on 100 acres in a history-rich and scenery-rich environment.

Pear Conserve

3 pounds pears, peeled, cored, cut into halves	2 lemons, seeded 1 pound raisins, chopped
3 pounds sugar	1 pound black walnut kernels
3 oranges, seeded	

- Place the pears in a large bowl. Cover with the sugar, and let stand overnight. Drain the syrup into a medium pan, and cook the syrup until thickened.
- Grind the pears with the oranges and lemons in a grinder, and add to the syrup. Cook until the fruit is tender, stirring occasionally. Add the raisins and nuts. Cook the fruit mixture until thickened, stirring occasionally. Spoon into pint jars, and seal.
- This conserve is best canned in pint jars since it is apt to mold in large jars once opened.
- Makes 6 to 8 pints

This recipe is from ALICE FISHER'S great-grandmother and dates back to the late 1800s. Alice is from Luray, Virginia, and is a member of the John Rhodes Chapter of the Virginia DAR.

Pineapple Casserole

2 (15-ounce) cans pineapple
   tidbits, drained
$^1/_2$ cup sugar
3 tablespoons all-purpose
   flour
1 cup shredded cheddar
   cheese

$^1/_2$ roll Ritz crackers,
   crushed
$^1/_2$ cup (1 stick) butter or
   margarine, melted

- Preheat the oven to 350°F. Combine the pineapple, sugar, flour, and cheese in a large bowl, and mix well. Spoon into an 8-inch round casserole or glass pie plate.
- Top with the crushed crackers. Drizzle the butter or margarine over the crackers. Bake for 25 to 30 minutes or until golden brown.
- Makes 4 to 6 servings

BARBARA A. KONAT, a member of the Montpelier Chapter of the Virginia DAR in Madison, submitted this recipe.

GRANDMOTHER SAUNDERS'
Watermelon Pickles

1 good-size watermelon
   rind, cut into bite-size
   pieces
Salted water, not too strong
1 teaspoon alum

1 stick cinnamon
8 whole allspice
16 whole cloves
1 quart vinegar
4 cups sugar, or to taste

- Soak the watermelon rind in the salted water in a large pot overnight. Drain the water, "squeezing" the watermelon rind against the side of the pot and rinsing the rind with water. Add the alum and water to cover, and boil until the watermelon rind is tender. Let the watermelon rind stand in the alum water until crisp.
- Prepare a spice bag with the cinnamon, allspice, and cloves.
- "Squeeze" out the water from the watermelon rind, and drain the water from the pot. Pour in the vinegar, and stir in the sugar. Add the spice bag. Bring to a rolling boil. Turn off the heat, and let stand until cool. Spoon into jars, and seal.
- Note: Don't forget to eat the watermelon.
- Servings depend on the size of the watermelon

The recipe is from the family of JOANNE SAUNDERS BERKLEY of Norfolk, Virginia, one of our biggest community assets and someone who never gives up if she thinks it will benefit the wonderful state of Virginia. It was copied from the original handwritten notes of Grandma Saunders and was difficult, but fun, to read and decipher.

VIRGINIA TIMELINE

1856—Woodrow Wilson, twenty-eighth U.S. president (1913-1921), is born at the First Presbyterian Church in Staunton. Booker T. Washington, who would later become the founder of Tuskegee Institute, is born in Franklin County.

1860—Virginia's number of slaves approaches one-half million, nearly 40 percent of the state's total population.

1861—On April 17, Virginia becomes the eighth state to secede from the Union. Richmond is designated the capital of the Confederate States of America. Virginian Winfield Scott is the senior U.S. army officer. The Confederate Army scores the first large-scale victory in the War Between the States when it defeats its Union counterpart at Manassas (Bull Run).

1862—During the Peninsula Campaign, the Union Army under General George B. McClellan occupies Williamsburg. Union forces fail to occupy Richmond. Confederate General Robert E. Lee, commander of the Army of Northern Virginia, is defeated at Antietam. The *Monitor* and the *Merrimack* fight it out near Hampton Roads in what becomes the first confrontation between ironclad warships.

1863—Fifty western Virginia counties hold a constitutional convention and vote to organize a separate state called

West Virginia. Confederate General Thomas "Stonewall" Jackson dies from wounds suffered at Chancellorsville.

1864—Confederate General J.E.B. Stuart is killed at Yellow Tavern. Total victory eludes the Union army, now under the command of General Ulysses S. Grant, at Spotsylvania, Richmond, and Petersburg. Union General Philip Sheridan defeats General Jubal Early's Confederates in the Shenandoah Valley, leaving a path of destruction behind him.

1865—Richmond and Petersburg are abandoned by the Confederate army. Confederate President Jefferson Davis and his cabinet flee the capitol. The War Between the States finally ends at Appomattox Court House on April 9.

1870—U.S. military rule ends in Virginia, and the state is readmitted into the Union.

1872—The Virginia Agricultural and Mechanical College is established at Blacksburg.

1889—The Association for the Preservation of Virginia Antiquities (APVA) is organized.

1890—John Mercer Langston becomes the first African-American Virginian in history to be seated in the U.S. Congress.

1900—Virginia's population reaches 1,854,184.

Cashew Rice

$^1/_4$ cup plus 2 tablespoons ($^3/_4$ stick) butter or margarine
1 medium onion, chopped
1 red or green pepper, chopped
$1^1/_4$ cups long grain rice

2 ($10^3/_4$-ounce) cans chicken consommé or broth
1 (4-ounce) can sliced mushrooms
1 (9-ounce) can cashew nuts

- Preheat the oven to 350°F. Melt the butter or margarine in a medium skillet. Sauté the onion and pepper lightly.
- Add the rice, and stir to moisten. Place in a 2-quart casserole dish. Add the consommé or broth, mushrooms, and cashews, and mix well. Bake, covered, for 45 minutes.
- Makes 8 to 10 servings

This makes a great side dish. Or, by adding browned ground beef or chopped chicken, it can be used as a quick main dish. A very close friend gave this to me. It is one of our favorites for a crowd.

DOTTIE CURLEY is from Chesapeake, Virginia. She loves to cook and is a great homemaker and a wonderful friend with whom it is fun to share thoughts and ideas.

EVA'S
Rice Casserole

$^1/_2$ cup (1 stick) butter or margarine
1 (7-ounce) can mushrooms
1 (8-ounce) can water chestnuts

1 cup rice
1 (10 $^3/_4$-ounce) can French onion soup

- Preheat the oven to 350°F. Melt the butter in a 8×10-inch baking dish. Drain the mushrooms and water chestnuts, reserving the liquid. Combine the rice, melted butter or margarine, mushrooms, water chestnuts, onion soup, and reserved liquid in a bowl, and mix well. Add a small amount of water if more liquid is needed. Spoon into the baking dish. Bake for 45 minutes, stirring occasionally.
- Makes 4 servings

Men love this.

This recipe was sent by VIRGINIA MORRIS JONES, Regent of the Judith Randolph-Longwood Chapter of the Virginia DAR.

ROWENA'S KITCHEN TIPS

Use confectioners' sugar instead of flour when rolling out cookie dough. This prevents your dough from toughening as happens sometimes when rolled out on a floured board.

THE Macaroni and Cheese

1 (8-ounce) package elbow
  macaroni
1 (10³/4-ounce) can cream
  of mushroom soup,
  undiluted
1/2 cup mayonnaise

1/4 cup (1/2 stick) butter or
  margarine, melted
1/4 cup chopped onion
1/2 to 1 pound grated cheese
1¹/2 to 2 cups crushed butter
  cracker crumbs, such as Ritz

- Preheat the oven to 350°F. Prepare the macaroni according to the package directions, and drain. Combine the soup, mayonnaise, butter or margarine, onion, and cheese in a large bowl. Add the macaroni, and mix well.
- Spoon the macaroni mixture into a 3-quart casserole dish, and top with the cracker crumbs. Bake, uncovered, for 30 to 40 minutes or until the top is lightly browned.
- Makes 10 to 12 servings

I have taken this recipe to funerals, church suppers, and family gatherings. When I took it to a family night church supper, ten people wanted the recipe right then and they named this recipe, "THE Macaroni and Cheese."

This recipe is from the kitchen of ANNE WEAVER, someone who never stops baking and cooking. She was born and reared in Virginia.

MADISON COUNTY

Madison County was named in honor of President James Madison. It was formed from Culpeper County in 1792. Madison County contains three hundred twenty-four square miles and is home to 12,520 residents. The county seat is Madison.

Hebron Church, the oldest (about 1740) Lutheran congregation in the South, is located in Madison County. On October 1, 1784, George Washington spent the night in this county at the widow Early's house.

MATHEWS COUNTY

Mathews County, one of Virginia's smallest, was formed in 1790 from Gloucester County and was named in honor of Colonel Thomas Mathews, a veteran of the Revolution. Its size is ninety-four square miles, and its population is 9,207. Its county seat is Mathews.

Windsor, the home of early botanist John Clayton, was located in Mathews County. The only female ever granted a commission in the Confederate Army, Captain Sally Tompkins, was born here in 1833.

A FUTURE KING OF FRANCE TOURS VIRGINIA

In 1797, Louis-Philippe was a young man on a fling. With his two younger brothers and a manservant, Louis had arrived in Philadelphia in October of the previous year with a mission in mind to tour the United States. Louis carried royal blood in his veins and claimed descent from King Louis XIII. Now, however, he was a refugee, having fled his native country during the French Revolution and wandering for some years across Europe. During his American tour, he kept a day-by-day journal, and his writings reveal that by the spring of 1797, he and his party were in the backwoods of Virginia, near the North Carolina line. The primitive conditions of the Virginia frontier made quite an impression on Louis-Philippe's regal sensibilities. Of visitors' accommodations of the region, he wrote:

The food in the inns is nothing much; generally it amounts to no more than fried fatback and cornbread. Eggs have disappeared and the potatoes are finished. In the better places they make us little wheatcakes that are rather good. There is coffee everywhere, but bad, very weak. The sugar is always black muscovado, or unrefined maple sugar, which I like better. We had tea only once and it was good, but it is not to be found.

In 1830, Louis-Philippe was crowned king of France, a position he held for the next eighteen years. His tour in democratic America had influenced him greatly, and he ruled his country with a down-to-earth approach, even wearing a business suit and carrying an umbrella.

Tortellini Bella Monte

12 ounces Bella Monte
  marinara
2 button mushrooms, sliced
1/4 cup grated Parmesan
  cheese
2 sun-dried tomatoes,
  julienned
3 ounces heavy whipping
  cream
9 ounces cheese tortellini,
  cooked
Chopped fresh parsley and
  basil for garnish

- Combine the marinara and mushrooms in a large sauté pan over medium to high heat, and mix well. Sauté for about 2 minutes or until the marinara is heated.
- Stir in the Parmesan cheese, sun-dried tomatoes, and whipping cream. Sauté until the sauce turns a pinkish color. Add the tortellini, and sauté for about 2 minutes or until the tortellini is heated through. Spoon into a pasta bowl, and garnish with parsley and basil.
- Makes 4 servings

Bella Monte of Virginia, Inc. was formed in Virginia in 1968 by an Italian family from New York trying to find a warmer climate and warmer place to live. The Montinino family and the Carauana family, joined by marriage, masterminded the association of two Italian family recipes to create the foods sold today. Salads, soups, bread, and sausages were the fare for the first few years. The Virginia Beach area, yearning for Italian specialties, brought in great business. In 1986 TOM and ROBIN TUITE purchased Bella Monte. With a background in retail and food service, Robin tackled the job of extending the grocery selections. The restaurant now seats 100 inside and 25 outside. The menu is Italian based, but over the years has taken on some other European specialties as well as an influence from the South. The Tuite's daughter, Barbie, now runs the operations as general manager and has begun to change the product mix once again to entertain the younger homemaker. Robin Tuite was born and raised in Norfolk, Virginia, and still sells to the friends she grew up with. They come for miles to chat and get information about food.

DID YOU KNOW THAT:

During the War Between the States, more men served and died in Virginia than in any other state, North or South? Likewise, more military engagements occurred in Virginia (2,154) than in any other state.

Taking Care of Your Vegetables

The following advice comes from *A Treatise on Gardening*, issued in Richmond in 1793. Supposedly written by John Randolph of Williamsburg, the book was the first gardening work ever published in Virginia. The spelling has been modernized for ease of reading.

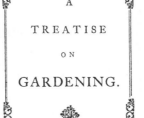

A
TREATISE
ON
GARDENING.

Written by a native of this State.

RICHMOND:
Printed by T. NICOLSON;—1793

JANUARY

Prepare hot beds for Cucumbers; as little can be done this month in a garden, I would advise the preparing of your dung, and carrying it to your beds, that it may be ready to be spread in February.

FEBRUARY

Sow Asparagus, make your beds and fork up the old ones, sow Sugar Loaf Cabbages, latter end transplant Cauliflowers, sow Carrots and transplant for feed, prick out endive for seed, sow Lettuce, Melons in hot beds, sow Parsnips, take up the old roots and prick out for seed, sow Peas and prick them into your hot beds, sow Radishes twice, plant Strawberries, plant out Turnips for seed, spade deep and make it fine, plant Beans.

MARCH

Slip your Artichokes, if fit, plant kidney Beans, Cabbages, Celery, Parsley, Cucumbers, Currants, Chamomile, Celandine, Nasturtium, Featherfew, Fennel, Ivy, Horse Radish, Hyssop, Lavender, Lettuce, Radishes twice, Marjoram, Marsh Mallow, Mint, Melons, Millet, Mugwort, Onions and for feed, Peas twice, Potatoes, Raspberry, Rosemary, Rue, Spinach, Tansy, Thyme, Turnips;—You may begin to mow your grass walks, and continue so to do every morning, and roll them, turf this month, plant Box.

APRIL

If Artichokes not slipped last month, do it this; Bushel and garden Beans, sow Cabbages, 12th, sow Cauliflowers, sow Celery, Cresses, Nasturtium, Lettuce, Peas, sow Radishes twice, Sage will grow in this or any other month, Turnips, sow Salsify early, Pepper, Turf this month.

MAY

Latter end Broccoli, Celery, Cucumbers for pickles, Endive, Featherfew, Hyssop, cuttings of M. Mallow, Melons, Peas, sow Radishes twice, Kidney Beans, turf this month.

JUNE

Cabbages should be sown, sow Radishes twice, transplant Cabbages, Prick out Cauliflowers, do. Broccoli, Draw up by the roots all your weeds.

JULY

Transplant Broccoli, sow Cabbages, Coleworts, transplant Cauliflowers to stand, Endive, gather Millet seed, take up Onions, sow Radishes twice, sow Turnips, plant Kidney Beans to preserve.

AUGUST

Sow Cabbages, latter end Carrots, get your Cucumber seed, sow Cresses, prick out Endive, early sow Lettuce, Mullein, gather Onion seed, plant Garlic, get Parsnip seed, 12th, sow Peas for the fall, sow Radishes, middle sow Spinach, tho' some say not till after the 20th, sow Turnips.

SEPTEMBER

Sow Cabbages, 10th, sow Cauliflowers, plant cuttings of Currants, Clary, Comfrey, Gooseberries, sow radishes, plant layers or suckers of Raspberries, Rosemary, plant out Strawberries, string your Strawberries, and dress your beds, plant Tansy.

OCTOBER

Latter end cut down your Asparagus, and cover your beds with dung, plant Beans for spring, sow Cabbages, 20th, transplant Cauliflowers, plant Horse Radish, prick Lettuce into boxes, sow Peas for the hot bed, Radishes, turf this month.

NOVEMBER

Take up your Cabbages, sow Cabbages, take up your Cauliflowers, such as are flowered and house them, take up your Carrots, trench all your vacant land, prune your trees and vines, plant out every thing of the tree or shrub kind, that has a root to it, if any thing is done to your Artichokes, this is a good month, plant Box, turf early.

DECEMBER

Cover your Endive with brush, cover Celery, and every thing else that needs shelter, if the weather will admit turn over your ground that is trenched, in order to mellow it, and pulverize it.—Whatever will prevent delay and enable you to begin spading in February should be done this month.

CHAPTER SIX

Delicious
and
Decadent Desserts

*Old recipes called for lots of eggs because the hens were not
fed like our hens today, so the eggs were smaller.*

Cakes

Apple Cake

4 medium apples, peeled,
  cored, finely chopped
2 cups sugar
2 large eggs, lightly beaten
1 cup (2 sticks) butter,
  melted, cooled
3 cups flour
2 teaspoons baking soda

2 teaspoons cinnamon
$^1/_2$ teaspoon grated nutmeg
$^1/_2$ teaspoon allspice
1 cup finely chopped
  walnuts
1 cup apple cider
$^1/_2$ cup confectioners' sugar

- Preheat the oven to 350°F. Place the apples in a large bowl. Sprinkle with the sugar, stirring well. Set aside for 15 minutes, stirring frequently. Beat the eggs and butter in a large bowl until smooth. Combine the flour, baking soda, cinnamon, nutmeg, allspice, and walnuts in a separate large bowl, and mix well. Add the butter mixture and apples, stirring well.
- Pour the batter into a buttered nonstick 12-cup bundt pan. Smooth the top of the batter with a spatula, and bake for about 45 minutes or until a wooden pick inserted in the center comes out clean. Let the cake stand in the pan for 10 minutes. Invert onto a wire rack.
- Bring the cider to a boil in a small saucepan over high heat. Boil until reduced by half. Cool slightly, and stir in the confectioners' sugar. Drizzle over the warm cake. Let the cake cool completely before slicing.
- Makes 10 to 12 servings

Use flavorful cooking apples such as Rome Beauty, Crispin, Granny Smith, or Golden Delicious for best results.

Many thanks to CHOWNING'S TAVERN for providing this recipe.

MECKLENBURG COUNTY

Mecklenburg County was organized in 1764 from part of Lunenburg County. It was named in honor of Princess Charlotte, consort of King George III and native of the Mecklenburg-Strelitz region of Germany. It contains six hundred sixty-nine square miles, and its population is 32,380. The county seat is Boydton.

The second William Byrd had extensive land holdings in the present-day county during the 1730s. The original Randolph-Macon college was located here, beginning in 1832 until it moved to Ashland in 1868.

Applesauce Cake

2 eggs
$3/4$ cup butter or margarine, melted
$2^1/2$ cups sugar
3 cups applesauce
3 teaspoons baking soda
1 (15-ounce) package raisins
1 cup walnuts or pecans
$3^1/2$ cups all-purpose flour
1 teaspoon salt
1 teaspoon cinnamon
$1/2$ teaspoon ground cloves
$1/2$ teaspoon nutmeg

- Preheat the oven to 350°F. Combine the eggs and melted butter or margarine in a large bowl, and mix well. Blend in the sugar until creamy. Heat the applesauce in a small saucepan, and stir in the baking soda. Add the applesauce mixture to the creamed mixture, and mix well.
- Combine the raisins and nuts in a large bowl. Sprinkle a small amount of the flour over the nuts and raisins, and mix well. Combine the remaining flour, salt, cinnamon, cloves, and nutmeg in a large bowl, and mix well. Add the flour mixture to the applesauce mixture, beating well after each addition. Fold in the nuts and raisins. Note: Coating the nuts and raisins with flour helps to prevent them from sinking to the bottom of the cake.
- Pour the batter into a greased and floured tube pan or 5×9-inch loaf pan. Bake for $1^1/2$ hours for a tube pan and about 1 hour for a loaf pan.
- Makes 8 to 10 servings

This recipe was given to me by a friend from Galax, Virginia, whose mother-in-law had been baking it for more than fifty years. That was 25 years ago, and I've been baking it ever since.

JEANNE POPYACK in Woodbridge, Virginia, a member of the Bill of Rights Chapter of the Virginia DAR, sent this recipe.

MIDDLESEX COUNTY

Middlesex County was organized in 1673 from Lancaster County. Its namesake is the English county of the same name. It contains one hundred forty-six square miles and has a population of 9,932. The county seat is Saluda.

In June 1608, Captain John Smith was injured by a stingray near the confluence of the Rappahannock River and Chesapeake Bay. Christopher Robinson, a noted statesman and one of the founding trustees of the College of William and Mary, was an early resident of this county.

VIRGINIA TIMELINE

1908—Staunton becomes the first city in the United States to adopt a city-manager form of local government.

1918—Shipyards in Hampton Roads produce more naval tonnage than all other U.S. facilities combined.

1920—Virginia women win the right to vote.

1924—Sarah Lee Fain and Helen Timmons Henderson are elected to become the first women to serve in the Virginia House of Delegates.

1925—Harry Flood Byrd begins his forty-year influence on Virginia politics when he is elected the state's governor.

1926—John D. Rockefeller purchases the Ludwell-Paradise House in Williams-

burg for $8,000, thus beginning the long restoration of the colonial village.

1933—The Civilian Conservation Corps (CCC) opens its first camp in the George Washington National Forest. In the ten years following, CCC boys build nearly one thousand bridges and plant more than 15 million trees across Virginia.

1934—President Franklin D. Roosevelt attends opening ceremonies for the first phase of restoration at Williamsburg.

1935—Douglas Southall Freeman, a Richmond newspaperman, wins the Pulitzer Prize for *R.E. Lee: A Biography*.

1942—The Pulitzer Prize for literature is awarded to novelist Ellen Glasgow of Richmond, Virginia, for her novel, *In This Our Life*.

Grandmother's Applesauce Cake

2¹/2 cups applesauce
4 cups all-purpose flour
2 teaspoons cinnamon
1 teaspoon allspice
¹/2 teaspoon ground cloves
1 teaspoon nutmeg
1 tablespoon baking soda
1 cup (2 sticks) butter or margarine
2 cups sugar
1 pound (or more) raisins

- Preheat the oven to 350°F. Heat the applesauce gently in a medium saucepan, stirring occasionally. Combine the flour, cinnamon, allspice, cloves, nutmeg, and baking soda in a large bowl, and mix well. Beat the butter or margarine and sugar in a separate large bowl, adding the applesauce alternately with the flour mixture, and raisins. Pour the batter into 2 greased loaf pans. Note: The pans can be lined with brown paper if desired.
- Place a pan of water underneath the loaf pans. Bake for 30 minutes. Remove the water, and reduce the heat to 250°F. Bake for 1¹/2 to 2 hours longer or until the cakes test done. Let the cakes cool completely in the pans before serving.
- Makes 2 loaves

This recipe is my grandmother's, which has been used religiously for a Christmas cake (and a Thanksgiving cake most of the time) by her family (Keyser), my mother's family (Smith), and mine (Ticer) for many, many years. Now my children are using it also. It is not as heavy as fruitcake and it is festive without being overburdened with fruit.

This comes from the family of Virginia State Senator PATRICIA S. (PATSY) TICER, who was elected to the Senate of the Commonwealth of Virginia in 1995 to represent the 30th Senatorial District. Previously she was on the Alexandria City Council, and then she became the first woman mayor in the history of the city. She is also the proud mother of four and the grandmother of five.

MONTGOMERY COUNTY

Montgomery County was formed in 1776 from Fincastle County. Its namesake is General Richard Montgomery, a casualty at the Battle of Quebec in 1775. It contains four hundred one square miles. Its population is 83,629, and the county seat is Christiansburg.

In this county in 1872, Virginia Polytechnic Institute opened on the site of the Draper's Meadows massacre of 1755. The Future Farmers of Virginia, the precursor to the Future Farmers of America (FFA), was organized on the campus of Virginia Polytechnic Institute in 1925.

Cocoa Delight

CAKE

2 cups sugar	1 teaspoon baking soda
2 cups all-purpose flour	1/2 cup buttermilk
1/2 cup (1 stick) butter or margarine	2 teaspoons cinnamon
1/2 cup vegetable oil	1 teaspoon vanilla extract
4 tablespoons baking cocoa	2 eggs
1 cup water	Dash of salt

ICING

1/2 cup (1 stick) butter or margarine	1 teaspoon vanilla extract
1/4 cup baking cocoa	1 (1-pound) package confectioners' sugar
1/4 cup plus 2 tablespoons milk	1 cup chopped nuts, optional

- To prepare the cake, preheat the oven to 400°F. Combine the sugar and flour in a large bowl, and mix well. Combine the butter or margarine, oil, baking cocoa, and water in a medium saucepan, and bring to a boil. Pour the mixture over the flour and sugar, and mix well. Stir in the baking soda, buttermilk, cinnamon, vanilla extract, eggs, and salt. Pour into a 11×17-inch pan, and bake for 20 minutes.
- To prepare the icing, melt the butter or margarine in a large saucepan, and stir in the baking cocoa, milk, and vanilla extract. Bring to a boil. Remove from the heat. Add the confectioners' sugar, and mix well.
- Spread the icing over the hot cake. Sprinkle with nuts, if desired. Cut into squares to serve.
- Makes 24 servings

This is a wonderful no-fail recipe. It is especially good (1) for an unlimited number of servings; (2) to make a day ahead; (3) to transport easily;(4) as a last minute, quick dessert; (5) for choco-holics; and (6) for people who like to get compliments on their food.

From the kitchen of LENORA MATHEWS of Norfolk, Virginia, a special friend to all and the founder of Volunteer Hampton Roads, which brought together citizens and businesses in the spirit of volunteerism and philanthropy. She is also one of the best cooks I know. —Rowena

NELSON COUNTY

Nelson County was organized in 1807 from land belonging to Amherst County. It was named in honor of General Thomas Nelson (1738-1789), an early Virginia governor (1781). It contains four hundred seventy-three square miles and is home to 14,445 residents. The county seat is Lovingston.

William Cabell Rives (1792-1868), U.S. senator and member of the Confederate Congress, was born in this county. In 1969, Hurricane Camille poured more than twenty-five inches of rain in the region, causing millions of dollars worth of damage.

A FIRST LADY

Pittslyvania County's Rachel Donelson grew up in a family of eleven children whose father was a member of the House of Burgesses. The entire family migrated to Tanasi territory and Kantuckie before Rachel met the love of her life: Andrew Jackson.

Colonel John Donelson and his wife, Rachel Stockley, had seven sons and four daughters in their large cabin home beside the Banister River in Pittsylvania County. The Colonel (1725-1786) was an iron manufacturer, land surveyor, and member of the Virginia Assembly. The family migrated to East Tennessee to Fort Watauga and eventually floated on a historic river voyage led by John. Their flatboat, the *Adventure*, led dozens of other families' boats down the Holston and Tanasi Rivers to merge against the currents with the mighty Ohio and then, on the Colonel's instincts but using no map, to the tranquil Cumberland. They rendezvoused with James Robertson and other men from Watauga who had gone overland earlier and entrusted the Colonel with their families' lives. The reunion took place at Fort Nashborough on March 24, 1780. Colonel John Donelson, along with Robertson, is credited as a cofounder of Nashville, Tennessee.

Twelve-year-old Rachel Donelson often sang to the young ones and was known for her warm and reflective nature. Because Native Americans frequented the area around Nashborough, the Colonel temporarily moved the clan to Kantuckie for safety. At seventeen,

Rachel married, but it did not last. Afterwards, she joined her widowed mother in Nashville where the family had reestablished. Family friend John Overton and a red-headed, lanky newcomer named Andrew Jackson were two young lawyers who came to board at the Donelson Station.

Rachel and Andrew Jackson fell in love, married, and eventually built their beautiful home, the Hermitage, just outside Nashville. During Jackson's political campaigns for the presidency, some scoffed at the scandal of Rachel's prior marriage, but those who really knew Rachel knew she was a dedicated, fine-hearted woman. She and Jackson took care of her many nieces and nephews, adopting one and raising many as wards.

As Jackson lost his first presidential election in 1824, Rachel was secretly relieved. Private and humble, she really did not care to live in the spotlight, yet supported her husband's endeavors. Returning to her beloved Hermitage and her family, Rachel was contented. When Jackson won the 1828 election, her beautiful lace inaugural ball gown was fashioned in Nashville. But in December, Rachel became ill and died at home. She was buried in her beloved garden. A heartbroken Jackson left for Washington a few weeks later to resume responsibilities as the nation's leader. For the rest of his life, the first thing Andrew Jackson did every morning was look at her portrait.

Macadamia Fudge Nut Cake

FOR THE TOPPING
1 cup heavy cream or
    whipping cream
1/2 cup sugar
2 tablespoons butter
1 tablespoon corn syrup

4 squares semisweet
    chocolate
1 teaspoon vanilla extract
1 (7-ounce) jar macadamia
    nuts

FOR THE CAKE
1 cup flour
3/4 cup sugar
3/4 cup sour cream
1/2 cup (1 stick) butter,
    softened
1/4 cup bakin cocoa
1 1/2 teaspoons instant coffee

1/2 teaspoon baking soda
1/2 teaspoon baking powder
1/2 teaspoon vanilla extract
1/4 teaspoon salt
1 egg

- To prepare the topping, combine the cream, sugar, butter, corn syrup, and chocolate in a saucepan, and mix well. Bring to a boil, stirring constantly. Simmer for 5 minutes, stirring constantly. Remove from the heat. Stir in the vanilla extract. Let stand for 10 minutes. Stir in the macadamia nuts.
- To prepare the cake, preheat the oven to 350°F. Grease a 9-inch round cake pan, and line with waxed paper. Combine the flour, sugar, sour cream, butter, cocoa, coffee, baking soda, baking powder, vanilla, salt, and egg in a bowl, and mix well. Pour the batter into the prepared pan. Bake for 30 to 35 minutes. Cool in the pan for 10 minutes. Invert the cake onto a serving plate, and drizzle with the topping. Refrigerate for 1 hour.
- Makes approximately 10 servings

This recipe is from CATHY STINEBAUGH, owner of A Pinch of the Past Antiques, Poquoson, Virginia.

NEW KENT COUNTY

New Kent County was probably named for Kent County, England. It was formed in 1654 from York County. The county contains one hundred ninety-one square miles, and its population is 13,462. The county seat is New Kent.

Martha Washington was born in this county in 1731. The first game bird breeding facility in the world was opened in 1920 near Providence Forge.

ROWENA'S KITCHEN TIPS

Before creaming any kind of shortening with your electric mixer, heat the beaters under hot water for a few minutes. It really helps to prevent your shortening from sticking to the blades.

Mocha Fudge Cake

8 ounces semisweet
    chocolate
1 cup (2 sticks) butter
1 cup sugar
1/4 cup rum
1/4 cup strong coffee, such as
    instant espresso

4 eggs, beaten
1 teaspoon vanilla extract
1/4 cup currant jelly
1 cup heavy cream
Vanilla extract
Sugar
Fresh raspberries

- Preheat the oven to 350°F. Melt the chocolate in the top of a double boiler. Stir in the butter until melted. Add the sugar, and mix well. Pour the chocolate mixture into a large bowl, and add the rum, coffee, eggs, and 1 teaspoon vanilla extract, and mix well. Pour into a buttered 8-inch springform pan, and bake for about 1 hour. The cake will be very soft, but will show cracks around the edges. Let stand until cool. Refrigerate, covered, for 24 hours or up to 1 week.
- To serve, melt the currant jelly in a small saucepan, and spread over the top of the cake. Let stand for about 15 minutes or until the jelly is set. Whip the cream, and stir in vanilla extract and sugar to taste. Spread the whipped cream mixture over the top, and stud with fresh raspberries. Refrigerate or serve immediately.
- Makes about 10 servings

This recipe is from MRS. ROGER H. MARTIN, the wife of the president of Randolph-Macon. Mrs. Martin often serves this at new faculty dinners to rave reviews.

NORTHAMPTON COUNTY

Northampton County is one of Virginia's original shires, and it was formed in 1634 as Accomac. The name was changed nine years later to honor the English county of the same name. Northampton County contains two hundred thirty-nine square miles. Its population is 13,093, and the county seat is Eastville.

Governor Berkeley used the county as his stronghold during Bacon's Rebellion in 1676. Tidewater Institute, a facility dedicated to the education of Virginia's black youth, was established here in 1903 and operated for twenty-eight years.

DID YOU KNOW THAT:

Fredericksburg native Matthew Fontaine Maury was internationally known and respected for his scientific oceanic and meteorological researches? He was called the "Pathfinder of the Seas," and his book *The Physical Geography of the Sea*, was called the "bible" of the new science of oceanography.

VILLAGE VIEW

Village View, a Federal plantation home located in Emporia, is a Virginia Historical Landmark. Built in the 1790s by a young bachelor named James Wall, it overlooked the old village of Hicksford on the south bank of the Meherrin River. The history of Village View chronicles the lives of generations of the Wall, Land, and Briggs families. It now stands tall in a beautiful park-like setting in the city of Emporia. Now owned by the Village View Foundation, it is being restored and furnished to accurately reflect the period in which it was built. The Hicksford Chapter of the D.A.R. has an ongoing project to furnish the dining room in the style of 1837. Chapter members also serve as volunteers for hostessing, fund raising, and tours.

THE BRIAR PATCH TEA ROOM

Joseph and Rebecca May always dreamed of having a bed and breakfast establishment, but have found themselves enjoying their own tea room instead. The history of the Briar Patch Tea Room reaches back to newer traditions set by recent past owners. Certain menu items have remained since the tea room opened, no matter which owner was involved.

Becky May worked as cook, waitress, and dishwasher for three years at the tea room before owning it. Many of the patrons are close friends. One couple visits every Thursday, sits at table P-5, and orders the same foods. Becky and the staff have two cups of coffee waiting on the table for them. They call the tea room "the black hole." Many of the customers work at NASA Langley Center or Langley Air Force Base. Folks from Hampton, Newport News, and York County frequent the tea room for their favorite Broccoli-Cheese Soup.

Becky's specialties include Lemon Crab Casserole, Shepherd's Pie, and a Finger Sandwich Sampler. Famous desserts here include Chocolate Fudge Pie, Strawberry Trifle, and various cheesecakes.

Joe and Becky are sure that this adventure with their tea room will one day extend to their dream of owning a B & B. One thing is for sure, the food will be great!

BRIAR PATCH TEA ROOM
Raspberry Mud Cake

CAKE
2 cups all-purpose flour
2 cups sugar
2 teaspoons cinnamon
1/8 teaspoon salt
1 cup (2 sticks) butter
l cup water

1/4 cup baking cocoa
1 teaspoon baking soda
1/2 cup buttermilk
2 eggs
1 teaspoon vanilla extract

FILLING
10 ounces frozen raspberries
Lemon juice

2 tablespoons sugar

ICING
1/2 cup (1 stick) butter or
  margarine
1/2 cup baking cocoa
1/4 cup plus 2 tablespoons
  milk
1 package confectioners'
  sugar

1 teaspoon vanilla extract
1 cup chopped pecans
Raspberries and mint leaves
  for garnish, optional

- To prepare the cake, preheat the oven to 400°F. Combine the flour, sugar, cinnamon, and salt in a mixing bowl, and mix well. Combine the butter, water, and baking cocoa in a saucepan, and bring to a boil, stirring constantly. Pour over the flour mixture, and beat well. Dissolve the baking soda in the buttermilk. Stir in the eggs, buttermilk mixture, and vanilla extract. Pour into a large greased sheet cake pan. Bake for 20 minutes. Let stand until cool.
- To prepare the filling, thaw the frozen raspberries, reserving the syrup. Add enough lemon juice to the syrup to measure 2/3 cup. Pour the syrup mixture into a saucepan. Stir in the sugar, and cook over medium heat until thickened, stirring frequently. Stir for 1 minute longer, and add the raspberries.
- To prepare the icing, heat the butter or margarine, baking cocoa, and milk in a saucepan until the butter is melted. Remove from the heat, and stir in the confectioners' sugar, vanilla extract, and chopped nuts.
- To serve, slice the cake into halves lengthwise, and spread the raspberry filling over the top of 1 cake half. Place the remaining cake half over the filling, and spread the icing over the top. Garnish with raspberries and mint leaves, if desired.
- Makes approximately 18 servings

The recipe was shared by REBECCA RAE MAY, owner of the Briar Patch Tea Room, Poquoson, Virginia. I am a frequent customer. —Winette

DID YOU KNOW THAT:

Virginia's General Assembly is the oldest legislative body in the Western Hemisphere?

WILLARD SCOTT'S
Red Velvet Cake

CAKE

1/2 cup shortening	1 teaspoon salt
1 1/2 cups sugar	1 cup buttermilk
2 eggs	1 teaspoon vanilla extract
2 ounces red food coloring	1 tablespoon vinegar
2 tablespoons baking cocoa	1 teaspoon baking soda
2 1/4 cups all-purpose flour	

FROSTING

8 ounces light cream cheese, at room temperature	1/2 teaspoon vanilla extract
1/4 cup plus 1 tablespoon unsweetened pineapple juice concentrate	1/2 teaspoon finely grated orange zest

- To prepare the cake, preheat the oven to 350°F. Beat the shortening and sugar in a mixing bowl until creamy. Add the eggs, and beat well. Combine the food coloring and baking cocoa in a bowl to form a paste, and add to the creamed mixture, beating well. Sift the flour and salt together twice. Add the buttermilk to the creamed mixture alternately with the flour, mixing well after each addition. Stir in the vanilla extract. Place the vinegar in a deep bowl, and add the baking soda, stirring until foamy. Add to the batter. Do not beat the batter, but just blend well. Pour the batter into 2 greased and floured 9-inch cake pans, and bake for 25 to 30 minutes.
- To prepare the frosting, whisk the cream cheese, pineapple juice, vanilla extract, and orange zest in a bowl until smooth.
- Spread the frosting over the cake, and serve.
- Makes 8 to 10 servings

Shared with us by WILLARD SCOTT, a native son of Alexandria, Virginia. Owner of a farm in northern Virginia, he is now involved with TV specials for Home and Garden Television, as well as being part of the *Today Show*.

NORTHUMBERLAND COUNTY

Northumberland County was originally part of a region known as Chickacoan. It was established in 1648 and took its name from the English county. Northumberland County contains two hundred five square miles. The county's population is 12,259, and the seat of government is Heathsville.

The Potomac River releases its waters into the Chesapeake Bay in this county. The town of Reedville became the center for the Atlantic menhaden fishing fleet in the late 1800s.

Keeping up with Alexandria's Willard Scott has been a lively journey! His smile has greeted American mornings on NBC's Today Show *since 1980. For more than thirty years, he has lighted the national Christmas tree in Washington, D.C. The centenarians of the nation adore him, and who else could have been the original Ronald McDonald? Only Willard!*

As "ambassadors" from Virginia go, Willard Scott leads the pack. Born in Alexandria on March 7, 1934, Willard has long distinguished himself with his public service efforts and his delightful television personality. He began his career with NBC as a page at the Washington station in 1950. He was also a weekend disc jockey for Washington radio station WINX. He joined WOL Radio that same year and, with Ed Walker, formed the Joy Boys broadcast team, moving in 1953 to WRC-AM, the NBC Radio Station in Washington, D.C. He stayed there until 1972, then broadcasted for WWDC, Washington, from 1972 to 1974. He had weather reports on WRC-AM from 1956 until 1972. Similar duties were seen on WRC-TV, the NBC television station in Washington, beginning in 1968.

In March 1980, Willard joined the *Today Show*, reporting the weather. He has long saluted and honored those Americans over one hundred years old each Tuesday and Thursday mornings on *Today*. Willard has traveled with the show to China, Australia, South America, and Hawaii. He went with *Today* to Rome during Holy Week, traveled on the *Today* cruise of the

Po' Man's Fruitcake

2^1/$_2$ cups dried apples
1 cup chopped raisins
1 cup pecan or walnut
   kernels
4 cups all-purpose flour
2 cups sugar
1 heaping teaspoon
   cinnamon

^{1}/$_2$ teaspoon ground cloves
^{1}/$_2$ teaspoon allspice
Pinch of salt
2 heaping teaspoons baking
   soda
1 cup (2 sticks) butter or
   margarine, melted

- Preheat the oven to 325°F. Combine the apples with enough water to cover in a medium saucepan. Bring to a boil, and simmer until the apples are tender. Drain, reserving the liquid.
- Combine the apples, raisins, and pecans or walnuts in a large bowl, and mix well. Combine the flour, sugar, cinnamon, cloves, allspice, and salt in a separate bowl, and mix well. Dissolve the baking soda in 1 cup of the reserved liquid. Stir the the apple mixture into flour mixture, coating the fruit and nuts. Note: This should prevent the fruit and nuts from sinking to the bottom of the cake.
- Stir in the butter or margarine until smooth, adding enough of the remaining reserved liquid to prevent the batter from becoming too dry. Pour into a greased bundt pan or angel food pan, and bake for 1^1/$_4$ hours.
- Makes 12 to 16 servings

This recipe was submitted by MARY CARTER STONE of Danville, Virginia, a member of the Thomas Carter Chapter of the Virginia DAR. Mary Younger Stone (1889-1977) and Mary Stone Gregory, both members of the D.A.R., were sisters-in-law, and each married in the summer of 1916. This is Mary Gregory's recipe, which Mary Stone wrote on one endpaper of her cookbook. Mary Gregory called it a recipe for Applesauce Fruitcake, but in the Stone family it was known as Po' Man's Fruitcake.

NOTTOWAY COUNTY

Nottoway County, named for a local Indian tribe, was formed in 1788 from neighboring Amelia County. It contains three hundred ten square miles, and its population is 15,725. The seat of government is Nottoway.

Near Burkeville, in 1781, Peter Francisco, a Virginia militiaman, single-handedly defeated nine British dragoons. Civilian Conservation Corps (CCC) camp #1370 was located in this county during the late 1930s.

DID YOU KNOW THAT:

The remains of General Douglas MacArthur are buried beneath the rotunda at the General Douglas MacArthur Memorial in downtown Norfolk?

---

eastern seaboard, rode the rails with the *Today* Orient Express trip, and went through the heartland of America on the *Today* Express.

Willard has enjoyed anchoring coverage of Macy's Thanksgiving Day Parade since 1987, and he traditionally appears as Santa Claus at White House events for children. He has lighted the national Christmas tree in Washington, D.C., for over three decades. Willard has played Carnegie Hall in New York City, Symphony Hall in Boston, and the Grand Ole Opry in Nashville. And of course, he was also the first Ronald McDonald for McDonald's.

Willard has received various awards from many organizations for humanitarian service, including the Distinguished Virginian honor from the Virginia Association of Broadcasters in 1990. A distinct recognition came from President Ronald Reagan with the Private Sector Award for Public Service.

Willard readily admits that he loves food. In his travels, he manages to find the right "eating spots" and enjoys sharing his recipes.

The author of four books, Willard is a graduate of American University in Washington, D.C., with a B.A. in philosophy and religion. He is married to the former Mary Dwyer, and they are the parents of two daughters, Mary and Sally.

Mt. Vernon

Follow the road outside of Historic Old Town Alexandria to the home of George and Martha Washington to get a glimpse of the life that once flowed along the Potomac River's shores. The Father of Our Country actually had several farms that connected to form his large estate called Mt. Vernon. Here, many a minuet was danced, many a dinner was served to distinguished guests and family, many a Christmas was revered and celebrated, and many a fine wine was served (the President favored Madeira). Here, foxhunts were the sport of the times. And here was the home in which Martha Washington kept her vigil, waiting for her husband to come home and praying for his safety as he led an infant nation to victory in the Revolution miles away.

The first meal of the day at Mt. Vernon was breakfast around seven in the morning. An early riser, George would already have been up, reading and working on correspondence, before his first meal. Martha also liked to get up earlier than most. She would have set about her household duties and then strolled along the long piazza on the rear of the mansion facing the Potomac before breakfast. If George were not going hunting, he had the first meal with the family when the first bell summoned. If he had a hunt planned, one would find him eating breakfast before dawn by candlelight. He always inspected the horses in his stables by dawn.

The "sitting room" (probably the West Parlor) had all the latest newspapers laid out for the family and guests to read in the mornings. There, a typical Virginia breakfast was served from the detached kitchen connected to the main house by a colonnade. The menu offered tea, coffee, and chocolate for beverage choices. Meats included ham, cold corned beef, cold fowl, red herring, and cold mutton. Various vegetables and parsley from the garden added beautiful garnishes to each dish. George also liked to eat "three small mush cakes swimming in butter and honey" and "three cups of tea without cream," according to granddaughter Nelly. But ham was the Virginia staple of the times. Martha cured her own hams and had one boiled daily at Mt. Vernon throughout her years there. Guests could (and would) arrive unexpectedly on a daily basis, but the Mistress of Mt. Vernon was prepared. Late-rising guests were always served breakfast as they wakened, dining in their room, in the small dining room, or out on the piazza.

After breakfast, George made his usual eight- to fourteen-mile ride around his plantation, which consisted of five farms: Mansion House Farm, Union Farm, Dogue Run Farm, Muddy Hole Farm, and River Farm. Each had its own overseer and lots of servants to maintain daily the livestock, dairy, crops, and a proper harvest.

No estate in United America is more pleasantly situated than this. It lies in a high, dry, and healthy Country 300 miles by water from the sea, . . . on one of the finest Rivers in the world.

— George Washington on Mt. Vernon

Sometimes, George took along his *Farmers Luncheon Box* with some morsels to snack on as the day progressed. He even had a *Sandwitch Box* (the 4th Earl of Sandwich had invented the sandwich in Washington's time). He also looked over his English and French hounds, such as Vulcan, Sweetlips, Truelove, Ringwood, Singer, Forester, Music, and Rockwood. George usually returned to his house just before dinner, which was normally served at three in the afternoon. He rode with a moderate pace, yet would gallop as he heard the "first bell" at quarter to three if he found himself tarrying about the estate.

Immediately after breakfast, Martha would have been giving orders for dinner, which included such meats as a pair of ducks, a goose or a turkey, a small roasted "pigg," and of course the daily ham. She took full advantage of the estate's garden bounty, as well, instructing the gathering of such vegetables as peas, "lettice," artichokes, cucumbers, potatoes, onions, and cabbage on many days. Martha also saw to the bread baking. Each evening, the dough was prepared under her watchful eye. It was left to rise slowly overnight in the kitchen warmth, then baked the next morning in the beehive oven to the left of the fireplace. Family tradition holds there was no bad bread at Mt. Vernon! Martha tended to other family needs and then visited with guests. By noon, many of the ladies would begin to "dress for dinner" at three!

The Mt. Vernon kitchen was supplied with such culinary equipment as milk pans, waffle irons, frying pans, cake pans, "Chaffin Dishes," and trivets. Martha had some "receipt books" such as *The Art of Cookery, Made Plain and Easy; Which Far Exceeds Any Thing of the Kind Yet Published . . . by a Lady*, published in England in 1747. She also had her own manuscript, *Booke of Cookery*. Martha's table furnishings included many fine sets of china. Blue and white china was used every day. She garnished her platters with flowers at times and was known for having a chocolate pot for guests. The ingredients for Martha's

Great Cake included pears and pecans, along with Madeira wine.

The main meal was served in the small or large dining room, depending on the number of guests. It began at three with soup. The meats and vegetables Martha had planned for the day were served next. Three servants usually served the meal. Diners simply asked for the beverage they chose (usually wine, porter, or beer). Martha sat at the head of the table with her husband to her right. This placement was customary for Virginia in their time. Prayers were sometimes offered at both the beginning and end of the meal in Virginia during this period. The tablecloth was wiped off before the second course, which included tarts, cheese, and mince pies. Later, the cloth was removed altogether as two kinds of nuts, apples, and raisins were set out. Port and Madeira wine were then offered, as well. After some discussion with the gentlemen, the ladies usually retired to another room to resume conversation and the men kept talking further at the table or outdoors on the piazza.

Late in the day between six and seven, Martha took a little "tea and toast," which included breads, butter, and little "cakes" or cookies. Family and guests enjoyed the tea, as well. George said goodnight around nine in the evening after leafing through newspapers and reading some of the excerpts aloud. His single cup of tea was his "supper."

I can truly say I had rather be at Mount Vernon with a friend or two about me, than to be attended at the seat of government by the officers of State and the representatives of every power in Europe.

— George Washington, June 15, 1790

MARTHA WASHINGTON'S
Great Cake

MODERN ADAPTATION

10 eggs, separated
1 pound (4 sticks) butter
4 pounds (9 cups) sugar
1¼ pounds (20 ounces)
  all-purpose flour
1¼ pounds (20 ounces)
  fruit (see Note below)

2½ teaspoons ground mace
2½ teaspoons ground
  nutmeg
2 ounces Madeira wine
2 ounces French brandy

- Preheat the oven to 350°F. Beat the egg whites in a mixing bowl until soft peaks form. Beat the butter in a bowl until creamy. Add the beaten egg whites to the butter, 1 spoonful at a time, beating slowly. Add the sugar, 1 spoonful at a time, beating slowly. Beat in the egg yolks. Add the flour, beating slowly.
- Note: Try a fruit combination of 5 ounces pears, peeled, cored, chopped; 9½ ounces apples, peeled, cored, chopped; 3½ ounces raisins; and 2 ounces sliced almonds for a total of 20 ounces.
- Fold in the fruit. Add the mace, nutmeg, wine, and brandy, and mix well. Pour the batter into a lightly greased and floured 10-inch springform cake pan. Bake for about 1¼ hours or until the cake tests done. Let the cake stand until cool.
- Makes 12 to16 servings

Before, when I made the full-size cake, I used 2 pounds apples, 1 pound currants, and 2 pounds raisins. Since Mrs. Washington would have used anything that was seasonal or available dried, and since nuts were considered a fruit, for this scaled down version, I used the fruits listed above. I baked it for 1 hour, which was just slightly not enough for the very center. — LCB

This recipe was submitted by MARY V. THOMPSON, research specialist, Mount Vernon Ladies' Association, Mount Vernon, Virginia. It is from Louise Conway Belden's book, *The Festive Tradition: Table Decoration and Desserts in America, 1650-1900* reprinted by W.W. Norton & Company, 1983.

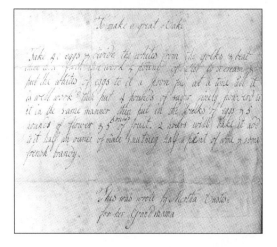

THE ORIGINAL
GREAT CAKE RECIPE

Take 40 eggs and divide the whites from the yolks & beat them to a froth then work 4 pounds of butter to a cream & put the whites of eggs to it a spoon full at a time till it is well work'd then put 4 pounds of sugar finely powdered [sic] to it in the same manner then put in the youlks [sic] of eggs & 5 pounds of flower [sic] & 5 pounds of fruit 2 hours will bake it add to it half an ounce of mace & nutmeg half a pint of wine & some frensh [sic] brandy.

Martha Washington's Great Cake recipe results in the type of cake traditionally served for Twelfth Night (January 6), also known as the Epiphany, which is the last of the twelve days of Christmas.

THE MONROE DOCTRINE

In his annual message to Congress on December 2, 1823, the nation's fifth President, Virginia-born James Monroe, stated,

With the governments who have declared their independence and maintained it . . . we could not view any interposition for the purpose of oppressing them or of controlling in any other manner their destiny by any European power in any other light than a manifestation of an unfriendly disposition to the United States.

With those words, Monroe put the world on notice that any foreign involvement in the political affairs of Western Hemisphere republics would be considered an assault on the U. S. This fundamental policy, known as the "Monroe Doctrine," was rigidly enforced until the mid-twentieth century when Washington politicians looked the other way during the Communist takeover of Cuba.

Nana's Jelly Roll

4 eggs
3/4 cup sugar
3/4 cup pancake mix
Confectioners' sugar
Jam, jelly, pudding, or
  whipped topping
Sliced fruits, such as
  bananas or strawberries,
  optional

- Preheat the oven to 400°F. Grease a 9×13-inch baking pan, and line with waxed paper. Grease the waxed paper. Note: It is not necessary to line the baking pan if it is sufficiently greased.
- Place the eggs in a blender. Add the sugar, and blend well. Blend in the pancake mix. Pour the batter into the prepared pan. Bake for 10 minutes in the middle of the oven.
- Invert the cake onto a dishtowel sprinkled with confectioners' sugar. Remove the waxed paper, and roll the cake in the dishtowel. Unroll the cake when cool, and spread with the jelly, pudding, or whipped topping. Add fruit to the whipped topping if desired. Roll up tightly. Refrigerate for at least 1 hour before slicing.
- Makes 10 servings

This is a wonderful, fun thing to do for younger children. I know some older children who love it, too. Make this and you will be a hit with all your grandchildren. My mother-in-law was—she put chocolate pudding inside. —Rowena

Raisin Cake

1 pound seedless raisins
2 cups water
1/2 cup shortening
1 cup cold water
2 cups sugar
1 teaspoon ground cloves
1 teaspoon allspice
1 teaspoon cinnamon
1 teaspoon nutmeg
1/2 teaspoon salt
1 tablespoon baking soda
4 cups all-purpose flour
1 cup chopped English or
  black walnuts, optional

- Preheat the oven to 300°F. Combine the raisins and 2 cups water in a medium saucepan. Bring to a boil. Cook for 15 minutes. Remove from the heat, and drain.
- Combine the shortening, cold water, and sugar in a large bowl. Add the cloves, allspice, cinnamon, nutmeg, salt, baking soda, and flour, and mix well. Fold in the raisins and chopped nuts, if desired. Pour into a greased 8 or 9-inch round cake pan. Bake for 1 1/2 hours.
- Makes 12 to 15 servings

This recipe was passed down from my grandmother, Jennie Turner, who got married in 1899.

The recipe was received from FLORENCE FOSTER NIXON of Madison Heights, Virginia. She is Regent of the Amherst Chapter of the Virginia DAR.

Wild Blackberry and Black Walnut Cake

CAKE

1 cup white raisins
1/2 pound dates, chopped
1 cup chopped black walnuts
1/2 cup chopped pecans
2 cups blackberry jam
4 cups all-purpose flour
1 teaspoon baking soda
1 teaspoon allspice

1 teaspoon cinnamon
1 teaspoon ground cloves
1/2 teaspoon salt
1 cup (2 sticks) butter or margarine
2 cups sugar
4 eggs
1 cup buttermilk

JIFFY CARAMEL ICING

1/2 cup plus 2 tablespoons (1 1/4 sticks) butter or margarine
2 cups firmly packed brown sugar

1/2 cup milk
3 cups confectioners' sugar

- To prepare the cake, preheat the oven to 350°F. Combine the raisins, dates, walnuts, pecans, and jam in a medium bowl, and mix well. Combine the flour, baking soda, allspice, cinnamon, cloves, and salt in a large bowl, and mix well Beat the butter, sugar, and eggs in a separate large bowl until creamy. Add the dry ingredients to the creamed mixture alternately with the buttermilk, beating well after each addition. Fold in the fruit mixture. Bake in a large greased and floured tube pan. Place a pan of water in the oven to keep the cake moist. Bake for 1 1/2 hours. Let stand until cool, and remove from the pan to a serving plate.
- To prepare the icing, melt the butter or margarine in a medium saucepan, and add the brown sugar. Bring to a boil. Add the milk, and boil for 3 minutes, stirring frequently. Remove from the heat, and cool. Add the confectioners' sugar, and beat until creamy.
- Spread the icing over the cake.
- Makes 18 to 22 servings

Blackberry jam cake is a favorite cake for my area. Blackberries grow naturally wild. It is a family tradition to pick blackberries the first week of July and make blackberry jam for cake. Also, black walnut trees are native trees. The walnuts are hulled and cracked in November, just in time for a cake for the holidays.

The recipe is shared by LINDA N. LAWSON, a member of the Major George Gibson Chapter of the Virginia DAR in Rose Hill, Virginia, at the far southwest corner of the state.

DID YOU KNOW THAT:

James Madison was the nation's smallest president?
He is reported to have stood about five feet, four inches tall
and weighed around one hundred pounds.

VESTAL'S GAP

Helen and Carl Franklin have a real interest in history, and they have researched an old road called Vestal's Gap. It ran from Alexandria, Virginia, to the Valley of Virginia. It was the only road west for about one hundred years and was used by George Washington so many times that a noted historian suggested it should be called the "Washington Road." Braddock's troops, including a young Daniel Boone, used it when en route to Fort Duquesne in the French and Indian War. An almost pristine portion of the road remains in Claude Moore Park in Sterling, Virginia.

WEEMS-BOTTS HOUSE

The Weems-Botts House is associated with the names and professional activities of two prominent early Virginians, Mason Locke (Parson) Weems and Benjamin Botts. The house is also one of the early structures surviving in the old Potomac port of Dumfries. Its earliest portion is a fine specimen of a small commercial structure of the late eighteenth century and is noteworthy for being a true story-and-a-half building, unusual for Virginia.

Mason Locke Weems bought the half-acre plot known as Lot 51 from two trustees of the Town of Dumfries in June 1798. It is likely that he built the earliest portion of the building for use as a bookshop and temporary lodging. Weems sold the property in June 1802 to Benjamin Botts, a successful criminal lawyer who was prominent among the team of attorneys who defended Aaron Burr during his treason trial. Botts and his wife died in the Richmond Theater fire of 1811, and the property was sold for taxes in 1835.

After brief periods of ownership by others, including the Bottses' sons, the Merchant family purchased the property in 1869 and held it until 1968. It was acquired by the Town of Dumfries and leased to Historic Dumfries Virginia, Inc., which maintains it as a museum.

The house was marked by the Bill of Rights Chapter of the Virginia Daughters of the American Revolution on October 6, 1996, during a special program.

RACHEL DONELSON JACKSON'S
Hickory Nut or Walnut Cake

Two cups of fine white sugar creamed with half a cup of butter, three eggs, two thirds of a cup of sweet milk, three cups of sifted flour, one heaping teaspoonful (level) of powered mace, a coffee cup of hickory nuts or walnut meats chopped a little. Fill the cake pans with a layer of the cake, then a layer of raisins upon that, then strew over these a handful of nuts, and so on until the pan is two-thirds full. Line the tins with well-buttered paper and bake in a steady, but not quick, oven. This is most excellent.

Reprinted from *Miss Daisy Celebrates Tennessee*, ©1995 by Daisy King, James A. Crutchfield, and Winette Sparkman, with permission.

BILL OF RIGHTS CHAPTER
Pound Cake

1¹/₂ cups (3 sticks) butter, softened, no substitution	1 teaspoon baking powder
3 cups sugar	1 cup sour cream
5 eggs	¹/₄ cup milk
3 cups all-purpose flour	2 teaspoons lemon extract
	1 teaspoon vanilla extract

- Beat the butter and sugar in a large bowl until creamy. Add the eggs, 1 at a time, and beat well after each addition. Combine the flour and baking powder in a medium bowl, and mix well. Beat the flour mixture into the creamed mixture alternately with the sour cream, milk, lemon extract and vanilla extract.
- Pour the batter into a well-greased and floured bundt pan and 1 loaf pan, or 3 loaf pans. Place in a cold oven. Bake at 275°F for about 1¹/₂ hours or until a wooden pick inserted in the center comes out clean. Remove to a wire rack to cool completely before removing from the pan.
- Makes 16 to 20 servings

For DAR functions, I slice the cooled pound cake in thin slices and place Rowena's Lemon Curd between slices, making delicate sandwiches. A big hit!

Please note that this recipe either uses ingredients that are noteworthy of our Commonwealth or is a food that is truly Southern! Submitted by JEANNE ROEDER PURKINS, Honorary Regent of the Bill of Rights Chapter of the Virginia DAR, Woodbridge, Virginia.

DID YOU KNOW THAT:

The first beer manufactured in North America was brewed in 1587 on Roanoke Island in Sir Walter Raleigh's Virginia Colony (now North Carolina)?

BARBARA CIARA'S
Old-Fashioned Pound Cake

1 cup (2 sticks) butter or margarine, softened	1 tablespoon lemon extract
1/2 cup shortening	1 tablespoon fresh lemon juice
6 eggs	3 cups all-purpose flour
3 cups sugar	1/2 teaspoon baking powder
1 tablespoon vanilla extract	1 cup milk

- Preheat the oven to 350°F. Beat the butter or margarine and shortening in a large mixing bowl until light and fluffy. Add the eggs, and mix well. Add the sugar 1/2 cup at a time, mixing well after each addition. Stir in the vanilla, lemon extract, and lemon juice. Combine the flour and baking powder in a bowl, and mix well. Add to the creamed mixture alternately with the milk, beating well after each addition.
- Pour the batter into a greased and floured 10-inch tube pan. Bake for 1 hour and 20 minutes to 1 1/2 hours or until a wooden pick inserted in the center comes out clean. Cool for 15 minutes on a wire rack. Remove to a serving plate.
- Makes 12 to 16 servings

My mother, Georgia, was taught this recipe by my grandmother, Roberta. With regret, my adult son, Robert, is "kitchen challenged," so I will pass it on you and my grandchildren. But I can tell you that this family dessert brings back such wonderful memories. Just imagine cold winters when we couldn't help but smell the tasty treat that would come following our big family dinner. You can enjoy the pound cake alone, or load it up with your favorite fruit toppings. For adult gatherings I enjoy a mixture of rum and brown sugar heated and drizzled over the cake while it is still cooling in the tube pan.

The recipe is from the family of BARBARA CIARA, who has more than 20 years experience as a broadcast journalist. She has won numerous community and professional honors for her work on camera and in the community. Barbara started the year 2000 by completing her degree Summa Cum Laude at Hampton University, winning an Emmy for her series "Guilty 'Til Proven Innocent" and receiving honors from Columbia University Graduate School of Journalism for her reports on race and ethnicity. Her co-honorees were CBS broadcaster Dan Rather and producers from 60 Minutes. Barbara is currently managing editor at WTKR NewsChannel 3 and also is a strong believer in public service, donating her time to many non-profit organizations.

ROWENA'S KITCHEN TIPS

When baking or broiling any kind of meat such as a chop, steaks, or meat loaf, line your pan with aluminum foil. This saves you from having to scour the pan—plus the foil collects the sauce created by what you are cooking.

JACK JOUETT'S RIDE

The "Southern" Paul Revere

No book including overall Virginia history should forget young twenty-seven-year-old Jack Jouett of Louisa County. His patriotism and gallant ride to warn of British maneuvers have inspired many children in Virginia who have heard his tale.

In the summer of 1781, while the Revolutionary War was ongoing and British invasion at hand, Thomas Jefferson and other legislative members trekked to Charlottesville from the capital city of Richmond. Jefferson's home Monticello boasted such guests as Richard Henry Lee, Thomas Nelson, Benjamin Harrison, Edmund Randolph, and Patrick Henry on one particular night as their host spoke with them about plans to protect Virginia and rally the new nation's cause. Six foot, four-inch-tall Jack Jouett happened to be at Cuckoo Tavern forty miles away that evening when he looked out to see British Colonel Banastre Tarleton's troops ride by on the main Charlottesville Road.

Jouett jumped on his thoroughbred horse and dashed off toward Monticello to warn Jefferson and the others. It is said that he rode the forty miles without stopping, and arrived at 4:30 a.m. Tales of Thomas Jefferson going out the back door as Tarleton's troops came up the mountain to the other side of Monticello still echo throughout the Charlottesville area as word of Jack Jouett's ride is spoken of today. Due to his bravery and quick actions, Virginia (and America) can truly thank and remember this young Virginia hero of Revolutionary times.

Deep Chocolate Pound Cake

4 (1.5-ounce) bars plain milk chocolate bars	2 cups sugar
1¹/2 (16-ounce) cans chocolate syrup	4 eggs
	¹/2 teaspoon baking soda
2 teaspoons vanilla extract	2¹/2 cups all-purpose flour
1 cup (2 sticks) butter or margarine	1 cup buttermilk
	1 cup chopped pecans

- Preheat the oven to 350°F. Melt the chocolate bars and syrup in a double boiler. Stir in the vanilla extract, and set aside to cool. Beat the butter or margarine and sugar in a large bowl until creamy. Add the eggs, 1 at a time. Beat in the chocolate mixture.
- Combine the baking soda and flour in a small bowl, and mix well. Add to the creamed mixture alternately with the buttermilk, beating well after each addition. Fold in the nuts.
- Pour the batter into a greased and floured large tube pan or bundt pan. Bake for 1¹/4 hours to 1¹/2 hours or until the cake tests done. Frost the cake if desired or serve unfrosted.
- Makes 12 to 16 servings, if you can stop eating it

This is one of my favorite recipes, loved by all my chocolate-loving family members. I submitted this to the newspaper and won a $25 prize. Try it; you'll love it.

This recipe is from the kitchen of BLAIR WILLIS of Norfolk, Virginia, a childhood friend and wonderful southern cook. Our mothers used to make old-fashioned bread and butter pickles together during World War II. —Rowena

ORANGE COUNTY

Orange County was named for the Prince of Orange, consort to Princess Anne, the daughter of King George II.
It was established in 1734 from Spotsylvania County. The county contains three hundred fifty-nine square miles and is home to 25,881 residents. The county seat is Orange.

President James Madison (1751-1836) resided here at his home Montpelier, and President Zachary Taylor (1784-1850) was in this county, as well. In May 1864, from his base near the town of Orange, General Robert E. Lee marched his command to commence the Wilderness Campaign.

DID YOU KNOW THAT:

Walter Reed, an army physician from Gloucester County, first demonstrated that the dread disease, yellow fever, was spread by the mosquito?

FORT LEWIS LODGE

Peach Pound Cake

3 cups all-purpose flour
¹/₂ teaspoon salt
¹/₄ teaspoon baking soda
1¹/₄ cups (2¹/₂ sticks) butter
   or margarine, softened
2¹/₂ cups sugar
6 eggs, at room temperature
1 teaspoon vanilla extract

¹/₂ teaspoon almond extract
¹/₂ cup plain yogurt or sour
   cream
2 cups chopped peeled ripe
   peaches
Sweetened whipped cream
   or ice cream of choice
Nutmeg

- Preheat the oven to 350°F. Combine the flour, salt, and
  baking soda in a large bowl, and mix well. Beat the butter
  or margarine and sugar in a separate large bowl until
  creamy. Add the eggs, 1 at a time, beating for 1 minute
  after each addition. Stir in the vanilla and almond extracts.
  Add the flour mixture alternately with the yogurt or sour
  cream, beating until smooth. Fold in the peaches.
- Pour the batter into a greased and floured 10-inch tube pan.
  Bake for 1 to 1¹/₄ hours. Cool in the pan for 20 minutes.
  Remove from the pan, and cool completely.
- To serve, dollop with sweetened whipped cream or ice
  cream, and sprinkle with nutmeg.
- Makes 16 servings

Caryl has a reputation of being a great cook.

This recipe is shared by LETA L. WIMER of Staunton,
Virginia, Regent of the Sarah Murray Lewis Chapter of the
Virginia DAR. In 1762, Col. Charles Lewis, who married
Sarah Murray of New York, took up residence on the
Cowpasture River in Bath County. He called this plantation
"Fort Lewis." Today's owners, John and Caryl Cowden,
operate a full-service country inn, located at the heart of a
3,200-acre mountain estate. Caryl prepares delicious meals,
highlighted by contemporary American-style cuisine served
in this historic Lewis country getaway.

THE PENTAGON

The Pentagon, headquarters of the
United States Department of Defense,
is one of the world's largest office
buildings. It is twice the size of the
Merchandise Mart in Chicago, and has
three times the floor space of the
Empire State Building in New York. The
National Capitol could fit into any one of
its five wedge-shaped sections.

The Pentagon is virtually a city in itself.
Within its confines, approximately 23,000
military and civilian employees contribute
to the planning and execution of the
defense of our country. These people
arrive daily from Washington, D.C. and
its Northern Virginia suburbs over
approximately thirty miles of access
highways, including express bus lanes
and one of the newest subway systems
in the country. They ride past two
hundred acres of lawn to park approximately 8,770 cars in sixteen parking lots;
climb 131 stairways or ride nineteen
escalators; and travel 17.5 miles of
corridors to reach offices that occupy
3,705,793 square feet. While in the
building, they tell time by 4,200 clocks,
drink from 691 water fountains, utilize
284 rest rooms, consume 4,500 cups of
coffee, 1,700 pints of milk and 6,800 soft
drinks prepared or served by a restaurant
staff of 230 persons and dispensed in one
dining room, two cafeterias, six snack

bars, and an outdoor snack bar. The restaurant service is a privately run civilian operation under contract to the Pentagon.

Within this massive complex, more than 200,000 telephone calls are made daily through phones connected by 100,000 miles of telephone cable. The Defense Post Office handles about 1,200,000 pieces of mail monthly. Various libraries support personnel in research and completion of their work. The Army Library alone houses 300,000 publications and 1,700 periodicals in various languages.

The original site was nothing more than wasteland, swamps, and dumps. Nearly six million cubic yards of earth, and 41,492 concrete piles contributed to the foundation of the building. Additionally, 680,000 tons of sand and gravel, dredged from the nearby Potomac River, were processed into 435,000 cubic yards of concrete and molded into the Pentagon form. The building was constructed in the remarkably short time of sixteen months and was completed on January 15, 1943, at an approximate cost of $83 million. It consolidated seventeen buildings of the War Department and returned its investment within seven years.

Courtesy of the Pentagon's official website.

Sour Cream Pound Cake

3 cups all-purpose flour
1/4 teaspoon baking soda
1 cup (2 sticks) butter, softened
3 cups sugar

2 extra-large whole eggs
4 egg yolks
4 egg whites, stiffly beaten
1 cup sour cream

- Preheat the oven to 325°F. Combine the flour and baking soda in a bowl, and mix well. Beat the butter and sugar in a bowl until creamy. Beat in the whole eggs and the egg yolks, mixing well. Add half of the flour mixture, mixing just until moistened. Beat in the sour cream. Add the remaining flour mixture, and mix well. Fold the stiffly beaten egg whites into the batter, beating at low speed.
- Pour the batter into a 12-cup bundt pan sprayed with nonstick vegetable cooking spray. Coat the edges of the bundt pan with flour. Bake for 1 1/2 hours or until the cake tests done. Cool in the pan on a wire rack for 5 minutes. Invert the cake onto a wire rack to cool completely.
- Variations: For Marble Cake, spoon half the batter into a bundt pan. Combine 1/2 cup chocolate syrup and 1/8 teaspoon baking soda in a bowl, and add to the remaining batter, mixing well. Pour over the batter in the bundt pan. Do not stir. Bake for approximately 5 minutes longer than the Sour Cream Pound Cake. For Almond Cake, add 1 teaspoon almond extract. For Lemon Cake, add 1 teaspoon vanilla extract and 1 tablespoon lemon extract.
- Makes 16 servings

The recipe is shared by THOMAS TILLETT, who says he's just an "old" man, but he's not, of course. He's loving to all he meets and absolutely cannot stop baking. In fact, his mother baked a cake in 1938 for President Franklin D. Roosevelt, and that is what started Tommy baking. I call him my warm and woolly baking friend. We exchange cakes, and when he bakes one, it is absolutely perfect and delicious. —Rowena

PAGE COUNTY

Page County was named for John Page (1744-1808), an early governor of Virginia (1802-1805). It was founded in 1831 from Shenandoah and Rockingham Counties. Page County contains three hundred twenty-two square miles, and its population is 23,177. The county seat is Luray.

The world-famous Luray Caverns are located in Page County. Several frontier forts protected this area, including Fort Long, built around 1740.

SPARKMAN FAMILY'S

Vanilla, Butter, and Nut Cake and Frosting

CAKE

1 cup (2 sticks) margarine
2 cups sugar
1 teaspoon baking soda
1 cup buttermilk
1 teaspoon salt
3 cups sifted all-purpose flour

1 tablespoon vanilla extract
1 tablespoon butter extract
1 tablespoon nut extract
3 eggs, separated

FROSTING

1 (8-ounce) package cream cheese
1 package confectioners' sugar
1/4 cup (1/2 stick) margarine, melted

1 tablespoon vanilla extract
1 tablespoon butter extract
1 tablespoon nut extract
1 cup pecans, chopped, toasted in margarine

- To prepare the cake, let the ingredients stand at room temperature. Preheat the oven to 350°F. Grease a bundt pan or 10-inch tube pan, and dust with flour. Beat the margarine and sugar in a bowl until creamy. Dissolve the baking soda in the buttermilk in a bowl, stirring until foamy. Combine the salt and flour, and mix well. Add the flour mixture to the creamed mixture alternately with the buttermilk, mixing well after each addition. Add the vanilla extract, butter extract, nut extract, and egg yolks, 1 at a time, beating well after each addition. Beat the egg whites until stiff peaks form, and fold gently into the batter. Pour the batter into the prepared pan, and bake for 1 hour or until cake tests done.
- To prepare the frosting, blend the cream cheese and confectioners' sugar in a mixing bowl. Add the margarine, vanilla extract, butter extract, and nut extract gradually, beating well after each addition. Stir in the pecans.
- Frost the cake as desired.
- Makes 10 to 12 servings

This recipe originally comes from author Winette Sparkman Jeffery's mother, EDWINA CLENDENON SPARKMAN. Reprinted from *Miss Daisy Celebrates Tennessee*, ©1995 by Daisy King, James A. Crutchfield, and Winette Sparkman, with permission.

DID YOU KNOW THAT:

Thomas Jefferson, recognized today as one of the United States' greatest influences upon the exploration and expansion of the American West— primarily through his purchase of Louisiana Territory and his support of the Lewis and Clark Expedition to the Pacific Ocean—never traveled farther west than the Blue Ridge Mountains of his native state.

VIRGINIA TIMELINE

1952—A federal court of appeals decision in *Davis v. County School Board of Prince Edward County, Va.* anticipates by two years the unconstitutionality of segregation ruling in the 1954 landmark case *Brown v. Board of Public Education of Topeka, Kansas.*

1964—The Chesapeake Bay Bridge-Tunnel is completed, connecting Virginia Beach with the Eastern Shore.

1965—The election of Mills E. Godwin Jr. to Virginia's governor's chair ends the forty-year dominance of the state's politics by Harry F. Byrd.

1966—The Virginia poll tax is ruled unconstitutional, thus setting the stage for the elimination of poll taxes in all states.

1970—A. Linwood Holton from Roanoke becomes Virginia's first Republican governor in nearly one hundred years. The present State Constitution is adopted by voters. It becomes effective the following year. Archaeologists discover the remains of Martin's Hundred on the grounds of Carter's Grove.

1972—Tropical storm *Agnes* spawns devastating floods across the state.

1975—Annie Dillard wins the Pulitzer Prize for *Pilgrim at Tinker Creek*.

1981—The last volume in Dumas Malone's six-volume work *Jefferson and His Times*, a project that began in 1948, is published.

Whiskey Cake

1 cup (2 sticks) butter or margarine	1 pound pecans, chopped
2 cups sugar	3 cups raisins, such as puffy baking raisins
6 eggs	1 cup firmly packed brown sugar
1 teaspoon cinnamon	
1/2 teaspoon nutmeg	1/2 cup whiskey, such as Jack Daniels or Virginia Gentleman
4 cups all-purpose flour	
1 teaspoon baking powder	

- Preheat the oven 300°F. Beat the butter or margarine and sugar in a large bowl until creamy. Add the eggs, 1 at a time, beating well after each addition. Add the cinnamon, nutmeg, flour, and baking powder, blending well. Fold in the pecans and raisins.
- Pour the batter into a 10-inch tube pan lined with greased brown paper, and bake for 1 3/4 hours. Invert the cake onto a serving plate while hot. Sprinkle the top with the brown sugar, and drizzle with the whiskey. Store, covered with cotton, in an airtight container to age. Add additional whiskey if desired. This makes a very large dense cake.
- Makes about 24 servings

This recipe is from my mother, Mrs. Richard H. Jones of Nashville, Tennessee. I remember having this as early as the 1940s. We always had it for Christmas dinner and during the holiday season to serve the guests, sometimes side by side with my mother's made-from-scratch eggnog. When the Whiskey Cake was made, then we all knew Christmas was really coming. Mother covered it with an old linen napkin, and put it in a tin. Naturally, because we were a Tennessee family, the whiskey used was Jack Daniels-no substitute.

ELAINE DUNNING, a good friend who has lived in Alexandria, Virginia, for more than 35 years, shared this recipe. Elaine is a consummate cook and loves to try new recipes and new food products. Fred, her husband, has been playing golf with my husband for more than 30 years. (But you know, in Virginia, we'd use Virginia Gentlemen as the whiskey.) —Rowena

PATRICK COUNTY

Patrick County was named in honor of Patrick Henry. Organized in 1790, it contains four hundred eighty-five square miles. Its population is 19,407, and its county seat is Stuart.

The locale of Patrick County is the westernmost point traversed by Colonel William Byrd's survey of the Virginia-North Carolina border in 1728. General James Ewell Brown (J.E.B.) Stuart (1833-1864), one of the Confederacy's most eminent cavalry commanders, was born in this county.

Myrtle's White Cake

AS WRITTEN IN 1900 BY GRANDMA GIBSON

2 scant cups sugar
$^2/_3$ cup butter
A cup ice water
Unbeaten whites of 5 eggs
3 cups flour

5 level teaspoons baking
  powder
$^1/_2$ teaspoon vanilla extract
$^1/_2$ teaspoon lemon flavoring

- Cream butter, gradually add sugar. Sift $^1/_2$ teaspoon of flour and add to sugar and butter, next add unbeaten whites, beat well. Then add ice water, flour and baking powder, sift flour 5 or 6 times. Add flavoring. Put in a rectangle pan. Start checking for doneness after 30 minutes. Cooked originally in a wood stove and of course, later in a gas stove so there is no temperature, but a moderate stove of 350°F should be used.
- Makes 15 servings

MARY JANE IRWIN DAVIS, who is the State Regent of the Virginia Daughters of The American Revolution and a member of the Great Bridge Chapter, supplied this recipe. She is highly energized and totally organized, traveling the state regularly to each of the districts and chapters. She has been incredibly helpful to me by providing access to the wonderful resources of the women of the Daughters of The American Revolution, which covers the full spectrum of Virginia cuisine mixed with the DAR's strong focus on history and patriotism. As far back as Mary Jane can remember this cake was never served with icing. It was Mary Jane's favorite of all cakes and as taken from her grandmother's actual recipe.

PITTSYLVANIA COUNTY

Pittsylvania County was named in honor of the English statesman William Pitt. It was organized in 1766 from Halifax County. Containing one thousand fifteen square miles, this is the largest county in Virginia. The population is 61,745, and the county seat is Chatham.

In 1781, Revolutionary War General Nathaniel Greene hospitalized his troops in this county following the battle at Guilford Court House. Claude A. Swanson (1862-1939), who in addition to holding numerous elected offices, served in President Franklin D. Roosevelt's administration as secretary of the navy (1933-1939), was born here.

ROWENA'S KITCHEN TIPS

When making meatballs, keep your fingers wet to prevent stickiness. For uniformly sized meatballs, spread the mixture into a rectangle and cut into 1-inch strips lengthwise. Now cut again making 1-inch squares. Form each square into a meatball.

OLD-FASHIONED STYLE APPLE BUTTER

The Farm Basket, located in Lynchburg, Virginia, began as a fruit stand marketing the Flippin family's mountain-grown Silver Creek apples from their working farm in Nelson County. Making apple butter here is an age-old tradition. They make it the old-fashioned way—in huge, copper kettles outside over an open fire. Kettles are filled with a variety of apple slices, sauce, and cider in the early morning, and ten copper pennies are thrown into each kettle to prevent the apple butter from sticking to the pot. The fragrant mixture is continually stirred until the color and consistency are just right. Then sugar and spices are added, and the hot, sweet apple butter is ladled into jars. Finding the ten copper pennies, now bright and shiny, in each kettle, adds to the fun and festivities at the end of the day. Biscuits and warm apple butter are enjoyed by the hard working crew, as the sun goes down and the kettle is washed.

VIRGINIA'S FIRST WEDDING

John Laydon set sail from London in December 1606; six months later, he was one of the first colonists who established Jamestown. As a carpenter, his skills were very much in demand and greatly needed.

Just over a year later, the ship *Mary Margaret* arrived with seventy-two new colonists. Two were women—the wife of Thomas Forrest and a thirteen-year-old maidservant, Anne Burras. Despite her youth, in this outpost settlement of all men, her arrival created considerable excitement. In the end, it was twenty-six-year-old John Laydon, the carpenter, who won Anne's hand; in December 1608, the first wedding occurred in Virginia.

Their first child, a girl, was born a year later; she was named Virginia in honor of the new colony. And eventually three more girls were added to their family.

This family not only survived the terrible Starving Time in the winter of 1609 to 1610, but was also listed in the census taken after the first Indian massacre in 1622. By this time, they were living on a farm in the Poquoson and Warwick River area. The mystery is what happened to them after 1622. There is no more mention of them in any of the later records. But one thing is for certain: they were the beginning of the very first families of Virginia.

—George Tucker
The Virginian Pilot, June 9, 2002.

Second-Day Wedding Cake

1 cup molasses	1 tablespoon plus 1 teaspoon
1 cup sugar	ginger
1 cup lard or solid vegetable	1 cup boiling water
shortening	7 cups all-purpose flour
1 tablespoon baking soda	Real apple butter
1 tablespoon salt	

- Preheat the oven to 400°F. Combine the molasses, sugar, and lard or vegetable shortening in a large saucepan, and mix well. Bring to a boil. Remove from the heat. Place the baking soda, salt, and ginger in a measuring cup, and fill with the boiling water, and mix well. Stir into the molasses mixture.
- Add the flour, stirring until the dough is stiff enough to handle. Roll out the dough thinly. Place a plate of desired size onto the dough, and cut into circles. The recipe will make enough dough for seven layers.
- Place the dough circles on baking sheets, and bake for about 12 to 15 minutes or until brown. Do not overcook. The layers will be very hard. Stack the layers, spreading the apple butter between each layers. The cake will improve if wrapped and stored in a cool place for several days.
- Makes 16 to 20 servings

In the late 18th century and the early part of the 19th century, the Second Day Wedding cake was popular in Tennessee, Kentucky, and parts of Virginia. The wedding took place at the home of the bride with her nearest kin and closest friends present. A great feast was set out for the bride's dinner, and a dark wedding cake with fruits and nuts was served.

Another dinner was prepared at the groom's home on the second day of the marriage. The bride wore her second-day wedding dress, and guests who were more distant relatives and friends were invited. Each guest brought a thin layer of the cake, which was stacked as they arrived and spread with apple butter. The more guests, the higher the cake, thus the alternate name "Stack Cake." Real apple butter was made with sweet apples, no sugar or spices added. It was done when it was so thick it would not pour from a jar when turned upside down.

This recipe was sent by EFFIE KING BROWN, a 91-year-old, very special lady of great energy and enthusiasm. When she was young, she taught in a one-room schoolhouse in Floyd County, where there were no real roads, and she boarded with the parents of some of the children. She is a master quilter as were her mother and grandmother before her. She is a member of the Floyd Courthouse Chapter of the Virginia DAR.

Zuccotto Falletta

1 (1½-pound) sponge cake, sliced into thin rectangles about ⅜ inch thick
1 cup maraschino cherry juice
6 cups whipping cream
1 cup confectioners' sugar
1¼ cups chopped toasted almonds

1 (6-ounce) package bittersweet chocolate chips
1 cup finely chopped orange peel
Maraschino cherry juice and confectioners' sugar for garnish

- Line a 1½-quart glass bowl with the cake slices, reserving enough slices to cover bowl. Sprinkle the slices in the bowl with enough of the maraschino juice to moisten. Whip the whipping cream in a large bowl, gradually adding 1 cup confectioners' sugar, and beating until stiff peaks form.
- Fold in the almonds, chocolate chips, and orange peel. Spoon over the cake slices in the bowl. Cover the whipped cream with the reserved cake slices, and moisten with the remaining maraschino cherry juice. Cover the bowl with a plate, and freeze for 24 hours.
- Remove the cake from the freezer about 2 hours before serving time, and unmold onto a serving plate.
- Sprinkle with maraschino cherry juice, and dust with confectioners' sugar just before serving.
- Makes 8 to 10 servings

This recipe is from the kitchen of JOANN FALLETTA, hailed by *The New York Times* "as ...one of the finest conductors of her generation." She currently holds the position of music director of the Buffalo Philharmonic Orchestra as well as the Virginia Symphony Orchestra. She is an effervescent and exuberant figure on the podium and is in great demand as a guest conductor all over the world. With her as its conductor, the Virginia Symphony is today Virginia's premiere, full-time professional orchestra. It is an exciting and versatile ensemble that attracts first-rate musicians from around the world. In August 2000, the Virginia Symphony was accepted into the International Conference of Symphony and Opera Musicians, officially entering the "major leagues" and joining ranks with the Boston Symphony, the New York Philharmonic, and more than 40 prestigious ensembles.

VIRGINIA SYMPHONY
JOANN FALLETTA MUSIC DIRECTOR

ROWENA'S KITCHEN TIPS

My mother, a great cook, always added a spoonful or dash of sugar to season her tomato dishes or meat and vegetable sauces. Try a pinch of sugar when sautéing onions. I love the flavor, and the sugar improves the browning. It's good when cooking bacon, too.

CONRAD KNEW THE "FLAVOR" OF THE TIMES

Bright ideas come from bright minds, and Conrad Frederick Sauer was thinking of business on his twenty-first birthday in 1887. He began a venture in Richmond that day that led to a tradition of quality with many fine Virginia food products. Conrad developed the manufacturing and packaging of pure flavoring extracts in five-and ten gram- sized, specially designed bottles. Immediate acceptance and sales convinced the young man to eventually locate his company to 2000 West Broad Street in the growing capital city.

By 1929, C. F. Sauer, Jr. had expanded the business and acquired the Interstate Commerce Company and the Duke's Products Company. Now, household drugs and remedies along with a whole line of salad dressings and mayonnaise were among the Sauer Company's most successful products. The plant in Richmond grew, and by 1956 vegetable oil production was added. Sales in retail and foodservice began to develop. 1967 saw the company begin a line of barbecue sauces as well by purchasing Alford's Barbecue Sauce.

Many a Virginia kitchen is stocked with products that families enjoy daily. Some of the favorites are Duke's Mayonnaise, Mrs. Filbert's Mayonnaise, Sauer's Salad Dressing, and Sauer's Spices, Flavorings, and Extracts. Many commercial products from the company form the basis for several recipes served to diners in the Commonwealth as well.

This large business came from a bright young man with ideas that still "flavor" Virginia today!

18th Century Icing Recipe from one of Martha Washington's Cookbooks

THE ORIGINAL RECIPE
Take two Pound of double refin'd Sugar, beat and sift it very fine, and likewise beat and sift a little Starch and mix with it, then beat six Whites of Eggs to Froth, and put to it some Gum-Water, the Gum must be steep'd in Orange-flower-water, then mix and beat all these together two Hours, and put it on your Cake: when it is baked, set it in the Oven again to harden a quarter of a Hour, take great Care it is not discolour'd. When it is drawn, ice it over the Top and Sides, take two Pound of double refin'd Sugar beat and sifted, and the Whites of three Eggs beat to a Froth, with three or four Spoonfuls of Orange-flower-water, and three Grains of Musk and Amber-grease together: put all these in a Stone Mortar, and beat these till it is as white as Snow, and with a Brush or Bundle of Feathers, spread it all over the Cake, and put it in the Oven to dry; but take Care the Oven does not discolor it. When it is cold paper it, and it will keep good five or six Weeks.

THE MODERN ADAPTATION

3 egg whites	1 teaspoon grated lemon
1 to 2 cups plus	peel
2 tablespoons	2 tablespoons orange-flower
confectioners' sugar	water

- Beat the egg whites and 2 tablespoons of the confectioners' sugar in a large bowl for 3 minutes. Add additional confectioners' sugar until 1 to 2 cups have be incorporated. Add the lemon peel and orange-flower water. Beat until stiff enough to remain separated when cut through with a knife. Spread over the top and sides of a cake. Let it stand in a 200°F oven for 1 hour or until hardened. Note: The icing will be brittle and shatter when the cake is sliced.
- Makes approximately 2 cups

The recipe was provided by MARY V. THOMPSON, research specialist, Mount Vernon Ladies' Association, Mount Vernon, Virginia. It is originally from Louise Conway Belden's book, *The Festive Tradition: Table Decoration and Desserts in America, 1650-1900* reprinted by W.W. Norton & Company, 1983.

POWHATAN COUNTY

Powhatan County was named in honor of the Indian leader of the same name. It was organized in 1777 from Cumberland and Chesterfield Counties. It contains two hundred seventy-three square miles and is home to 22,377 residents. The county seat is Powhatan.

Powhatan County was the site for a large Huguenot settlement in 1699-1700. On April 14, 1865, returning home from his surrender at Appomattox Court House, General Robert E. Lee stopped overnight in this county to visit his brother.

Candy and Cookies

Dixie Peanut Brittle

STOVETOP METHOD

2 cups sugar
1 cup light corn syrup
1/2 cup water
1/2 teaspoon salt
3 cups shelled fresh peanuts
  with skins

2 tablespoons (1/4 stick)
  butter or margarine
2 teaspoons baking soda

• Combine the sugar, corn syrup, water, and salt in a heavy saucepan, and mix well. Bring to a rolling boil, stirring constantly. Stir in the peanuts. Reduce the heat. Cook until a candy thermometer reaches 293°F or hard-crack stage, stirring constantly. Remove from the heat. Stir in the butter and baking soda. Beat rapidly, and pour onto a buttered surface, such as a cookie sheet or marble, spreading to 1/4-inch thickness. Break into pieces when cool. Store in an airtight container.
• Makes about 2 pounds

MICROWAVE METHOD

1 cup sugar
1/2 cup light corn syrup
1/8 teaspoon salt
1 1/2 cups shelled peanuts
  with skin

1 teaspoon butter
1 teaspoon vanilla extract
1 teaspoon baking soda

• Combine the sugar, syrup, salt, and peanuts in a 1 1/2-quart glass dish, and mix well. Microwave on High for 8 minutes, stirring well after 4 minutes. Stir in the butter and vanilla extract. Microwave on High for 2 minutes longer. Add the baking soda, and stir quickly until light and foamy. Pour immediately onto a lightly greased baking sheet, spreading thinly. Break into pieces when cool. Store in an airtight container.
• Makes about 1 pound

JOANNE FOX, Regent of the Hicksford Chapter of the Virginia DAR, shared this recipe. It is from *All About Cooking Peanuts*.

PRINCE EDWARD COUNTY

Prince Edward County was formed in 1753 from land once part of Amelia County. It was named in honor of Edward Augustus, the grandson of King George II. It contains three hundred fifty-six square miles and is home to 19,720 residents. The county seat is Farmville.

Hampden-Sydney College, one of America's foremost seats of learning, was opened in this county in 1776. Much of the Battle of Sailor's (or Sayler's) Creek was fought here on April 6, 1865, resulting in a mass surrender by Confederate forces.

Martha Washington Candy

½ cup (1 stick) butter or
    margarine, softened
3 (1-pound) packages
    confectioners' sugar
1 can sweetened condensed
    milk, such as Eagle Brand
2 teaspoons vanilla
    extract

2 (10-ounce) jars
    maraschino cherries,
    drained, chopped
1 quart chopped pecans
1 block paraffin
1 (6-ounce) package
    semisweet chocolate bits
1 (9-ounce) bar chocolate

- Combine the butter or margerine, 2 packages of the confectioners' sugar, condensed milk, and vanilla extract in a large bowl until blended. Stir in the cherries and pecans, and chill, covered, in the refrigerator.
- Roll the mixture into balls, keeping hands powdered with the remaining confectioners' sugar. Melt the paraffin and chocolate bits in a double boiler. Dip the chilled balls in the chocolate mixture. Place on waxed paper to cool.
- Makes 16 dozen candies

This is a fun recipe shared by NATASSIA and ROSELLE TAYLOR of the Carter's Fort Chapter of the Virginia DAR in Scott County.

DESSIE'S
Potato Candy

1 small white potato,
    peeled, boiled, mashed
¼ cup (½ stick) butter or
    margarine
¼ cup evaporated milk
1 teaspoon vanilla extract

Dash of salt
1 (1-pound) package
    confectioners' sugar
Peanut butter, crunchy or
    creamy

- Combine the mashed potato, butter or margerine, evaporated milk, vanilla extract, and salt in a bowl, and mix well. Add the confectioners' sugar a small amount at a time until a stiff dough forms. Roll out thinly. Spread with peanut butter. Roll up. Let stand for 1 hour at room temperature or until set. Cut into ¼-inch to ½-inch slices.
- Makes about 2 dozen

This recipe was submitted by BARBARA DOUGHTERY BISHOP, Regent of the Carter's Fort Chapter of the Virginia DAR. Carter's Fort happens to be in Daniel Boone country, and he had a real fondness for potatoes, especially sweet potatoes. It is said that he died from an overindulgence of sweet potatoes in 1820 at the age of 86.

INTERESTING STATISTICS ABOUT VIRGINIA

- Virginia's population, according to the 2000 Census, is 7,078,515.
- Virginia's statewide population has increased by 14.4 percent since 1990.
- With a population of 425,257, Virginia Beach is the state's largest city.
- A total of 68.1 percent of Virginians own their homes.
- The average Virginian's annual income is $40,209.
- There are 2,699,173 households in Virginia.
- The average Virginia household consists of 2.54 persons.
- Women outnumber men in Virginia by a ratio of 51 percent to 49 percent.
- The highest point in Virginia is Mount Rogers, at 5,729 feet above sea level.
- The state's lowest point is sea level.
- The mean elevation of the state is 950 feet.
- Virginia's highest temperature ever recorded was 110 degrees Fahrenheit, taken on July 15, 1954, at Balcony Falls.
- The state's lowest-ever temperature was 30 degrees below zero Fahrenheit, taken on January 22, 1985, at Mountain Lake Biological Station.
- Virginia has a shoreline that measures 3,315 miles.
- Virginia contains 39,594 square miles, making it the thirty-seventh largest state in the Union.

NATURAL BRIDGE

More than fifty natural bridges have been discovered in the United States. Of these, none is more graceful or beautiful than Virginia's Natural Bridge, located in Rockbridge County, just a few miles south of Lexington. The bridge stands 215 feet high and its span is nearly 100 feet long. George Washington surveyed the region around the bridge in 1750 and carved his initials upon the rock. In 1774, Thomas Jefferson purchased the bridge and the surrounding 157 acres from King George III, for twenty shillings. The bridge has remained in private hands ever since.

Jefferson built a two-room log cabin on the premises and supposedly entertained guests there. After his death, his heirs disposed of the property, and its new owners built the Forest Inn as a tourist attraction. Today, Virginia's Natural Bridge is listed as both a Virginia and a National Historic Landmark. For information, contact: 800-533-1410.

Fresh Apple Squares

1³/4 cups sugar	1 teaspoon cinnamon
3 eggs	2 cups chopped peeled
1 cup vegetable oil	apples
1 teaspoon baking soda	1 cup chopped nuts
¹/4 teaspoon salt	Confectioners' sugar for
2 cups all-purpose flour	dusting

- Preheat the oven to 350°F. Beat the sugar, eggs, and oil in a large bowl until well blended. Combine the baking soda, salt, flour, and cinnamon in a bowl. Add the dry mixture gradually to the egg mixture, and beat well. Fold in the apples and nuts. Pour the batter into a 9×13-inch pan, and bake for 1 hour. Let stand until cool. Dust with confectioners' sugar, and cut in squares to serve.
- Makes 12 servings

This recipe is from SHARON SNELL POWELL, Chesapeake Chapter of the Virginia DAR.

Chinese Noodle Cookies

2 (6-ounce) packages chocolate chips	2 (3-ounce) cans Chinese noodles, such as La Choy
2 (6-ounce) packages butterscotch chips	¹/2 cup peanuts
	³/4 cup raisins

- Melt the chocolate chips and butterscotch chips in a saucepan over low to medium heat. Add the noodles, peanuts, and raisins, and stir to coat. Drop by spoonfuls onto waxed paper, and refrigerate.
- Makes 18 to 24 cookies

My mother would always make these cookies for me during special events in my childhood, and I loved them so much that I now associate these cookies with those many wonderful times in my life. Just recently I gave birth to our first child, and guess what? My mom had these cookies waiting for me on our return from the hospital.

LORI JAAP is married to our son, Joe, who was raised in Norfolk. Lori loves to entertain and to try different recipes, and she is a great daughter-in-law. —Rowena

ROWENA'S KITCHEN TIPS

Do you want to use herbs from your garden all winter long? As winter approaches, I cut a handful of each type I want to keep, rinse them and place each bunch in a small, uncovered bowl in my refrigerator. As they dry out, not only are they available for me to use as seasonings all winter long, but they freshen my refrigerator, as well. You can also freeze herbs in plastic bags.

SENATOR JOHN WARNER'S
Favorite Cookies

1 cup (2 sticks) butter	1 teaspoon baking soda
1 cup firmly packed brown sugar	1 cup flaked coconut
$3/4$ cup sugar	$1^1/_2$ cups semisweet chocolate chips
2 eggs	$1/4$ cup chopped dates
1 teaspoon vanilla extract	$1/2$ cup sunflower seed kernels
$1^1/_2$ cups all-purpose flour	$1/4$ cup slivered almonds

- Preheat the oven to 325°F. Cream the butter, brown sugar, and sugar in a large bowl. Add the eggs and vanilla extract, and mix well. Stir in the flour and baking soda. Add the remaining ingredients, and mix well. Drop by spoonfuls onto cookie sheets. Bake for 12 minutes. Let stand until cool.
- Makes 2 to 3 dozen cookies

This was sent by SENATOR JOHN W. WARNER, senior senator from Virginia, who is serving his fifth term in the United States Senate. Prior to his service in the Senate, he served presidential appointments as Under Secretary of the Navy, Secretary of the Navy, and as administrator of the American Revolution Bicentennial Administration. He is one of just four elected officials in Virginia's political history to have won five or more statewide elections. Senator Warner is the senior Republican member of the Armed Service Committee and also serves on the Environment and Public Works, Health, Education, Labor and Pensions, and Rules and Administration committees.

PRINCE GEORGE COUNTY

Prince George County, formed in 1702 from Charles City County, was named in honor of Queen Anne's husband, Prince George of Denmark. It contains two hundred ninety-four square miles, and its population is 33,047. The county seat is Prince George.

The first windmill in America was built in this county by Governor George Yeardley in 1621. The Battle of the Crater was fought here in 1864.

PRINCE WILLIAM COUNTY

Prince William County was organized in 1730 from parts of Stafford and King George Counties. Named in honor of William Augustus, the second son of King George II, the county contains three hundred forty-five square miles and has a population of 280,813. The county seat is Manassas.

Simon Kenton (1755-1836), frontiersman and protégé of Daniel Boone and George Rogers Clark, was born here. Both the First and Second Battles of Manassas (Bull Run) were fought in this county.

OLD CAPE HENRY LIGHT

Old Cape Henry Light, our nation's first lighthouse, now stands silent and dark, a ninety-two-foot, copper-domed, sandstone-brick structure at the entrance to Chesapeake Bay. It gives mute testimony to its architectural and historic significance, as well as the part it played in history by keeping seafarers safe. Its site is near the spot where in 1607 Captain Christopher Newport and the first shipload of English colonists to Virginia raised a cross to offer thanks for their safe crossing of the treacherous Atlantic. In 1896, the Association for the Preservation of Virginia Antiquities (APVA) placed a tablet on the tower marking this event.

Though a lighthouse here had been a recognized need during Colonial days, Old Cape Henry was finally erected as the first Public Works construction project authorized and funded by the First Congress of the United States in 1789. In turn, in November 1789, the Virginia General Assembly conveyed title to the land at the headland of Cape Henry to the new government for the purpose of building the lighthouse. Erected in 1792 as a lighted and visual navigation aid to guide all shipping through the Virginia Capes to the Chesapeake and its commerce, Old Cape Henry Light served for eighty-nine years with its fish-oil burning lamps tended by an ever-vigilant light keeper. It was replaced in 1881 by the new Cape Henry Light, a black and white cast-iron lighthouse, erected just three hundred fifty feet away, which is still operating over one hundred twenty years later. In 2002, Old Cape Henry Light received new honors and a bronze plaque proclaiming it a National Historic Civil Engineering Landmark.

My Chocolate-Dipped Macaroons

$2/3$ cup sugar
3 tablespoons all-purpose flour
3 large, or 4 small egg whites
$1/4$ teaspoon salt
1 teaspoon real almond extract
$2^2/3$ cups coconut
12 ounces semisweet or bittersweet chocolate

- Preheat the oven to 325°F. Combine the sugar, flour, egg whites, salt, and almond extract in a large bowl, and mix well. Fold in the coconut. Drop the batter by rounded tablespoonfuls (or use a large cookie scoop) onto cookie sheets sprayed with nonstick cooking spray or lightly greased. Bake until lightly browned. Remove immediately to a wire rack using a spatula, and let stand until cool.
- Melt the chocolate in a double boiler. Dip each macaroon halfway into the chocolate, and place on waxed paper to harden. The macaroons can be frozen before coating with the chocolate. Thaw the macaroons before dipping.
- Makes 3 dozen macaroons

I have to hide these when I make them for a party or gift, because if my family spots them, they will be gone before I need them, even if I double the recipe. This has always been a secret recipe until now.

The recipe is from the kitchen of MARGIE GRIFFITH, who loves to cook, especially for family and friends. She is also the loving wife of Circuit Court Judge Chuck Griffith of Norfolk, Virginia.

PULASKI COUNTY

Named in honor of the Polish patriot Casimir Pulaski, who aided the American army during the Revolution, Pulaski County was formed in 1839 from parts of Wythe and Mongomery Counties. It contains three hundred thirty-three square miles. Its population is 35,127 and the county seat is Pulaski.

John Draper, an officer in the Point Pleasant Indian expedition of 1774, was an early settler in this county. The Battle of Cloyd's Mountain was fought here in May 1864.

RAPPAHANNOCK COUNTY

Rappahannock County was established in 1833 from Culpeper County. Its namesake is the Rappahannock River, which has its headwaters here. It contains two hundred seventy-four square miles and is home to 6,983 residents. The county seat is Washington.

Of the twenty-eight towns in the United States named Washington, the one in Rappahannock County, surveyed by George Washington himself in 1749, was the first to be named such (in 1796). William Randolph Barbee (1818-1868), a world-renowned sculptor, was born in this county.

SUSAN ALLEN'S LITHUANIAN GRANDMOTHER'S
Cranberry Cookies

$1/2$ cup (1 stick) butter or margarine
1 cup sugar
$3/4$ cup firmly packed brown sugar
$1/4$ cup milk
2 tablespoons orange juice
1 egg

3 cups all-purpose flour
1 teaspoon baking powder
$1/4$ teaspoon baking soda
$1/2$ teaspoon salt
1 cup chopped nuts
$2^1/2$ cups chopped fresh cranberries

- Preheat the oven to 375°F. Beat the butter or margarine, sugar and brown sugar in a large bowl until creamy. Combine the milk, orange juice, and egg in a separate large bowl, and mix well. Add the flour, baking powder, baking soda, and salt, and mix well. Stir the flour mixture into the creamed mixture, and blend well. Fold in the nuts and cranberries. Drop by teaspoonfuls onto greased cookie sheets. Bake for 10 to 15 minutes.
- Note: The cranberries are easier to chop if frozen.
- Makes 12 dozen cookies

A real favorite of the Allen family.

The recipe is from the family of SUSAN ALLEN, a lovely, energized mother of three and a leader on many children's issues. She served as the popular First Lady of Virginia from 1994 to 1998 during her husband's tenure as The Commonwealth's 67th Governor. A leader on cancer-related issues and children's issues among many other things, she is a true partner with her husband, now our 51st senator from The Commonwealth of Virginia. Susan Allen also wrote the preface for this book.

RICHMOND COUNTY

Richmond County was formed in 1692 from the first Rappahannock County and was named for the town of the same name in England. It contains two hundred four square miles, and its population is 8,809. The county seat is Warsaw.

Francis Lightfoot Lee (1734-1797), signer of the Declaration of Independence, spent his last days at Menokin, his home near Warsaw. Early statesman Cyrus Griffin (1748-1810) was born in this county.

ROWENA'S KITCHEN TIPS

Here's an old baking trick! Prevent raisins or any other fruit from sinking to the bottom of your baked goods by coating them with flour. Then add them to your batter towards the end of the mixing. They won't sink during baking.

JIM BECKWOURTH, MOUNTAIN MAN

"I was born in Fredericksburg, Virginia, on the 26th of April, 1798." Thus begins James P. Beckwourth's autobiography, published in New York in 1856. His book, *The Life and Adventures of James P. Beckwourth*, has been alternatively praised and criticized by historians ever since its appearance. In 1885, the historian, Hubert Howe Bancroft described Beckwourth as "a famous hunter, guide, Indian-fighter, chief of the Crows, and horse-thief." Bancroft also added, "No resume can do justice to his adventures, nor can the slightest faith be put in his statements." On the other hand, many fur trade historians rank Beckwourth as one of the outstanding mountain men of the era.

Beckwourth was a mulatto. His father was a plantation overseer and a former major in the Revolutionary War, and his mother was a slave. The family name was originally "Beckwith," but Jim later became known as "Beckwourth," and he used the new name forever afterwards. As a young boy, Jim moved to Missouri, where he was apprenticed to a blacksmith. In 1824, he enlisted with General William Ashley's third fur trading mission about to depart for the upper Missouri River.

During the next few years, Beckwourth pursued his newfound craft in the Rocky Mountains. Eventually, he was adopted by the Crow Indians and accepted as one of their chiefs. He supposedly married several times within the tribe and often accompanied his Indian brethren on war parties.

During the Second Seminole War (1835-1842), Beckwourth fought with Zachary Taylor for at least part of that time. He participated in the suppression of the Taos Revolt in 1847, and went back to California during the Gold Rush.

In 1860, Beckwourth married again and settled in Denver, where he ran a store and owned a small ranch. Four years later, he guided Colonel J. M. Chivington's Third Colorado Volunteers on their vicious attack upon Black Kettle's Cheyenne and Arapaho encampment at Sand Creek, a deed he later denounced and called "revolting."

Beckwourth's last job was as a scout and messenger at Fort Laramie. Hired to interpret among the Crows for Colonel Henry B. Carrington, Jim finally returned to his adopted people and died in one of their camps in 1866. According to Crow tradition, he was buried on a scaffold.

Mrs. James Monroe's
Cream Jumbles

2 cups sugar
2 cups (4 sticks) butter
2 eggs
1 cup cream

4 cups flour
1 teaspoon vanilla extract, optional

- Preheat the oven to 350°F. Beat the butter and sugar in a large bowl until creamy. Add the eggs, and mix well. Add the cream and flour alternately to the creamed mixture, beating well after each addition. Stir in the vanilla extract if desired.
- Chill the dough, covered, in the refrigerator for at least 1 hour. Roll the dough thinly, and cut into desired shapes. Place on cookie sheets, and bake for 8 to 10 minutes.
- Note: These cookies can be baked in a ring shape like the Waverly Jumbles (page 247), or baked as drop cookies.
- Makes about 5 dozen

The original recipe read 1 pound sugar, 1 pound butter, 2 eggs, 1 cup cream made into a stiff paste, rolled thin, and baked quickly.

Recipe submitted by CAROLYN HOLMES, Director, Ashlawn-Highland from *Monroe Family Recipes*, Judith E. Kosnik, editor, published by Ashlawn-Highland, October 1988.

Date-Nut Goodies

1 cup sifted confectioners' sugar
1 cup chopped dates

1 cup chopped pecans
1 egg white

- Preheat the oven to 350°F. Combine the confectioners' sugar, dates, and pecans in a bowl, and mix well. Stir the egg white.
- Drop by teaspoonfuls onto well-greased cookie sheets. Top each cookie with a piece of candied cherry or colored sugar if desired.
- Bake for 12 minutes or until light brown. Let stand to cool before removing from the cookie sheets.
- Makes approximately 30 to 40 cookies

VALLI LANEVE submitted this recipe in loving memory of her mother, Doris Laneve. This was her favorite cookie recipe.

ROWENA'S KITCHEN TIPS

When washing and shredding lettuce, place it in a bowl with paper towels on the bottom of the bowl and on top. Let it sit for about an hour, preferably in the refrigerator. The excess moisture is absorbed, and the lettuce becomes crisp.

Florentines

2/3 cup sugar
1/2 cup whipping cream
3 tablespoons butter or
   margarine
1 teaspoon orange liqueur,
   optional
1 cup slivered almonds or
   hazelnuts
1/2 cup chopped candied
   lemon peel
1/2 cup chopped crystallized
   ginger

3/4 cup chopped candied
   mixed fruits
1/3 cup plus 3 tablespoons
   all-purpose flour, unsifted
1/2 pound bittersweet
   chocolate, melted
1 teaspoon almond or
   orange extract
1 tablespoon heavy cream,
   optional

- Preheat the oven to 350°F. Combine the sugar, whipping cream, butter or margarine, and orange liqueur if desired in a medium saucepan. Bring to a boil. Remove from the heat, and stir in the almonds, lemon peel, ginger, mixed fruits, and flour. Drop by teaspoonfuls onto greased and floured cookie sheets, leaving ample space between each cookie, and flatten with a fork.
- Bake until golden brown. Let stand until cool. Combine the melted chocolate and almond or orange extract, and mix well. "Paint" the bottoms of each cookie with the chocolate mixture. Add heavy cream if the chocolate becomes too hard. Place the cookies, painted side up, on wire racks to cool. Store in an airtight container between layers of waxed paper in the refrigerator.
- Makes 50 to 60 cookies

These cookies make a delicious addition to any party, but I prefer to make them in December when the candied fruits are available. Enjoy them while reading your travel guide to Italy or a chapter of your favorite Italian author, and you will feel as if you have traveled, if not to paradise, at least to the Tuscan Woods.

This recipe is from the kitchen of DR. ROSEANN RUNTE, president of Old Dominion University in Norfolk, Virginia. Old Dominion University began in 1930 as the Norfolk Division of The College of William and Mary. In 1962 it became an independent institution, and in 1969 it achieved university status. It has close to 20,000 students and offers both undergraduate and graduate degrees. Its business and research initiatives contribute $600 million annually to the economy, making the University the largest generator of new jobs in the region.

The former capital of Tuscany, Florence—or Firenze in Italian—was a great center of art during the Middle Ages and Renaissance. Known for its palaces (Palazzo Veccio), cathedrals (Saint Mary of the Flowers), museums (Bargello, Pitti), its schools of painting, and sculpture, Florence is also known for this delicate cookie, which, since it contains fruit and nuts, would almost qualify as a healthy snack it were not so wonderfully decadent. This recipe is an original one, which Dr. Runte made after tasting these cookies in Europe. Thus all the ingredients are available here.

INAUGURATION WORDS: VIRGINIA'S PRESIDENTS

MARCH 4, 1793
GEORGE WASHINGTON

George Washington's second inaugural address was the shortest on record, consisting of only 135 words. Among his brief thoughts was the statement

That if it shall be found during my administration of the Government I have in any instance violated willingly or knowingly the injunctions thereof, I may (besides incurring constitutional punishment) be subject to the upbraidings of all who are now witnesses of the present solemn ceremony.

MARCH 4, 1801
THOMAS JEFFERSON

Long before he became President, Jefferson had entertained ideas about the exploration of the western lands beyond the Mississippi River. In his inaugural speech of 1801, he said

A rising nation, spread over a wide and fruitful land, traversing all the seas with the rich productions of their industry, engaged in commerce with nations who feel power and forget right, advancing rapidly to destinies beyond the reach of mortal eye—when I contemplate these transcendent objects, and see the honor, the happiness, and the hopes of this beloved country committed to the issue, and the auspices of this day, I shrink from the contemplation, and humble myself before the magnitude of the undertaking. . .

MARCH 4, 1817
JAMES MONROE

Following the War of 1812, Monroe was still concerned with national defense. He warned his inaugural listeners about "Dangers from abroad," and told them,

... the United States may be again involved in war, and it may in that event be the object of the adverse party to overset our Government, to break our Union, and demolish us as a nation.

In order to prevent such a catastrophe, Monroe suggested that

... our coast and inland frontiers should be fortified, our Army and Navy, regulated upon just principles as to the force of each, be kept in perfect order, and our militia be placed on the best practicable footing.

STRATFORD HALL PLANTATION
Ginger Cookies

1¹/₂ cups (3 sticks) butter or margarine, softened
¹/₂ cup molasses
2 cups sugar
2 eggs
4 cups all-purpose flour
¹/₄ cup baking soda
2 teaspoons cinnamon
1 teaspoon ground ginger
1 teaspoon ground cloves
Additional sugar for rolling

- Preheat the oven to 350°F. Beat the butter or margarine, molasses, sugar, and eggs in a bowl until creamy. Combine the flour, baking soda, cinnamon, ginger, and cloves in a bowl, and mix well. Add to the butter mixture, stirring until dough forms.
- Refrigerate the dough, covered, for several hours. Shape the dough into small balls, and roll in additional sugar. Place on cookie sheets, and bake for 8 to 10 minutes or until browned and firm. For large amounts, shape the refrigerated dough into a roll about 1 inch thick, and slice into ³/₄-inch slices. Dip the cut sides in sugar, and bake as above.
- Makes approximately 5 dozen cookies

This is the traditional ginger cookie that has been made and served in the dining room at Stratford for many years. It used to be served in the outside kitchen at the Great House.

STRATFORD HALL PLANTATION, Stratford, Virginia, shared this recipe. Stratford is the birthplace of Robert E. Lee and the ancestral home of four generations of the Lee family, including Richard Henry Lee and Francis Lightfoot Lee, the only brothers to sign the Declaration of Independence. The historic site includes the great house, four out buildings, coach house and stables, slave quarters, gristmill, Jessie Ball duPont Memorial Library, visitor center, log cabin restaurant, and gift shop. The 1,700-acre landscape includes three miles of nature trails, formal boxwood gardens, period gardens with 18th century varieties of flowers, vegetables, and herbs, the Potomac River overlook, and beachfront. Stratford Hall Plantation is open for tours daily.

Mountain Ranger Cookies

1 cup sugar
1 cup firmly packed brown sugar
1 cup (2 sticks) butter or margarine, softened
2 eggs
2 cups all-purpose flour
1 teaspoon baking soda
1/4 teaspoon salt
1/2 teaspoon baking powder
1 teaspoon vanilla extract
2 cups old-fashioned oats
2 cups cereal, such as Rice Krispies, Kellogg's Cornflakes, or 3/4 cup All-Bran
1 cup chopped walnuts or pecans
3/4 cup golden raisins

- Preheat the oven to 350°F. Beat the sugar, brown sugar, and butter or margarine in a large bowl until creamy. Add the eggs, and mix well. Beat in the flour, baking soda, salt, and baking powder. Stir in the vanilla extract. Fold in the oats, cereal of choice, walnuts or pecans, and raisins.
- Drop by tablespoonfuls onto ungreased cookie sheets, and bake for 12 minutes or until lightly browned. Cool on the cookie sheets on a wire rack for 1 minute. Remove the cookies to a wire rack to cool completely.
- Makes 6 dozen cookies

I've always loved a good homemade cookie. This one fits the bill. It's delicious, easy, and makes enough for the freezer.

The recipe is from the kitchen of MURIEL GREENHALGH of Virginia Beach, Virginia. She is one of the most creative gals I have ever known. With our Navy husbands, we have moved all over the country together, entertaining as we went, and we have been friends for more than 40 years. —Rowena

ROANOKE COUNTY

Roanoke County was probably named for the Roanoke River when it was organized in 1838 from parts of Botetourt and Montgomery Counties. The county contains three hundred five square miles, and its population is 85,778. The county seat is Salem.

Several early inns and stagecoach stops were located in Salem, a primary town in Virginia's Great Valley that led to the West. Virginia Institute, a coeducation liberal arts school, opened in this county in 1842, later changing its name to Roanoke College.

ROWENA'S KITCHEN TIPS

Many recipes call for baking soda. The added baking soda can promote faster action and browning of baked goods. Test your baking soda freshness by adding a few drops of vinegar to a small amount of baking soda. If it doesn't bubble, it is too old.

WHITE HOUSE APPLE CIDER VINEGAR

A Family Tradition

The Shenandoah Valley of Virginia graces many an American table with its production of apples and apple products. One well-known apple food brand is called White House, a label that is now part of a nationally acclaimed food producer. The National Fruit Product Company had its beginning in March of 1908 as Board, Armstrong, and Company in Alexandria. The Armstrong family has handed the business down through four generations. Today, the home office sits on 63 acres in Winchester where production has taken place since 1915.

Frank Armstrong Sr. and Jr. established quite a history with their early products. The White House label was created taking its name from the President's house in Washington D.C. Company legends tell of regular deliveries made by horse-drawn carriage of White House Apple Cider to the real White House in 1908.

Sugar Cakes or Sugar Cookies

ORIGINAL VERSION
Half a Pd butter well washed in Rose Water, the same quantity of fine sugar, a little mace, the yolks of three and whites of One egg; shake in a Pd of flour-work all well, till it becomes a light Paste, then roll it out and bake it on Tin Sheets.

MODERN ADAPTATION

1 cup (2 sticks) butter or margarine	1 whole egg
1 cup plus 3 tablespoons sugar	2 egg yolks
	2 cups all-purpose flour
	1/2 teaspoon nutmeg

- Beat the butter or margarine and 1 cup of the sugar in a large bowl until creamy. Add the whole egg and the egg yolks, and beat well. Beat in the flour and nutmeg. Turn the dough out onto a cookie sheet. Pat the dough into a rectangle about 1/2 inch thick with floured hands. Sprinkle with the remaining sugar. Bake for 20 minutes. Let stand until cool. Cut into squares. For individual cookies, pinch off dough, and roll into walnut-size balls. Flatten each ball with the bottom of a glass. Place on cookie sheets, and bake for 15 minutes.
- Makes 3 dozen cookies

The recipe was submitted by the GEORGE WASHINGTON BIRTHPLACE MEMORIAL ASSOCIATION. Both the original and modern versions are from *The Old Washington Recipes* published by this association.

America's first and greatest hero, George Washington, was born on his father's Pope's Creek tobacco plantation in 1732. Located in the Northern Neck of Virginia, thirty-eight miles east of Fredericksburg, the George Washington Birthplace National Monument preserves the heart of Augustine Washington's plantation, the seventeenth-century home site of the immigrant John Washington, and the Washington family burial ground. First marked in 1815, George Washington's birthplace contains a Memorial House and dependencies constructed in 1931 near the site of the original Washington home. Here in the peace and beauty of this place untouched by time, the staunch character of our hero comes to the imagination.

In time, Frank Armstrong, III learned the family business inside and out. After college, he worked in every aspect of the business at one time or another to gain insight for management. As business and world economics changed, Frank III expanded the company's product line to offer new products and locations beyond Virginia's borders. Today, instead of local apple companies as the competition, White House (National Fruit) competitors are large corporations nationwide.

National Fruit Product Company is one of the largest apples growers in the United States. During peak season, more than 100,000 bushels of apples are delivered to the Winchester plant in a day. Careful monitoring of the quality and traditions set by the Armstrong family is now the focus of Frank Armstrong IV, the fourth generation Armstrong to run the company.

The company now boasts such products as applesauce, apple juice, apple cider, apple butter, apple cider vinegar, and white distilled vinegar for families throughout the southeastern United States. This Virginia company has come a long way from horse-drawn deliveries to 1600 Pennsylvania Avenue!

Ginger's Lemon Sugar Cookies

$1/2$ cup butter-flavor shortening, such as Crisco	1 tablespoon milk
$3/4$ cup sugar	$1^1/4$ cups flour
1 egg	$1/8$ teaspoon salt
1 tablespoon lemon extract	$1/4$ teaspoon baking powder

• Preheat the oven to 350°F. Beat the shortening in a large bowl until creamy, and add the sugar gradually. Beat until light and fluffy. Add the egg, lemon extract, and milk, and beat well. Add the flour, salt, and baking powder, and blend well. Drop by teaspoonfuls onto buttered cookie sheets. Bake for 12 to 15 minutes or until lightly browned. Remove to a wire rack to cool.
• Makes 45 to 55 cookies

Ginger Hill Bed and Breakfast is a country home located on fourteen and a half wooded acres in central Virginia, with a walking path, fishing pond, beaver ponds, and lots of wildlife. It is convenient to Charlottesville, Richmond, Lake Anna, and Fredericksburg. Many Civil War sites, other historical sites, and recreational areas are nearby. The innkeeper is GINGER ELLIS, who shared this recipe.

Harris Family's
Welsh Cookies

1 cup shortening	$7^1/2$ cups all-purpose flour
1 cup (2 sticks) butter or margarine	1 teaspoon each salt, nutmeg, cream of tartar, and baking soda
2 cups sugar	
3 eggs, beaten	2 teaspoons baking powder
$1/4$ cup milk	1 pound currants

• Beat the shortening, butter or margarine, and sugar in a large bowl until creamy. Add the eggs and milk, and mix well. Combine the flour, salt, nutmeg, cream of tartar, baking soda, and baking powder in a separate bowl, and mix well. Add to the creamed mixture, beating well. Stir in the currants. Roll the dough out onto a lightly floured board to about $1/4$-inch thickness, and cut into circles with a juice glass or biscuit cutter. Bake on an ungreased griddle over low heat until lightly browned, turning once.
• Makes 100 or more cookies

From the Harris family recipes, sent by KATHERINE HARRIS KLEMMER of Fairfax Station, Virginia. She is a member of the Providence Chapter of the DAR.

JEFFERSON IN RETIREMENT

Retirement from the presidency did not dull Thomas Jefferson's quick wit and his mastery for government. An example of his far-thinking philosophy, even in his senior years, can be seen in a letter written from Monticello on March 22, 1812. In the epistle, Jefferson suggested that *The only...object of... government is to secure the greatest degree of happiness possible to the general mass of those associated under it....[and] unless the mass retains sufficient control over those entrusted with the powers of their government, these will be perverted to their own oppression, and to the perpetuation of wealth and power in the individuals and their families selected for the trust. Whether our Constitution has hit on the exact degree of control necessary, is yet under experiment.*

MRS. JAMES MONROE'S SYRUP OF ROSES

Infuse three damask rose leaves in a gallon of warm water in a well-glazed earthen pot with a narrow mouth for eight hours. Stop so close that none of the virtue may exhale. When they have infused so long, heat the water again, squeeze them out, and put in three pounds more of rose leaves to infuse for eight hours more; then press them out very hard. To every quart of this infused, add four pounds of sugar and boil to a syrup.

MRS. JAMES MONROE'S
Waverly Jumbles

1 cup (2 sticks) butter	¹/₂ teaspoon nutmeg
2 cups firmly packed light brown sugar	2 tablespoons rosewater or 2 teaspoons vanilla extract
2 eggs	4 cups flour

- Preheat the oven to 350°F. Beat the butter and sugar in a large bowl until light and fluffy. Add the eggs, nutmeg, and rosewater or vanilla, and mix well. Stir in the flour. Chill the dough, covered, in the refrigerator for 1 hour or longer.
- Pinch off pieces of dough and roll into ropes. Join the ends of each rope to form a ring shape. Place on cookie sheets, and bake for 10 to 12 minutes.
- Makes about 5 dozen

The original recipe reads, One pound of flour; one-half pound of butter; three-fourths pound of brown sugar; two eggs; one-half teaspoon of nutmeg; two tablespoons of rosewater. Roll out long and cut into strips; join into rings and bake. *Rosewater was the preferred flavor for baked goods in the 18th century and well into the 19th century when vanilla became the most popular flavoring.*

Recipe submitted by CAROLYN HOLMES, Director, Ashlawn-Highland from *Monroe Family Recipes*, Judith E. Kosnik, editor, published by Ashlawn-Highland, October 1988.

ROCKBRIDGE COUNTY

Rockbridge County, named for the famous Natural Bridge located here, was formed in 1778 from Augusta and Botetourt Counties. Containing six hundred sixteen square miles, its population is 20,808, and the county seat is Lexington.

Sam Houston (1793-1863) and Cyrus McCormick (1809-1884) were born in this county, and Robert E. Lee (1807-1870) and Stonewall Jackson (1824-1863) are buried here. The noted educational institutions Virginia Military Institute and Washington and Lee University are located here, as well.

ROCKINGHAM COUNTY

Rockingham County was name for the Marquis of Rockingham, a British statesman. Organized in 1778 from Augusta County, it contains eight hundred seventy-six square miles and has a population of 67,725. The county seat is Harrisonburg.

Tennessee's first governor, John Sevier (1745-1815), was born here, as was Thomas Lincoln, father of President Abraham Lincoln. Dr. Jesse Bennett performed the first successful Caesarian section in America in this county in 1794.

Pies

Apple Pie with Cheese Crust

2 cups all-purpose flour	7 to 8 medium apples
1/2 teaspoon plus 1/4 teaspoon salt	2/3 cups sugar
1 1/2 cups finely grated extra-sharp cheddar cheese	2 tablespoons cornstarch
	1/2 teaspoon cinnamon
	1/4 teaspoon nutmeg
2/3 cup shortening	3 tablespoons butter or margarine
1/3 cup ice water	

- Combine the flour and 1/2 teaspoon of the salt in a large bowl. Cut in the cheese and shortening with a pastry blender or 2 knives until the mixture resembles coarse meal. Add enough of the ice water to moisten the mixture. Shape into a ball, and chill, covered, for 30 minutes.
- Preheat the oven to 450°F. Peel, core, and slice the apples into a bowl. There should be about 7 cups. Combine the sugar, remaining salt, and cornstarch in a bowl, and mix well. Sift over the apples, and toss to coat well. Sprinkle with the cinnamon and nutmeg.
- Cut the dough into 2 equal portions. Roll out 1 portion of the dough, and fit into a 9-inch pie plate. Arrange the apple slices in layers over the crust. Dot the top with the butter or margarine. Roll out the remaining dough, and cover the pie, cutting a few vents in the top for steam to escape. Bake for 10 minutes. Reduce the oven temperature to 350°F. Bake for 45 minutes longer or until the apple slices are tender but not mushy. Cool slightly before serving.
- Makes 8 to 10 servings

This recipe is an easy and wonderful apple pie especially well suited to the fall and winter months when tart apples, such as Granny Smith or Braeburn, are most fresh and abundant. The cheddar cheese in the crust is a surprising and tasty treat. Tom and I look forward to sharing this apple pie with friends when the leaves begin to turn and the air starts getting crisp.

This recipe is from TERRI SUIT. Terri is a young woman of uncommon energy and courage, a wife and mortgage loan officer, who in the year 2000 was elected to the Virginia House of Delegates, 81st District. She represents parts of the cities of Virginia Beach and Chesapeake.

RUSSELL COUNTY

Russell County was formed in 1786 from part of Washington County. It was named in honor of General William Russell, a Revolutionary War veteran. It contains four hundred ninety-six square miles. Its population is 30,308, and the county seat is Lebanon.

Several defensive works were built in this county during the late 1700s, including Glade Hollow, Elk Garden, and Russell's Forts. Among the early settlers in the region were Isaiah, John Benjamin, and Zachariah Salyer.

Brown Sugar Pie

3 large eggs
2 cups firmly packed brown
  sugar
1/2 cup (1 stick) salted
  butter, melted

1 (9-inch) frozen deep-dish
  piecrust
1/3 cup large pecan halves
  for decorating

- Preheat the oven to 350°F. Beat the eggs with the brown sugar in a large bowl just until blended. Add the butter, and beat until creamy. Pour into the piecrust. Bake for 10 minutes or until a slight crust forms over the surface of the pie filling. Decorate the surface of the pie with the pecan halves. Bake for about 35 minutes or until the filling puffs up. The filling will settle when cool.
- Note: Baking the pie before decorating with the pecan halves prevents them from sinking into the filling.
- Makes 8 to 10 servings

This is a family favorite and appears on every Thanksgiving and Christmas menu. Enjoy!

Virginia's Finest

ANGELA BARKSDALE and MARGERY WRIGHT established The Added Touch in 1981. Becoming a licensee for Colonial Williamsburg was exciting for them with the creation of some recipes for Wassail, Mint Julep, and Syllabub. They sell gourmet blends of herbs and spices in special gift packaging.

Lemon Chess Pie

3 cups sugar
2 tablespoons all-purpose
  flour
2 tablespoons white
  cornmeal
6 eggs

Juice of 2 lemons
1/3 cup butter or margarine
1/2 cup milk
1/4 cup grated lemon rind
2 unbaked (9-inch) pie
  shells, chilled

- Preheat the oven to 450°F. Combine the sugar, flour, and cornmeal in a large bowl, and mix well. Add the eggs, lemon juice, butter or margarine, milk, and lemon rind, and mix well. Pour into the pie shells, and bake for 10 minutes. Reduce the oven temperature to 375°F, and bake for 35 minutes longer.
- Makes 8 to 10 servings

This church pie recipe is shared by MARGUERITE GORDON DIERAUF, Regent, Shadwell Chapter of the Virginia DAR in Charlottesville, Virginia. It is from *Good Eating From Willis Gordon, Garnett Country Kitchens*. It is an old family favorite and is always found at family reunions. The pies are sometimes called church pies because they are thin, can easily be eaten with fingers, and show up at church picnics.

FUN FACTS IN HISTORY

Check out some of these facts from the 1500s and 1600s, which explain many of the sayings we have heard all our lives.

My father, Em Stanley, always said, "Sleep tight! Don't let the bed bugs bite," every time he kissed us good-night as children and even as adults. And for many years, I never understood what it meant. But now I do! In the early days, beds had ropes instead of box springs to support the mattress. These ropes would work loose and have to be tightened during the night so you wouldn't end up on the floor. Hence, "Sleep tight." The mattresses were made of straw and, of course, contained vermin—so it was important to say, "Don't let the bed bugs bite."

Most floors were made of dirt; only the wealthy could afford true flooring. Therefore, the saying "dirt poor" became popular.

Most couples got married in June because as the weather warmed up, they would take their yearly bath and thus be ready and presentable. If the wedding was delayed, the brides would carry a bouquet of nosegay flowers to hide any body odor.

—Rowena

GERMAN-AMERICAN ENGLISH

In today's hurried and complex world, it seems that the annual influx—legal and illegal—of tens of thousands of immigrants to the United States is placing an almost impossible task upon educators and administrators. The dilemma, of course, is which language should the newly-arrived people primarily use in their new home, English or their native tongue? Back in the days when German emigration to America was in its prime, the same problem existed. As early as 1794, recently arrived German farmers in Virginia requested from the U.S. Congress that they be provided German-language information about the laws of their adopted home. Frederick Augustus Conrad Muhlenberg, the reigning speaker of the House of Representatives, disappointed his fellow countrymen when he refused their request, stating instead that they should learn English as rapidly as possible to become better Americans. Still, in the U.S., as late as 1980, more than fifty newspapers and other periodicals were published in German serving nearly three hundred thousand German-speaking subscribers.

DOCTOR BALL'S
Chocolate Pie

3 tablespoons butter or margarine	2 squares unsweetened chocolate
1 cup sugar	1 teaspoon vanilla extract
1/2 cup all-purpose flour	1 baked (8-inch) pie shell
1 egg, beaten	Sweetened whipped cream
1 1/4 cups milk	or whipped topping

- Beat the butter or margarine in a medium bowl, and add the sugar and flour, beating until creamy. Combine the egg and milk in a bowl, and mix well. Add to the creamed mixture, and beat until well mixed.
- Break up the chocolate squares, and add to the creamed mixture. Pour into a double boiler, and cook until smooth and thickened, stirring constantly. Remove from the heat, and stir in the vanilla extract. Pour into the pie shell. Chill in the refrigerator. Top with sweetened whipped cream or whipped topping before serving.
- Makes 8 servings

Years ago Doctor Ball was a professor of English at the University of Richmond. Over the years, and one by one, his colleagues received a recipe as the seal of his admiration.

This one was shared by MRS. JAMES P. COX, JR., member of the Mount Vernon Chapter of the Virginia DAR.

SCOTT COUNTY

Scott County was organized in 1814 from Lee, Washington, and Russell Counties. Named in honor of General Winfield Scott, it contains five hundred forty-three square miles and has a population of 23,403. The county seat is Gate City.

Daniel Boone cut a road to Kentucky through Big Moccasin Gap in this region in 1775. Defense against Indians was important business to the county's early settlers, and several forts were erected throughout the area.

SHENANDOAH COUNTY

Renamed for the Shenandoah River in 1778, Shenandoah County was originally called Dunmore County when it was first formed in 1772 from Frederick County. It contains five hundred ten square miles and has a population of 35,075. The county seat is Woodstock.

The Battle of New Market was fought in this county on May 15, 1864, where the cadets from Virginia Military Institute distinguished themselves in combat. Confederate General Jubal Early and Union General Phil Sheridan matched wits here at the Battle of Fisher's Hill on September 22, 1864.

THE WILLIAMSBURG WINERY
Raspberry Chocolate Pie

FILLING

3 egg yolks
1 (14-ounce) can chocolate
  sweetened condensed milk
1 (10-ounce) package frozen
  whole raspberries in syrup,
  thawed

3 ounces Dominion Wine
  Cellars Raspberry Merlot,
  optional
1 (9-inch) chocolate
  graham cracker or Oreo
  piecrust

TOPPING

1 cup heavy cream
3 tablespoons confectioners'
  sugar

Semisweet chocolate
  sprinkles, optional

- To prepare the filling, preheat the oven to 350°F. Combine the egg yolks and sweetened condensed milk in a bowl. Beat at high speed for approximately 5 minutes or until light and fluffy. Beat in the raspberries and Merlot, if desired, gradually. (If Raspberry Merlot is used, drain the thawed raspberries.) Pour into the piecrust. Bake for 6 to 8 minutes or until the filling is firm. Remove from the oven, and cool to room temperature. Refrigerate for 4 hours.
- To prepare the topping, beat the cream in a chilled bowl until soft peaks form. Add the confectioners' sugar, and beat until stiff peaks form. Chill in the refrigerator.
- To serve, spread the topping over the pie, and garnish with chocolate sprinkles, if desired.
- Note: Serve within 1 hour of adding the topping for best results. Serve with Dominion Wine Cellars Raspberry Merlot.
- Makes 8 servings

Virginia's Finest

In the late 1970s, Patrick G. Duffeler became involved in the wine industry in Burgundy, France, and developed relationships with Burgundian and other French producers. In 1983 he and his wife, Peggy, purchased a 300-acre farm in Williamsburg and then founded The Williamsburg Winery, an operation which has grown to become the largest winery in Virginia and a well-respected producer of premium wines. This is an original recipe from his son, J. PATRICK MIFFLETON, the retail manager for the Williamsburg Winery.

SMYTH COUNTY

Smyth County, named in honor of General Alexander Smyth, was created in 1832 from Wythe and Washington Counties. It contains four hundred thirty-five square miles and has a population of 33,081. The county seat is Marion.

In 1750, Samuel Stalnaker built a log cabin in the area that would become Smyth County. At the time, the cabin was the westernmost building in Virginia. Author Sherwood Anderson lived in this county from 1925 until his death in 1941.

THE QUEEN'S ENGLISH

Even today, in the remote nooks and crannies of the Blue Ridge and Allegheny Mountains of Virginia, one can still hear evidences of the times when Queen Elizabeth's swashbuckling adventurers, such as Sir Walter Raleigh, scoured America's coastline for suitable settlement sites. Raleigh, of course, was directly responsible for the ill-fated colonization of Roanoke Island in 1585, in today's North Carolina. By the time the Jamestown settlers arrived in present-day Virginia in 1607, James I had succeeded Elizabeth to the throne, but Elizabethan English was still the rage in the homeland.

Here are a few words, still used today, that at first sight appear "hillbilly" or "country." Actually, if we transported ourselves back in time four centuries, these same words would be universally accepted in England and on the Continent.

Arn—Iron (The marker is made from wrought arn). Also, the tool with which one presses clothes (I don't like to arn my shirts).

Ast— Asked; to interrogate (I ast him if I could go with him).

Barn—Born (She was barn on October 2).

Blowed—Blown or Blew (The wind blowed off the tree branches).

Cheer—Chair (That cheer doesn't fit well under the table).

Drap—Drop (If you're not careful, you'll drap those dishes).

Fitten—Fit (That spoiled meat isn't fitten to eat).

Git—Get (He's going to git that chocolate all over his face).

Git shet uv—To dispose of (I'll git shet uv this book after I read it.)

Hit—It (She knew that was hit when she first saw hit).

Jine—Join (John's boys are going to jine the Scouts).

Learn—Teach (If I had the time, I would learn you how to cook).

Nary—None (There's nary a drop of water in that bucket).

Recken—Believe (I recken I'll help Sam build his house).

Salet—Salad or greens (That poke salet should was good).

Smidgen—A small quantity (It doesn't take but a smidgen of salt).

Sky High Coconut Cream Pie

³/₄ cup sugar
¹/₄ cup cornstarch
Dash of salt
2 cups whole milk
5 extra-large eggs
1 tablespoon butter or margarine

1 teaspoon vanilla extract
¹/₂ cup flaked coconut
1 (9-inch) deep-dish pastry shell
Additional flaked coconut for sprinkling

- Preheat the oven to 350°F. Combine ¹/₂ cup of the sugar, cornstarch, and salt in a heavy medium saucepan, and mix well. Stir in the milk. Cook over low heat until the mixture thickens and comes to a boil, stirring constantly. Separate the eggs into 4 egg yolks and 5 egg whites into 2 medium bowls, discarding the extra yolk. Beat the egg yolks well, and stir in ¹/₂ cup of the hot mixture gradually. Add the beaten egg yolks to the hot mixture. Cook for 1 minute, stirring constantly. Remove from the heat. Stir in the butter or margarine, vanilla extract, and coconut. Pour into the pastry shell.
- Beat the egg whites until foamy, and add the remaining sugar gradually, beating until stiff peaks form. Spoon over the filling. Seal the edges, and swirl into peaks. Sprinkle with the remaining coconut. Bake for 12 minutes or until the meringue is toasty brown. Cool on a wire rack for at least 5 hours before cutting.
- Makes 8 to 10 servings

This is a very hard recipe to find, but it has been worth the search.

This is from the collection of PHYLLIS WITCHER, who is always trying new recipes.

SOUTHAMPTON COUNTY

Southampton County was formed in 1748 from Isle of Wight County, with a section of the now extinct county of Nansemond added later. It was most likely named after Southampton, England. It contains six hundred four square miles and has a population of 17,482. The county seat is Courtland.

Nat Turner's slave revolt, in which sixty people were murdered, occurred in this county in 1831. General George Thomas (1816-1870), "The Rock of Chickamauga," was born hear Courtland.

DID YOU KNOW THAT:

After his prodigious service to Queen Elizabeth and his great influence upon the settling of Virginia, Sir Walter Ralegh (or Raleigh), was finally beheaded in London in 1618 at the hands of King James I?

JENNIE McDAVID'S
Cushaw Pie

1 cup mashed cooked
  cushaw
1 cup evaporated milk
2 eggs
1 cup firmly packed brown
  sugar
1 tablespoon cornstarch or
  flour

Dash of salt
1/4 teaspoon cinnamon
1/4 teaspoon nutmeg
1 unbaked (9-inch)
  deep-dish pie shell

- Preheat the oven to 450°F. Combine the cushaw, milk, and eggs in a large bowl, and mix well. Add the sugar, cornstarch or flour, salt, cinnamon, and nutmeg, and beat well. Pour into the pie shell.
- Bake for 10 minutes, and reduce the oven temperature to 325°F. Bake for 40 minutes longer.
- Makes 6 to 8 servings

Cushaw is an edible gourd that stores well in the winter. They have been grown throughout the Appalachian mountain region since pioneer times. Cushaws may be purchased in most grocery stores today.

This recipe was sent by MARY MCDAVID WINEGAR of the Carter's Fort Chapter of the Virginia DAR in Scott County.

SEVIER FAMILY
One-Hundred-Fifty-Year-Old Lemon Pie

1/2 cup (1 stick) butter
2 cups sugar
3 soda crackers, finely
  rolled, sifted

Juice and rind of 2 lemons
6 whole eggs, well beaten
2 unbaked pie shells

- Preheat the oven to 375°F. Cream the butter and sugar thoroughly. Add the cracker crumbs. Add the lemon juice and rind. Blend well until smooth. Add the eggs, and blend well. Pour the mixture into the pie shells, and bake from 35 to 40 minutes.
- Makes 2 small pies

Reprinted from *Miss Daisy Celebrates Tennessee*, ©1995 by Daisy King, James A. Crutchfield, and Winette Sparkman, with permission.

John Sevier, originally from an old Virginia family, later became governor of the Lost State of Franklin, in Tennessee. The (then) 16th state only officially existed from 1784- 1788.

OLD ENGLISH RECIPES

These recipes are in Old English. When reading them, please substitute "s" for most "f". An example of this is "fugar," which means "sugar". Fun to read, so enjoy!

TO MAKE A MINCE PYE WITHOUT MEAT: Chop fine three pounds of fuet, and three pounds of apples, when pared and cored, wafh and dry three pounds of currants, ftone and chop one pound of jar raifins, beat and fift one pound and a half of loaf fugar, cut fmall twelve ounces of candied orange peel, and fix ounces of citron, mix all well together with a quarter of an ounce of nutmeg, half a quarter of an ounce of cinnamon, fix or eight cloves, and half a pint of French brandy, pot it clofe up, and keep it for ufe.

TO MAKE A SOLID SYLLABUB: Take a quart of rich cream, and put in a pint of white wine, the juice of four lemons, and fugar to your tafte, whip it up very well and take off the froth as it rifes, put it upon a hair fieve, and let ftand till the next day in a cool place, fill your glaffes better than half full with the thin, then put on the froth, and heap it as high as you can, the bottom will look clear, and keep feveral days.

These recipes are from the historic Willoughby-Baylor House in downtown Norfolk. It offers visitors a gracious view of a middle-class family lifestyle of late 18th century Norfolk. In 1636, twenty-six years after he arrived in the New World, Thomas Willoughby was granted 200 acres of land, including that on which his descendants' home now stands. The parcel passed through several owners following Willoughby's death until part of it became the city of Norfolk in 1682.Thomas Willoughby's descendant William, owner of a prosperous construction business, purchased the lot and brought it back into the family in 1794. You will see two recipes from *The Experienced English House-Keeper* by Elizabeth Raffald, published in Dublin in the 1790s, that were likely used by the family at that time. His granddaughter, Elizabeth Sharp Baylor, inherited the house after her father's death in 1871, and it served as her family's home until 1890. The Willoughby-Baylor House now takes its name from these two families.

Osgood Pie

2 cups sugar	1 teaspoon ground cloves
1 tablespoon butter or margarine	4 egg whites, stiffly beaten
4 egg yolks, lightly beaten	1 cup chopped pecans
3 teaspoons vinegar	1 cup raisins
1 teaspoon cinnamon	2 unbaked (9-inch) pie shells

- Preheat the oven to 300°F. Beat the sugar, butter or margarine, and egg yolks in a large bowl until well mixed. Stir in the vinegar, cinnamon, and cloves. Fold in the stiffly beaten egg whites. Add the pecans and raisins, and mix well. Pour into the pie shells, and bake for 30 to 45 minutes.
- Makes 16 servings

This pie was in my mother's family for many years. At all Thanksgiving and Christmas dinner celebrations, my mom, Maxine Fitch, would bake and serve these. We all enjoyed them and expected these pies as part of the holiday tradition. They were one of my dad's special favorites. I have no idea where the peculiar name came from.

The recipe is from the family of BETSY BENTON, a very special teacher and friend in Norfolk, Virginia.

The Henry Clay Inn

Peanut Butter Pie

$^1/_2$ cup creamy peanut butter	2 cups sugar
1 (8-ounce) package cream cheese, softened	8 ounces whipped topping, such as Cool Whip
$^1/_4$ cup milk	1 baked (9-inch) piecrust

- Blend the peanut butter, cream cheese, milk, and sugar in a large bowl. Fold in the whipped topping gently. Spoon into the piecrust, and chill for at least 4 hours.
- Makes 8 to 10 servings

This is a favorite family recipe. It is very quick and easy to make and quite tasty.

This came from THE HENRY CLAY INN, a charming country inn with massive white columns and a generous porch on which to enjoy a summer breeze. It is located in historic downtown Ashland, Virginia, tucked away just minutes from bustling I-95. The inn is a stunning replica of the original 1906 Georgian Revival-style building destroyed by fire in 1946. Every detail speaks of authenticity, but it hasn't forsaken modern amenities. It has fourteen guest rooms, a restaurant, meeting/reception/banquet facilities, and an art and gift gallery.

THE BELLE GRAE INN
Chocolate Peanut Butter Pie

PIE

1¹/₂ cups confectioners'
  sugar
¹/₂ cup creamy peanut
  butter

¹/₄ cup (¹/₂ stick) butter or
  margarine, melted
1 baked (9-inch) piecrust,
  cooled

FILLING

1¹/₂ ounces unsweetened
  chocolate
1 tablespoon butter or
  margarine
2 cups scalded milk
1 cup sugar

3 egg yolks, beaten
2 to 3 tablespoons
  cornstarch
¹/₃ cup milk
¹/₂ teaspoon vanilla extract
Whipped cream

- To prepare the pie, combine the confectioners' sugar, peanut butter, and butter or margarine in a bowl with a pastry blender until crumbly. Sprinkle over the bottom of the piecrust, reserving some for the garnish.
- To prepare the filling, melt the chocolate and butter or margarine in a double boiler over gently simmering water. Add the scalded milk, and blend until smooth. Whisk in the sugar, stirring until dissolved. Stir in the egg yolks. Add a mixture of the cornstarch and remaining milk, and cook for about 20 minutes or until thickened, stirring constantly. Remove from the heat. Blend in the vanilla extract. Let stand until room temperature, stirring frequently. Pour the mixture into the prepared crust. Refrigerate until set. Top with whipped cream, and sprinkle with the reserved peanut butter mixture.
- Makes 8 to 10 servings

Chocolate Peanut Butter Pie is offered courtesy of MR. KEN HICKS, owner of The Belle Grae Inn. He was enticed to do so by Carolyn D. Bell, Regent of the Beverly Manor Chapter of the Virginia DAR of Staunton, who is proud of the Belle Grae Inn, located in the heart of Staunton, as among the best inns in the Queen City of the Shenandoah Valley. Staunton is the first Virginia city recognized and honored with the designation of "Great American Cities" award by the National Trust for Historic Preservation. The Belle Grae Inn is a memorable experience as Historic Staunton's Premier Country Inn in a neighborhood of thirteen restored, turn-of-the-century, Victorian homes dating from 1870 to the early 1900s.

DID YOU KNOW THAT:

Virginia Military Institute at Lexington, often referred to as the "West Point of the South," is the oldest state-supported military college in the United States? Such notables as Matthew Fontaine Maury and Thomas J. "Stonewall" Jackson, both native-born Virginians, taught there, and among its alumni is five-star General George C. Marshall, of World War II fame.

SURVEYOR, MAPMAKER, LAND SPECULATOR

In 1760, King George III inherited the British crown from his father, George II. One of the first official acts promulgated by the new king was the issue—on October 7, 1763—of his so-called "Proclamation." The Proclamation of 1763 prohibited the settlement by American colonists of any land west of a line that stretched north and south along the crest of the Appalachian Mountains. Even before the act became law, however, settlers were already clamoring across the mountains to stake their claims on the rich land that lay beyond. One of these eager colonists was a young George Washington, who early in his career was a surveyor and mapmaker. Washington issued instructions to his land agent "to secure some of the most valuable lands in the King's part...notwithstanding the proclamation that...prohibits the settling of them at all."

FUN FACTS
IN HISTORY

Bathing in hot water was a special privilege. The men of the household bathed first, then the women, and finally the babies. By this time, the water was so dirty you could almost lose someone in it—hence the saying "Don't throw out the baby with the bath water."

Houses had thatched roofs made of thick straw. In many cases, it was the only place where dogs, cats, and other animals could get warm. But when it rained, it often became slippery. Animals could be seen slipping off the roof—hence the saying "Raining cats and dogs."

SURREY HOUSE
Peanut Raisin Pie

3 eggs
1 cup sugar
1/4 cup firmly packed brown sugar
1/4 cup (1/2 stick) butter or margarine, softened
1 tablespoon vanilla extract
1 tablespoon cider vinegar
1/2 cup dark corn syrup
1 1/4 cups ground roasted peanuts
3/4 cup raisins
1 unbaked (9 or 10-inch) piecrust

- Preheat the oven to 325°F. Combine the eggs, sugar, brown sugar, and butter or margarine in a large bowl, and mix well. Add the vanilla extract, vinegar, and corn syrup, and mix well. Fold in the peanuts and raisins. Spoon into the piecrust.
- Bake for approximately 35 minutes or until the pie wiggles, but does not slosh. Let stand for 1 hour.
- Makes 8 to 10 servings

THE SURREY HOUSE RESTAURANT AND COUNTRY INN gave us this recipe. It has been serving visitors to the south side of the James River since 1954. It is a true Virginia landmark.

Chocolate Pecan Pie

4 eggs
3/4 cup sugar
1/4 cup firmly packed brown sugar
1 teaspoon vanilla extract
2 tablespoons bourbon
1 cup white corn syrup
1/2 cup (1 stick) butter or margarine, melted
1 tablespoon all-purpose flour
1 cup chopped pecans
1 cup chocolate chips
1 unbaked (10-inch) pie shell

- Preheat the oven to 350°F. Beat the eggs in a large bowl. Add the sugar, brown sugar, vanilla extract, bourbon, corn syrup, butter or margarine, and flour, and mix well. Sprinkle the pecans and chocolate chips over the bottom of the pie shell. Pour the filling into the prepared pie shell. Bake for 45 minutes. Garnish with whipped cream.
- Makes 8 to 10 servings

I have the honor of serving as Congressman for the Seventh District of Virginia, a seat once held by former President James Madison. I hope you enjoy this recipe as much as my family and friends do.

This recipe was sent by CONGRESSMAN ERIC CANTOR.

Highland Inn

"Pride of the Mountains Since 1904"

Famous Maple Pecan Pie

$^1/_2$ cup light corn syrup
$^1/_2$ cup pure maple syrup
1 tablespoon cornstarch
3 eggs

1 cup firmly packed brown
  sugar
1 cup pecans
1 unbaked (9-inch) pie shell

- Preheat the oven to 350°F. Combine the corn syrup, maple syrup, cornstarch, eggs, and brown sugar in a large bowl, and mix until well blended. Sprinkle the pecans into the pie shell. Pour the filling over the pecans, and bake for 1 hour.
- Makes 8 servings

The recipe is shared by GREGG and DEBORAH MORSE, owners of The Highland Inn, which is nestled in the foothills of the Allegheny Mountains. The quaint, picturesque village of Monterey is the county seat and is fondly referred to as "Virginia's Switzerland." The inn, a grand Victorian structure, was built in 1904, is listed on the National Register of Historic Places, and is a Virginia Historic Landmark. Meals are served in the main dining room, which features continental American cuisine.

LEWIS AND CLARK'S VOYAGE OF DISCOVERY

Although Virginia is just about as far east in the United States as you can get, if it had not been for three of the Commonwealth's most eminent sons, our present-day knowledge of the American West would be much lacking. Long before he became the U. S. president in 1801, Thomas Jefferson had dreamed of an expanded American empire poised west of the Mississippi River. In early 1803, in order to learn more about what secrets that vast territory held, Jefferson quickly persuaded Congress to appropriate funds for an exploration that would take its members all the way to the Pacific Ocean. The American purchase of the 828,000-square-mile Louisiana Territory from France in April, 1803, only served to redouble Jefferson's determination to fulfill his long-held ambitions.

The man the President chose to lead the expedition was Meriwether Lewis, his personal secretary and a close neighbor. Lewis, in turn, prevailed upon his friend and one-time army commander,

William Clark, to share in the expedition's planning and responsibilities. In May, 1804, after close to a year of planning and supply and equipment gathering, the Lewis and Clark Expedition, sometimes called the "Voyage of Discovery," pushed off from the St. Louis waterfront on its way up the mighty Missouri River. Before it was over twenty-eight months later, the journey would carry the expedition's forty-two-member crew eight thousand miles to the mouth of the Columbia River and back again. Amazingly, during the entire trip, only one man died and that was from an attack of appendicitis.

The Lewis and Clark Expedition was the precursor to the opening of the American West. The exploration party had hardly returned to St. Louis in 1806, before fur entrepreneurs were sending bands of trappers to the headwaters of the Missouri River in search of beaver. Although Lewis did not live long enough following his successful journey to witness the exploitation of the spacious land he had helped chart (he either committed suicide or was murdered in Tennessee in 1809), his partner in discovery, William Clark, lived a long life, eventually serving as governor of the Missouri Territory, a region that included much of the land he had earlier explored.

GREGORY'S
Derby Pie

3/4 cup (1 1/2 sticks) butter or margarine, melted	1 teaspoon vanilla extract
3/4 cup sugar	3/4 cup chopped pecans
3/4 cup light corn syrup	1/2 cup chocolate chips
3 eggs	1 unbaked (9-inch) pie shell
	Whipped cream

- Preheat the oven to 350°F. Beat the butter or margarine and sugar in a large bowl until creamy. Add the corn syrup, eggs, and vanilla extract, and beat well. Stir in the pecans and chocolate chips.
- Pour the mixture into the pie shell, and bake for 1 hour. Serve warm topped with whipped cream. Enjoy!
- Makes 8 to 10 servings

This is one of our favorite desserts. It is a recipe so old we no longer can remember who Gregory is, but his Derby Pie is terrific.

FANN and BILLIE GREER, two of the most fun, but dedicated, people I know shared this recipe. Billie Greer is the president of Virginia Wesleyan College, a four-year, liberal arts institution located on a wooded, 300-acre campus astride the Norfolk/Virginia Beach border. Many of the 5,700 graduates remain in Virginia and are contributors to the professions, the arts, and the business community. —Rowena

Prune Pie

1/4 cup (1/2 stick) butter or margarine	1 1/2 cups chopped prunes
1 cup sugar	1 1/2 cups milk
3 eggs	1/2 teaspoon vanilla extract
2 tablespoons all-purpose flour	1/8 teaspoon salt
	1 unbaked (9-inch) pie shell

- Preheat the oven to 350°F. Blend the butter and sugar in a large bowl. Add the eggs, flour, prunes, milk, vanilla extract, and salt, and mix well. Spoon into the pie shell, and bake for 50 minutes.
- Note: Do not chop the prunes in a food processor.
- Makes 8 to 10 servings

This is a recipe of Virginia Bonner Hoolser Oden, affectionately known as Mother Oden, and shared by her granddaughter, DR. CATHERINE ODEN FULTON, a member of the Old Donation/Borough of Norfolk Chapter of the Virginia DAR. It originated with Mother Oden's mother, Virginia Bonner, who was born in 1864 and married Walter Hooker in 1883. Mother Oden's Prune Pie is served every Thanksgiving and Christmas at Oden family gatherings. If you decide to serve the pie, don't tell your guests what they are eating until after they have asked for a second slice. Otherwise, they might turn their noses up at this delicious dessert.

CONGRESSMAN ED AND JUDY SHROCK'S
Mile High Strawberry Pie

1 (10-ounce) package frozen
strawberries, thawed
1 cup sugar
2 egg whites
1 tablespoon lemon juice
Dash of salt

$^1/_2$ cup heavy cream,
whipped
1 teaspoon vanilla extract
1 (10-inch) graham cracker
piecrust

- Combine the strawberries, sugar, egg whites, lemon juice, and salt in a large mixing bowl. Beat for 15 minutes or until stiff. Fold in the whipped cream and vanilla extract. Spoon into the piecrust, and freeze until firm.
- Makes 8 to 12 servings

This incredible taste treat was given to JUDY SHROCK by an aunt in Long Beach, California. The Schrocks always give this to friends and others who need food provided. For those who are ill, they become well instantly after a piece of this delicacy. Judy Schrock, teacher extraordinaire and wife of Congressman Ed Schrock, traveled extensively with her husband during his military career and now as Congressman for Virginia's Second District, where good food is served. Now retired, Judy has time to experiment with the many recipes she and her husband have collected since they were married in September 1967.

Sweet Potato Coconut Pie

2 cups mashed cooked sweet
potatoes
2 eggs
$^3/_4$ cup sugar
$^3/_4$ cup milk
$^1/_4$ cup ($^1/_2$ stick) butter or
margarine

$^1/_4$ teaspoon allspice
$^1/_8$ teaspoon nutmeg
$^1/_2$ cup flaked coconut
1 unbaked (9-inch) piecrust

- Preheat the oven to 375°F. Beat the sweet potatoes, eggs, sugar, milk, butter or margarine, allspice, and nutmeg in a large bowl at low speed until well blended. Stir in the coconut. Spoon into the piecrust. Bake for 35 to 45 minutes or until the crust is brown and a knife inserted in the center comes out clean.
- Makes 8 servings

This is Grandma Josephine Newton's recipe. She never used exact measurements of ingredients, but this is her approximation as told to my mother.

The recipe comes from the family of SHIRLEY WELLS of the Chancellor Wythe Chapter of the Virginia DAR.

EARLY ADVICE TO A VIRGINIA HOUSEWIFE

Professor George Tucker's introduction to Mrs. Randolph's *Virginia Housewife*, as reprinted in his granddaughter Mary Stuart Smith's *Virginia Cookery-Book*, copyright 1884 by Harper & Brothers.

Management is an art that may be acquired by every woman of good-sense and tolerable memory. If, unfortunately, she has been bred in a family where domestic business is the work of chance, she will have many difficulties to encounter, but a determined resolution to obtain this valuable knowledge will enable her to surmount all obstacles. She must begin the day with an early breakfast, requiring each person to be in readiness to take their seats when the muffins, buckwheat cakes, etc., are placed on the table ... No work can be done until breakfast is finished. The Virginia ladies, who are proverbially good managers, employ themselves, while their servants are eating, in washing the cups, glasses, etc., arranging the cruets, the mustard, salt-sellers, pickle-vases, and all the apparatus for the dinner-table ... Let all the articles intended for the dinner pass in review before her, have the butter, sugar, flour, meal, lard given out in proper quantities, the catsup, spice, wine, whatever may be wanted for each dish, measured to the cook ... There is economy as well as comfort in a regular mode of doing business.

The prosperity and happiness of a family depend greatly on the order and regularity established in it. The husband who can ask a friend to partake of his dinner in full confidence of finding his wife unruffled by the petty vexations attendant on the neglect of household duties ... will feel pride and exultation in the possession of a companion who gives to his home charms that gratify every wish of his soul and render the haunts of dissipation hateful to him. The sons bred in such a family will be moral men, of steady habits, and his daughters, if the mother shall have performed her duties of a parent in the superintendence of their education as faithfully as she has done those of a wife, will each be a treasure to her husband, and being formed on the model of an exemplary mother, will use the same means for securing the happiness of her own family which she has seen successfully practised under the parental roof.

Sweet Potato Pie

1 recipe pie pastry
1¹/₂ cups mashed canned
   sweet potatoes
²/₃ cup sugar
2 tablespoons (¹/₄ stick)
   unsalted butter, melted

¹/₂ teaspoon mace
¹/₂ teaspoon vanilla extract
¹/₂ teaspoon salt
2 tablespoons lemon juice
2 large eggs, lightly beaten
1 cup light cream

- Roll out the pastry to a ¹/₈-inch thickness on a floured surface. Fit into a 9-inch pie pan. Prick all over with a fork, and refrigerate, covered with plastic wrap, for 30 minutes.
- Preheat the oven to 425°F. Cover the pastry-lined pie pan with parchment paper or foil. Add pie weights, dried beans, or rice to prevent the pastry from puffing while baking. Bake the pastry for about 10 minutes or until lightly browned around the edges. Remove the weights and paper or foil carefully. Reduce the oven temperature to 375°F, and bake for 5 minutes longer or until the center of the pastry is white and dry. Remove from the oven, and cool.
- Combine the sweet potatoes and sugar in a large bowl, and mix well. Beat in the butter, mace, vanilla extract, salt, and lemon juice. Stir in the eggs and cream gradually until smooth. Pour into the pie shell, and bake for 35 to 40 minutes or until a wooden pick inserted in the center comes out clean. Cool before serving.
- Makes 8 servings

Serve this delicious Southern favorite with whipped cream, and sprinkle with mace. Mace is the dried membrane that surrounds a nutmeg seed. Along with clove, cinnamon, and nutmeg, Williamsburg cooks often used mace to flavor sweet dishes.

Thanks to SHIELD's TAVERN for sharing this recipe.

SPOTSYLVANIA COUNTY

Spotsylvania County was organized in 1720 from parts of Essex, King and Queen, and King William Counties. It was named in honor of Alexander Spotswood (1676-1740), who served as Virginia's lieutenant-governor (1710-1722). It contains four hundred thirteen square miles. The population is 90,395, and the county seat is Spotsylvania.

Numerous skirmishes and battles during the War Between the States occurred in this county, including the Battles of Chancellorsville, Fredericksburg, Spotsylvania, and part of the Wilderness. One of the Confederacy's most brilliant leaders, General "Stonewall" Jackson, died from wounds received from his own men at Chancellorsville.

Colonial Williamsburg

Pie Pastry

2 cups flour
1 teaspoon salt
2 tablespoons sugar, optional
1/3 cup chilled unsalted
   butter, cut into small
   pieces

1/3 cup chilled vegetable
   shortening or lard
1/3 cup (or more) ice water

- Sift the flour, salt, and sugar if using, together into a large bowl. Cut the butter and shortening into the flour mixture with 2 knives or a pastry blender until mixture resembles coarse meal. Or, combine the flour, salt, and sugar in a food processor, and process once or twice. Add the butter and shortening, and process for about 10 seconds or until the mixture resembles coarse meal. Remove to a large bowl.
- Make a well in the center of the mixture, and add the ice water. Stir quickly with a fork to form a soft dough. Add 1 to 2 tablespoons ice water if the dough appears to be too dry. Turn out the dough onto a floured work surface, and knead gently into a rough ball. Refrigerate, wrapped in plastic wrap, for at least 30 minutes.
- Note: The pastry dough can be made 1 day ahead.
- Makes enough for 1 single-crust 10-inch pie

Thanks to the COLONIAL WILLIAMSBURG INN for sharing this recipe.

STAFFORD COUNTY

Stafford County derives its name from Staffordshire, England, and was formed in 1664 from Westmoreland County. It contains two hundred seventy-four square miles. Its population is 92,446, and the county seat is Stafford.

Pocahontas was kidnapped by the English from a village in this region in 1612. The first English Roman Catholic settlement in Virginia was made here in 1647.

SURRY COUNTY

Surry County was formed in 1652 from James City County and named for Surry County, England. It contains two hundred seventy-eight square miles. The population is 6,829, and the county seat is Surry.

Bacon's Castle, which figured prominently in the Rebellion of 1676, is located in this county. The first automobile ferry service across the James River was inaugurated here in 1925.

More Desserts

Monticello

Travel back through time to walk with Thomas Jefferson where he greeted the mountain dawn, listened for the early morning laughter of his grandchildren, began his daily routines—pleased to be home again, back from his time in the White House. He is still, in his heart, the young red-headed man who had run the trails through the woods of Shadwell and grown into a learned scholar at William and Mary. He was the same young man who had fallen desperately in love with Martha Wayles Skelton, making her his Virginia bride, written the beloved words of a nation's independence, traveled on behalf of his country to France. Imagine him again, his long political life over, enjoying the view as he scanned the morning dew on his gardens and the Blue Ridge. What a morning—almost two hundred years ago!

The busy day at Monticello began about 8 a.m. with breakfast for the family and any guests in the house. It was the first of only two meals served each day. The menu was usually cold meats and hot breads, with bacon and eggs. Fried Virginia apples were always a favorite. "Batter-cakes" or the French *pannequaiques* were served, as well. In 1809, Margaret Bayard Smith reported, "Our breakfast table was as large as our dinner table . . . we had tea, coffee, excellent muffins, hot wheat and corn bread, cold ham and butter . . . . Here indeed was the mode of living in general [of] that of a Virginia planter." Jefferson's grandchildren (the Randolph children) were so well behaved, Smith said, that "you would not know, if you would not see them, that a child was present." Jefferson read while waiting for his family (numbering twelve in 1809) beside the white and blue dining room mantle. He sat on one of a pair of low French armchairs. His candle stand between the chairs always held a candlestick and a book or two.

After breakfast, the nation's third president retired to his quarters to attend to correspondence or research. Sometimes he walked out to the gardens with some of his grandchildren. By one in the afternoon, he rode a horse around his large plantation. Jefferson once said, "The whole of my life has been a war with my natural tastes, feelings, and wishes." But at Monticello, he felt at home.

Monticello's kitchen was one of the best equipped in all of Virginia. Jefferson had been left a widower early in life, and the household duties had fallen upon him until his daughters were of age to assist. After being a Minister to France for the United States, he had richly taken to the French cuisine and come home to "blend" it with standard Virginia fare from his upbringing. He stocked the kitchen with fine copper pots, unlimited utensils, and such foodstuffs as "macaroni, Parmesan cheese, figs of Marseilles, Brugnoles, raisins, mustard, almonds, vinaigre d'Esrtagon, other good vinegar, oil, and anchovies." He employed exquisite French chefs at times in Washington City and also at his beloved Monticello.

Through the years, as guests were taken with the hospitality at Monticello, they were duly intrigued with "new dishes" of fare. Ice cream was a curiosity at Monticello just as it had been when he had served it in the White House as small balls enclosed in cases of warm pastry. Mutton, pork, beef, and fish were served on a standard basis at his home. Through the years, James and Dolley Madison were frequent guests.

Monticello's elaborate thousand-foot-long terrace garden on the southeastern side of his "little mountain" overflowed with delights for the table—cabbages, radishes, beets, beans, carrots, turnips, kale, Jerusalem artichokes, apples, asparagus, peaches, figs, berries, and

nineteen varieties of his favorite food, English peas! He ardently enjoyed his community's annual "Early English Pea" contest. Oregano, basil, and other herbs were grown on the plantation, as well.

Jefferson's notations about his gardens were meticulous, defining growth times as well as harvest times. He also made a point to arrange his vegetable garden into squares reflecting different shades with seeds from beans sprouting purple, red, scarlet, and white. Adjacent rows of purple, white, and green broccoli, along with purple or white eggplant, made his garden a palette of colors interspersed with sesame and okra growing around tomatoes!

The second meal of the day was served in the late afternoon between 3:30 and 5 p.m. The first "summoning bell" was usually rung at 3:30, and the second at 4 p.m. In 1824, visitor Daniel Webster wrote that Jefferson "enjoys his dinner well, taking with his meat a large proportion of vegetables." Beer and cider were served with the meal, but wine was not served until the cloth was removed from the table. Salads were an important part of Jefferson's diet. He also liked light "splashes" of dressings and sauces on his foods.

Beautiful china and silver pieces adorned the dining table. One serving piece the grandchildren were fond of was a silver askos used as a chocolate-pot. It resembled a Roman pouring vessel. They nicknamed the piece the "silver duck." Another piece that delighted the children was what they called "the glass tree." It was actually an epergne—with small glass cups dangling on a "trunk" holding nuts and mincemeats. "The dinner was always choice," George Ticknor wrote, and "served in the French style." Jefferson favored dumb-waiters—sets of shelves on casters—which were placed between and behind the diners, thus allowing guests to serve themselves or enjoy their host filling their plates. Wine was delivered cold from the cellar by dumbwaiter pulleys hidden in the sides of the fireplace mantle. Webster wrote, "Dinner is served half Virginian, half French style, in good taste and abundance."

Meals were sometimes served in the Tea Room, Jefferson's "most honorable suite." Located on the north corner of the house, the polygonal room was filled with portraits and busts of family and friends, some who had influenced him, such

as Lafayette, Franklin, John Paul Jones, and Washington. The glass double pocket doors that led from the Dining Room slid open to reveal a large space combining the two rooms for large gatherings. Large, tall windows brought in the light and favorite views from the mountain. An unusual feature found in the Tea Room was a comfortable reading-and-writing arrangement for Jefferson. A revolving comb-back Windsor chair with an attached writing arm was placed near a sofa or Windsor couch. Here, he would stretch out his legs as he read or wrote.

Jefferson has been credited with many "food legends," many of which are facts. There is no proof of his eating a tomato or "poison love apple" in public, yet countless stories indicate that it happened more than once (Lynchburg offers much on this occurrence) to prove that the fruit was indeed a safe delicacy. He also is thought to have served ice cream in America first (bringing the recipe home from France). He certainly brought vanilla beans (pods) for initial distribution and shared his find of endive lettuce. More varieties of green peas were shared than ever before! Tales are told that he was the first to instruct that sliced potatoes be cooked in hot oil. There is not always proof, yet stories through the years abound about some favorite "American" foods. His introduction of macaroni to America really happened. He also began the wine industry here. To these adventures in food, most Americans say, "Thank you, T.J.!"

Jefferson's White House years have been described by many who enjoyed the festive flavors of meals there and the French-Virginia flair with which they were served. Over a century later, at a Nobel Peace Prize dinner, President John F. Kennedy noted that such unlimited brilliance represented by the attendees had not been gathered in the White House before in history—except perhaps when Thomas Jefferson had dined alone!

Apple Crisp

¹/4 cup (¹/2 stick) cold
  unsalted butter, cut into
  pieces
¹/2 cup firmly packed light
  brown sugar
¹/2 cup all-purpose flour
¹/2 cup rolled oats
1 teaspoon ground
  cinnamon

¹/2 cup chopped walnuts
2 tablespoons fresh lemon
  juice
4 apples, such as Granny
  Smith, peeled, cored,
  cut into ¹/2-inch cubes
Vanilla ice cream or plain
  cream, optional

- Preheat the oven to 350°F. Combine the unsalted butter, brown sugar, flour, oats, and cinnamon in a bowl, mixing with the fingertips until the mixture resembles coarse meal. Add the walnuts.
- Drizzle the lemon juice over the apples, and spoon into a buttered 8×8inch baking dish. Sprinkle the topping mixture evenly over the apples. Bake in the center of the oven for 1 hour or until bubbly and the apples are tender. Let cool slightly. Serve warm topped with ice cream or plain cream if desired.
- Makes 6 servings

I have a great affection for Virginia. My daughter was born at Portsmouth Naval Hospital, and I lived in Northern Virginia for more than thirty years. My business, The Protocol School of Washington®, was created and nurtured in Virginia until I relocated to Maine in the summer of 2001. When my dear friend Rowena asked me to contribute to this book, I immediately thought of my granddaughter, Liv Tyler, a popular actress in her own right. Liv attended first and second grade at Congressional School in Falls Church, and we had fun times cooking. If I want to prepare a dessert that reminds me of Virginia and fun times, I'd know exactly what to do: prepare Apple Crisp. Not even the most sophisticated, finely tuned gourmet can resist or complain about this simple, but extraordinarily succulent, dessert. I would take great care to serve my Apple Crisp with a scoop of slightly softened ice cream on my finest dessert plates, to be eaten with a dessert fork and spoon. Apple Crisp is one of the easiest desserts that a non-baker can make. So easy, in fact, that Liv was making it when she was six years old. I peeled and chopped the apples, and measured everything. Liv loved to butter the baking dish, mix the topping, and place everything in the baking dish. Apple Crisp remains our favorite dessert, which we prepare often for family and friends. Liv recently called me from England to make sure she had her ingredients in order. She later reported that the Apple Crisp was a huge hit with her English friends.

DOROTHEA JOHNSON, a talented and beautiful woman who is also a founder and director of The Protocol School of Washington®, shared this recipe.

THE PATRIOT INN FRUIT CRISP

This delicious treat was received from co-innkeeper, VERLE WEISS, who is also a member of the Fort Nelson Chapter of the Virginia DAR. The inn-keeper noted that they have many military guests at The Patriot Inn and that men often ask for this recipe for their wives. And in truth, many women will call for the recipe.

Located in a National Historic District, The Patriot Inn is filled with furnishings enabling guests to step back in time and experience the spirit of Colonial America. The inn is an architectural gem built in 1784 and located in the Olde Town Portsmouth Historical District. Shopping, antiquing, and the busy Elizabeth River waterfront are just a few steps way.

Preheat the oven to 375°F. Peel, core, and slice 5 large cooking apples. Arrange the apple slices in an 8- or 9-inch square pan. Sprinkle with 1 tablespoon lemon juice and 1 tablespoon water. Combine 1/4 cup firmly packed brown sugar, 1/2 cup all-purpose flour, 1/4 cup rolled oats, and 1 teaspoon cinnamon in a large bowl, and mix well. Cut in 1/2 cup (1 stick) chilled butter or margarine with a pastry cutter until the mixture is crumbly. Sprinkle the mixture over the apples. Bake for 40 to 45 minutes or until the apples are tender.

For an added twist, substitute peaches or pears for the apples. Serve warm with cinnamon-flavored whipping cream, or top with whipped topping and sprinkle with cinnamon. As a breakfast treat, serve in individual ramekins.

Makes 6 servings

Big Apple Bake

1 recipe plain pastry
5 to 7 tart apples, cored, sliced
1/2 cup sugar
1 teaspoon cinnamon
1/4 teaspoon nutmeg
3/4 cup all-purpose flour
1/2 cup (1 stick) butter or margarine

- Preheat the oven to 450°F. Cut a 15-inch circle of foil about the size of a pizza pan. Prepare the plain pastry recipe using 2 cups flour or use purchased pie pastry. Roll out the pastry on the foil to fit the circle. Place the foil and pastry on a baking sheet or pizza pan.
- Overlap the apple slices around the circle, beginning 3/4 inch inside the edge of the pastry. Make as many rows of apple slices as needed to fill the circle. Combine the sugar, cinnamon, nutmeg, and flour in a bowl, and mix well. Cut in the butter until crumbly. Sprinkle over the top of the apples. Turn up a 3/4-inch rim of pastry and foil to flute the edges. Bake for 20 to 25 minutes or until the crust is brown and the apples are tender.
- Note: Sprinkle the apples with 1 1/2 tablespoons lemon juice if they are not tart.
- Makes 10 servings

This has been a great recipe to serve a lot of people with the least amount of effort and no pie plate. I used this recipe to gain my husband's attention while we were dating. You see, he had a prolific apple tree, and the guys in the engineering lab were mostly single with good appetites. I didn't have a pie plate, so Mom suggested this recipe from The Better Homes and Gardens Magazine *of September 1958; she said that she used to take it to PTA meetings when I was little, and she never lost her pie plate.*

ELOISE SCHOOLEY of the Chesapeake Chapter of the Virginia DAR, shares this recipe.

SUSSEX COUNTY

Sussex County was established in 1753 from lands belonging to Surry County. It was named for Sussex County, England. It contains five hundred fifteen square miles and has a population of 12,504. The county seat is Sussex.

In Sussex County, around the year 1842, Dr. Matthew Harris is reported to have grown the first commercial peanut crop in the United States. Nationally recognized folk artist Miles B. Carpenter (1889-1985) lived in this county for most of his life.

DID YOU KNOW THAT:

Fort Monroe in Hampton is the largest enclosed fort in the United States?

Upside-Down Macadamia Nut-Crusted Cheesecakes

CRUST

1 cup graham cracker
  crumbs
$^{1}/_{2}$ cup unsalted macadamia
  nuts, crushed

$^{1}/_{4}$ cup ($^{1}/_{2}$ stick) butter,
  melted

CHEESECAKES

$1^{1}/_{4}$ pounds cream cheese,
  softened
$^{3}/_{4}$ cup plus 2 tablespoons
  sugar
$1^{1}/_{2}$ tablespoons all-purpose
  flour

2 tablespoons lemon juice
1 tablespoon vanilla extract
3 whole eggs
1 egg yolk

FLAMBÉ

$^{1}/_{4}$ cup ($^{1}/_{2}$ stick) butter,
  preferably unsalted
$^{3}/_{4}$ cup firmly packed light
  brown sugar
$^{1}/_{2}$ teaspoon ground
  cinnamon
Pinch of ground nutmeg

4 ripe bananas, cut into
  $^{1}/_{2}$-inch slices
$^{1}/_{4}$ cup banana liqueur
$^{1}/_{2}$ cup spiced rum
$^{1}/_{4}$ cup heavy cream or
  half-and-half

- To prepare the crust, combine the graham cracker crumbs and macadamia nuts in a mixing bowl, and mix well. Add the melted butter, a small amount at a time, until the crumb mixture holds together when pinched with the fingers. Divide the crumb mixture equally into 4 ramekins. Press down lightly on the crumb mixture to form a crust.
- To prepare the cheesecakes, preheat the oven to 250°F. Combine the cream cheese, sugar, and flour in a mixing bowl. Beat at low speed until blended. Add the lemon juice and vanilla extract, beating at medium-high speed. Beat in the eggs and egg yolk, 1 at a time, until blended, scraping the side of the bowl after each addition. Place $^{3}/_{4}$ cup of the batter into each of the prepared ramekins. Place the ramekins in a large pan. Fill with enough water to come halfway up the sides of the ramekins. Bake for about 45 minutes to 1 hour or until a wooden skewer inserted in the center comes out clean. Increase the oven temperature to 500°F, and bake for 5 to 7 minutes longer or until golden brown. Turn off the oven, and with the door ajar, let the cheesecakes cool. Invert the cheesecakes onto a serving plate when cool enough to handle. Tap the ramekins against the countertop to loosen.
- To prepare the flambé, melt the butter in a large skillet over medium heat. Add the brown sugar, cinnamon, and nutmeg, and cook about 2 minutes or until the sugar dissolves, stirring constantly. Add the bananas and banana liqueur, and cook for 3 minutes or until the bananas begin to brown on both sides. Add the rum carefully, and move

A BLUE HIPPO IN NORFOLK

An upscale casual restaurant in downtown Norfolk, the Blue Hippo has received rave reviews for the menu of celebrated chef Chad Martin. Martin is much sought after in the Hampton Roads area—a string of popular restaurants have begun with his touch.

Appetizer selections include Drunken Jumbo Coconut Shrimp "Martini," Pan-Seared Ostrich, and Iced Russian Caviar. The Blue Hippo features the largest martinis served in Norfolk. The appetizers prepare diners for such delicious entrees as Fresh Arctic Char, Tenderloin of Beef and Sesame Shrimp Wontons, Peanut Crusted Red Snapper, and Grilled Ahi Tuna Steak. Martin believes his clientele are happy, for they return again and again. Its convenience to the downtown cultural centers, the waterside, and MacArthur Center Mall makes the Blue Hippo a favorite dining choice before a play, concert, cruise, or shopping.

Martin also teaches cooking classes at Bouillabaisse in Norfolk's historic Ghent, as well as the Chateau de Villette in Versailles, France. A visit to the Blue Hippo is a wonderful Virginia experience!

HISTORIC RECIPE FROM THOMAS JEFFERSON

BISCUIT DE SAVOYE
(BISCUIT CAKE)

Separate 6 eggs. Beat the yolks until lemon colored and light. Add 6 table-spoons of sugar and the grated rind of one orange. Beat well; add 6 tablespoonfuls of sifted flour mixed with 1/8 teaspoonful of salt. Beat the egg whites until stiff and dry. Fold into the first mixture. Butter a cake mould and dust with sugar. Turn the mixture into this and set in a slow oven. Bake from thirty to forty minutes or until the cake shrinks from edge of pan.

This historic recipe was provided by SUSAN STEIN and the staff of Monticello, from *Thomas Jefferson's Cookbook*, by Marie Kimball, University Press of Virginia.

---

the pan back and forth to warm the rum and ignite the pan, or remove the pan from the heat, and ignite the pan carefully with a match. Shake the pan back and forth until the flame subsides, basting the bananas with the rum mixture. Stir in the heavy cream or half-and-half.
- To serve, place each cheesecake on an individual serving plate. Arrange the bananas slices carefully around the top of each cheesecake using tongs. Pour the remaining sauce around or on top of each cheesecake. Garnish with cocoa powder and edible flowers if available.
- Makes 4 servings

CHAD MARTIN, chef, The Blue Hippo, Norfolk, shared this recipe.

Easy Peach Cobbler

---

1 cup all-purpose flour	1 cup milk
1 tablespoon baking powder	3 to 4 cups fresh or thawed
1/2 cup (1 stick) butter or	frozen peaches
margarine, melted	

- Preheat the oven to 350°F. Combine the flour and baking powder in a large bowl, and mix well. Stir in the melted butter or margarine and milk. Spoon into an 8-inch round casserole dish. Add the peaches. Bake until the top is golden brown.
- Makes approximately 6 to 8 servings

This is an old family recipe from Irvine Hill's mother's family. It was submitted by IRVINE B. HILL, one of, if not the most, community-minded personalities in all of Hampton Roads. By the way, the "B" stands for Byrd. The Byrds of Virginia, a well-known family, were on his mother's side. After serving as Mayor of Norfolk and president of WCMS radio, he joined Cox Communications almost two decades ago and began "Hampton Roads Speaks Out." He's done more than 5,000 programs and interviewed more than 15,000 people in his dark suits, white shirts and ties, and gentle manner. He has contributed to more community projects than one can count, working many times seven days a week, morning, noon, and often nights. He has been a cheerleader for hundreds of charities, people, and projects. As Mr. Bower, vice-president and general manager of Cox Communications, put it, *He's an original, a one of a kind. He puts every fiber of his body into making Hampton Roads a better place in which to live. His heart is in this community.* Irvine stands tall physically at 6 feet 5 inches, and also as a personality, a friend to all. He is a Hampton Roads folk hero.

TIM AND DAPHNE REID'S
Peach Cobbler

1 cup unbleached all-purpose flour	1 teaspoon cinnamon
$^1/_4$ cup plus 2 tablespoons unrefined sugar	$^1/_2$ teaspoon nutmeg
1$^1/_2$ tablespoons baking powder	$^1/_4$ teaspoon grated orange peel
3 tablespoons soft shortening	$^1/_4$ cup cornstarch
$^1/_3$ cup milk	$^1/_3$ cup water
5 to 6 ripe Virginia peaches	2 tablespoons ($^1/_4$ stick) butter or margarine
	Additional unrefined sugar

- Preheat the oven to 400°F. Combine the flour, 2 tablespoons of the unrefined sugar, and baking powder in a medium bowl, stirring to make a soft dough. Cut in the shortening with a pastry blender until the mixture resembles cornmeal. Add the milk, and shape into a smooth soft ball. Divide the dough into 2 equal portions. Cover the bottom of a 1$^1/_2$ to 2-quart casserole dish or a 9×13-inch baking pan with 1 portion of the dough.
- Fill a medium saucepan half full with water, and bring to a boil. Place the peaches carefully in the boiling water, and roll around with a large slotted spoon for about 3 minutes. Immerse the peaches in cold water and remove the skin. Slice the peaches into a bowl.
- Combine the remaining sugar, cinnamon, nutmeg, and orange peel in a small saucepan, and mix well. Place over low heat. Stir the cornstarch into the water in a small bowl, and add to the heated sugar mixture. Spoon the peaches over the dough in the casserole dish or baking pan. Pour the sugar mixture over the peaches. Roll out the remaining dough, and place over the top. Dot with the butter, and sprinkle with additional unrefined sugar. Place the casserole dish on a baking sheet lined with foil. Bake for 40 minutes or until brown and bubbly. Let cool to serve.
- Makes enough to serve 6 hungry or 10 polite eaters

North meets South in this compromise to Tim's Southern style taste and my Northern style cooking. We both enjoy this one.

TIM REID, a native of Norfolk, and DAPHNE MAXWELL REID, a native New Yorker, live in Charlottesville, Virginia, and produce feature film and television programming at their full-film service facility, New Millennium Studios, in Petersburg, Virginia. They are a wonderful, fun couple and give back in many ways to their community.

DID YOU KNOW THAT:

Virginia is one of only two states in the Union to furnish native sons to the presidency of foreign countries? Sam Houston, born near Lexington in 1793, became president of the Republic of Texas in 1836. The other native-born American to become a foreign president was a Nashvillian, William Walker, who was elected president of Nicaragua in 1856.

THE FIRST TOBACCO IN VIRGINIA

When Jamestown's first English colonists arrived in 1607, they discovered the local natives were smoking a form of tobacco that was raised in their village gardens. Although the Englishmen were familiar with tobacco - the plant was imported to the island nation around 1565 and smoking had become so commonplace by 1604 that King James had condemned the habit - the variety grown by the Indians was different. One colonist complained that the native tobacco was "not of the best kind, it is but poore and weake, and of a byting tast . . . ." It remained for John Rolfe, whose name went down in history as the husband of the Indian princess, Pocahontas, to experiment with other varieties of tobacco and to develop a blend capable of satisfying the tastes of all good Englishmen.

Rolfe imported a quantity of Spanish tobacco from Trinidad and South America, and before long, he was experimenting with a variety that "no doubt but after a little more triall and expense in the curing thereof . . . will compare with the best in the West Indies." Rolfe's efforts paid off quickly.

GRANDMOTHER DICKENS'
Custard

¹/₂ gallon whole milk	Pinch of salt
4 eggs, beaten	1 teaspoon vanilla extract
1 cup sugar	

- Combine the milk, eggs, sugar, and salt in a heavy pot, and mix well. Cook over medium heat until the mixture begins to get hot, stirring frequently. Reduce the heat. Cook until the custard coats a spoon, stirring frequently. Cool slightly, and add the vanilla extract. Serve chilled with cookies.
- Makes about 12 servings

Once a year DANA DICKENS, insurance executive and Suffolk, Virginia mayor, becomes king of the grill and chief cook at the Crittenden, Eclipse, Hobson, Ruritan Chicken Barbecue Dinner. Although willing to share culinary tips regarding the cooking, Dickens' secret sauce from an old family recipe remains a closely guarded secret. Although the barbecue sauce is a well-kept secret, Mayor Dickens shares other family specialties, which he remembers from Sunday trips to his grandparents' farm. He always enjoyed the homemade custard and cookies at the round oak table that welcomed folks to Grandma's kitchen, and he has provided her recipe for custard.

Brannock Sweet Potato Custard

3 medium sweet potatoes	4 eggs, beaten
¹/₂ cup (1 stick) unsalted butter	1 tablespoon vanilla extract, bourbon, or Bailey's Irish Cream
1 cup sugar	
2 cups whole milk	

- Preheat the oven to 325°F. Cook the sweet potatoes in a medium saucepan for 20 minutes or until tender. Peel the sweet potatoes, and mash in a large bowl. Add the butter, sugar, milk, and eggs, and mix well. Stir in the vanilla extract, bourbon, or Bailey's Irish Cream.
- Makes 4 to 6 servings

This is my good friend Boyce Brannock's recipe, for which I have to give him credit; it is now served at every holiday at our house.

The recipe was shared by Virginia delegate CHRIS SAXMAN, who represents the 20th District in the Virginia House of Delegates. Delegate Saxman is general manager of Shenandoah Valley Water and is very involved in his community. He is married to Michelle Lynn Frick and is the father of four children.

When the colonists discovered that a good tobacco crop was worth up to six times more than any other agricultural commodity they could grow, tobacco culture mushroomed. By 1618, more than forty thousand pounds of tobacco were shipped from Jamestown to England.

In an interesting, but almost tragic aside, the greedy colonists became so enamored with growing the highly profitable tobacco, that they neglected growing crops for food and, on more than one occasion, nearly starved to death. Indeed, the official records of the Virginia Company reveal that as early as 1617, a visitor to Jamestown "found the marketplace, and streets, and all other spare places planted with Tobacco."

THE FAMILY'S
Never-Fail Custard

1 quart (32 ounces) whole
   milk (no skim or low-fat)
5 eggs
1/4 cup plus 2 heaping
   tablespoons sugar

1 teaspoon vanilla extract
1/2 teaspoon almond extract
Nutmeg

- Preheat the oven to 325°F. Heat the milk gently in a large saucepan. Separate the eggs into 2 medium bowls. Beat the egg yolks and sugar until creamy, and add the milk, vanilla extract, and almond extract, beating well.
- Beat the egg whites until foamy, but not too stiff. Fold the egg whites gently into the milk mixture. Pour into glass ramekins, and sprinkle with nutmeg. Place the ramekins in a pan large enough to hold 2 inches of water. Add the water, and bake for 1 hour. Let stand until cool, and refrigerate.
- Makes 6 servings

In our family, the Never-Fail Custard was Maemar's remedy of choice for any bump in the road, illness, or disappointment. If we were sick, Maemar would always appear with custard. During the last few months of Mother's illness, the family custard was her sustenance. In addition to being easy to swallow and digest, we girls thought it was probably comfort food, transporting her in taste and thought to the tender loving care of her mother. It is our gift to you.

This recipe was sent by ASHLEY and ALDEN in memory of their mother, JANE BLACK CLARK. Jane was a gifted and giving human being who touched the lives of hundreds of people with her incredible faith as she struggled with several bouts of cancer until her death. The girls' cousin, Jane Hudgins Frasier, compiled a cookbook of treasured Taylor/Black family recipes handed down from their maternal grandmother, Aileen Taylor Black, or Maemar as she was called.

TAZEWELL COUNTY

Tazewell County was established in 1799 from parts of Wythe and Russell Counties. Named for Senator Henry Tazewell (1753-1799), it contains five hundred thirty-one square miles and its population is 44,598. The county seat is Tazewell.

Mathias Harmon Sr. (1736-1832), an early settler in what later became eastern Kentucky, lived in this area. Bluefield College, a liberal arts school for men and women, was chartered here in 1920.

MOSES MYERS HOUSE FLOATING ISLAND

This recipe is in Old English. When reading it, please substitute an "s" for most "f". An example of this is "fugar," which means "sugar". Fun to read, so enjoy!

TO PREPARE A FLOATING IFLAND
Grate the yellow rind of a large lemon into a quart of cream, put in a large glafs of Madeira wine, make it pretty fweet with loaf fugar, mill it with a chocolate mill to a ftrong forth, take it off as it rifes, then lay it upon a fieve to drain all night, then take a deep glafs difh, and lay in your froth, with a Naples biscuit in the middle of it, then beat the white of an egg to a ftrong froth, and roll a fprig of myrtle in it to imitate fnow, ftick it in the Naples biscuit, then lay all over your froth currant jelly cut in very thin flices, pour over it very ftrong calf's foot jelly, when it grows thick lay it all over, till it looks like a glafs, and your difh is full to the brim; let it ftand till it is quite cold and ftiff, then lay on rock candied fweet meats upon the top of your jelly, and fheep and fwans to pick up the myrtle; flick green sprigs in two or three places on top of your jelly, amongft your fhapes; it looks very pretty in the middle of a table for fupper. You muft not put the fhapes on the jelly till you are going to fend it to the table.

This recipe is from the MOSES MYERS HOUSE, which remains preserved in Norfolk. The Moses Myers House and its collection draw an exceptionally accurate picture of the late18th century life of this prosperous Jewish merchant's family. Born in New York in 1752, Moses Myers was the eldest son of Hyam Myers, a Dutch immigrant, and his New York-born wife, Rachel Louzada. In 1787, Moses married Elizabeth Judah Abraham. They moved to Norfolk and eventually had twelve children, nine of whom lived to adulthood. A prominent businessman and citizen, Moses Myers purchased a large lot in which he created the house in 1792. Unfortunately, his prosperity did not last since Moses fell victim to the First National Bank crash in 1819. His son Frederick purchased the house and furnishings from bankruptcy auction so that the family could remain in the residence. In 1823, Eliza Myers died, and at times during the next twelve years, Moses served as consul to the Netherlands and collector of Port Norfolk. It is from Mrs. Myers' personal collection of cookbooks, The Experienced English House-Keeper by Elizabeth Raffald, published in Dublin in the 1790s, that we have taken this recipe.

EARL HAMNER'S "GOOD NIGHT JOHN BOY"
Peach Ice Cream

5 cups sliced peaches, crushed	Almond extract
4¹/₂ cup sugar	1¹/₂ tablespoons vanilla extract
¹/₄ tablespoon salt	3 cups half-and-half
Lemon juice	3 cups whipping cream

- Combine the peaches, ³/₄ cup of the sugar, and salt in a bowl, and mix well. Stir in a few drops of lemon juice and almond extract. Chill, covered, in the refrigerator.
- Prepare an ice cream churn according to directions. Combine the vanilla extract, remaining sugar, half-and-half, and cream in a bowl, and mix well. Chill, covered, in the refrigerator at least 1 hour. Pour the chilled cream mixture into the freezer container. Churn until partially frozen. Add the peach mixture. Churn until the ice cream is thick, and the churn stops.
- Makes 1 gallon

Most of my novels were inspired by my growing up in a large family in the Blue Ridge during the Depression. I remember those days as rich and happy and free of want, yet the criticism I receive most often is that I portray my family and the times as too idyllic. It is true that city people often went hungry, but in the country, we kept a cow for milk and butter, raised vegetables, hunted wild game, and slaughtered pigs. All summer long, there was generous supply of fresh fruits and berries. And everything that wasn't eaten was "put up" in Mason jars to sustain us through the winter. There was a peach tree in my Grandmother Giannini's yard, and as long as I live, I will remember the peach ice cream we made from its fruit. In a word, it was "idyllic." Today we celebrate each Fourth of July with a truly all-American family custom. The memory comes from Virginia. The recipe comes from my wife, Jane's, Iowa family cookbook, and we enjoy it with our daughter from California and our son from Vermont!

This recipe was generously provided by EARL HAMNER, JR., originally from Nelson County, Virginia, and creator of *The Waltons* television series.

WARREN COUNTY

Warren County was organized in 1836 from parts of Frederick and Shenandoah Counties. It was named in honor of General Joseph Warren, a hero of the Battle of Bunker Hill during the Revolution. It contains two hundred sixteen square miles. Its population is 31,584, and the county seat is Front Royal.

In May 1862, the 1st Maryland Regiment of the U.S. Army fought the 1st Maryland Regiment of the Confederate Army near Front Royal. William E. Carson, a driving force in the establishment of the Shenandoah National Park and the Colonial National Historical Park at Williamsburg, lived here.

A Blue Ridge Boy Remembers

The writing and production talents of Nelson County's Earl Hamner Jr. have led many to Virginia to share the wonderment of the Blue Ridge and look for the "Walton's Mountain" in their hearts. Earl Hamner Jr. is truly the real "John-Boy."

There really is no Walton's Mountain on any Virginia map, yet it rises in the hearts of fans all around the world and is as real as the light in Earl Hamner Jr.'s eyes when he wistfully remembers his boyhood home. Earl was born the oldest of eight "tall, lean, fine-boned, red-headed youngsters" on July 10, 1923, in Schuyler. His parents, Earl Sr. and Doris, were proud of what his father called "his thoroughbreds" as they grew up. Earl has shared that his family lived during the Depression, but they were not depressed!

Secretly yearning to be a writer, Earl kept a journal of those wonder-filled childhood days he shared with his brothers, sisters, parents, and grandparents. When Earl was six, he wrote a poem about a wagon full of puppies and it was published in *The Richmond Times Dispatch*. Earl graduated from Schuyler High School and entered the University of Richmond on a scholarship. After being drafted into the United States Army in 1943 and serving in a Quartermaster Corps unit in Paris, Earl returned to civilian life and worked at radio station WMBG in Richmond. Later, he went to Northwestern University and then graduated from the University of Cincinnati.

New York was next to see Earl's writing talent, as he became a radio writer for NBC. There, he wrote his first novel, *Fifty Roads To Town* and then *You Can't Get There From Here*. His striking book *Spencer's Mountain* was based on his family and became a Warner Brothers film starring Henry Fonda and Maureen O'Hara. By 1961, Earl found himself in Hollywood writing feature scripts for *The Twilight Zone* and CBS *Playhouse*. Well-known author E.B. White then chose Earl to script the film adaptation of *Charlotte's Web*.

Success never made Earl forget his roots. In 1970, when Lorimar Productions asked him to write a television special based on his book *The Homecoming*, the overwhelming response was so great that CBS invited him to write the series that became *The Waltons*. His family and their life in Nelson County were once again something to share and to learn from as he created the "television family" so close to over fifty million fans in the United States! Earl let his character as big brother "John-Boy" once again lead a small troop of siblings. His brother Clifton was the model as the musical son "Jason." Sister Marion was the series' tomboy, "Mary Ellen." Audrey inspired the pretty, love-challenged "Erin." Brothers Bill and Paul were represented as the independent "Ben." James was the model for the "big-dreaming "Jim-Bob." Nancy, as the youngest, became the character of "Elizabeth" in the series.

Earl received countless awards for *The Waltons* including six Emmy Awards. The series ran for nine seasons on CBS and still has "specials". Syndication keeps the "Walton" family very popular even today. The show has also been embraced internationally. Earl went on to write many more books and productions (including television's *Falcon Crest* series). He continues to write and recently was co-executive producer of *Snowy River: The McGregor Saga* on the Family Channel. His latest book, *Goodnight John-Boy* (co-written with Ralph Giffin) recalls the heritage and bliss of his family in the Blue Ridge. He shares some visions that his father had and the varied wisdom of his grandfathers. He honors his mother and grandmothers' stamina to be strong through the generations. An overview of each season's episodes is shared along with pictures and comments throughout the book's pages.

Earl and his wife Jane now live in Los Angeles, California. They have two children, Scott and Caroline. Earl and Jane "come home" to Virginia frequently. Here, he is assisting with the development of a Nelson County Museum. The white clapboard Hamner home place still stands near the "Walton's Mountain" Museum in Schuyler. Fish still wait for Earl in the Rockfish River when he visits. The rest of the remaining Hamner siblings are still living in Virginia, except one.

In his recent book, *Goodnight John-Boy*, Earl relates:

Our parents were resourceful in feeding us. My father would go out at dawn and come back with bobwhite quail that my mother cooked with dark brown gravy. There were bass and catfish in the Rockfish River, and always plenty of venison, both in and out of season. We kept pigs and always had a cow out grazing somewhere. I am probably the only writer in Hollywood who knows how to milk a cow, not that I get called on much to use that particular talent. I dream of the day when my agent will call and say: "Twentieth Century Fox is looking for a writer who can milk a cow." It won't happen.

In the television show's first episode, titled "The Foundling," Earl wrote this narration (below) for the closing and then a brotherly exchange.

Those were lean years, and for many Americans a harsh and bitter time. On Waltons Mountain we were sustained with poems and gingerbread and laughter and sharing, but most of all by a remarkable mother and father. The house in which we were born and raised is still there, still home, and on the winds that sigh along those misted blue ridged mountains our voices must echo still.

— Ben: John-Boy, you awake?

— John-Boy: What'd you want, Ben?

— Ben: Are you going to marry Marcia Woolery?

— John-Boy: You want me to?

— Ben: She makes good gingerbread.

— John-Boy: Huh huh. Well I'll think about it. Goodnight now.

— Ben: Goodnight.

Sleeping Meringue

1 angel food cake, sliced
  horizontally into halves
6 egg whites
1/4 teaspoon salt
1/2 teaspoon cream of tartar
1 1/2 cups sugar

1 teaspoon vanilla extract
1 cup whipping cream
2 cups sliced fruit, such as
  strawberries, peaches,
  blueberries, or a
  combination

- Preheat the oven to 450°F. Place half the angel food cake in a buttered deep-dish springform pan with a hole. Beat the egg whites in a large bowl until stiff peaks form, adding the salt and cream of tartar while beating. Add the sugar and vanilla extract gradually, and beat for 15 minutes. Pour the meringue over the angel food cake half in the pan. Place in the oven. Turn off the heat, and go to bed (8 to 10 hours). Remove the dessert from the pan to a serving plate just before serving time. Whip the whipping cream in a bowl, and spread over the top of the dessert. Garnish with the fruit.
- Makes 8 to 10 servings

There is half a cake left over, so you can double the recipe and make two desserts, or just nibble on that extra half of the cake. I consider that a cook's benefit.

From CAROL FULLINWIDER, my mother-in-law and one of the first volunteers to serve in the U.S. Navy's Woman Auxiliary Volunteer Service (WAVES) in September 1942. Carol makes everyone feel good with her never-ending cheerfulness and zest for life. She's absolutely amazing. —Rowena

ROWENA'S
Forgotten Dessert

6 egg whites
1/4 teaspoon salt
1/2 teaspoon cream of tartar
1 teaspoon vanilla extract

1 1/2 cups sugar
1 cup whipping cream
2 cups crushed strawberries,
  or other fruits

- Preheat the oven to 450°F. Beat the egg whites in a large bowl until stiff peaks form, adding the salt and cream of tartar while beating. Add the vanilla and sugar, 1 tablespoon at a time, beating constantly for 15 minutes. Spoon the meringue into an ungreased 9x9-inch pan. Place in the oven, and turn off the heat. Do not open the oven door for 8 to 10 hours or overnight. Whip the whipping cream in a bowl, and spread over the dessert, sealing to the edges. Cut into 6 or 8 servings, and top with the strawberries, or other fruits.
- Makes 6 to 8 servings

This is another version of Sleeping Meringue. Everyone who has tried this recipe has made it over and over. It is quick and pretty to serve. My children loved the fact they couldn't open the oven door until the next morning. It was a race to see who could get there first. —Rowena

THE NORFOLK BOTANICAL GARDENS

Wonderful things come alive in our Virginia gardens, both from the past and present. Hampton Roads is blessed to have the incredible Norfolk Botanical Gardens nearby, where one can enjoy brilliant floral displays, peaceful waters, as well as unique programs and special events. Even sighting a bald eagle, our country's symbol of freedom, is possible. Surrounded by the waters of Lake Whitehurst, Norfolk Botanical Gardens is a collection of more than twenty-four themed gardens encompassing 155 beautiful acres. Open year-round, the gardens feature one of the largest collections of azaleas, camellias, roses, and rhododendrons on the East Coast. It is also the only garden offering both tram and boat tours. Both tours are absolutely delightful and educational at the same time. It is from this garden that we have received a list of edible flowers and herbs and a recipe for Candied Flowers.

Edible flowers and herbs include:
  Nasturtiums, rose petals and rose hips, calendulas, day lilies, zucchini flowers, marigolds, pansies, violas, Johnny-jump-ups, squash blossoms, anise, hyssop, borage, mums, carnations, clover, hollyhocks, jasmine, daisies, cornflowers, lilac, primrose, tulips, and herb blossoms—basil, chives, cilantro, garlic, lavender, marjoram, onion, oregano, rosemary, sage, and thyme.

Eat only organically grown flowers and herbs; do not eat any of these named if they were purchased at a nursery or sprayed with pesticide.

CANDIED FLOWERS

1 egg white

1 teaspoon water

3 tablespoons superfine sugar

Use clean, dry, edible, pesticide-free flowers. In a small bowl, with a fork beat together the egg white and water until frothy. Using a brush, paint the petals with the egg mixture, and then set them on a plate covered with superfine sugar. Sprinkle some of the sugar on top of the petals, and shake off the excess. Lay the petals on waxed paper, and allow them to dry overnight; or place them on a baking sheet, and dry in a warm oven with the door ajar.

Use some of these ideas for a treat for your family or to surprise and delight your friends. Gather them directly from your garden, or look for them in your neighborhood grocery store. Their popularity for home use is growing.

Authentic Derbyshire Bakewell Pudding

PASTRY

$1/2$ cup (1 stick) butter or margarine	$1/2$ teaspoon salt
2 cups all-purpose flour	$1/4$ cup water
1 teaspoon baking powder	Juice of 1 lemon

PUDDING FILLING

4 to 6 ounces black currant jam or lemon curd	3 egg yolks
$1/2$ cup (1 stick) butter or margarine	1 egg white
$1/2$ cup plus 1 tablespoon sugar	Almond essence
	2 ounces ground almonds

- To prepare the pastry, cut the butter or margarine into a mixture of the flour, baking powder, and salt in a large bowl until it resembles coarse meal. Add enough of the water and lemon juice to form a smooth dough.
- To make the base for a tart, roll out the dough to a $1/4$-inch thickness, and line an 8-inch sandwich tin (pie plate). Trim the edges, and set aside for the pudding filling.
- To prepare the pudding filling, preheat the oven to 350°F. Spread a thin $1/4$-inch-thick layer of jam or lemon curd over the pastry in the sandwich tin. Beat the butter or margarine and sugar in a large bowl until creamy. Add the egg yolks and egg white, 1 at a time, beating well after each addition. Stir in the almond essence and ground almonds, and mix well. Spread the mixture over the jam to fill the pie $3/4$ full. Place on a hot baking tin (baking sheet). Bake for 40 minutes.
- Makes 8 servings

The town of Bakewell sits in an area of natural beauty in the countryside of Derbyshire in the United Kingdom. Derbyshire itself sits in the middle of the United Kingdom. Bakewell Pudding was born of a happy accident in the kitchen of the Rutland Arms Pub over 200 years ago.

This was sent by the lovely SALLY FORBES, wife of Admiral Ian Forbes, Royal Navy, Deputy Supreme Allied Commander, Atlantic. The North Atlantic Treaty Organization (NATO) staff and forces are a very real and welcome presence in Norfolk and Hampton Roads, and we are proud that NATO is headquartered in this area. The North Atlantic Treaty was signed in Washington on April 4, 1949, creating an alliance of twelve independent nations committed to mutual defense. Between 1952 and 1982, four more European nations acceded the treaty. In March 1999, the Czech Republic, Hungary, and Poland were welcomed into the alliance, which now numbers nineteen members. Today it has transformed its political and military structures in order to adapt to peacekeeping and crisis management tasks undertaken in cooperation with other international organizations.

Dunderfunk
(Bread Pudding)

$^1/_2$ loaf white bread, such as
    challah, potato, and
    cinnamon raisin, sliced,
    buttered
2 cups mixed fruit, such as
    raisins, sultanas, and
    apricots

6 eggs
$1^1/_2$ cups sugar
2 pints half-and-half
1 teaspoon vanilla extract

- Preheat the oven to 350°F. Layer the bread and fruit in a buttered 9×13-inch ovenproof dish. Combine the eggs, sugar, half-and-half, and vanilla extract in a large bowl, and mix well. Pour over the layers, and let stand for 30 minutes.
- Bake in the center of the oven for 45 minutes or until the custard is set.
- Makes 10 to 12 servings

Dunderfunk refers to an Age of Sail dish discussed in Herman Melville's *White-Jacket.* Traditionally the dish was made of a hard biscuit, mashed and mixed with beef fat and molasses, and then baked. Fortunately, the modern dish is deliciously appealing since local CHEF DAVID BLACKSTOCK created it specifically for the Dunderfunk Society of Hampton Roads Naval Museum, which consists of a group of naval history enthusiasts who meet bi-monthly for a lunch and lecture. The Hampton Roads Naval Museum is one of eleven officially sponsored U.S. Navy museums in the country and the only one located in the State of Virginia. Located on Norfolk's downtown waterfront in the National Maritime Center, the museum is dedicated to preserving regional naval history and shares a rich collection of maritime artifacts with the public. The museum also oversees it own battleship, the USS Wisconsin.

WASHINGTON COUNTY

Washington County was formed in 1776 from Fincastle County, with part of Montgomery County being added at a later date. It was named for General George Washington (1732-1799) and was the first county in the country to honor him. It contains six hundred four square miles and has a population of 51,103. The county seat is Abingdon.

Militia under the command of Colonel William Campbell gathered here in late 1780 and marched on to victory against American loyalists at Kings Mountain, South Carolina. Emory and Henry College, the first institute of higher learning in southwestern Virginia, was founded here in 1836.

USS WISCONSIN

The battleship Wisconsin (BB-64), one of the famous Iowa-class ships, began her career in the middle of World War II. Commissioned in April 1944, the powerful new warship joined Admiral William F. Halsey's Third Fleet when the liberation of the Philippines was underway and in 1945 supported the landings on Iwo Jima and Okinawa. The battleship's brief but active World War II career concluded with the transport of war-weary GI's back to the U.S. during Operation Magic Carpet. In 1948 the Wisconsin entered the Atlantic Reserve Fleet at Norfolk, where she has stayed. The battleship provided gunfire support for American, Korean, and other United Nations troops on the Korean peninsula until relieved by her sister ship, the Iowa, in April 1952. In 1988 she was reactivated again. The ship was given new Tomahawk and Harpoon missiles in addition to her 16-inch guns when she steamed to the Persian Gulf in 1990 for Operation Desert Storm. After effective use of missiles and high explosives in the desert conflict, the battleship returned home to be decommissioned for the third time in 1991. She now resides in downtown Norfolk, waiting patiently for any new call to duty.

CUMBERLAND GAP: GATEWAY TO THE WEST

Poised astride the Virginia-North Carolina-Tennessee border sits Cumberland Gap. Situated 1,600 feet above sea level, the Gap provides a natural passage across the two- to three-thousand-feet-high Appalachian Mountains. Local Indians called the Gap, *Quasioto*, meaning "mountains where deer are plenty." The first known white man to traverse the pass was a Virginian, Dr. Thomas Walker, who in 1750 crossed through, explored parts of Kentucky, and named Cumberland Gap, the Cumberland Mountains, and the Cumberland River all in honor of the Duke of Cumberland. Walker was born in King and Queen County in 1715, and was the chief agent for the Loyal Company, a large land speculation company. He later served in the House of Burgesses.

The famed woodsman, Daniel Boone, and his associates blazed the forerunner of the Wilderness Road through Cumberland Gap during the summer of 1769, when they traveled from North Carolina to reconnoiter future homes in Kentucky. The Gap was quickly capitalized upon by westward-looking white settlers who later traveled the Wilderness Road through the Gap in increasing numbers to carry their families to the promised lands across the mountains. The Union Army also used Cumberland Gap as the invasion route into Tennessee during 1862-63.

Charlotte Russe

1 package unflavored gelatin	Pinch of salt
2 cups milk	1 cup whipping cream
2 eggs	$^1/_2$ cup rum, optional
$^1/_2$ cup confectioners' sugar	$^1/_4$ pound macaroons or
$^1/_2$ teaspoon vanilla extract	2 dozen ladyfingers
	$^1/_2$ cup slivered almonds

- Dissolve approximately 1 tablespoon of the gelatin (see gelatin package for more directions) in a small amount of the milk in a small bowl.
- Separate the eggs into 2 separate bowls. Beat the eggs yolks and sugar until creamy. Add the vanilla extract and salt, and mix well.
- Heat the remaining milk in a saucepan over low heat, stirring constantly. Stir in the egg yolk mixture and the dissolved gelatin when the milk begins to boil. Cook until thickened, stirring constantly. Remove from the heat, and set aside to cool.
- Whip the whipping cream in a large bowl. Beat the egg whites until stiff peaks form, and fold into the whipped cream. Pour the rum over the macaroons or ladyfingers if desired.
- If using macaroons, fold the macaroons into the pudding mixture. Combine the pudding mixture with the whipped cream mixture, and pour into a 2-quart bowl.
- If using ladyfingers. line a 2-quart bowl with the ladyfingers. Fold the whipped cream mixture into the pudding mixture lightly, and pour into the center of the ladyfingers.
- Sprinkle the slivered almonds over the top. Chill, covered, in the refrigerator for 8 to 10 hours.
- Makes 6 to 8 servings

These recipes are a large part of our memories and history, the names alone evoking many warm thoughts of beautiful meals in our grandmother's gracious home. Our grandmother, Maemar, had a wonderful cook, Daisy Barnes, who usually prepared these recipes, although Maemar also was an excellent cook in her own right. We remember that Maemar had a button installed in the floor where her right foot rested that was hidden by the rug. It rang a bell in the kitchen to alert Daisy that we were ready for the next course. As children, we were mystified that Daisy always arrived just as we finished each course without being called.

This recipe was sent by ASHLEY and ALDEN in memory of their mother, JANE BLACK CLARK. Jane was a gifted and giving human being. She touched the lives of hundreds of people with her incredible faith as she struggled with several bouts of cancer from 1969 until her death. She was a beautiful and special lady, and we will all miss her. The girls tell us their family recipes were handed down from their maternal grandmother, Aileen Taylor Black.

GRANDMA WALTHALL'S
Christmas Dessert

BLANCMANGE
2 envelopes unflavored
  gelatin
$2^{1}/_{2}$ cups milk
$^{2}/_{3}$ cup sugar
$1^{1}/_{2}$ cups cream
1 teaspoon vanilla extract

Pinch of salt
2 to 3 drops of green food
  coloring
$^{1}/_{2}$ cup blanched, chopped
  or slivered almonds

WINE JELLY
2 envelopes unflavored
  gelatin
1 cup cold water
1 cup sugar
1 cup boiling water

1 cup sherry wine
Juice of 1 lemon
4 drops of red food coloring
Whipped cream

- To prepare the blancmange, combine the gelatin, milk, sugar, cream, vanilla extract, salt, and food coloring in a large bowl, and mix well. Let stand for 5 minutes. Heat the mixture in a saucepan over medium heat until the sugar and gelatin are dissolved, stirring frequently. Pour into a ring mold. Chill in the refrigerator until the custard begins to thicken. Stir in the almonds gently.
- To prepare the wine jelly, soften the gelatin in the cold water in a large bowl for 5 minutes. Add the sugar and boiling water, stirring until the sugar is dissolved. Stir in the sherry wine, lemon juice, and food coloring. Pour into a small deep mold. Chill in the refrigerator until set.
- To serve, unmold the blancmange onto a serving platter. Unmold the wine jelly, and place in the center of the blancmange. Top with whipped cream.
- Makes 8 to 10 servings

This is my family's traditional Christmas dessert. It's from my great-grandmother, who lived with her husband, Howard Walthall, a Confederate veteran, in Richmond in the Gay '90s of the 1800s. You can use all milk in the blancmange rather than part cream. They didn't worry about cholesterol in the 19th century.

GRACE KARISH, a member of the Fairfax County Chapter of the Virginia DA, shared this recipe.

WESTMORELAND COUNTY

Westmoreland County was established in 1653 from King George and Northumberland Counties. It contains two hundred fifty-two square miles and has a population of 16,718. The county seat is Montross.

George Washington's mother, Mary Ball, lived in this county as a youth and was married to Augustine Washington here. Westmoreland County was the birthplace of George Washington (1732-1799), James Monroe (1758-1831), and Robert E. Lee (1807-1870).

COMMONWEALTH OF VIRGINIA SEALS

According to Sections 7-26 and 7-27 of the Code of Virginia:

The Great Seal of the Commonwealth of Virginia shall consist of two metallic discs, two inches and one fourth in diameter, with an ornamental border one fourth of an inch wide, with such words and figures engraved thereon as will, when used, produce impressions to be described as follows: On the obverse, Virtus, the genius of the Commonwealth, dressed as an Amazon, resting on a spear in her right hand, point downward, touching the earth, and holding in her left hand, a sheathed sword or parazonium, pointing upward, her head erect and face upturned, her left foot on the form of Tyranny represented by the prostrate body of a man, with his head to her left , his fallen crown near by, a broken chain in his left hand and scourge in his right. Above the group and within the border conforming therewith, shall be the word Virginia, and, in the space below, on a curved line, shall be the motto, Sic Semper Tyrannis. On the reverse, shall be placed a group consisting of Libertas, holding a wand and pileus in her right hand, on her right Aeternitas, with a globe and phoenix in her right hand, on the left of Libertas, Ceres, with a cornucopia in her left hand and an ear of wheat in her right over this device, in the curved line, the word Perseverando.

The Lesser Seal of the Commonwealth shall be one and nine sixteenths inches in diameter, and have engraved thereon the device and inscriptions contained on the obverse of the Great Seal.

Cottage Berry Pudding

SYRUP

$^1/_2$ cup sugar
2 cups boiling water

$^1/_2$ teaspoon vanilla extract

PUDDING

$^1/_4$ cup ($^1/_2$ stick) butter or margarine
$^3/_4$ cup sugar
2 eggs
$2^1/_4$ cups all-purpose flour

1 tablespoon baking powder
$^1/_2$ teaspoon salt
$^3/_4$ cup milk
1 teaspoon vanilla extract
1 to 2 cups black raspberries

- To prepare the syrup, combine the sugar and boiling water in a bowl, stirring until the sugar is dissolved. Add the vanilla extract, and mix well. The syrup should be thin.
- To prepare the pudding, preheat the oven to 400°F. Beat the butter, sugar, and eggs in a medium bowl until creamy. Sift the flour, baking powder, and salt together into a separate bowl. Add the flour mixture to the creamed mixture alternately with the milk, beating well after each addition. Stir the vanilla extract, and mix well. Fold in the "Black Caps" (the black raspberries) with a wooden spoon. Spoon into a greased 8×8-inch or 9×9-inch baking pan. Bake for 20 to 25 minutes.
- Serve the warm pudding topped with warm syrup.
- Makes 6 to 9 servings

This really isn't a pudding, but that's what my great-grandmother called it, so that's what Mom and I call it. Mom says that my great-grandmother always made this for the Fourth of July and that she would fret herself that the "Black Caps" (black raspberries) wouldn't be ready in time or that the wildlife would get them first. Growing up on the farm, we would watch our berries mature on the vine and hope we too would get them first and on time. It has been a Fourth of July tradition that I love to continue, but today I have to buy my berries.

CAROLYN ARMSTRONG DRAKE BALEY of the Chesapeake Chapter of the Virginia DAR shared this recipe.

WISE COUNTY

Wise County, named in honor of Henry A. Wise (1806-1876), a Virginia governor (1856-1860), was formed in 1856 from Scott, Russell, and Lee Counties. It contains four hundred twenty square miles and has a population of 40,123. The county seat is Wise.

As early as 1750, the noted frontiersman Christopher Gist explored the region that became Wise County. Popular novelist John Fox Jr., author of *Trail of the Lonesome Pine*, lived near Big Stone Gap.

Molasses Pudding

4 cups cream	1 teaspoon salt
1/4 cup plus 1 tablespoon white cornmeal	1 teaspoon cinnamon
	1/2 teaspoon ground ginger
2 eggs, beaten	1/4 teaspoon nutmeg
1 cup dark molasses	3/4 cup cold milk

- Preheat the oven to 325°F. Combine 1 cup of the cream and cornmeal in a small bowl, stirring just until moistened. Heat the remaining cream in a large saucepan. Add the moistened cornmeal, and cook until the mixture begins to simmer, stirring constantly. Reduce the heat to low, and cook for 20 minutes, stirring constantly. Remove from the heat.
- Beat the eggs in a medium bowl until foamy, and stir in the molasses, salt, cinnamon, ginger, and nutmeg. Add the egg mixture to the cornmeal mixture, beating quickly to combine. Pour the mixture into a buttered 2-quart baking dish. Pour the milk gently over the top. Bake for 1 hour or until a silver knife inserted in the center comes out clean.
- Serve warm or cold from the baking dish. The pudding will taste completely different, but just as good, when cold.
- Makes 8 to 10 servings

This recipe was from my Shelton grandmother and is a favorite of my family.

The recipe was submitted by APRIL MILLER of Chatham, Virginia, author of the cookbooks *Southern Cooking on a Country Road*, and *My Table at Brightwood*. She is also a member of the Dorothea Henry Chapter of the Virginia DAR.

GRAYSON COUNTY
Rice Pudding

1 cup rice	2 eggs, slightly beaten
1 quart milk, scalded	1 tablespoon butter,
1/2 cup sugar	optional
1/4 teaspoon salt	Flavoring, optional

- Prepare the rice according to package directions. Stir the cooked rice into the milk in a bowl, and add the sugar, salt, and eggs, mixing well. Add butter and flavoring, if desired. Spoon into a buttered shallow baking dish, and bake or steam until firm. Meringue may be added if desired.
- Makes 4 servings

This very old recipe had no baking temperature or time given because it was probably baked in a wood stove. It was a recipe passed on to my mother by her mother, and was one of my mother's favorite recipes.

The recipe was sent to us by ALICE COX PHILLIPS, a native of Grayson County, Virginia, and now a resident of Poquoson, Virginia.

BACON'S REBELLION

On September 19, 1676, the Virginia Colony's primary settlement at Jamestown was destroyed by fire. The devastation was the result of a short-lived revolt that took place in Eastern Virginia, spearheaded by a young backwoodsman named Nathaniel Bacon. Bacon had repeatedly petitioned Royal Governor William Berkeley to provide his region of Virginia with protection from marauding Indians. Attempt after attempt to persuade the governor to send military personnel to thwart continued native attacks fell on deaf ears, as Berkeley steadfastly refused assistance.

In early 1676, Bacon took matters into his own hands, as he and his followers massacred a number of Occaneechi Indians, even though this tribe was on friendly terms with the English colonists. Later, when Berkeley refused to sign a commission making Bacon the colony's commander-in-chief, an honor already bestowed upon him by the

Assembly, Bacon and his disgruntled men marched on Jamestown, setting it ablaze. Among the buildings burned was the old church, the remains of which can still be seen today.

Bacon did not enjoy his revenge for long. He died of dysentery five weeks after torching Jamestown. A gleeful Berkeley wrote, "God so infected his blood that it bred lice in an incredible number, so that for twenty days he never washed his shirts but burned them." Just to be sure Bacon's Rebellion was really over, the governor inaugurated a witch hunt unsurpassed in Virginia history. He ordered anyone having any connection with the ill-fated Bacon and his revolt to be executed.

Mrs. Patrick Henry's Tipsy Pudding

ORIGINAL VERSION

Make a sponge cake, the weight of a dozen eggs sugar, half their weight in flour, a little salt, with grated rind and juice of a lemon to season. Have ready a gallon of custard, allowing 5 eggs to each quart of milk, a pound of sugar to a gallon. Blanch a pound of almonds, with which to fill the cake, after first having cut it round through, saturated it with wine, and put it together with jelly (if you fancy it). Then place the cake in a large deep dish and pour the custard over it, covering the whole with syllabub.

To make syllabub, take fresh rich cream, sugar and good wine, whipped to a stiff froth.

Tipsy pudding, a variation of English trifle, literally translated means "something of little consequence." It is said to have been the favorite dessert of William Wirt Henry, who married Lucy Gray Marshall of "Villeview" in Charlotte Court House on February 8, 1854. The recipe was handed down to Mrs. Henry from her mother. Mrs. William Wirt Henry was the first state Regent of the Virginia Daughters of the American Revolution, serving from 1891 to 1898. Mr. and Mrs. Henry lived in Richmond, but made Red Hill, the home of Patrick Henry, their summer home until William Wirt Henry's death in 1900.

This information was obtained through the efforts of the curator of the Patrick Henry Memorial Foundation, EDITH POINDEXTER, and SERENA GREEN, Regent of the Red Hill Chapter of the DAR.

WYTHE COUNTY

Wythe County was established in 1789 from Montgomery County and named for George Wythe of Williamsburg (1726-1806), an early patriot and signer of the Declaration of Independence. It contains four hundred seventy-nine square miles. Its population is 27,599, and its county seat is Wytheville.

Lead mines discovered in this county in 1756 furnished much-needed lead for the American patriots during the Revolution. The Old Wilderness Road that leads to Cumberland Gap and Kentucky passed through this region.

Woodford Pudding
(CIRCA 1872)

1 cup sugar
1/2 cup (1 stick) butter or
   margarine, melted
3 eggs, beaten
1 tablespoon baking soda
1 tablespoon sour milk
3/4 cup all-purpose flour

1/2 teaspoon nutmeg
1/2 teaspoon cinnamon
1 (15-ounce) can sour
   cherries, drained, sliced
1 (8-ounce) package dates,
   chopped

- Preheat the oven to 275°F. Beat the sugar and butter or margarine in a large bowl until creamy. Add the beaten eggs, and mix well. Dissolve the baking soda in the sour milk in a bowl. Add the baking soda mixture, flour, nutmeg, and cinnamon to the creamed mixture, and blend well. Note: For sour milk, add 2 drops of vinegar to whole milk.
- Toss the cherries and dates in a small amount of flour in a bowl. Note: The flour coating will help to prevent the cherries and dates from sinking to the bottom of the pudding while baking. Fold the cherries and dates into the pudding mixture. Pour the mixture into a baking mold of your choice or a 2-quart casserole. Bake for 1 hour.
- Makes approximately 6 servings

This recipe was sent by ANNE BOWEN SMITH. It is her husband's grandmother's recipe, and it has been used for four generations at Smithfield, which was built in 1850 by Dr. John Taylor Smith and has been the home of nine generations of Smiths.

1957 STYLE
French-Fried Strawberries

2 pounds extra-large
   strawberries, capped
1 bottle of kirsch
2 egg yolks, beaten
2/3 cup milk
1 tablespoon butter, melted
1 cup flour
Dash of salt

2 egg whites, stiffly beaten
Oil for deep frying
1 package confectioners'
   sugar
1 can whipping cream,
   whipped cream, or
   non-dairy whipped
   topping

- Soak the strawberries in the kirsch in a bowl for 20 minutes, and chill in the refrigerator. Combine the egg yolks, milk, butter, flour, and salt in a bowl, and mix well. Fold the stiffly beaten egg whites into the batter. Dip the strawberries into the mixture, and fry in a deep fryer on medium heat. Drain on paper towels. Sprinkle with confectioners' sugar, and top with whipped cream or whipped topping.
- Makes 12 servings

Adapted from the *350th Festival Foods of Virginia Commemorative Cookbook* which is no longer in print.

USEFUL MEASUREMENTS

1 tablespoon	=	3 teaspoons
	=	15ml
1/4 cup	=	4 tablespoons
	=	60ml
1/3 cup	=	5 1/3 tablespoons
	=	79ml
1/2 cup	=	8 tablespoons
	=	118ml
1 cup	=	16 tablespoons
	=	237ml
2 tablespoons	=	1 fluid ounce
	=	30ml
1 cup	=	8 fluid ounces
	=	237ml
2 cups or 1 pint	=	16 fluid ounces
	=	473ml
4 cups or 1 quart	=	32 fluid ounces
	=	946ml

VIRGINIAN BY CHOICE

This fruit torte consistently receives rave reviews from hungry critics. One woman who owns restaurant chains said, "I've always been partial to chocolate. Once I ate your excellent fruit torte, I now prefer fruit desserts." I had lived on the West Coast all my life. When my husband said he wanted to find a job on the East Coast, I took a poll of my friends who had lived there. After I listed the possible locations, they unanimously said, "Choose Virginia. Virginia is the best." I flew out to investigate the area before John sent any resumes. A friend picked me up at the airport and asked if I wanted to see the Washington Mall. I agreed even though I secretly couldn't understand why he needed to go shopping. That night, as I thought of all the amazing historical places I'd seen that day, I dozed off wondering how anyone could choose California over Virginia.

—Bonnie Johnson Fite

BONNIE'S
Fruit Torte

CRUST
1/2 cup (1 stick) butter or margarine, melted

1 cup all-purpose flour
1/4 cup confectioners' sugar

FILLING
1 teaspoon vanilla extract
8 ounces cream cheese, softened
1/3 cup sugar

Sliced fruit of choice, such as kiwifruit, strawberries, peaches, or berries, or 1 (11-ounce) can mandarin oranges

GLAZE
2 tablespoons cornstarch
1 cup prepared limeade

1/2 cup sugar

- To prepare the crust, preheat the oven to 350°F. Combine the butter or margarine, flour, and sugar in a medium bowl, and mix well. Press over the bottom of a 10-inch springform pan, forming an edge around the sides. Bake for 8 to 10 minutes until light brown. Let stand until cool. Note: Substitute 1/3 cup finely ground rolled oats for 1/3 cup of the flour if desired.
- To prepare the filling, beat the vanilla extract, cream cheese, and sugar in a large bowl until creamy. Spread over the cooled crust. Top with the sliced fresh fruit.
- To prepare the glaze, combine the cornstarch, limeade, and sugar in a medium bowl, and mix well. Microwave at 45-second intervals until thickened. Let stand until cool. Pour over the fruit, and chill for 2 hours or longer before serving.
- Makes 8 to 12 servings

This delicious recipe was provided by BONNIE JOHNSON FITE, who is the author of *Effective Discipline* and *The Twelve New Days of Christmas*. She inspires hundreds of teachers and parents from coast to coast and has been featured on several nationally syndicated radio shows such as Janet Parshall's "America." Bonnie, her husband, John, and their four children truly enjoy their life in Virginia.

YORK COUNTY

York County was one of the original Virginia shires established in 1634. It was first called Charles River County, but in 1643, it assumed its current name in honor of the town of Yorkshire, England. It contains one hundred thirty-six square miles and has a population of 56,297. The county seat is Yorktown.

An early experiment with grape culture was launched in this county in 1769. The turning point of the American Revolution occurred at Yorktown on October 19, 1781, when George Washington's troops defeated those of Lord Cornwallis.

Tea, A Little History

Did you know that tea is nearly five thousand years old? Legend has it that a Chinese Emperor, known for his interest in science, actually discovered tea by accident. This Emperor believed in boiling drinking water for health purposes, something unheard of in that time. Once, while resting during a journey, leaves from a bush fell into the water he was boiling. The brown color of the water created by the leaves intrigued the Emperor. Drinking some, he found it invigorating. Thus began the story of tea, with all its enjoyment, rituals, and uses.

Tea even became a form of art, as we see in the famous Japanese Tea Ceremony. Years later, it became a much desired import for the European countries, primarily France and Holland. By the mid- to late 1600s, tea had spread to England where it became as popular as ale.

Tea-time with sandwiches and sweets became popular in the late 1700s and early 1800s because the English traditionally had only two meals, breakfast and dinner. Imagine how inviting was this afternoon treat of tea with sandwiches and sweets. From this, the idea of tea gardens developed. Ladies and gentlemen could take tea out of doors and be entertained at the same time.

By the early 1700s, tea had migrated to America but was heavily taxed. It was this taxation that ultimately brought about the Boston Tea Party in 1773, during which colonists threw hundreds of pounds of tea into the harbor rather than pay tax to the king. In retaliation, England closed the port of Boston, shutting off the city's sea trade. In due course and with other grievances, the colonists rebelled and a revolution was declared.

In the late 1800s, tearooms and tea dances became popular in both America and England. When a heat wave hit the St. Louis World's Fair in 1904, a creative tea plantation owner dumped ice into hot tea—and iced tea was born! A few years after that, a New York merchant started sending samples of his tea out in small silk pouches. To his amazement, restaurants started brewing these samples in his bags, thus avoiding having to strain tea leaves out of their mixture. Thus, the tea bag was born.

Tea is not only a way to relax and revitalize, but studies suggest it has health benefits also and may play a role in reducing the risk of some cardiovascular diseases and certain cancers.

The three main types of tea are black, oolong, and green. But all three come from the same plant, *Camellia sinensis*. The processing makes the difference. The leaves of black tea are allowed to oxidize before steaming and drying, producing a full-bodied tea. Green tea leaves, however, are steamed and dried immediately after picking. And oolong teas are semi-oxidized, which make it stronger than green tea but gentler than black tea. It's really a cross between the two. Black and oolong teas are both perfect for the afternoon.

TYPES OF TEA OFTEN SERVED

- **AFTERNOON TEA:** The proper afternoon tea is served between 3 p.m. and 5 p.m., though the hours are often stretched slightly in either direction. Along with choice of tea, there are three distinct courses: tiny sandwiches first to blunt the appetite, then scones, and finally, pastries.
- **CREAM TEA:** A light repast that originated in the southwestern part of England around Devon and Cornwall, cream tea calls for some scones, jam, clotted cream, and choice of tea.
- **LIGHT TEA:** A lighter version of afternoon tea. The menu includes scones, sweets, dessert, and choice of tea.
- **ROYAL TEA:** Choice of tea and a four-course menu of finger sandwiches, scones, sweets, dessert, and a glass of champagne or sherry.
- **HIGH TEA:** The term "high tea" is often misused. High tea is a simple supper, the most substantial of the tea meals, much like a family supper.

—Dorothea Johnson, *The Protocol School of Washington* ©

Enjoying Tea

*Tipping as a response to proper service developed in the
Tea Gardens of England. Small, locked wooden
boxes were placed on the tables throughout the Garden.
Inscribed on each were the letters "T.I.P.S." which
stood for the sentence "To Insure Prompt Service." If a
guest wished the waiter to hurry (and so insure the tea arrived
hot from the often distant kitchen), he dropped a coin into
the box on being seated "to insure prompt service."
Hence, the custom of tipping servers was created.*

Enjoying Tea

Scones Made Easy

1 package Rowena's Scone   Various ingredients
Mix

- Prepare Rowena's Scone Mix according to directions.
- For sweet scones, add any of the following: raisins, chopped blueberries, lemon zest, poppy seeds, or mashed strawberries.
- For savory scones, add any or all of the following: cheese, chopped green onions, chopped jalapeño peppers, or chopped olives.
- Makes 8 scones

Either way, you will enjoy these scones. —*Rowena*

The
Painted Lady

Candied Ginger Scones

2 cups all-purpose flour $^1/_4$ pound unsalted butter
$^1/_2$ cup sugar $^3/_4$ cup heavy cream
$^3/_4$ tablespoon baking soda
$^1/_2$ cup chopped candied
    ginger

- Preheat the oven to 350°F. Combine the flour, sugar, baking soda, and ginger in a large bowl, and mix well. Cut in the butter using fingers or a pastry blender until the mixture resembles coarse cornmeal. Add the cream, and stir until blended.
- Turn the dough out onto a lightly floured board, and knead for about 1 minute. Pat or roll the dough about $^3/_4$ inch thick, and cut with a biscuit cutter. Place on a lightly greased baking sheet, and bake for about 17 minutes.
- Makes 12 scones

This recipe was generously shared by THE PAINTED LADY TEAROOM, located in Ghent Gardens, Norfolk, Virginia.

Fruit Scones

2 cups all-purpose flour
2 tablespoons sugar
1 tablespoon baking powder
1 teaspoon salt
2 teaspoons grated orange
  peel
$^1/_4$ cup ($^1/_2$ stick) butter or
  margarine
$^1/_3$ cup milk

2 eggs, beaten
1 cup dried tropical fruit
  mixture
$^1/_2$ cup white chocolate
  chips
1 cup confectioners' sugar
2 to 3 tablespoons orange
  juice

- Preheat the oven to 400°F. Combine the flour, sugar, baking powder, salt, and orange peel in a large bowl, and mix well. Cut in the butter or margarine with a pastry blender or process in a food processor until the mixture resembles coarse crumbs. Add the milk and eggs, blending well. Stir in the dried fruit and white chocolate chips until well mixed.
- Knead the dough 6 to 7 times on a flourred pastry cloth until smooth. Divide the dough into 2 portions. Pat each portion into a 6-inch circle. Cut each circle into 4 wedges with a floured knife. Place the wedges 2 inches apart on a greased baking sheet. Bake for 12 to 16 minutes or until golden.
- Combine the confectioners' sugar and orange juice in a small bowl, mixing until smooth. Drizzle over the top of each scone. Serve warm. These fruit scones freeze well.
- Makes 8 large wedges

APRIL MILLER of Chatham, Virginia, and author of the cookbooks *Southern Cooking on a Country Road* and *My Table at Brightwood*, sent this recipe. She is also a member of the Dorothea Henry Chapter of the Virginia DAR and a Shelton.

Crunchy Cake Fingers

1 Rowena's Pound Cake

- Preheat the oven to 250°F. Slice the pound cake into 1-inch slices. Cut each slice into 3 or 4 fingers. Place the fingers on a baking sheet, and place in the oven. Let stand in the oven for several hours or until the cake is dry.
- Makes 2 to 3 fingers per person

Toasty and yummy! Wonderful served with a salad for lunch or dinner. —Rowena

DID YOU KNOW THAT:

The Newport News Shipbuilding Company in Newport News is one of the world's largest and oldest privately owned shipyards? The company was founded in 1886.

SAVING THE BOXWOOD INN

After the expense of saving a house over one hundred years old that was scheduled to be torn down for a fast food restaurant and gas station, Barbara Lucas somehow manages to keep from fainting when her oil bills arrive every winter. Her two children say that "bed and breakfast" is something Mom has always made, but now she gets paid for it! "Yes," says Barbara, "we'd do it all over again!"

Barbara and Bob Lucas are a retired U.S. Air Force couple who have saved the former Simon "The Bossman of Warwick County" Curtis home in the village of Lee Hall, between Williamsburg and the rest of "The Peninsula." After six years of overcoming codes issues and working with renovation crews that "would start a job on Monday and after getting paid on Friday would never be heard from again," the Lucases believe that moving into their Inn has been worth the effort. They call their "B&B" and Tea Room the Boxwood Inn.

The community of Lee Hall is situated within the city limits of Newport News where the city borders James City County. Carter's Grove (owned by the Colonial Williamsburg Foundation) is nearby. Neighbors to the Boxwood Inn are the beautiful Lee Hall Plantation (built in 1850 by Richard Decauter Lee) and Endview Plantation (home of

William Harwood before 1720). The current renovation of the Lee Hall Depot takes place right next door!

Barbara enjoys people. As an Air Force wife, she has traveled to many places around the world and been involved with various Wives' Clubs and hospitality venues. Her background in sales and marketing, coupled with her degree from a French culinary institute, help her today from promotion to actual cooking to presentation.

The four rooms available for guests in the Inn are tastefully decorated and private. The Lucas family offers some weekend packages that are hard for locals to pass up. Weddings are a mainstay of Boxwood Inn's business. Bob Lucas makes sure the grounds are immaculate for ceremonies and receptions. (A former CPA, he minds the books as well!)

The Inn is open to the public through the weekdays as a true Tea Room, offering memorable desserts. The grand staircase greets visitors who enter the foyer to await a table in the Blue Willow room or another favorite part of the house.

Formerly a hotel for officers during World Wars I and II, a country store, and a post office, the Boxwood Inn would tell many stories if only its walls could talk. The Inn is included in the book *Haunted Inns of the Southeast*. Barbara and Bob Lucas welcome all . . . even ghosts.

THE BOXWOOD INN
Teacup Brownies

1 package brownie mix	¹/₂ cup half-and-half
1 cup chocolate chips	Ice cream, any flavor

- Spray large café au lait cups with nonstick cooking spray. Prepare the brownie mix according to the package directions, but do not bake. Place 1 scoop of the prepared brownie mix in each of the prepared cups using a 4-ounce ice cream scoop.
- To serve, microwave the chocolate chips with the half-and-half in a bowl until melted. Microwave the teacup brownies, 1 cup at a time, for 60 to 90 seconds. Mixture should be moist and soft; do not overcook.
- Drizzle the chocolate fudge sauce around the rims of individual plates. Place the teacup brownies in the center of each plate, and top with a scoop of ice cream and the chocolate fudge sauce. Dust the edges of the plates with confectioners' sugar, and garnish with fresh mint.
- Makes 6 to 8 servings

The recipe was ssent by BARBARA W. LUCAS, owner and manager, The Boxwood Inn, Historic Lee Hall Village, Newport News.

TASTE
Tea Salon & Gifts

Honey Madeleines

3 egg whites	¹/₄ cup plus 2 tablespoons
1 cup sifted confectioners'	(³/₄ stick) unsalted butter,
sugar	melted, cooled to
¹/₂ cup all-purpose flour,	lukewarm
sifted	1 tablespoon honey
¹/₃ cup finely ground	
blanched almonds, sifted	

- Preheat the oven to 400°F. Butter 2 madeleine molds. Beat the egg whites in a bowl until soft peaks form. Add the sugar gradually, beating until stiff peaks form. Fold in the flour and almonds alternately in 2 or 3 additions. Stir the butter and honey together in a small bowl. Fold the mixture gently into the egg whites until incorporated. Spoon into the molds, filling about ²/₃ full. Bake for 8 to 10 minutes or until edges are golden. Let cool in the pan for 5 minutes, and invert onto a rack to cool completely.
- Makes about 40 madeleines

This recipe was kindly provided by CHERRI FIORENZA and DIANA DEAN, Taste Tearoom's co-owners.

Green Spring Gardens

Manor House Clotted Cream

1 cup whipping cream
2 tablespoons confectioners'
  sugar

1 cup sour cream

- Pour the whipping cream into a chilled bowl. Add the confectioners' sugar. Beat until stiff peaks form. Stir in the sour cream. Spoon into a serving dish, and serve with scones.
- Makes 20 servings for a tea

The recipe is shared by JAN DOWNING of the Henry Clay Chapter of the Virginia DAR.

Green Spring Gardens is a twenty-seven-acre Fairfax County site dedicated to the preservation and interpretation of the area's horticultural, historical, and natural resources. Green Spring invites visitors to explore more than twenty different gardens, visit an Eighteenth Century Manor House, and meander along forested paths and pond edges while exploring the horticulture and history of Northern Virginia. Clotted cream is served with freshly baked scones at the Manor House tea programs.

LAUREL BRIGADE INN

Lemon Curd

1/2 cup fresh lemon juice
Zest of 1 lemon
1 cup sugar

4 whole eggs plus 1 egg yolk
4 ounces cold unsalted
  butter, cut into 8 pieces

- Combine the lemon juice, lemon zest, sugar, eggs, and egg yolk in the top of a stainless steel double boiler. Do not let the water touch the top pan. Cook until the mixture begins to thicken, stirring frequently to prevent the eggs from scrambling. Remove from the heat when the mixture thickens, and whisk in the cold butter 1 piece at a time. Let stand until cool, and refrigerate, covered. Lemon curd will keep for up to 3 days.
- Makes approximately 1 1/2 cups

To serve, spoon the curd over slices of pound cake, arrange any fresh berries on the curd, and top with a little fresh whipped cream. Sprinkle with confectioners' sugar, garnish with a lemon twist, and you will wow your guests with a very simple, but elegant, dessert.

The LAUREL BRIGADE INN, Leesburg, Virginia, sent this recipe.

THE STORY OF THE LAUREL BRIGADE INN

Aptly named for a local Confederate unit that operated gallantly and wore a sprig of laurel in their hatbands for distinction.

A proud heritage of welcoming visitors to Leesburg has been in place since the 1760s at the Laurel Brigade Inn. Leesburg's original plan, drawn in 1759, shows the structure on lot number 30 as a public house with bed and board. The "ordinary" (as such was called) served weary travelers journeying between Winchester and Alexandria. During the 1780s, the building became the home of celebrated Revolutionary War hero John Thornton. Later in the 1820s, the Inn became "a tavern, the finest in Leesburg." Indeed, while Henry and Eleanor Peers called the building the Peers Hotel, the Marquis de Lafayette was entertained in the finest manor as he visited Leesburg with President James Monroe.

During the Civil War, the Inn was once again a private residence owned by Dr. A.R. Mott and his family. He instituted some fine changes, including unusual Swiss door fixtures, marble mantle pieces from France, and elaborate gardens in the rear. Wounded Confederate soldiers were brought to the front parlors, which served as a makeshift field hospital. During this era, the Laurel Brigade, commanded by Colonels Ashby and White, was recognized.

Laurel Brigade INN

In 1945, the property was sold at a local auction. Roy Flippo made many renovations and opened the property as the Laurel Brigade Inn in the fall of 1949. After fifty years, the Flippos sold the Inn to Peter and Priscilla Miller. Recently, Elizabeth Coppersmith bought the property. Her brother, Executive Chef Spenser May, is a graduate of the Culinary Institute of America. Having worked all over America (including the Foundry Restaurant in Georgetown), Spenser has created a fine regional cuisine while the Inn houses guests from near and far. Weddings are a specialty as well!

"Saturday Teas" are a feature at the Laurel Brigade Inn. Romantic evenings and nearby historic-district shopping are other attractions. Historic Leesburg is entitled to such a place.

PERFECT TO A TEA

Earl Grey Mock Devonshire Cream

1 cup heavy whipping cream
2 tablespoons Earl Grey tea leaves or 4 tea bags

$1/2$ cup confectioners' sugar
$1/2$ cup sour cream

- Whisk $1/2$ cup of the whipping cream, tea leaves or bags, and 2 tablespoons of the confectioners' sugar in a heavy saucepan until combined. Heat over medium-low heat, stirring frequently until the mixture steams and begins to bubble around the edges. Place on a wire rack to cool. Let cool to room temperature.
- Remove the tea bags, and strain through a fine sieve. Press to extract all the liquid. Pour into a container, and refrigerate, covered, for several hours. Place the tea-infused cream in a deep mixing bowl, and add the remaining whipping cream and confectioners' sugar. Beat at high speed until stiff. Fold in the sour cream. Place in a covered container, and refrigerate until using. Serve with warm scones. Mixture will keep for 1 to 2 days in the refrigerator.
- Makes $1^1/2$ cups

Earl Grey is the world's most popular tea. The delicate taste of the essence of bergamot in the Earl Grey blend and the sweetness of the cream are the perfect accompaniment to freshly baked scones. You won't need any jam.

This comes to us from MARTHA CRIMMINS, who established Perfect To A Tea in 1999 in Fredericksburg, Virginia. As tea mistress, she conducts presentations and lectures for organizations, fundraisers, and business or social occasions on the legend, lore, and etiquette of "taking tea". Perfect To A Tea also features many fine tea accoutrements so you may savor this timeless ritual at home.

Grilled Tea Sandwiches

1 jar Rowena's Peach Orange Clove Jam, or any other favorite jam
1 loaf white bread, crusts removed

4 ounces cream cheese, softened, optional
$1/2$ cup (1 stick) unsalted butter

- Spread the jam on 1 side of half the bread slices. Add a thin layer of the cream cheese if desired. Top with another bread slice. Butter both pieces lightly, and cook gently in a skillet until lightly browned. Cut into squares or triangles. Serve warm.
- Makes $1^1/2$ sandwich per person

ROWENA'S
Old-Fashioned Sandwiches

- *RAISIN AND NUT SANDWICHES:* Process 1¹/2 cups seeded raisins and ¹/2 cup chopped nuts through a meat chopper. Combine the mixture with mayonnaise or whipped cream, and mix well. Spread between slices of bread.

- *CHICKEN SANDWICHES:* Combine 1 cup cold, finely chopped boiled or baked chicken, 1 finely chopped hard-cooked egg, and ¹/4 cup mayonnaise in a bowl. Season to taste, and mix well. A small amount of chopped celery may be added if desired. Spread between slices of bread.

- *CHEESE AND OLIVE SANDWICHES:* Combine 1 cup grated cheese, 1 small bottle of chopped pimientos, ¹/4 cup chopped olives, 1 pinch of cayenne, 1 pinch of dry mustard, and salt in a bowl, and mix well. Spread on thinly sliced bread.

- *EGG SANDWICH:* Spread a layer of mayonnaise on a thin slice of bread. Place a lettuce leaf over the mayonnaise. Combine chopped hard-cooked eggs and mayonnaise in a bowl, and mix well. Spread over the lettuce leaf. Top with another thin slice of bread.

- *CHEESE AND NUT SANDWICH:* Place a lettuce leaf on a thin slice of buttered bread, and spread with mayonnaise. Sprinkle with grated cheese and minced English walnuts. Top with another thin slice of buttered bread.

- *CHEESE AND PIMIENTO SANDWICHES:* Combine ¹/2 pound cheddar cheese, 4 pimientos pieces processed through a meat grinder, and salt to taste in a bowl, stirring until smooth. Add mayonnaise, stirring until the consistency of a soft paste. Spread on thinly sliced bread.

- *GROUND HAM SANDWICHES:* Combine 1 cup ground ham, 1 cup finely chopped pecans, 1 stalk celery, finely chopped, and enough mayonnaise to make of spreading consistency in a bowl, and mix well. Spread on thinly sliced bread.

- *TOMATO SANDWICH:* Spread a layer of mayonnaise on a thin slice of bread. Place a lettuce leaf and a slice of tomato over the mayonnaise. Spread with additional mayonnaise, and top with another thin slice of bread.

- *ORANGE MARMALADE AND CHEESE SANDWICHES:* Combine orange marmalade, softened cream cheese, minced pecans or almonds, and sweet cream in a bowl, and spread on white or brown bread.

These sandwiches make wonderful tea sandwiches. They are very old-fashioned, and I can remember my mother making them when I was a child. These recipes are from The King's Daughters Cook Book, *published in 1924 and compiled by the Circle of Service of the King's Daughters in Norfolk, Virginia. The book sold for one dollar. —Rowena*

THE MAGIC OF ROWENA'S TEAROOM

They said she was "in" today. Busy as a bee in her kitchen, where all those wondrous goodies originate, ready with a smile, and always quick with a greeting that encourages one to return to Norfolk again and again. She is the one who really needs that hot cup of apricot tea you just finished, but doesn't take time for herself. Oh, there she is! As you scan the scrumptious gift shop, you find her signing one of her storybooks for a new grandmother to give to her first grandchild. Yes, here is the ever-energetic and creative Rowena asking you how your day is and never too busy to share her time.

Tearoom elegance and Rowena's "touch" greet you outside the front door. Whimsical paintings on the outside and the larger-than-life "bunny" remind you that you are in for a treat. The street is lined with cars carrying young ladies anticipating their first tea, couples on an anniversary trip, and tourists lucky enough to just "stumble" across Norfolk's hidden jewel in the historic section of Ghent. Rowena's Tearoom is nestled comfortably within the Cake and Jam Factory. The tearoom was just a natural extension of the beautiful operations Rowena has provided for two decades.

Virginia's Finest

It is a wonder that Rowena, involved as she is with civic duties, has the time to chat with her customers, yet she does so regularly.

Rowena's Tearoom offers five tea selections from the light Cream Tea to the Full Afternoon Tea. The scones, made with a touch of oatmeal, are baked fresh daily. The jams and jellies are made in the next room in large vats simmering on huge stoves. The fresh cakes brim with flavors that make your mouth water. Assorted tea sandwiches placed on elegant silver and china complete the scene as you are served fresh tea from a beribboned teapot. And, of course, special teas and etiquette classes are available for children and adults alike. There's always a reason to celebrate at Rowena's Tearoom.

Congealed Slaw

1 (3-ounce) package lemon gelatin	1 tablespoon vinegar
1 cup boiling water	$^1/_2$ cup shredded cabbage
$^3/_4$ cup cold water	$^1/_2$ cup shredded carrots
1 tablespoon minced onion	$^1/_2$ cup chopped celery
$^1/_2$ teaspoon salt	1 tablespoon chopped pimiento

- Empty the gelatin into a quart bowl. Add the boiling water, stirring to dissolve. Stir in the cold water. Add the onion, salt, and vinegar, and mix well. Chill in the refrigerator for 1 hour or until thick and syrupy. Fold in the cabbage, carrots, celery, and pimiento. Pour into a loaf pan. Chill in the refrigerator until firm.
- Makes 6 to 8 servings

This makes wonderful tea sandwiches.

The recipe comes from JEANETTE VEAL BRASWELL of the Chesapeake Chapter of the Virginia DAR.

SPOONER HOUSE
Tea Toddy

3 cups cold water	4 tablespoons dark rum, or
3 bags spiced apple tea, or herbal tea	1 tablespoon rum extract
	4 pieces cinnamon stick
2 teaspoons firmly packed dark brown sugar	

- Bring the water to a boil in a teakettle. Place the tea bags in a warm 4-cup teapot, and pour the boiling water over the bags. Let steep, covered, for 3 minutes. The tea will be slightly weak. Warm 4 mugs with hot water. Place $^1/_2$ teaspoon brown sugar in the bottom of each mug.
- To serve, remove the tea bags, and stir. Pour $^2/_3$ cup of the tea into each mug. Add 1 tablespoon of the dark rum or $^1/_4$ teaspoon rum extract to each mug, and stir. Garnish with a cinnamon stick.
- Makes 4 (6-ounce) servings

This recipe comes to us from MARTHA CRIMMINS, who established Perfect To A Tea in 1999 in Fredericksburg, Virginia.

The Spooner House in Fredericksburg was built in 1793 on land Charles Washington purchased from the Lewis plantation (now Kenmore) in 1761. His brother George most likely surveyed the property. Charles built on one lot, and many years later sold what is now the Spooner House property. The house has welcomed guests since then as a home to early Fredericksburg merchants, as a tavern (1809), and today as a private residence featuring a bed and breakfast suite catering to business travelers.

Hosting the Perfect Tea Party

The most important thing about hosting any event is that your guests are comfortable and relaxed. So here are a few rules:

1. Don't invite more people than you can personally attend to.

2. Don't invite people who don't get along. Why put anyone in an uncomfortable position? Have two parties, if necessary.

3. Do prepare refreshments in advance.

For an informal party, phoning your guests with an invitation is fine, but for a more formal gathering, an invitation should be sent several weeks in advance. You can make your own (cut them out in the shape of a tea cup) or, of course, buy them. Whichever way you go, keep it simple.

The time of your party depends on your guest list. If most of your company have school-age children, a morning affair might be best. For an older crowd, 3 or 4 P.M. might be nice.

If you have seating enough around your dining table, use it. It makes for better conversation than spreading out around the room. Again, keep it simple. Put a single flower at each place, or use one large centerpiece. A mix of china is nice, too. If you have linen napkins, by all means use them. Your flatware and glasses should sparkle.

Unless you have individual serving tiers, a buffet is best. Different heights make for an interesting way to display your refreshments. Use cake stands or build your own—use a large plate and place a sturdy vase or candle stick on it, then top that with another plate.

The food you serve depends on the time of day. A lighter fare is appropriate for the morning. Try some of the following:

- Scones
- Crumpets
- Fruit
- Clotted Cream or Devonshire Cream
- Jams or Curds
- Small Cake Fingers or Petits Fours

Afternoon tea should be heavier. Here are some suggestions:

- Assorted finger sandwiches cut into different shapes (possible fillings: egg salad, chicken salad—not chunky, cucumber, water crest, pimiento cheese, turkey, tomato)
- Scones
- Crudités (assorted small cut vegetables with a dip)
- Fruit
- Cakes
- Jams and Curds
- Candies

As host, you should always pour the tea. If this is not possible due to the number of guests, ask a close friend or relative to assist. This should be considered an honor. Don't make your guests carry a plate and a teacup. Experiment with different teas before your party. Choose one that is full-bodied but not overbearing. Once the tea is poured, sit back and enjoy your company.

To Brew a Perfect Pot of Tea

1. Choose high-quality loose tea.

2. Select the proper size pot.

3. Fill the pot with hot water; then empty it (this warms the pot).

4. Place 1 teaspoon of tea for every serving into a tea sock or tea ball, and place that into the pot.

5. Pour freshly boiled water over the leaves.

6. Let the tea seep for 3 to 5 minutes—the longer, the stronger.

7. Remove the sock or ball.

8. Put the lid on the pot and pour.

A few more tea tips:
- Sugar cubes are much easier to handle than a spoonful of sugar.
- Always serve milk with tea—never cream.
- Milk should be used only with black teas.
- For those who prefer lemon, place a thin slice in the hot tea. The hot liquid draws the citrus into the tea.

Cooking with Children

Cooking with children is a delightful adventure for young and old. It's a wonderful way to spend some quality time with your children, because you will always be there to supervise. Cooking provides children with an opportunity to peek into the adult world they so often imitate—and it's fun! The adventure begins when the special child in your life tries some of these easy and delicious recipes.

All recipes have been adapted from *The Adventures of Rowena & The Wonderful Jam and Jelly Factory* and *The Adventures of Rowena & Carrot Jam, the Rabbit*, both by Rowena Jaap Fullinwider, and illustrated by Deborah G. Rogers, by permission.

Sunshine Fruit Tea

YOU WILL NEED:
a measuring cup
a sharp knife
1 teapot or covered pitcher
tea cups or glasses

5 cups water
1 lemon or lime
1 tangerine or orange
1 family-size tea bag or 4 small
  tea bags
Dash of cinnamon, allspice,
  and cloves
Honey or sugar

- Heat the water to boiling in a saucepan.
- While the water is getting hot, cut the lemon or lime, and tangerine or orange into 4 slices. Place $1/2$ of each kind of fruit in the teapot. Add the tea bag(s) and spices to the teapot.
- When the water comes to a boil, carefully pour the water over the fruit in the teapot. Cover the teapot and let stand for 5 minutes. Remove the tea bags and fruit.
- Cut the rest of the fruit into halves, and place in the tea cups. Pour the tea into the tea cups. Add honey or sugar to sweeten the tea.
- This tea can also be served in a glass with ice.
- Makes 4 to 5 cups

Shortbread Pizza

YOU WILL NEED:
a large bowl
a large cookie sheet or a
   pizza pan
a measuring cup
clean hands
spreading knife
pot holders

1 cup (2 sticks) butter, softened
2 cups flour
$1/2$ cup confectioners' sugar
$1/2$ cup lemon curd or any flavor jam
Sliced fruit, such as strawberries,
   grapes, blueberries, any kind of fruit
   you like, optional

- Preheat the oven to 350°F.
- Combine the butter, flour, and sugar in a large bowl, and shape into a 9-inch flat circle on a large cookie sheet or pizza pan.
- Bake for 25 to 30 minutes or until lightly browned.
- While still warm, slide the crust onto a serving platter. Spread with the lemon curd or jam.
- It's great now but it's even better if you decorate it with sliced fruit. So pretty! Cut it into wedges to serve. So good!!
- Makes 1 (9-inch) pizza

Pinwheel Sandwiches

YOU WILL NEED:
a sharp knife
a rolling pin
a spreading knife

1 loaf unsliced bread
Peanut butter or cream cheese
Raisins
Fruit jelly or Rowena's Thick & Quick Jam

- With an adult's help, cut the crusts off the bread. Now slice the bread horizontally into $1/4$-inch slices.
- With a rolling pin, flatten each slice. Spread with peanut butter and jam, and sprinkle with raisins. Start at one short end and roll up.
- Wrap each roll in plastic wrap, and refrigerate for 1 hour. Slice each roll into the number of sandwiches you will need.
- Makes 8 to 12 sandwiches

Bunny Salad

YOU WILL NEED:

waxed paper

a rolling pin

a knife

a can opener

1 (1-pound) can pear halves
(6 halves)

12 raisins

6 red-hot candies

6 large marshmallows

Shredded lettuce

6 carrot sticks

- Place each pear half, round side up, on a bed of shredded lettuce on a serving plate.
- Cut each marshmallow into halves vertically. Cut 1 marshmallow half into 2 pieces.
- Place each smaller piece between 2 pieces of waxed paper, and roll out until flattened, and look like bunny ears. Repeat with the remaining marshmallows.
- Pat the pear half dry, and place 2 ears on each half. Place raisins where the bunny should have eyes. Place the red-hot candies where the bunny's nose should be.
- Stick the remaining marshmallow half to the back of the bunny for a tail.
- Now arrange the carrot stick to look like the bunny is having a snack.
- Makes 6 salads

Carrot Cone Cakes

YOU WILL NEED:

1 (12-cup) muffin tin

a medium mixing bowl

a small mixing bowl

a mixing spoon

a spreading knife

1 (15-ounce) package carrot
cake mix

12 flat-bottom ice cream cones

1 can prepared cream cheese frosting

2 tablespoons Rowena's Carrot Jam or
any marmalade

- Preheat the oven to 350°F.
- Prepare the carrot cake mix by following the directions on the package.
- Spoon the batter into the cones, filling 3/4 full.
- Place each cone in a muffin cup for support when baking.
- Bake for 30 minutes. The cake should rise above the rim of the cones.
- Remove the cones carefully from the oven. Cool to room temperature.
- Combine the frosting and the Carrot Jam in a small mixing bowl, and dip each cone cake into the frosting mixture with a swirling motion. Use a spreading knife to spread the frosting, if necessary.
- Makes 12 cone cakes

Wabbit Wrap-Ups

You Will Need:
a small mixing bowl
a spoon
a spreading knife

2 tablespoons mustard
3 tablespoons mayonnaise
1 teaspoon chopped chives
6 thin slices smoked turkey
6 thin slices Swiss cheese
6 carrot sticks
6 bread sticks

- Combine mustard, mayonnaise, and chives in a small mixing bowl.
- Spread each slice of turkey and cheese with the mixture.
- Wrap 1 slice of turkey around 1 carrot stick. Make 2 more.
- Wrap 1 slice of turkey around 1 bread stick. Make 2 more.
- Wrap 1 slice of cheese around 1 carrot stick. Make 2 more.
- Wrap 1 slice of cheese around 1 bread stick. Make 2 more.
- Arrange 6 turkey and 6 cheese wrap-ups on a serving plate.
- Makes 12 wrap-ups

You could use roast beef, salami or other cheeses as the wrappers and pickles, celery, or cucumbers as the sticks to be wrapped. Have fun!

Mix and Match Fun Fruit Drinks

You Will Need:
tall glasses
a knife
a cutting board

Various fruits and fruit juices
  of choice

- Rinse fresh fruit, such as pineapple chunks, banana slices, seedless white grapes, melon balls, and blueberries carefully, and pat dry. Place fruit on a cutting board and cut very carefully into small bite-size pieces. Drop small pieces of fruit into a tall glass and pour in your favorite fruit juice, such as cranberry juice, orange juice, grape juice, lemonade, and limeade. Add some ice and a drinking straw and enjoy!
- Makes 1 drink or more

Histories of the Contributing Virginia DAR

ALBEMARLE CHAPTER HISTORY: The Albemarle Chapter was organized in Charlottesville on February 19, 1892, the second chapter to be organized in Virginia. The chapter was named for the County of Albemarle, which had been named for William Ann Keppel, Earl of Albemarle, a colonial governor of Virginia from 1737 to 1754.

AMHERST CHAPTER HISTORY: Lord Jeffrey Amherst was born in Kent, England, in 1717. He joined the Army and by 1758 was appointed Commander in Chief of the British Army in America. Later, he was appointed Governor of Virginia by the King of England, but living in the colony was not really to his liking.

Nevertheless, leaders greatly respected Lord Amherst, and when a new county was formed in Southern Albemarle, they named it for him (1761). Because of this rich history connected with the War of the American Revolution and the French and Indian War, the chapter selected Amherst as its name.

ANNA MARIA FITZHUGH CHAPTER HISTORY: Organized in 1982, the Anna Maria Fitzhugh Chapter is named after Anna Maria Sarah Goldsborough Fitzhugh. Born to the prominent Goldsborough family of the Eastern Shore of Maryland in 1796, she later married William Henry Fitzhugh III, owner of the Ravensworth estate in Fairfax County and related to the most prominent families in Virginia.

When Fitzhugh died unexpectedly in 1830, Anna Maria became the richest and largest landowner and slave-owner in Fairfax County. Anna Maria remained close to her sister-in-law, Mary Lee Fitzhugh Custis, and her niece, Mary Ann Randolph Custis, who would become the wife of Robert E. Lee in 1831 and mistress of Arlington House.

ARLINGTON HOUSE CHAPTER HISTORY: George Washington Parke Custis named Arlington House for the old Custis Mansion on Virginia's Eastern Shore. Slaves on the estate manufactured the bricks for the solid brick home with cement plaster exterior. Construction began in 1802. The estate is now part of Arlington National Cemetery, which was named for the house, as was Arlington County.

The grandson of Martha Washington, George Washington Parke Custis was also descended from the Calverts and Lord Baltimore. He married Mary Lee Fitzhugh; their daughter Mary Ann Randolph Custis, born 1808, became the wife of Robert E. Lee.

BERMUDA HUNDRED CHAPTER HISTORY
The town of Bermuda Hundred was established in 1613 by Sir Thomas Dale. It became the first incorporated town in 1614. An early port for Richmond, Bermuda Hundred was home to John Rolfe, Colony Recorder, who was married to Pocahontas.

BEVERLY MANOR CHAPTER HISTORY: Beverly Manor Chapter was organized at historic Stuart House in Staunton, Queen City of the Shenandoah Valley. Located in Augusta County, Staunton hosted members of the Colonial Assembly when they fled the British during the Revolutionary War. Augusta County, which boasts the largest number of Revolutionary War soldiers' graves in Virginia outside of Yorktown, was formed from a land grant to William Beverly, which became known as Beverly Manor and later Staunton.

BLACK'S FORT CHAPTER HISTORY: In 1760, Daniel Boone hid in a cave to escape a pack of howling wolves. Today, the cave is situated under Cave House—an old Victorian House. In 1774, settler Joseph Black built a log fort there and named the settlement "Black's Fort." But it was not until after the Revolutionary War, that the town of Abingdon was chartered.

BLUE RIDGE CHAPTER HISTORY: Established in 1894 in Lynchburg, the Blue Ridge Chapter was the sixth chapter to be chartered in Virginia. The first meetings were held at a home on Floyd Street, which is on one of the highest elevations in the city with a splendid view of the Blue Ridge Mountains. At an early meeting, during a discussion of a name for the chapter, Richmond visitor Mrs. Davidson, suggested, "There should be none other, when you have the Blue Ridge."

BOTETOURT COUNTY CHAPTER HISTORY: Botetourt County (pronounced "bot-e-tot") was formed from Augusta County in 1770 and is named in honor of Norborne Berkley, Lord Botetourt, Royal Governor of the Colony of Virginia. Botetourt County originally extended from the Blue Ridge Mountains to the Mississippi River and the Great Lakes, including portions which later became the states of Kentucky, Illinois, Indiana, Ohio, West Virginia, and Wisconsin.

Thomas Jefferson, George Washington, and Patrick Henry owned land in Botetourt County. Explorers Lewis and Clark visited Botetourt County. William Clark married the daughter of a prominent Botetourt family.

CAMERON PARISH CHAPTER HISTORY: Parishes were created in Colonial America by the Church of England. Truro Parish, encompassing lands in both Fairfax and Loudoun counties in Northern Virginia, was divided in 1748, and Cameron Parish was established. *Cameron* was one of Lord Fairfax's many titles, and thus in a way honored him, as he was holder of the land grants in the Northern Neck of Colonial Virginia. Fairfax County (Truro Parish) and Loudoun County (Cameron Parish) represent this division.

CARTER'S FORT CHAPTER HISTORY: Located in Scott County, Carter's Fort is where Daniel Boone's Wilderness Trail travels through the Moccasin Gap of the Clinch Mountains leading from the western reaches of the Great Valley of Virginia into the interior of the Alleghenies. The Great Warriors Path crosses the Wilderness Trail at Moccasin Gap; early settlers poured through the gap into Kentucky, violating a treaty with the Shawnee that led to Dunmore's War of 1774.

In later years, Maces Springs became well known as the home of the original Carter Family, where some of the finest mountain music was ever played.

CHANCELLOR WYTHE CHAPTER HISTORY: Established November 30, 1921, in Ashland, the Chancellor Wythe Chapter was named for George Wythe—lawyer, judge, statesman, and signer of the Declaration of Independence. He wrote the original Virginia protest against the Stamp Act in 1764 and participated in the Constitutional Convention of 1787. In 1786, he became Chancellor of the State. The Wythe House is in Williamsburg.

CHANTILLY CHAPTER HISTORY: Covering both Richmond and Westmoreland Counties, the Chantilly Chapter is named for the colonial plantation and manor house of Colonel Richard Henry Lee, who was born at Stratford in Westmoreland County in 1732. A delegate to the Continental Congress in Philadelphia, Colonel Lee, on June 7, 1776, introduced the resolution calling for independence from England. Westmoreland County was established in 1653 by the colonial government in Jamestown. It is the birthplace and home of more statesmen of national stature than any other county in the United States.

CHARLES PARISH CHAPTER HISTORY: Charles Parish was derived from Charles River Shire, one of the eight original Shires of Virginia, later becoming York County. The Charles Parish Church, located in York County in the old Poquoson district, served the surrounding community from 1636 until after the Revolutionary War.

It is a small, quiet city bordered by the marshes of the Chesapeake Bay. These days, generations of watermen and farmers who have lived in Poquoson since the 1700s share the city with residents who work at nearby NASA Langley or Langley Air Force Base.

CHESAPEAKE CHAPTER HISTORY: The chapter is named for the USS *Chesapeake*, which was launched from the Gosport Shipyard (today's Norfolk Naval Shipyard) at the southern branch of the Elizabeth River in Norfolk County in 1799. She saw extensive service in the War with France, the Tripolitan Wars, and the War of 1812. Her last battle was in Boston in 1813. The British were maintaining effective blockade of every American major port, but the British frigate *Shannon* was the only ship blockading Boston.

While the men on the *Shannon* were experienced, the men on the *Chesapeake* were very new, save one, Captain James Lawrence, a seasoned naval hero. On June 7, 1813, the battle ensued savagely on both sides. Captain Lawrence was mortally wounded, but as he was helped below, he commanded "Don't give up the ship!"

In September 1813, Captain Oliver Hazard Perry (a close friend of Captain Lawrence) unveiled his battle standard, a new flag of blue bunting on which had

been sewn in big white muslin letters "Don't give up the ship." It is an inspiration to to every U.S. warship that goes to sea.

COLONEL ABRAM PENN CHAPTER HISTORY: The Colonel Abram Penn Chapter was established February 25, 1950 in Stuart. Abram Penn was captain of militia at Point Pleasant and in Lord Dunmore's War in 1774. After moving to Pittsylvania County, later Henry County, Penn served as delegate to the General Assembly. Penn and seven of his sons served as "Gentleman Justices." His home Poplar Grove, the oldest frame house in Patrick County, sits on a hill overlooking the North Mayo River. Penn was buried there in 1801.

COLONEL JAMES PATTON CHAPTER HISTORY: Colonel James Patton Chapter was organized in October 1970 in Waynesboro. A Scotch-Irish sea captain who settled near Waynesboro in 1738, Colonel Patton was instrumental in the early development of Augusta County. He served the county until his death during the French and Indian War uprisings at Draper's Meadow in 1755.

COLONEL THOMAS HUGHART CHAPTER HISTORY: Colonel Thomas Hughart was born in 1729 and died in Augusta County in 1810. He was one of the largest and wealthiest landowners of the county. After honorably serving in the army, the governor of Virginia appointed Hughart one of the gentleman justices of the county. He served in this office or as High Sheriff almost to the time of his death.

Many members of this chapter trace their descent from Colonel Hughart or from members of the Augusta County Riflemen that he, in part, commanded.

COLONEL WILLIAM PRESTON CHAPTER HISTORY: The Colonel William Preston Chapter was established July 12, 1923, in Roanoke. Colonel Preston came to America in 1736 at the age of eight; his family settled near Staunton. He held three important frontier offices at the same time: County Lieutenant, Surveyor, and Justice of the Peace. He also served as a member of the House of Burgesses. In 1757, Preston received an Indian Commission and negotiated a treaty with the Shawnee and Delaware Indians. He tried and hanged Tories on treason charges. Married to Susanna Smith in 1761, Preston named his one-hundred-nineteen-thousand-acre plantation home Smithfield in her honor. He died in 1783 while supervising a regimental muster, and left twelve children.

COMMONWEALTH CHAPTER HISTORY: The Commonwealth Chapter was established on February 6, 1902, in Richmond. Members had previously belonged to Old Dominion Chapter, which was large enough to sustain two chapters.

CONSTANTIA CHAPTER HISTORY: The Constantia Chapter was established on February 21, 1924, in Suffolk. John Constance built his home, Constantia

House, on a bluff overlooking his warehouse on the Nansemond River. It survived with restoration for over one hundred seventy years. He had built his warehouse and wharf to increase trading along the river's shores. When this was accomplished, the Virginia Legislature under Governor Gooch passed an Act to establish a town on the river, to be called Suffolk. The chapter rebuilt the colonial home, and by 1944, debt-free ownership had been realized.

CRICKET HILL CHAPTER HISTORY: Cricket Hill Chapter was established on December 31, 1923, in Mathews, naming it for the old fort on the mainland of Mathews County, across from Gwynns Island. A decisive battle of the Revolution was fought there, following the burning of Norfolk.

DOROTHEA HENRY CHAPTER HISTORY: The Dorothea Henry Chapter was established March 4, 1894, in Danville. It was named for Patrick Henry's second wife.

FAIRFAX COUNTY CHAPTER HISTORY: One of the oldest organizations in Vienna, the Fairfax County Chapter was chartered on October 14, 1905, at the beautiful Victorian home of the chapter's first registrar, Kate Strong Summy. On October 13, 1995, the chapter placed a historical marker on this home as part of the ninetieth anniversary celebration. Annette Gibson Berry, a charter member and regent of the chapter from 1924 to 1926, lived in the house. As the chapter's one hundredth anniversary approaches, the current membership includes several descendants of Mrs. Berry.

FALLS CHURCH CHAPTER HISTORY: Mary Edwards Riley married Samuel H. Styles in June 1892. As a result of her interest in libraries and her children's gift of land, the library in Falls Church was named for her. Mary Riley Styles and two of her sisters were charter members of the Falls Church Chapter, established in 1910. Mary was Chapter Regent 1922-1924. Her daughter, Elizabeth (Betty) Styles wrote the introduction for the *Cherry Hill Cookbook* in 1976.

FAUQUIER COURT HOUSE CHAPTER HISTORY: Fauquier Court House was chosen as the chapter name for its significance as the name of the crossroads settlement at the intersection of the old Winchester-Falmouth Road with the post road from Charlottesville to Alexandria, where the courthouse of the newly formed county of Fauquier was to be located in May 1759. This thriving settlement, almost at the exact center of the county, kept its original name until 1810 when the town was incorporated and became Warrenton in honor of General Joseph Warren of Revolutionary fame.

FLOYD COURTHOUSE CHAPTER HISTORY: Floyd Courthouse Chapter was named in honor of the county and Governor John B. Floyd. In 1940, the chapter placed a bronze plaque in the courthouse lobby containing the names of eighteen patriots of the Revolutionary War who are buried in Floyd County.

FORT CHISWELL CHAPTER HISTORY: Fort Chiswell Chapter was organized in Bristol in November 1922. It was named for the 1758 fort built by Colonel John Chiswell to protect his vital lead mines located on the "New" River in what was then West Augusta County.

FORT MAIDEN SPRING CHAPTER HISTORY: Established November 8, 1924, in Tazewell, Fort Maiden Spring Chapter was named for a fort built by Captain Rees T. Bowen and settlers. The area was the common hunting ground of both North and South Indians, and the scene of much fighting between them. In 1773, the construction of Fort Maiden Spring stockade, to protect the settlers from Indian raids, was begun near an unusually fine spring, originating from a cavern at the foot of an enormous limestone cliff about twelve miles west of Tazewell. During the Revolutionary War, the fort was the rallying point for men who participated in the Battle of King's Mountain, where Captain Bowen died in action.

Today the fort forms part of a residence occupied by the eighth generation of the Bowen Family.

FORT NELSON CHAPTER HISTORY: The Fort Nelson Chapter of Portsmouth was formed in 1896 with twelve charter members. The chapter celebrated its hundredth anniversary on May 9, 1996, with seventy-seven members.

Fort Nelson was the name of a fort built for the defense of Portsmouth and Norfolk. An engagement with the British took place at this location May 9, 1779.

FRANCIS LAND CHAPTER HISTORY: Francis Land built his home, the Francis Land House, in 1732 in lower Norfolk County (later Princess Anne County and now the city of Virginia Beach). He owned over a thousand acres when he died in the mid-1650s. Six generations of the Land family (all six heads of the households were named Francis) operated the plantation. The house that still stands on the property was probably built by the fifth or sixth generation of the Land family.

FREEDOM HILL CHAPTER HISTORY: Freedom Hill Chapter was named after the location of the first Fairfax County Court House, which was built in 1742 on Freedom Hill, located about a mile or two north of the village of Vienna. This land was deeded to the county by William Fairfax, the agent for, and cousin of, Lord Fairfax, who owned six million acres of land between the Potomac and Rappahannock Rivers. In 1752, the Court House was abandoned because of Indian hostilities in the area. The Court House was moved to Alexandria for a short time and then reestablished in the village of Providence, now Fairfax.

FRONT ROYAL CHAPTER HISTORY: Front Royal is the county seat of Warren County and the northern entrance to Shenandoah National Park and Skyline Drive. Located in the Shenandoah Valley, the county was named for General Joseph Warren, killed at Bunker Hill in 1775.

GREAT BRIDGE CHAPTER HISTORY: The Great Bridge Chapter, organized in 1894, was named for the first land battle of the America Revolution fought in the South against the British on December 9, 1775, twelve miles from Norfolk. Colonel William Woodford, commanding the Patriots, declared it was the Bunker Hill of the South, resulting in colonial control of the largest port in the colony.

HAMPTON CHAPTER HISTORY: This chapter is named for the city of Hampton, which is the oldest continuous English-speaking community in the nation. Hampton's history includes many rich stories, including one about Blackbeard, a much-feared pirate who ravaged ships, towns, and farms along the Virginia and Carolina coasts and waterways. In fact, the Governor of Virginia in 1718 ordered the Royal Navy to put an end to Blackbeard's pirate operations. A great battle occurred at Okracoke Sound in November. His head was returned to Hampton for public display, as a warning to would-be pirates.

HENRY CLAY CHAPTER HISTORY: The Henry Clay Chapter was confirmed as Annandale Chapter on October 15, 1958. The chapter members greatly admired Henry Clay, who was born during the Revolution on April 12, 1777, in Hanover County, so his name was proposed in the expectation that the chapter would accomplish much.

HICKSFORD CHAPTER HISTORY: Hicksford Chapter was formed in 1911. Its name comes from the original Hicks' Ford on the Meherrin River, a ford that was on Captain Robert Hicks land in the early 1700s. In 1781, the General Assembly put the county seat of Greensville County there. In 1798, plats were laid out across the river and called Belfield. The two communities combined in 1886 and renamed Emporia.

JACK JOUETT CHAPTER HISTORY: In early June 1781, General Cornwallis detached Colonel Tarleton, one hundred eighty dragoons and seventy mounted infantrymen to capture Governor Thomas Jefferson and the Virginia Legislature, then meeting in Charlottesville. The British were successful in concealing their movements until they reached Cuckoo Tavern in Louisa County, only forty-odd miles from Charlottesville. There, a young Virginia Captain, Jack Jouett, observed the British, grasped the significance and danger of their presence, and made a historic decision to sound the alert. Among those he warned were Patrick Henry and three signers of the Declaration of Independence, Richard Henry Lee, Benjamin Harrison, and Thomas Nelson, plus Jefferson, author of the Declaration. Some believe that had these leaders been captured, the Revolution might have failed. To honor this courageous man, the Jack Jouett Chapter was formed in 1922.

JAMES RIVER CHAPTER HISTORY: This chapter was actually located in Lynchburg on the James River. Lynchburg, founded in the 1780s, was named after John Lynch, who put a ferry across the James River.

Batteauxs (boats using poles to pull themselves along) carried goods down to Richmond and on to the coast. Thomas Jefferson country retreat Poplar Forest is nearby.

JOHN ALEXANDER CHAPTER HISTORY: The John Alexander Chapter was organized in Alexandria on May 17, 1932, and the first meeting was held at Gadsby's Tavern. A gavel made from material from George Washington's birthplace was used. The chapter was named by Eleanor Washington Howard (the last child born at Mount Vernon) for the patriot John Alexander, for whom the City of Alexandria is named.

JOHN RHODES CHAPTER HISTORY: Formed on August 8, 1935, in Luray, the John Rhodes Chapter was named for the Mennonite Minister Reverend John Rhodes, who, along with his wife and seven children, was one of the first settlers in the area. In August 1764, Rhodes' wife and six of their children were killed in the last Indian Massacre in what is now Page County.

The Indians ransacked the cabin and took hostage sixteen-year-old Michael Rhodes. He lived for three years with the Indians in the Ohio Territory before escaping and returning home. Michael fought in the Revolutionary War and later settled in Maurertown.

JUDITH RANDOLPH-LONGWOOD CHAPTER HISTORY: Named for the wife of Richard Randolph of Bizarre in Cumberland County, the Judith Randolph-Longwood Chapter was established October 8, 1925, in Farmville. Judith Randolph was a descendant of William Randolph of Warrickshire, England, who emigrated to Virginia and settled at Turkey Island. When Bizarre was destroyed by fire in 1813, she lived in Farmville. She is buried at Tuckahoe Plantation.

Longwood Chapter, named for Longwood Estate, the birthplace of General Joseph Eggleston, for whom Longwood College is also named, was formed in 1965. It merged with Judith Randolph Chapter in 1988.

LEEDSTOWN CHAPTER HISTORY: King George County, named after King George I of England, was formed by an act of the General Assembly, passed November 24, 1720. Leedstown was in King George County when the Leedstown Resolutions were drawn up and signed on February 27, 1766. Thomas Ludwell Lee called upon one hundred fifteen patriots who met, adopted, and signed the famous Leedstown Resolutions, a declaration of independence, the first, drafted by Lee's brother, the illustrious Richard Henry Lee.

LOUISA COURT HOUSE CHAPTER HISTORY: The Louisa Court House Chapter took its name from the county courthouse located in the town of Louisa. Louisa County was created in 1742 when it separated from Hanover County. The county was named after Princess Louisa, the youngest daughter of King George III.

LYNNHAVEN PARISH CHAPTER HISTORY: Parishes were grants of land along rivers. The boundaries of the Lynnhaven Parish were first defined by the Assembly at Jamestown in 1642. These same boundaries were used when Princess Anne County was formed out of lower Norfolk in 1691. The county in turn became the City of Virginia Beach in 1963.

MAJOR GEORGE GIBSON CHAPTER HISTORY: Major Gibson came from Ireland in 1743 and settled in Augusta County. He served as a Lieutenant in the Southern Division of Lord Dunsmore's Army and in Valley Forge during the "terrible winter." He moved to Lee County next to Cumberland Gap in the 1800s. Today, this is called Gibson Station, and some of his descendants still live there. Cumberland Gap is the most southwestern part of Virginia where Virginia, Tennessee, and Kentucky come together.

MONTPELIER CHAPTER HISTORY: Montpelier Chapter honors James Madison, the fourth President of the United States, and is the name of his family estate in nearby Orange County. Madison County was established in 1792, and the new county was named for James Madison, then an opposition leader in Congress who had played a major role in the adoption of the Federal Constitution.

MOUNT VERNON CHAPTER HISTORY: The third oldest chapter in Virginia, the Mount Vernon Chapter in Alexandria was organized on May 13, 1893, on the porch of Mount Vernon Mansion, the home of George Washington. The first project of the chapter was the restoration of Jamestown with the Society for Preservation of Antiquities. In 1912, the chapter erected a fountain next to Gadsby's Tavern in Alexandria, recording Revolutionary events. The fountain is made from a cannon that experts believe was manufactured about 1750 and used by General Braddock. A dolphin sits above the cannon and spouts water into a small basin for birds above two automatic fountains for man. The main fountain is for horses, with a base for dogs and cats. It was dedicated "in memory of the Colonial and Revolutionary Events of the town of Alexandria."

In 1926, the chapter received from the U.S. Congress the deed to Jones Point Lighthouse (1855) in Alexandria. It is the oldest "light" on the Potomac River. The chapter restored the lighthouse that same year.

NANCY CHRISTIAN FLEMING CHAPTER HISTORY: The Nancy Christian Fleming Chapter was established March 14, 1922, in Roanoke. It was named in honor of Nancy Christian Fleming, the oldest daughter of Israel Christian of Staunton and the wife of Dr. William Fleming. A Colonial surgeon, Dr. Fleming was wounded at the Battle of Point Pleasant, where he commanded the Botetourt troops. In 1788, he voted in the Virginia Convention to ratify the Constitution and was a member of the first Board of Trustees at Washington and Lee University. Both Flemings are buried on a hill at Belmont.

NELLY CUSTIS CHAPTER HISTORY: The Nelly Custis Chapter was organized on February 22, 1928, as the Irvine-Wells Chapter and renamed in 1994 in honor of Eleanor Parke Custis, Martha Washington's granddaughter. Born at Abingdon in 1779, Nelly was adopted by George Washington and lived with his family from an early age in New York and Mount Vernon. Nelly married Washington's nephew, Lawrence Leuns, and they lived and reared a large family at Woodlawn Plantation. Nelly, noted for her beauty and grace, as well as for her intelligence and political acumen, died in 1852.

NORTHAMPTON COUNTY CHAPTER HISTORY: On one side of Northampton County is the Atlantic Ocean; on the other side is the Chesapeake Bay, first explored by Captain John Smith in 1608. The county seat is Eastville and has been so since 1715. Court records dating from 1632 are housed there. They are the oldest continual court records in the United States. Originally, this county had been named "Ye Plantacon of Accawmacke," meaning "over the water" or "on the other side of the water" place. In 1643, the name was changed to Northampton after Northamptonshire in England, birthplace of two prominent local citizens.

OLD DONATION-BOROUGH OF NORFOLK CHAPTER HISTORY: The Old Donation-Borough of Norfolk Chapter was established on October 1, 1925, in Lynnhaven and changed to Norfolk in 1928. It was named for Old Donation Church in Princess Anne County, one of the oldest churches in America. Erected in 1694, Old Donation Church was the mother church of Lynnhaven Parish. When Borough of Norfolk Chapter was organized in 1951, Norfolk had been a borough three years longer than it had been a city, so the chapter recognized that history. The two chapters merged in 2001.

PATRICK HENRY CHAPTER HISTORY: Patrick Henry County, created in 1776, was named in honor of the great orator of the Revolution, Patrick Henry, who did so much to overthrow the royal establishment in Virginia. The Patrick Henry Chapter was named in tribute to this great man who was also an early Governor and lived in Leatherwood in this County from 1780 to 1784.

POINT OF FORK CHAPTER HISTORY: The Point of Fork Chapter was established on December 8, 1936, in Fort Union. The name was chosen because this wedge of land at the confluence of the Rivanna and James Rivers is that corner of Fluvanna most closely connected with the Revolution. The natural "V" was the setting in early 1781 for the Point of Fork Military Establishment, the principal depot for the assembly of military stores and the training ground for Continental recruits under Major-General Baron von Steuben.

POPLAR FOREST CHAPTER HISTORY: The Poplar Forest Chapter takes its name from Thomas Jefferson's country retreat Poplar Forest, located in Bedford County. Jefferson favored simple food when visiting Poplar Forest and was fond of such foods as mashed potatoes and ice cream.

PRINCE WILLIAM RESOLVES CHAPTER HISTORY: Prince William Resolves Chapter is located in the Dale City area of Prince William County. Formed in 1731, the county was named for William Augustus, Duke of Cumberland, second son of King George II. The territory, which included Fairfax, Arlington, Alexandria, Loudon, and Fauquier, was reduced to its present size in 1759. Prince William County now covers three hundred forty-eight square miles. Dale City is located west of I-95 and is about thirty miles south of Washington, D.C.

PROVIDENCE CHAPTER HISTORY: The chapter name of Providence comes from the name of the town at which the Fairfax County Courthouse was built. Around 1632, English traders from Maryland began expanding into the area followed by Jamestown colonists in 1649, who came from the South. It was not until 1742 that the area became known as Fairfax County. Descendants of these settlers figured prominently in the Revolution and were important to the young country. In 1798, land was purchased in Providence for the price of one dollar to establish a county courthouse. It opened on April 21, 1800 and it is still in use today. On file there are the wills of George and Martha Washington. While Providence grew as the center of a largely agricultural area, it was more commonly referred to as "Fairfax Courthouse," for its primary use, but it wasn't until 1874 that the town assumed the name "Fairfax."

RED HILL CHAPTER HISTORY: Red Hill Chapter was organized in April 1977 in Brookneal and was named for the last home of Patrick Henry. It was also the home of Mrs. William Wirt Henry, the first State Regent of the Virginia DAR, serving from 1891 to 1898.

ROANOKE VALLEY CHAPTER HISTORY: The Roanoke Valley Chapter was established November 6, 1961, in Vinton (outside Roanoke) and was named for the valley where its members lived. In the latter part of the eighteenth century, settlers were mostly descendants of the Cavaliers who came along the Blue Ridge Mountains down the Great Trail, the Scotch-Irish, and the Swiss-German Protestants who came in from the North.

ROYAL OAK CHAPTER HISTORY: The Royal Oak Chapter was established on October 13, 1979, in Marion. Marion is situated on the Royal Oak Tract, surveyed and so named by Colonel John Buchanan in 1747. He was the first verified explorer in Southwest Virginia.

SARAH MURRAY LEWIS CHAPTER HISTORY: Colonel Charles Lewis was born in 1736 at Lewis Fort, northeast of present-day Staunton. Lewis was the youngest and only American-born son of John and Margaret Lynn Lewis, who fled County Donegal, Ireland, in the 1730s to seek a new life in the Valley of Virginia. Charles Lewis married New York-born Sarah Murray in 1761, and the couple came to live at Fort Lewis. As Commander of the Augusta County Regiment, Lewis led the initial charge of Virginians that morning of October 10, 1774, at the Battle of Point Pleasant, where he was mortally wounded, leaving a widow and five children.

SHADWELL CHAPTER HISTORY: Shadwell Chapter was named for the birthplace of Thomas Jefferson. Peter Jefferson owned a thousand-acre tract in what is now Albemarle County. He acquired an additional hundred acres of adjoining land from William Randolph for "consideration of Henry Weatherbourne's biggest bowl of arrack punch." A house was built on the site in 1737 and named "Shadwell" after the parish in London where Peter Jefferson's wife was born. Thomas Jefferson, son of Peter Jefferson and Jane Randolph Jefferson, was born at Shadwell on April 13, 1743. He lived there 1743-1745 and 1752-1770, and moved on to Monticello after the house was destroyed by fire in 1770.

SHENANDOAH RIVER CHAPTER HISTORY: Shenandoah River Chapter was organized in October 1986. The Shenandoah River has been the lifeblood of the Shenandoah Valley throughout Virginia's history. A mode of travel for the people and their industry, the river weaves through the history of the valley. In fact, the valley takes its name from the river, which the Native Americans called "Daughter of the Stars."

VIRGINIA FRONTIER CHAPTER HISTORY: The Virginia Frontier Chapter of Rockbridge County is rich in history and lore. Forty years after the first settlers came to what is now Rockbridge County, the War for Independence began. The future county seat was named for the Battle of Lexington, 1775, and many men from the Virginia frontier fought under their new Commander-in Chief, George Washington. The chapter's name honors those rugged frontiersmen and women.

WILLIAM PITT CHAPTER HISTORY: The William Pitt Chapter was established on January 29, 1911. Chatham William Pitt, Earl of Chatham, in 1776 urged the repeal of the Stamp Act in the House of Commons and continued to champion the American cause in the House of Lords. His portrait hangs in the Pittsylvania Court Room.

WILLIAM TAYLOR CHAPTER HISTORY: William Taylor was a patriot who provided much-needed food to the troops. He later served as Clerk of the Court in Lunenberg County for almost half a century, the longest anyone has ever served in that position in Virginia. This chapter covers Brunswick County (1720) and Lunenberg County (1746).

WILLIAMSBURG CHAPTER HISTORY: The Williamsburg Chapter, organized in 1925 in Williamsburg, was named for the town. The favorite meeting place from 1929 to 1946 was Ye Poor Debtor's Prison in Williamsburg, owned by Annie Gault, a member. After 1946, the chapter met in the Bruton Parish House. Now with more than two hundred members, the chapter has cosponsored, with the Colonial Williamsburg Foundation, a special December Naturalization Ceremony in the Hall of the House of Burgesses for twenty-eight years. On July 4, an annual wreath-laying ceremony takes place at Berkley Plantation in honor of Benjamin Harrison, a signer of the Declaration of Independence.

Virginia Today

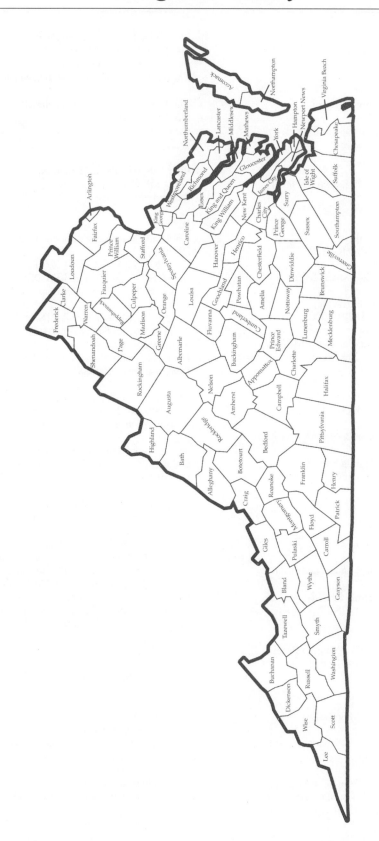

Resources

"A"

The Added Touch [Petersburg]
(804) 732-8738
Brown Sugar Pie

A.J.'s On The Creek [Chincoteague]
(575) 336-5888
www.chincoteague.com/rest/ajs/html
*Deep-Fried Artichoke Hearts with
Horseradish Sauce*

Anderson's Showplace CafÈ [Newport News]
(757) 599-3510
Chicken Salad

The Apple House [Linden]
(540) 636-6329 Fax (540) 636-4470
www.applehouseva.com
Five-Star Broccoli and Yellow-Squash Salad

Ashlawn-Highland [Charlottesville]
(434) 293-9539 Fax (434) 293-8000
www.monticello.avenue.org
*Mrs. James Monroe's Cream Jumbles, Mrs. James
Monroe's Waverly Jumbles, Mrs. James Monroe's Syrup
of Roses*

Ashman Manufacturing Company [Virginia Beach]
(757) 428-6734 Fax (757) 437-0398
www.ashmanco.com
Virginia Gentleman Bourbon Baby-Back Pork Ribs

Azar's Natural Foods [Virginia Beach]
(757) 486-7778 Fax (757) 486-2034
Poulet a l'Oriental

"B"

Bay Beyond, Inc. [Melfa]
(800) 221-2722 Fax (757) 787-3430
www.bluecrabbay.com
Blue Crab Bay Bloody Mary Shrimp and Pasta

Beach Smokehouse [Virginia Beach]
(757) 428-2281 Fax (757) 428-2335
Smoked Fish Salad

Bella Monte of Virginia, Inc. [Virginia Beach]
(757) 425-6290 Fax (757) 491-6654
Tortellini Bella Monte

The Belle Grae Inn [Staunton]
(540) 886-5151 Fax (540) 886-6641
Chocolate Peanut Butter Pie

The Blue Hippo [Norfolk]
(757) 573-9664
*Drunken Coconut Shrimp "Martini" with Ginger-Scented
Tomato Chutney, Upside-Down Macadamia Nut-Crusted
Cheesecake with a Flambé of Bananas, Spiced Rum, and
Brown Sugar*

Blue Ridge Beverage Company [Salem]
(540) 380-2000 (800) 868-0354
www.blueridgebeverage.com
Chicken and Dumplings, Chili Tomato Dip

The Boxwood Inn [Newport News]
(757) 888-8854
www.boxwood-inn.com
Teacup Brownies

Briar Patch Tearoom [Poquoson]
(757) 858-6843
Raspberry Mud Cake

"C"

Christ and Saint Luke's Episcopal Church
[Norfolk]
(757) 627-5665 Fax (757) 626-1334
www.CHRISTANDSTLUKES.ORG
Remoulade Sauce for Cold Shrimp

The Chrysler Museum of Art [Norfolk]
(757) 664-6200 Fax (757) 664-6201
www.chrysler.org
*Ham-and-Peanut-Stuffed Chicken Breasts with Cider
Sauce and Apple Garnish*

The Civil War at Endview Plantation [Newport News]
(757) 887-1822; www.endview.org
A Soldier's Favorite Fare: Hardtack

The Colonial Williamsburg Foundation (Including:
Chowning's Tavern, Christiana Campbell Tavern,
Colonial Williamsburg Tavern, Golden Horseshoe
Clubhouse, Golden Horseshoe Clubhouse Gold Grill,
King's Arms Tavern, Shield's Tavern, Williamsburg
Inn, Williamsburg Lodge) [Williamsburg]
(757) 229- 1000
www.colonialwilliamsburg.com
*Apple Cake, Berry Shrub, Chesapeake Crab, Corn, &
Potato Chowder, Cream of Peanut Soup, The Fairway,
Gingered Pumpkin Bisque with Maple, Mulled Apple
Cider, Mushroom-Crusted Loin of Lamb, Oyster Fritters
with Dipping Sauce, Pie Pastry, Rosemary-Scented Sweet
Red Pepper Bisque, Rummer, Sweet Potato Pie, Wassail*

Cookin' Cheap
www.cookincheap.com
Chicken & Crabmeat in Sun-Dried Tomato Sauce

Covered Bridges in Virginia
(757) 484-4404
Email: vabridgelady@aol.com

Creative Memories [Vienna]
(703) 734-7893
Email: allynfj@aol.com
Lemon Cajun Barbecue Sauce for Chicken or Beef

308

"D"

The Duck-In [Virginia Beach]
(757) 481-0201
www.duck-in.com
Fisherman's Chowder

"E"

Eastern Shore of Virginia Historical Society [Onacock]
(757) 787-8012
www.esva.com/kerrplace.htm
Eastern Shore Sweet Potato Casserole

"F"

Fort Lewis Lodge [Millboro]
(540) 925-2314 Fax (540) 923-235
www.fortlewislodge.com
Fort Lewis Lodge Peach Pound Cake

"G"

Gadsby's Tavern [Alexandria]
(703) 548-1288 Fax (703) 548-5324
www.gadsbys.org
Sally Lunn Bread

George Washington Birthplace Memorial Monument
[Washington Birthplace]
(804) 224-1732
www.nps.gov/gewa
To Make Sugar Cookies

Ghent Gardens [Norfolk]
(757) 627-8873
Franklin Sweet Potato Pudding

Ginger Hill Bed and Breakfast [Louisa]
(540) 967-3260
www.bbhost.com/gingerhill
Ginger's Lemon Sugar Cookies

Gourmet Cookies by Valli [Glen Allen]
(804) 360-1963 Fax: (804) 360-9504
Date-Nut Goodies

Greenway Haven Party House [Abingdon]
(276) 628-7511
Party House Rolls

The Greyhorse Inn [The Plains]
(540) 253-7000 Fax (540) 253-7031
www.greyhorseinn.com
Herb-Baked Eggs

"H"

Hampton Roads Naval Museum [Norfolk]
(757) 322-2987
www.hrnm.navy.mil
Dunderfunk(Bread Pudding)

The Henry Clay Inn [Ashland]
(800) 343-4565 (804) 798-3100
Fax (804) 752-7555
www.henryclayinn.co
Peanut Butter Pie

The Highland Inn [Monterey]
(540) 468-2143 Fax (540) 468-3143
www.highland-inn.com
Famous Maple Pecan Pie

The Homestead, 1766 [Hot Springs]
(540) 839-1766 Fax (540) 839-7670
www.thehomestead.com
Sautéed Mountain Trout Homestead

The Hotel Roanoke and Conference Center [Roanoke]
(540) 985-5900 Fax (540) 853-8290
www.hotelroanoke.com
Chicken Penne with Mushrooms

Hunt Country Foods, Inc. [Middleburg]
(540) 364-2622 Fax (540) 364-311
Sweet Yeast Bread

The Hunter House Victorian Museum [Norfolk]
(757) 623-9814 Fax (757) 623-0097
www.hunterhousemuseum.org
Season's Best Strawberry Bread

"I"

The Inn at Burwell Place, Inc. [Historic Salem]
(800) 891-0250 (540) 387-0250 Fax (540) 387-0250
www.burwellplace.com
Oven Puff Pancakes

Inn at Old Virginia [Staunton]
(877) 809-1146 (540) 248-4650 Fax (540) 245-4377
www.innatoldvirginia.com
Quail and Apple Bisque

"J"

J D & W, Inc. [Virginia Beach]
(757) 340-8411 Fax (757) 340-2082
www.info@jdwinc.co
Apricot and Brazil Nut Bread

Julie Plunkett Marketing [Charles City]
(804) 648-7833 Fax (804) 829-2911
Perfect Fried Oysters

"K"

Kingsmill Resort [Williamsburg]
800-982-2892 (757) 253-3948 Fax (757) 253-3993
www.kingsmill.com
Seafood Paella

"L"

La Petite Tea Room [Williamsburg]
(757) 565-3422
www.lapetitetearoom.com
Old Southern Pork Cake

The Laurel Brigade Inn [Leesburg]
(703) 777-1010 Fax (703) 777-9001
Email: LaurelBrigadeInn@aol.com
Lemon Curd

Lee Milteer, Inc. [Virginia Beach]
(757) 460-1818 Fax (757) 460-3675
www.milteer.com
Carrots in Mustard Glaze

The Lynnhaven House [Virginia Beach]
(757) 460-1688
Herbed Cornbread

"M"

Mabry Mill Restaurant and Gift Shop
[Meadows of Dan]
(276) 952-2947
Grits

MacArthur Memorial [Norfolk]
(757) 441-2965
sites.communitylink.org/mac
Pork Tenderloin

Magnolia House Tea Room [Hampton]
(757) 722-6851 Fax (757) 723-6821
jk.glass@verizon.net
Maple Pecan Scones

Martha Washington Inn [Abingdon]
(540) 628-3161
www.marthawashingtoninn.com
*Spinach and Potato Salad, Grilled Strip Steak with
Sorghum Cured Onions*

Michie Tavern ca. 1784 [Charlottesville]
(434) 977-1234 Fax (434)296-7203
www.michietavern.com
Black-eyed Peas, Murphy's Biscuits, Stewed Tomatoes

Mill Street Grill [Staunton]
(540) 866-0656 Fax (540) 886-0744
www.millstreetgrill.com
Filet Mignon Medallions Stuffed with Crab Imperial

The Mimslyn Inn [Luray]
(800) 296-5105 Fax (540) 743-2632
www.mimslyninn.com
Southern Peanut Soup

Monticello [Charlottesville]
(434) 984-9822; www.monticello.org
Biscuit de Savoye (Savoie Cake)

Moses Myers House [Norfolk]
(757) 333-1085 Fax (757) 333-1089
www.chrysler.org
To Make a Floating Ifland

The Mount Vernon Inn [Mount Vernon]
(703) 780-0011
*Mount Vernon Inn Tomato Cobbler, Mount Vernon
Rabbit Stew*

Mount Vernon Ladies Association [Mount Vernon]
(703) 780-2000
www.mountvernon.org
*Nelly Custis' Hoecakes, Martha Washington's
Great Cake, 18th Century Icing Recipe*

"N"

Nancy Thomas, Artist [Yorktown]
(757) 898-0748 Fax (757) 898-6400
www.nancythomas.com
Avocado and Cheese Dip

New Millennium Studios [Petersburg]
(804) 957-4200 Fax (804) 862-1200
Peach Cobbler

Norfolk Botanical Gardens [Norfolk]
(757) 441-5830 Fax (757) 853-8294
www.virginiagarden.org
Edible Flowers

Norfolk State University [Norfolk]
(757) 823-8600
www.nsu.edu
Jambalaya

"O"

The Oaks Victorian Inn [Christiansburg]
(540) 381-1500 Fax (540) 381-3036
www.bbhost.com/theoaksinn
Pasta Soufflé with Baked Salmon in Dill Sauce

The Old Chickahominy House [Williamsburg]
(757) 229-4689
Miss Melinda's Pancakes

Old Dominion University [Norfolk]
(757) 683-3159 Fax (757) 683-5679
www.odu.edu
Florentines

Our Daily Bread Bakery [Blacksburg]
(540) 953-2815
Portuguese Sweet Bread

Overhome Bed and Breakfast [Hardy]
(540) 721-5516
www.overhomebandb.com
Baked Fresh Pears

"P"

Page House Inn Bed and Breakfast [Norfolk]
(757) 625-5033 Fax (757) 623-9451
Eggs a la Stormi

The Painted Lady Tea Room [Norfolk]
(757) 623-8872 Fax: (757) 623-0635
Champagne Mashed Potatoes, Horseradish and
Dill Shrimp Croquettes

Paradise Nursery [Virginia Beach]
(757) 421-0201 Fax (757) 421-7043
www.paradisenursery.com
Wild Rice Salad with Fresh Figs

Pasta Valente [Charlottesville]
(888) 575-7670 Fax (434) 971-1511
www.pastavalente.com
Fran's Fast Pasta Dinner

The Patriot Inn Bed and Breakfast [Portsmouth]
(757) 391-0157 Fax (757) 391-9290
bbonline.com/va/patrio
Fruit Crisp

Perfect To A Tea
(540) 760-TPOT
Email: perfecttoatea@att.net
Earl Grey Mock Devonshire Cream, Mint Julep Iced Tea,
Spooner House Tea Toddy

Poor Mariner's Shanty Nautical Gifts
[Coles Point]
(804) 472-3270 Fax (804) 472-2420
Crab Appetizers

Profound Promises [Fairfax]
(703) 449-7751
www.profoundpromises.com
Bonnie's Fruit Torte

Prospect Hill Plantation Inn [Charlottesville]
(800) 277- 0844
www.prospecthill.com
Virginia Bacon and Corn Chowder

The Protocol School of Washington
[Yarmouth, ME]
(207) 781-6525 Fax (207) 781-6580
www.psow.com
Apple Crisp

"Q"

Quality Camera and Photo Imaging, Inc.
[Norfolk]
(757) 625-6726 Fax (757) 625-3408
www.qcpix.com
Chicken and Yellow Rice

"R"

Randolph-Macon College [Ashland]
Fax (804) 752-3042
www.rmc.edu
Mocha Fudge Cake

Randolph Macon Woman's College [Lynchburg]
(434) 947-8000
www.rmwc.edu
Salad Dressing

The Red Fox Inn [Middleburg]
(800) 223-1728 (540) 687-6301 Fax (540) 687-6053
www.redfox.com
Crab Cakes

Red Hill
The Patrick Henry Memorial Foundation [Brookneal]
(804) 376-2044 Fax (804) 376-2647
www.redhill.org
Dorothea Henry's Sally Lunn Bread, Mrs. Henry's
Tipsy Pudding

Rowena's, Inc., Creator and Producers of Gourmet
Foods [Norfolk]
(800) 627-8699 (757) 627-8699 Fax (757) 627-1505
www.rowenas.com
Carrot Jam Chicken Salad, Crunchy Cake Fingers,
Grilled Tea Sandwiches, Jelly Roll, Refrigerator Bran
Muffins, Scones Made Easy, Sleeping Meringue

"S"

Sea Gull Pier Restaurant, Chesapeake Bay Bridge and
Tunnel [Virginia Beach]
(757) 464-4641 Fax (757) 464-2103
www.cbbt.com
Clam Chowder

Shepherd's Joy [Abingdon]
(276) 628-3273 Fax (276) 628-6273
www.shepherdsjoy.com
Toffee Coffee Cake

Smithfield Foods, Inc. [Smithfield]
(757) 365-3000
www.smithfieldfoods.com
Peanut Crusted Pork with Bourbon Mushroom Cream,
Smithfield Inn Corn Custard, "The World's Largest Ham
Biscuit"

Stratford Hall Plantation [Stratford]
(804) 493-8038 Fax (804) 493-0333
www.stratfordhall.org
Ginger Cookies

Surrey House Restaurant and Country Inn [Surrey]
(757) 294-3389 Fax (757) 294-0076
www.surreyhouserestaurant.com
Peanut Raisin Pie

S. Wallace Edwards and Sons, Inc. [Surrey]
(757) 294-3121 Fax (757) 294-5378
www.edwardsham.com
Elegant Ham-Chicken Divan

"T"
Taste Tearoom [Williamsburg]
(757) 221-9550
Honey Madeleines

Taste Unlimited [Virginia Beach]
(757) 425-3011 Fax (757) 425-3928
www.tasteunlimited.com
Pan-Seared Tuna with Curry Dipping Sauce

Thomas Jefferson's Poplar Forest [Forest]
(434) 525-1806 Fax (434) 525-74252
www.poplarforest.org
Horseradish Mashed Potatoes

The Trellis [Williamsburg]
(757) 229-8610 Fax (757) 221-0450
www.thetrellis.com
*Grilled Tuna and Grilled Potatoes with Tomatoes, Green
Beans, and Onion Dressing*

"V"
Virginia Opera Association [Norfolk]
(757) 627-9545 Fax (757) 622-0058
www.vaopera.org
*Grilled Filet Mignon with Sweet Potato Hash, Spicy
Peanut Sauce, and Wilted Collards*

Virginia Stage Company [Norfolk]
(757) 627-6988
www.vastage.com
Everyday Meatloaf

Virginia Symphony [Norfolk]
(757) 466-3060 Fax (757) 466-3046
www.virginiasymphony.org
Zuccotto Falletta

Virginia Wesleyan College
[Norfolk/Virginia Beach]
(757) 455-3288 Fax (757) 466-8274
www.vwc.edu
Gregory's Derby Pie

Vision of Peace [Cobbs Creek]
(804) 725-1183
www.dorothyfagan.com
Pineapple Sunset

"W"
The Waltons Mountain Museum[Schuyler]
www.thewaltons.com
Peach Ice Cream

The Williamsburg Winery, Limited [Williamsburg]
(757) 258-0899 Fax (757) 229-0911
www.williamsburgwineryltd.com
Raspberry Chocolate Pie

Willoughby-Baylor House [Norfolk]
(757) 333-1085 Fax (757) 333-1089
www.Chrysler.org
Mince Pye

The Wilson-Lee House B&B [Cape Charles]
(757) 331-1954 Fax (757) 331-8133
www.wilsonleehouse.com
Blueberry French Toast Strata, Huevos Rancheros

Woodlawn Plantation [Alexandria]
(703) 780-4000 Fax (703) 780-8509
www.woodlawn@nthp.org

How to Convert to Metric

	When You Know	You Can Find	If you Multiply By
Length	Inches	Millimeters	25
	Feet	Centimeters	30
	Miles	Kilometers	1.6
Area	Square Inches	Square centimeters	6.5
	Square feet	Square meters	0.09
	Square yards	Square meters	0.8
	Square miles	Square kilometers	2.6
Weight	Ounces	Grams	28
	Pounds	Kilograms	0,45
Liquid	Ounces	Milliliters	30
Volume	Pints	Liters	0.47
	Quarts	Liters	0.95
	Gallons	Liters	3.8
Temp	Degrees	Degrees	$5/9$ (after
	Fahrenheit	Celsius	subtracting 32)

Recipe Index

314

Historic Reference Index